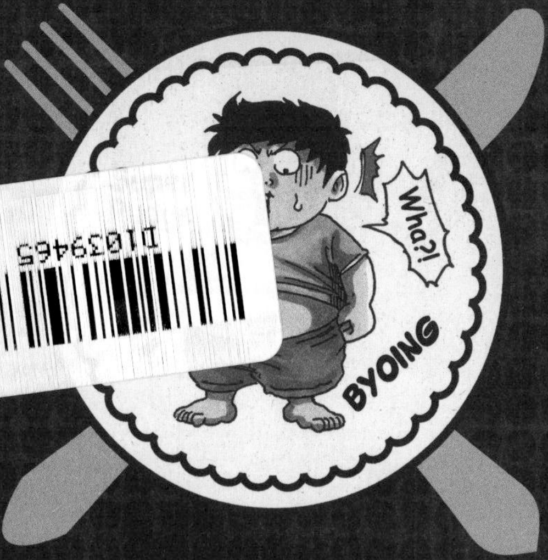
Wha?!
BYOING

Since the start of *Toriko*'s weekly serialization in *Weekly Shonen Jump*, my first new series in six years, I've gained a whopping ten kilograms. What the heck?! I can't stop freaking out! I mean, it's only been six months!! What kind of crazy phenomenon is my body undergoing that it'd gain a whole ten kilograms in half a year?! This can't be good!! Sure, I'm writing a manga about gourmet foods, but that is no excuse! And so I'm going to do what anybody my age would do and go on a serious diet! Right now, I weigh 74 kilograms (163 lbs). I'll update you with my new weight next volume. I wonder which will come first—losing ten kilos or wrapping up the *Toriko* series?! I'm on the edge of my seat...

–Mitsutoshi Shimabukuro, 2008

Mitsutoshi Shimabukuro made his debut in **Weekly Shonen Jump** in 1996. He is best known for **Seikimatsu Leader Den Takeshi!** for which he won the 46th Shogakukan Manga Award for children's manga in 2001. His current series, **Toriko**, began serialization in Japan in 2008.

TORIKO VOL. 2
SHONEN JUMP Manga Edition

STORY AND ART BY **MITSUTOSHI SHIMABUKURO**

Translation/Christine Dashiell
Adaptation/Hope Donovan
Touch-Up Art & Lettering/Jim Keefe
Design/Sam Elzway
Editor/Alexis Kirsch

TORIKO © 2008 by Mitsutoshi Shimabukuro
All rights reserved. First published in Japan in 2008 by SHUEISHA Inc., Tokyo.
English translation rights arranged by SHUEISHA Inc.

Printed in Canada.

Published by VIZ Media, LLC
P.O. Box 77010
San Francisco, CA 94107

10 9 8 7 6 5 4 3 2 1
First printing, September 2010

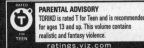

TORIKO

2

COCO!!

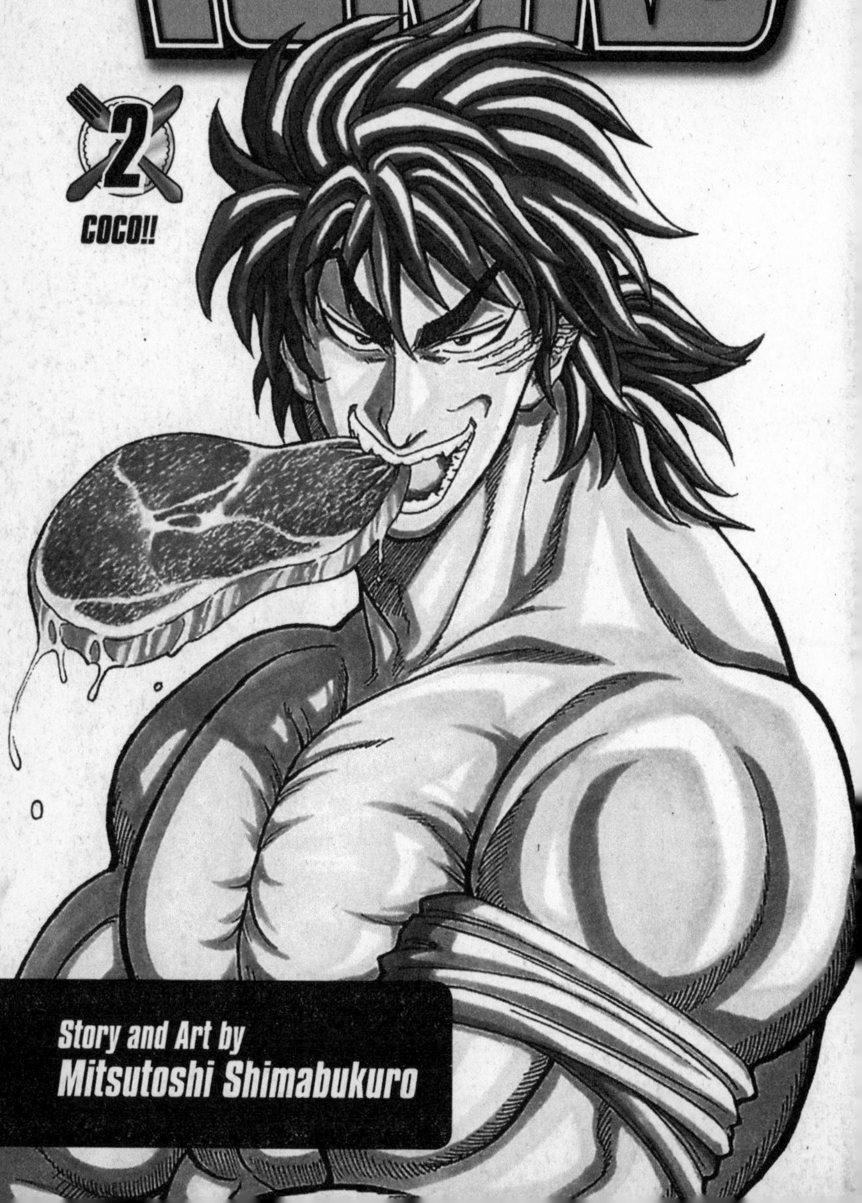

Story and Art by
Mitsutoshi Shimabukuro

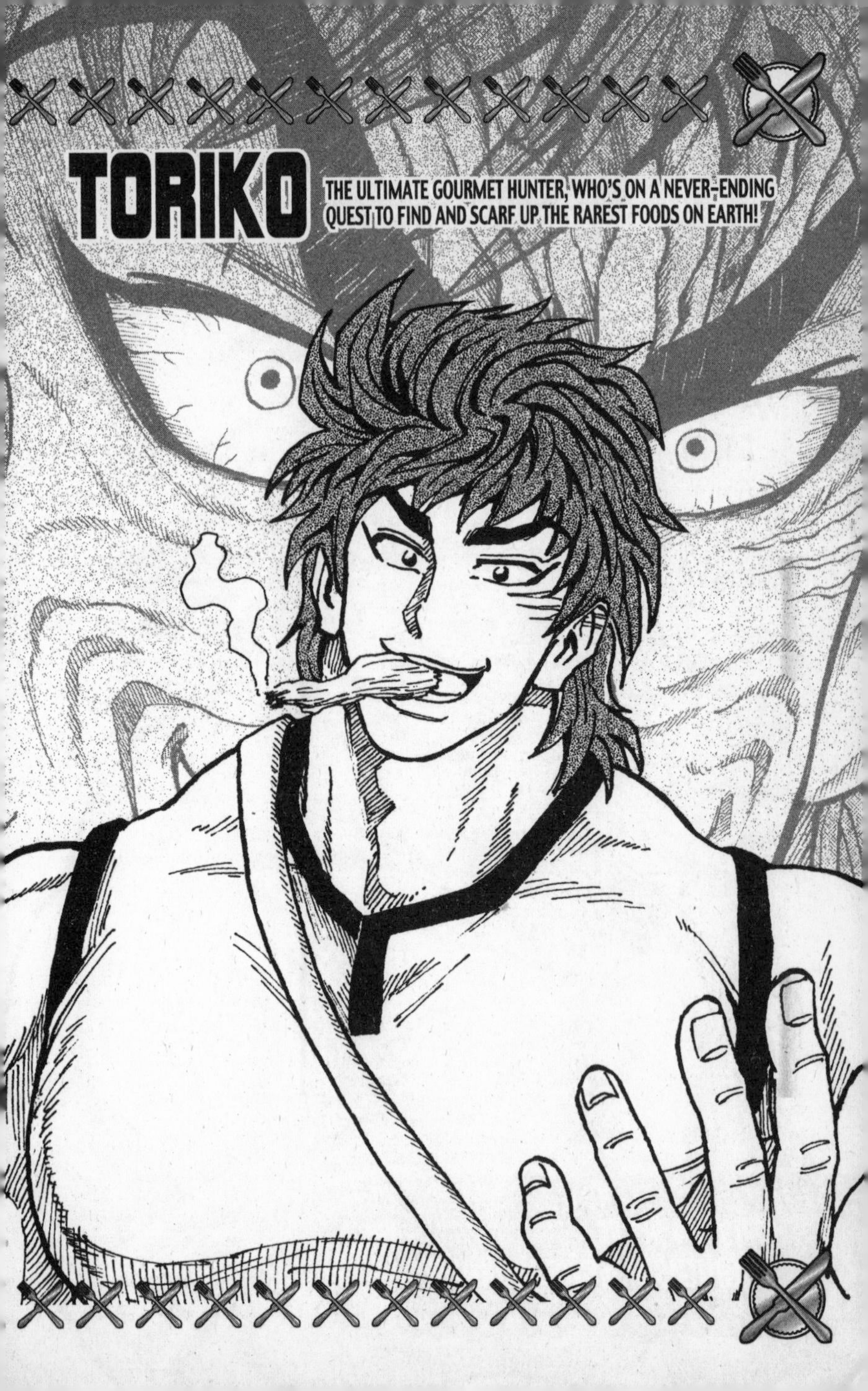
TORIKO
THE ULTIMATE GOURMET HUNTER, WHO'S ON A NEVER-ENDING QUEST TO FIND AND SCARF UP THE RAREST FOODS ON EARTH!

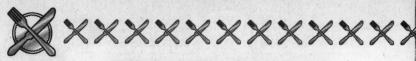

WHAT'S FOR DINNER

IT'S THE AGE OF GOURMET! KOMATSU, THE HEAD CHEF AT THE HOTEL OWNED BY THE *IGO* (INTERNATIONAL GOURMET ORGANIZATION), WAS ORDERED BY HIS BOSS TO CAPTURE A GARARA GATOR! TO HELP KOMATSU IN THIS TASK, THE *IGO* HIRED NONE OTHER THAN THE LEGENDARY TORIKO--A CHARISMATIC GOURMET HUNTER WHOSE IMPRESSIVE TRACK RECORD HAS EARNED HIM A TITLE AS ONE OF THE FOUR KINGS!!

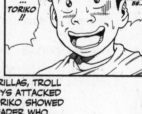

WHEN KOMATSU LEARNED THAT TORIKO'S DREAM IS TO DESIGN THE BEST FULL-COURSE MEAL OF HIS LIFE, HE WAS SO MOVED THAT HE DECIDED TO JOIN TORIKO ON THE HUNT. HOWEVER, AT THEIR DESTINATION, THE BABARIA ISLANDS, A MEAN, MASSIVE 300-YEAR-OLD GARARA GATOR THREW THEM A BLOODY WELCOME PARTY. PAYING NO MIND TO KOMATSU, WHOSE LEGS TURNED TO JELLY, TORIKO TURNED THE GARARA GATOR INTO A SHISH KEBAB, USING HIS BARE HAND AS THE SKEWER. AND THEN THERE WAS MUCH REJOICING AND EATING!

THEIR NEXT JOB WAS TO PLUCK A RAINBOW FRUIT FROM THE RAINBOW TREE. HOWEVER, IT WAS NO CAKEWALK, AS THE FRUIT LAY WITHIN THE NESTING GROUNDS OF A TROOP OF THE WORLD'S STRONGEST GORILLAS, TROLL KONGS. THE MALICIOUS MONKEYS ATTACKED ONE AFTER ANOTHER, UNTIL TORIKO SHOWED THEIR LEADER WHO WAS BOSS WITH THE MENACE OF HIS FRIGHTENING DEMONIC AURA. AND SO, THEY SUCCESSFULLY SECURED THE RAINBOW FRUIT.

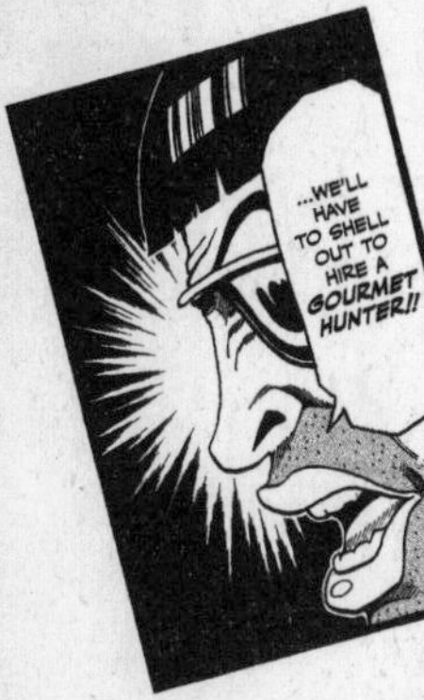

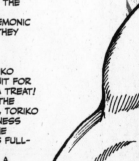

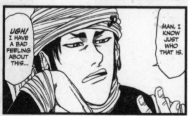

FINALLY, TORIKO TASTED THE FRUIT FOR HIMSELF. WHAT A TREAT! FASCINATED BY THE RAINBOW OF FLAVORS ON HIS TONGUE, TORIKO DECLARED THE DREAMLIKE DELICIOUSNESS OF THE RAINBOW FRUIT WORTHY OF THE POSITION OF DESSERT COURSE ON HIS FULL-COURSE MEAL!!

MEANWHILE, IN GOURMET FORTUNE, A FARAWAY TOWN KNOWN FOR FORTUNE-TELLING, THE FORTUNE-TELLER/GOURMET HUNTER COCO FORESEES TORIKO'S COMING VISIT...

...WE'LL HAVE TO SHELL OUT TO HIRE A GOURMET HUNTER!!

● **UUMEN UMEDA**
IGO BUREAU CHIEF

● **KOMATSU**
A HOTEL CHEF WHO ADMIRES TORIKO.

...WOULD BE...
...TORIKO!!

MAN, I KNOW JUST WHO THAT IS.
UGH! I HAVE A BAD FEELING ABOUT THIS...

● **COCO**
A FORETUNE-TELLER/ GOURMET HUNTER WHO LIVES IN GOURMET FORTUNE.

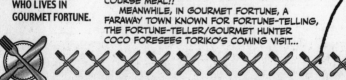

Contents

TORIKO

GOURMET 8: COCO!!

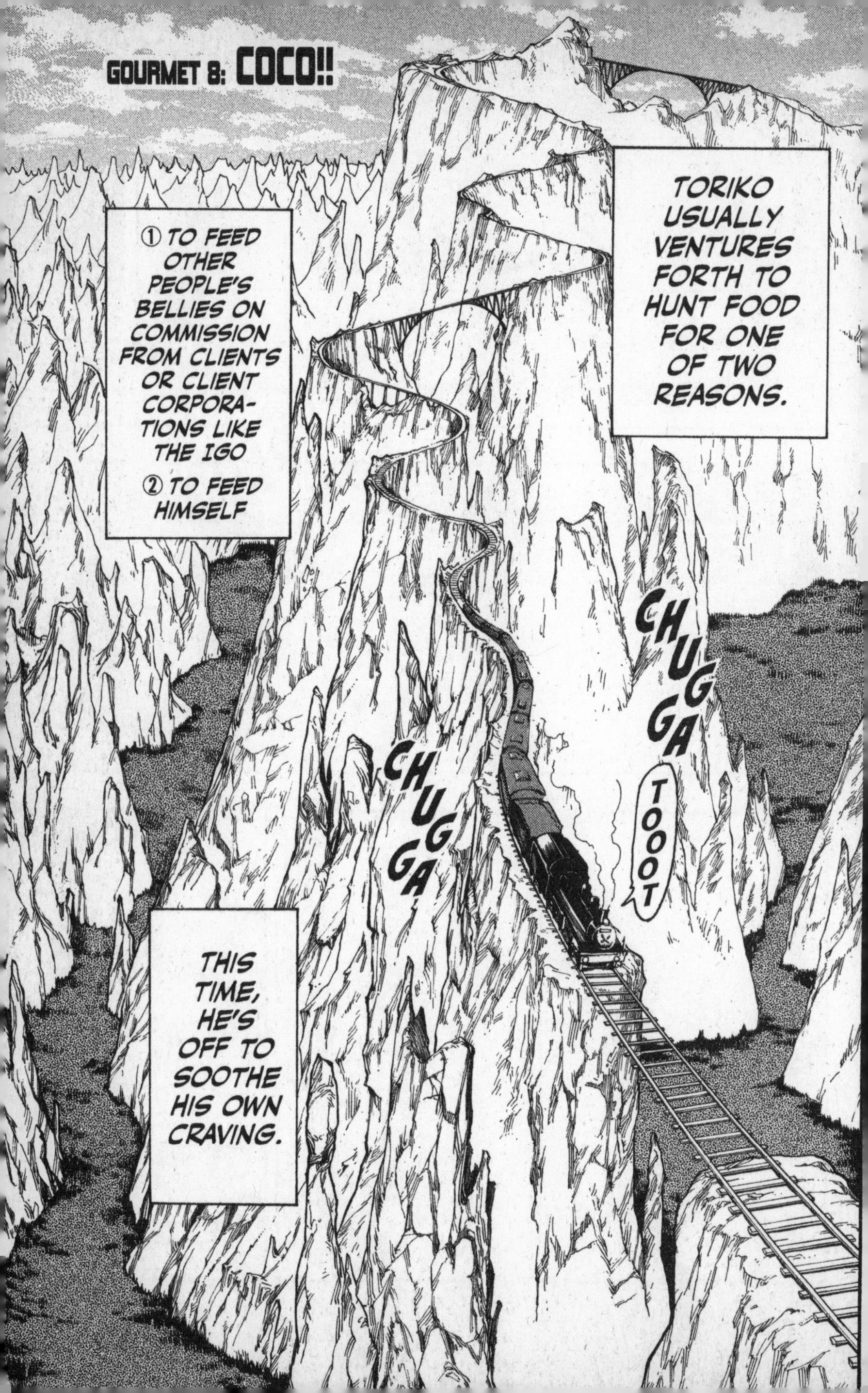
TORIKO USUALLY VENTURES FORTH TO HUNT FOOD FOR ONE OF TWO REASONS.
① TO FEED OTHER PEOPLE'S BELLIES ON COMMISSION FROM CLIENTS OR CLIENT CORPORATIONS LIKE THE IGO
② TO FEED HIMSELF
CHUGGA
TOOOT
CHUGGA
THIS TIME, HE'S OFF TO SOOTHE HIS OWN CRAVING.

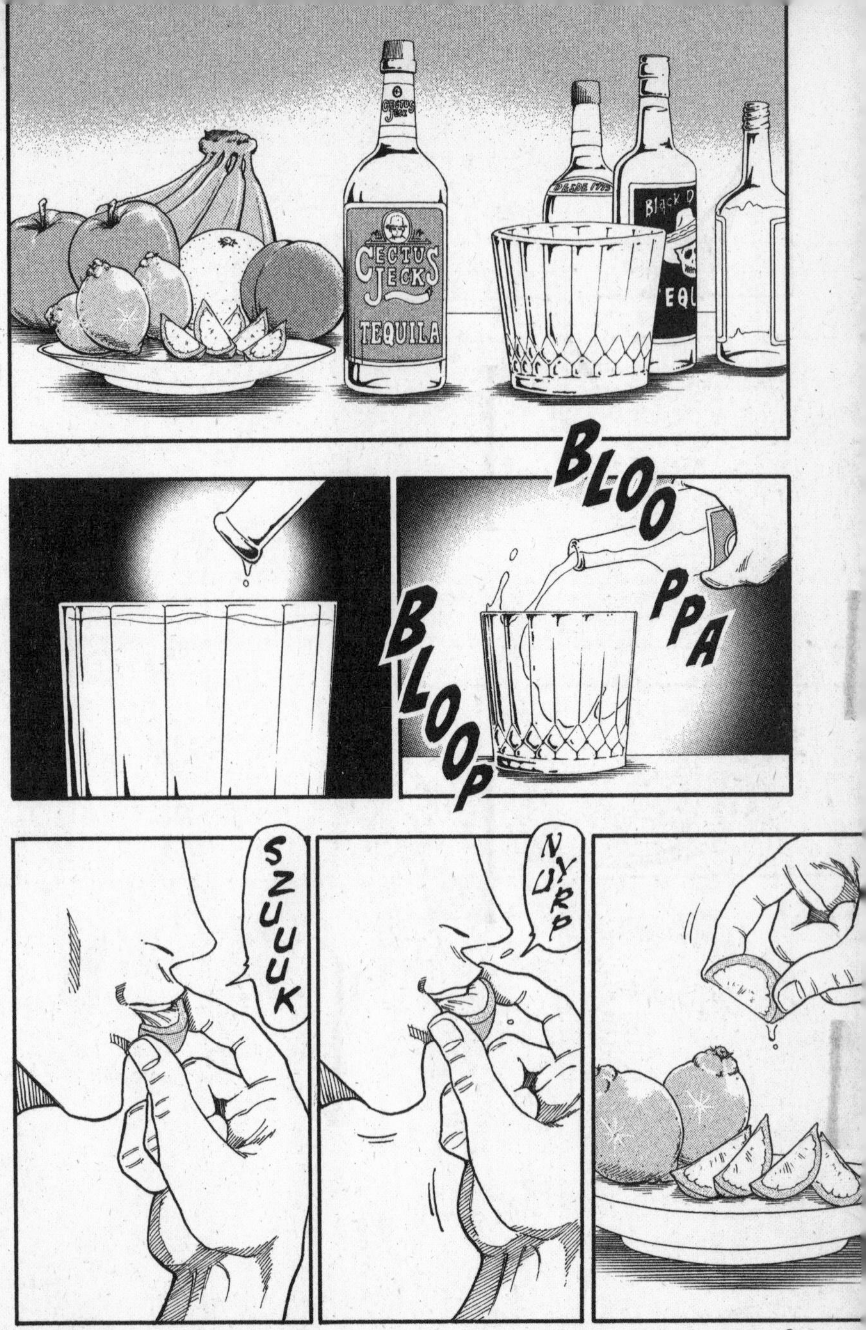
CECTUS JECK
TEQUILA
DESDE 1795
BLOOPPA
BLOOP
NYURP
SZUUUK

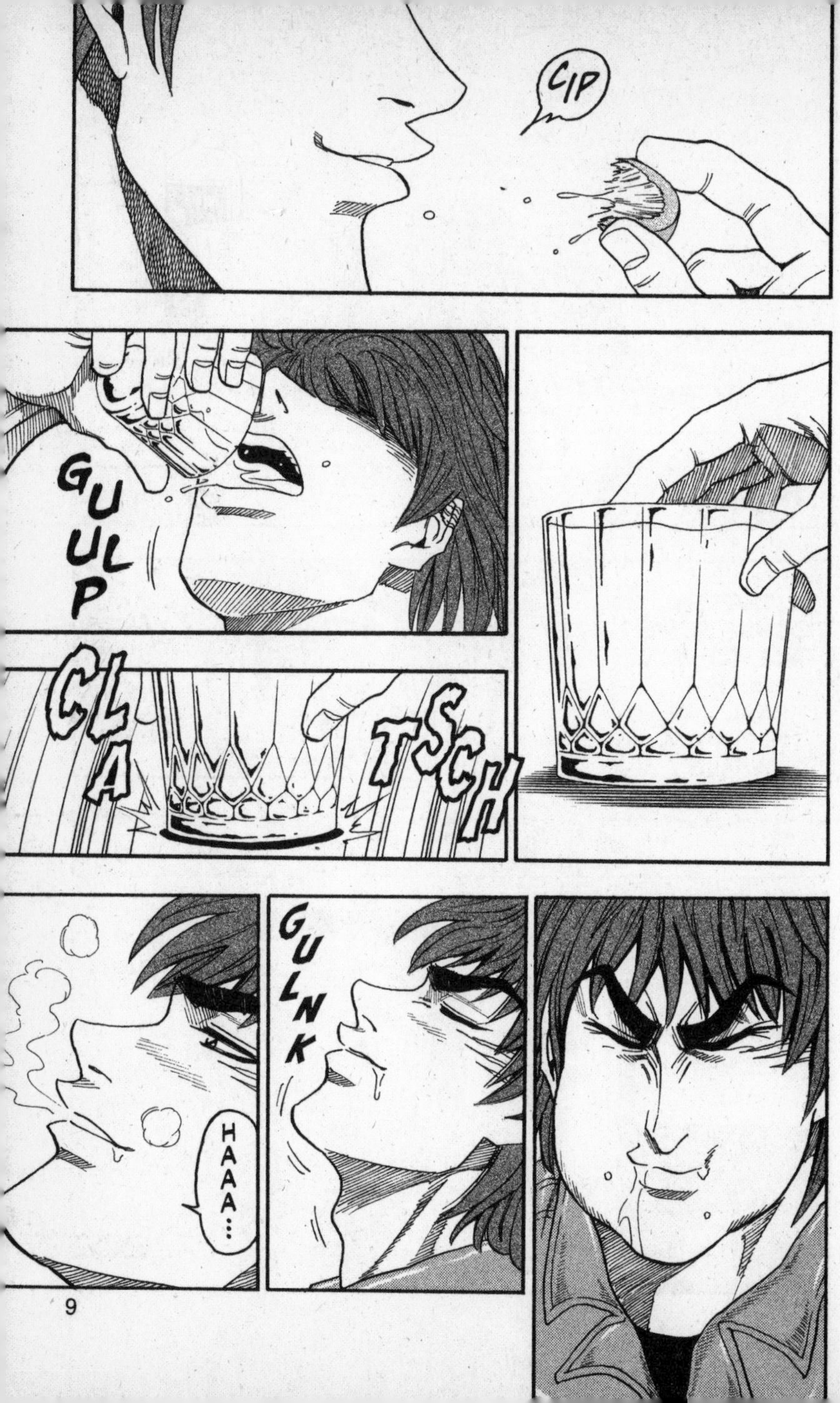
CIP
GUULP
CLATSCH
GULNK
HAAA...

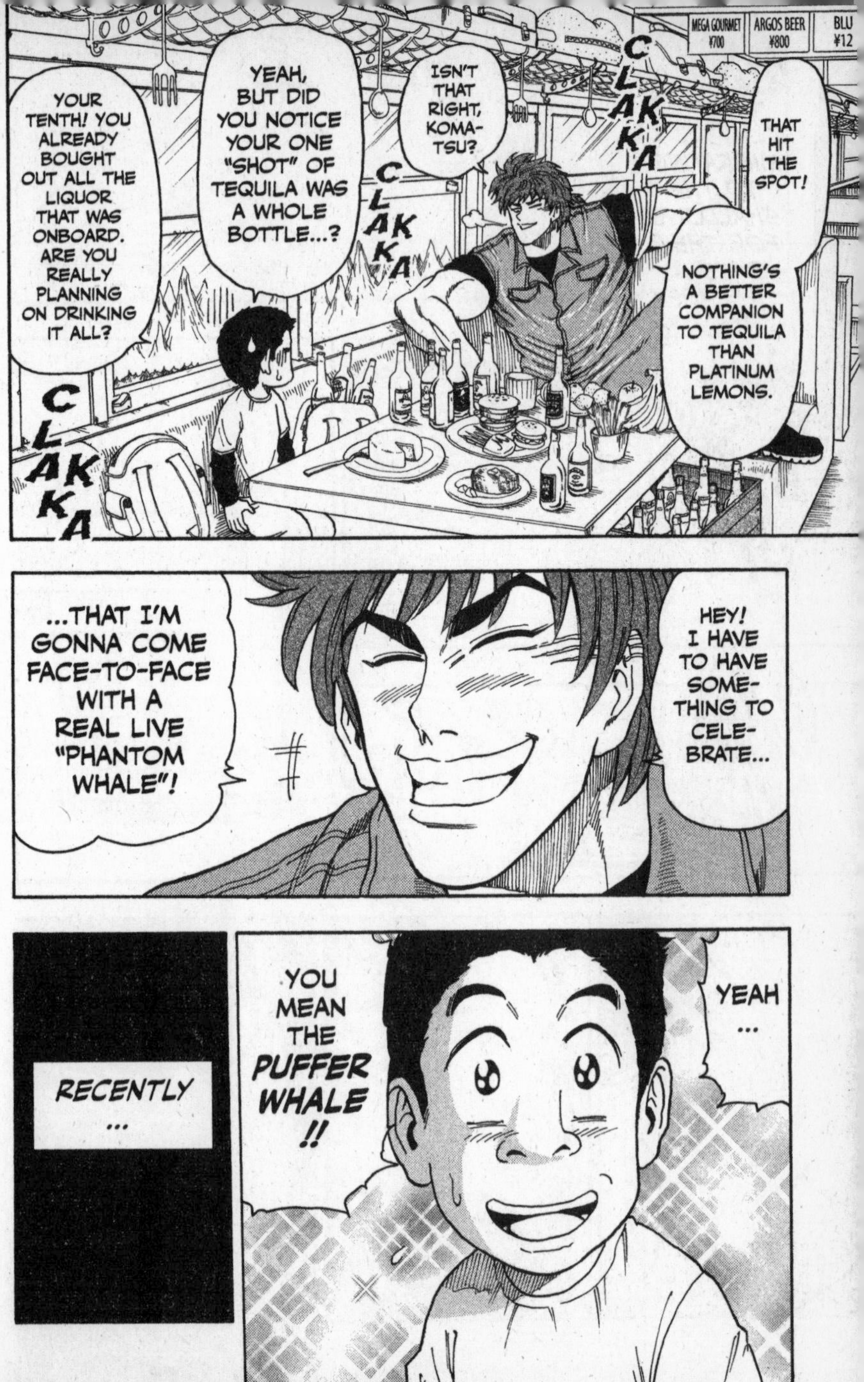
MEGA GOURMET ¥700
ARGOS BEER ¥800
BLU ¥12
THAT HIT THE SPOT!
NOTHING'S A BETTER COMPANION TO TEQUILA THAN PLATINUM LEMONS.
CLAKA
CLAKA
ISN'T THAT RIGHT, KOMATSU?
YEAH, BUT DID YOU NOTICE YOUR ONE "SHOT" OF TEQUILA WAS A WHOLE BOTTLE...?
YOUR TENTH! YOU ALREADY BOUGHT OUT ALL THE LIQUOR THAT WAS ONBOARD. ARE YOU REALLY PLANNING ON DRINKING IT ALL?
CLAKA
HEY! I HAVE TO HAVE SOMETHING TO CELEBRATE...
...THAT I'M GONNA COME FACE-TO-FACE WITH A REAL LIVE "PHANTOM WHALE"!
YEAH...
YOU MEAN THE *PUFFER WHALE*!!
RECENTLY...

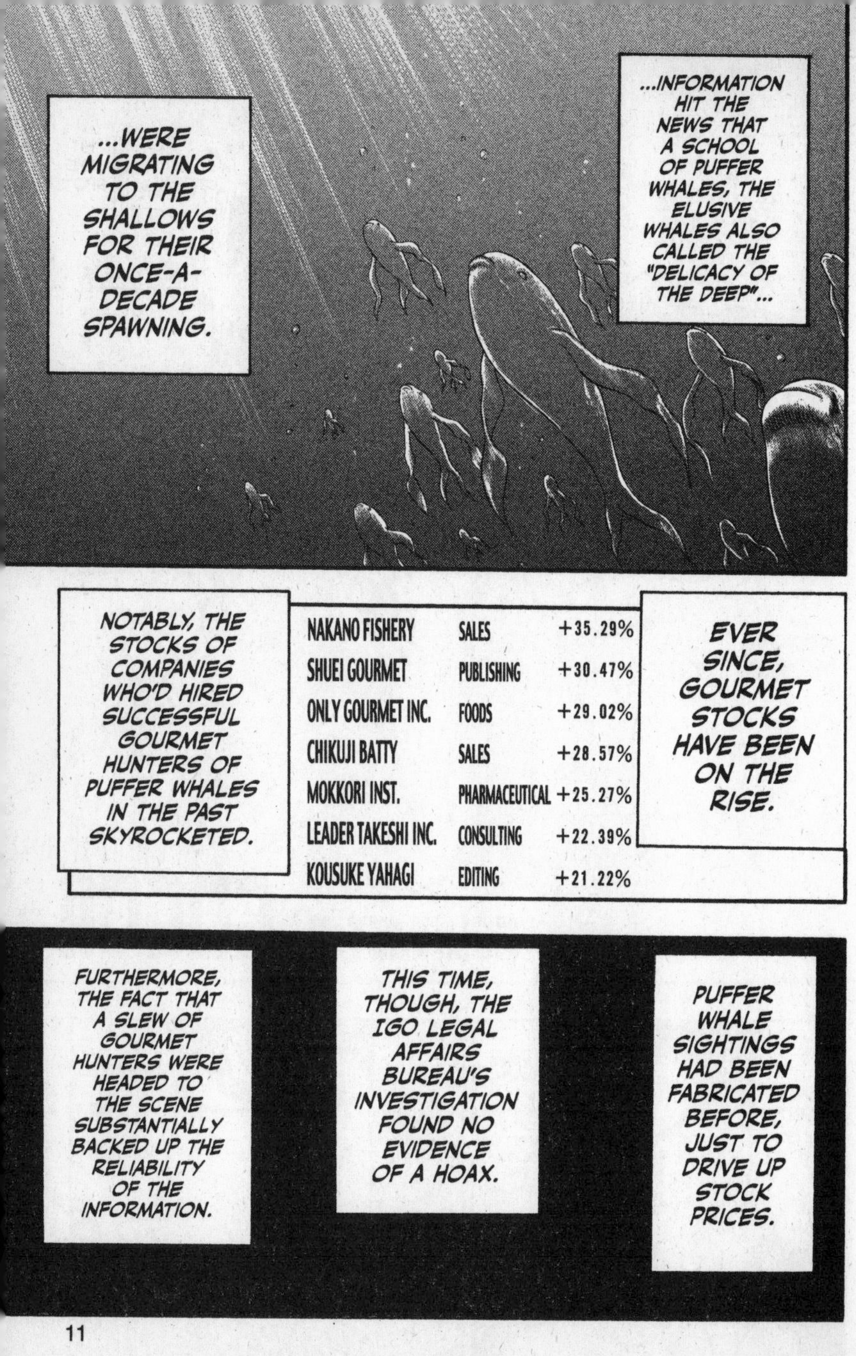
...INFORMATION HIT THE NEWS THAT A SCHOOL OF PUFFER WHALES, THE ELUSIVE WHALES ALSO CALLED THE "DELICACY OF THE DEEP"...
...WERE MIGRATING TO THE SHALLOWS FOR THEIR ONCE-A-DECADE SPAWNING.
EVER SINCE, GOURMET STOCKS HAVE BEEN ON THE RISE.
NAKANO FISHERY SALES +35.29%
SHUEI GOURMET PUBLISHING +30.47%
ONLY GOURMET INC. FOODS +29.02%
CHIKUJI BATTY SALES +28.57%
MOKKORI INST. PHARMACEUTICAL +25.27%
LEADER TAKESHI INC. CONSULTING +22.39%
KOUSUKE YAHAGI EDITING +21.22%
NOTABLY, THE STOCKS OF COMPANIES WHO'D HIRED SUCCESSFUL GOURMET HUNTERS OF PUFFER WHALES IN THE PAST SKYROCKETED.
PUFFER WHALE SIGHTINGS HAD BEEN FABRICATED BEFORE, JUST TO DRIVE UP STOCK PRICES.
THIS TIME, THOUGH, THE IGO LEGAL AFFAIRS BUREAU'S INVESTIGATION FOUND NO EVIDENCE OF A HOAX.
FURTHERMORE, THE FACT THAT A SLEW OF GOURMET HUNTERS WERE HEADED TO THE SCENE SUBSTANTIALLY BACKED UP THE RELIABILITY OF THE INFORMATION.

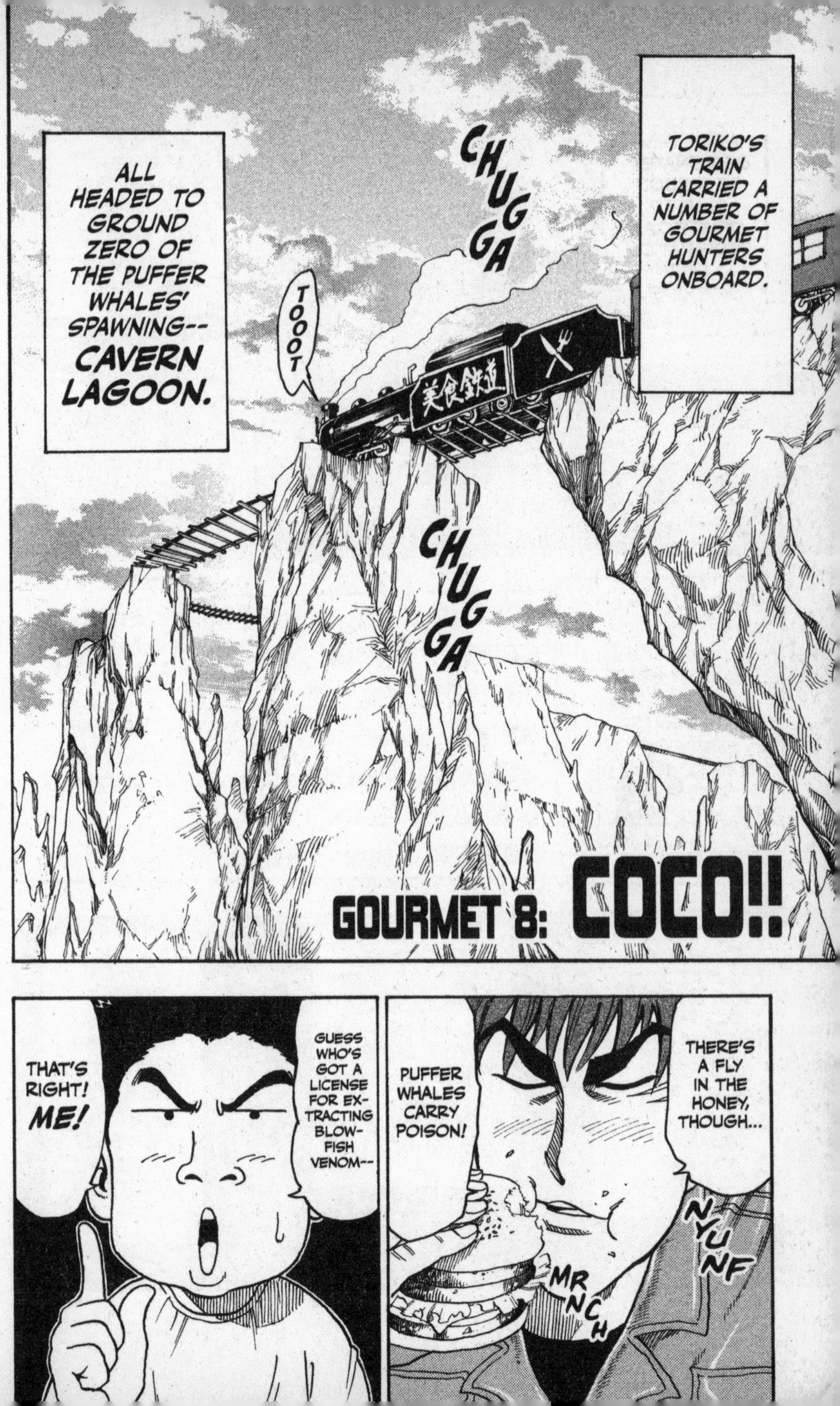
TORIKO'S TRAIN CARRIED A NUMBER OF GOURMET HUNTERS ONBOARD.
CHUGGA
美食鉄道
TOOOT
ALL HEADED TO GROUND ZERO OF THE PUFFER WHALES' SPAWNING-- CAVERN LAGOON.
CHUGGA
GOURMET 8: COCO!!
THERE'S A FLY IN THE HONEY, THOUGH...
PUFFER WHALES CARRY POISON!
NYUNF
MRNCH
GUESS WHO'S GOT A LICENSE FOR EX-TRACTING BLOW-FISH VENOM--
THAT'S RIGHT! ME!

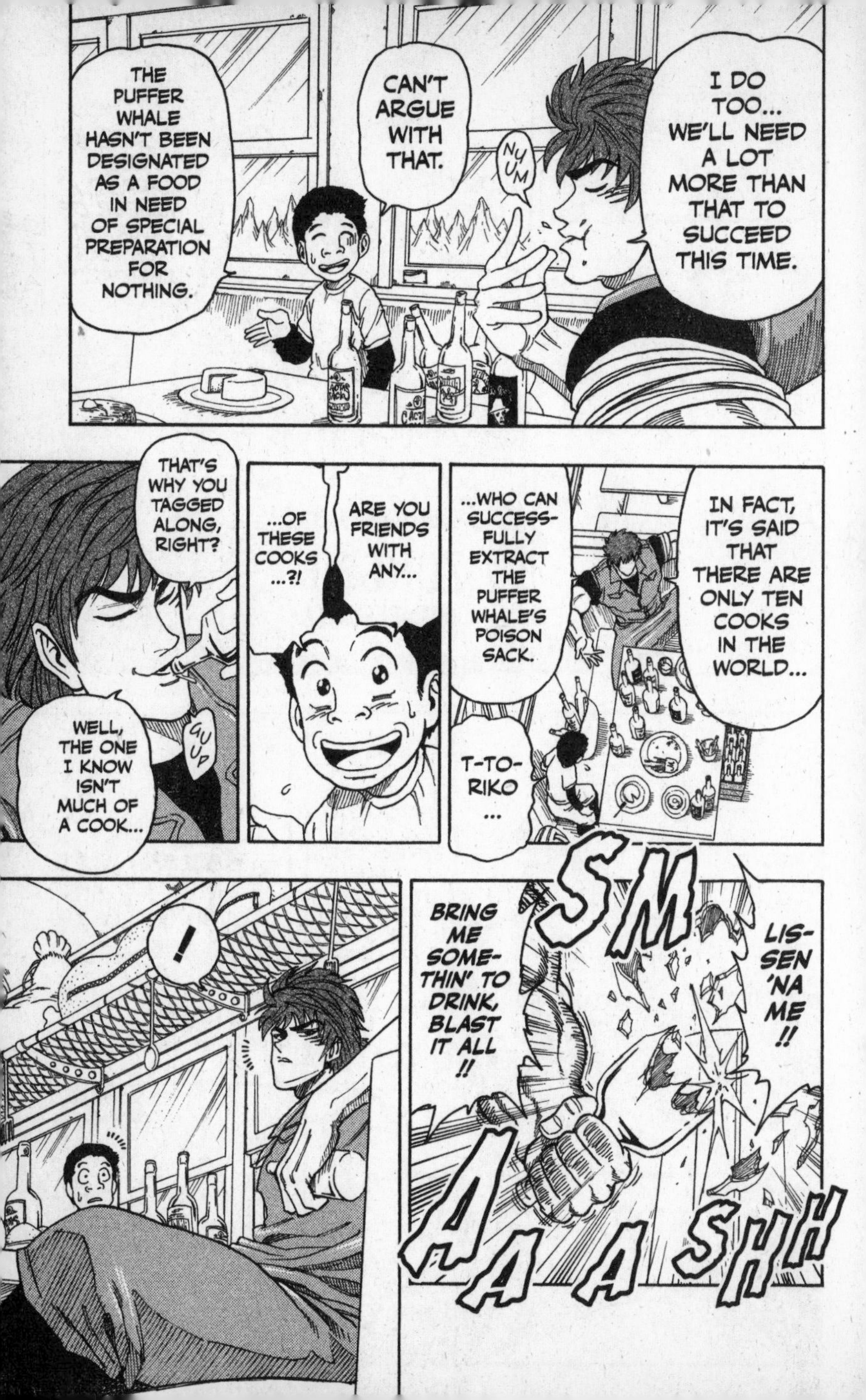
I DO TOO... WE'LL NEED A LOT MORE THAN THAT TO SUCCEED THIS TIME.
NUUM
CAN'T ARGUE WITH THAT.
THE PUFFER WHALE HASN'T BEEN DESIGNATED AS A FOOD IN NEED OF SPECIAL PREPARATION FOR NOTHING.
IN FACT, IT'S SAID THAT THERE ARE ONLY TEN COOKS IN THE WORLD...
...WHO CAN SUCCESS-FULLY EXTRACT THE PUFFER WHALE'S POISON SACK.
T-TO-RIKO ...
ARE YOU FRIENDS WITH ANY...
...OF THESE COOKS ...?!
THAT'S WHY YOU TAGGED ALONG, RIGHT?
GULP
WELL, THE ONE I KNOW ISN'T MUCH OF A COOK...
LIS-SEN 'NA ME !!
SMAAASHH
BRING ME SOME-THIN' TO DRINK, BLAST IT ALL !!
!

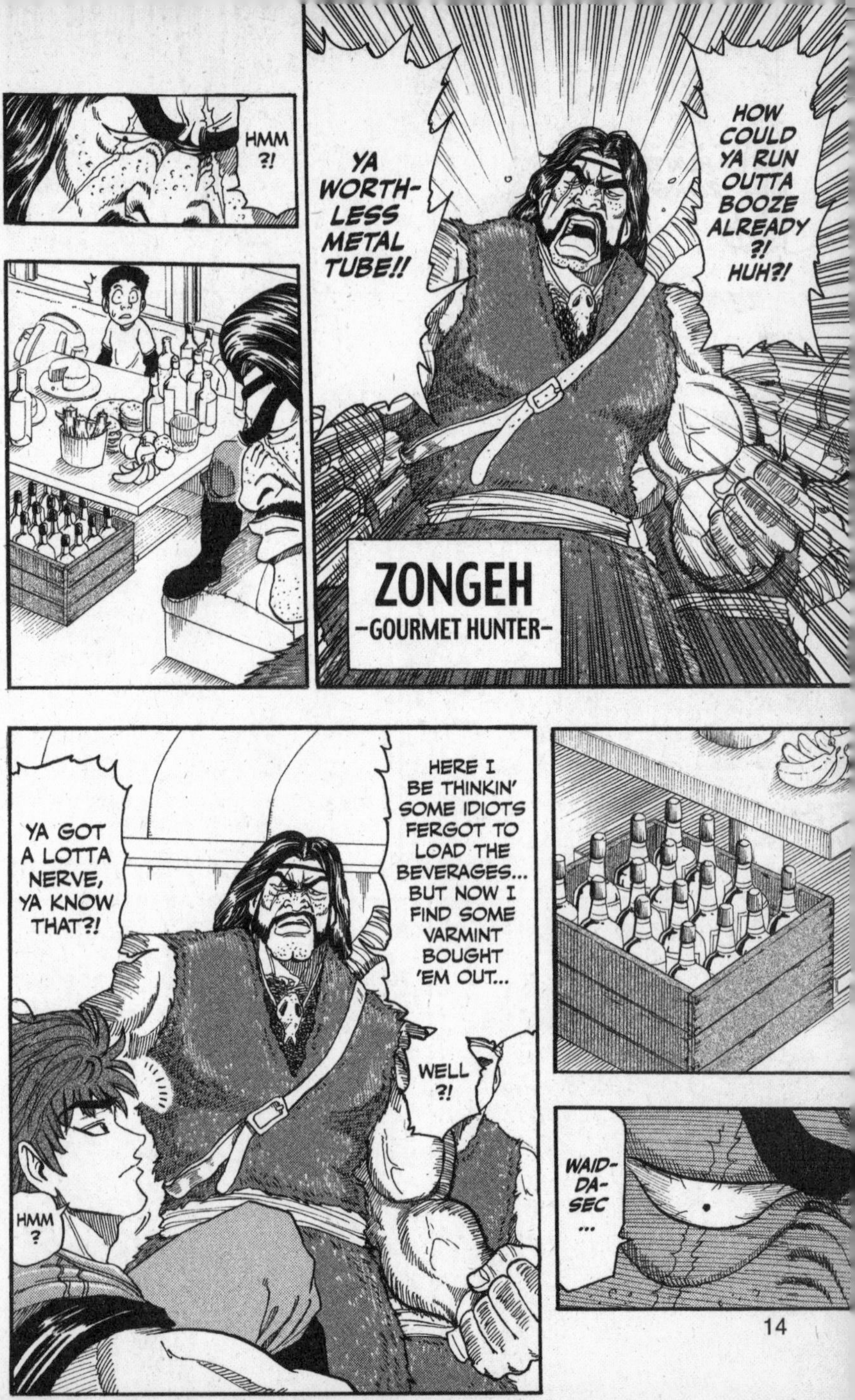
HOW COULD YA RUN OUTTA BOOZE ALREADY ?! HUH?!
YA WORTH-LESS METAL TUBE!!
ZONGEH
-GOURMET HUNTER-
HMM ?!
WAID-DA-SEC ...
HERE I BE THINKIN' SOME IDIOTS FERGOT TO LOAD THE BEVERAGES... BUT NOW I FIND SOME VARMINT BOUGHT 'EM OUT...
YA GOT A LOTTA NERVE, YA KNOW THAT?!
WELL ?!
HMM ?

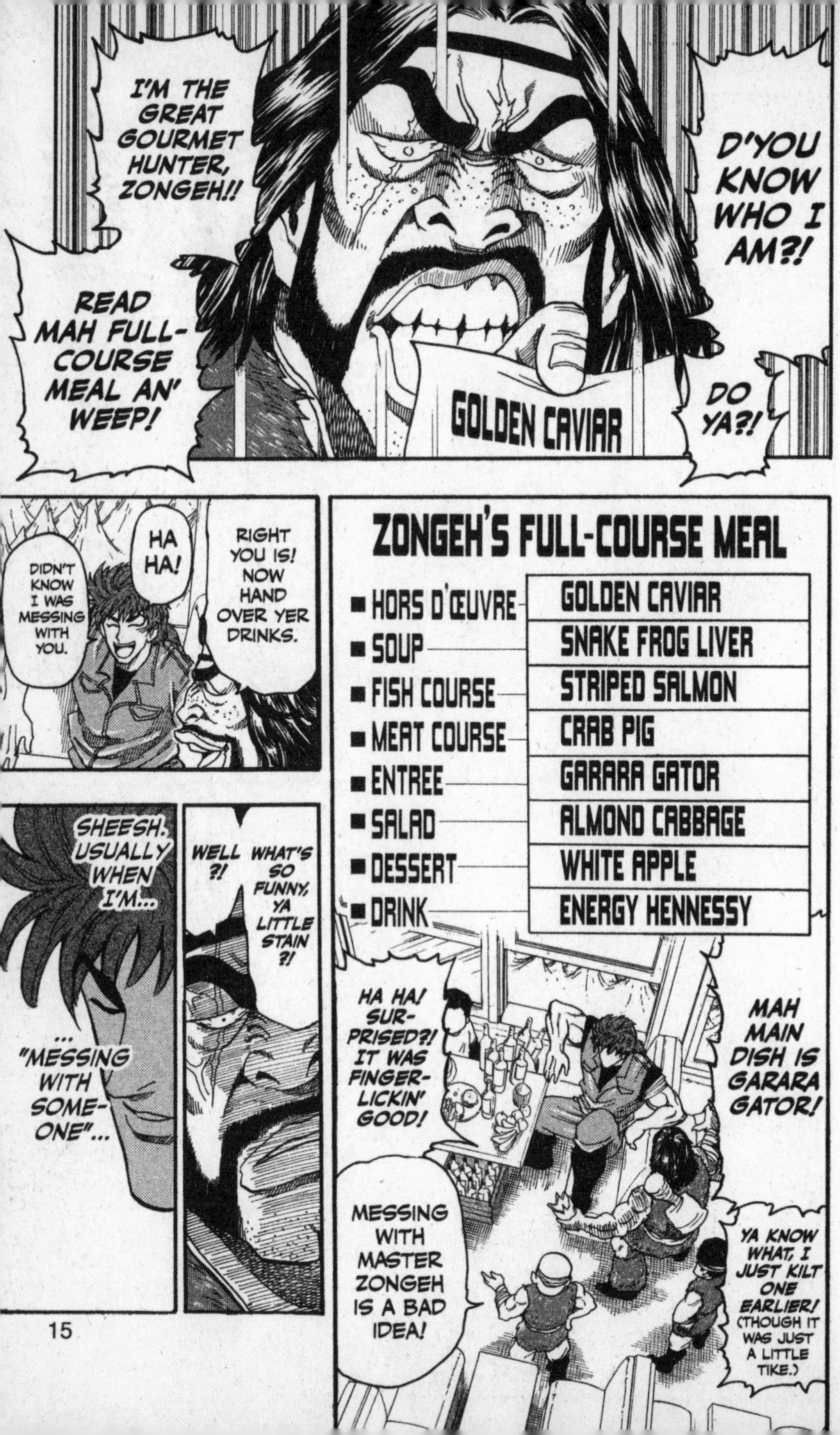

D'YOU KNOW WHO I AM?!
DO YA?!
I'M THE GREAT GOURMET HUNTER, ZONGEH!!
READ MAH FULL-COURSE MEAL AN' WEEP!
GOLDEN CAVIAR
ZONGEH'S FULL-COURSE MEAL
■ HORS D'ŒUVRE — GOLDEN CAVIAR
■ SOUP — SNAKE FROG LIVER
■ FISH COURSE — STRIPED SALMON
■ MEAT COURSE — CRAB PIG
■ ENTREE — GARARA GATOR
■ SALAD — ALMOND CABBAGE
■ DESSERT — WHITE APPLE
■ DRINK — ENERGY HENNESSY
MAH MAIN DISH IS GARARA GATOR!
HA HA! SUR-PRISED?! IT WAS FINGER-LICKIN' GOOD!
YA KNOW WHAT, I JUST KILT ONE EARLIER! (THOUGH IT WAS JUST A LITTLE TIKE.)
MESSING WITH MASTER ZONGEH IS A BAD IDEA!
RIGHT YOU IS! NOW HAND OVER YER DRINKS.
HA HA!
DIDN'T KNOW I WAS MESSING WITH YOU.
WHAT'S SO FUNNY, YA LITTLE STAIN?!
WELL?!
SHEESH. USUALLY WHEN I'M...
... "MESSING WITH SOME-ONE"...

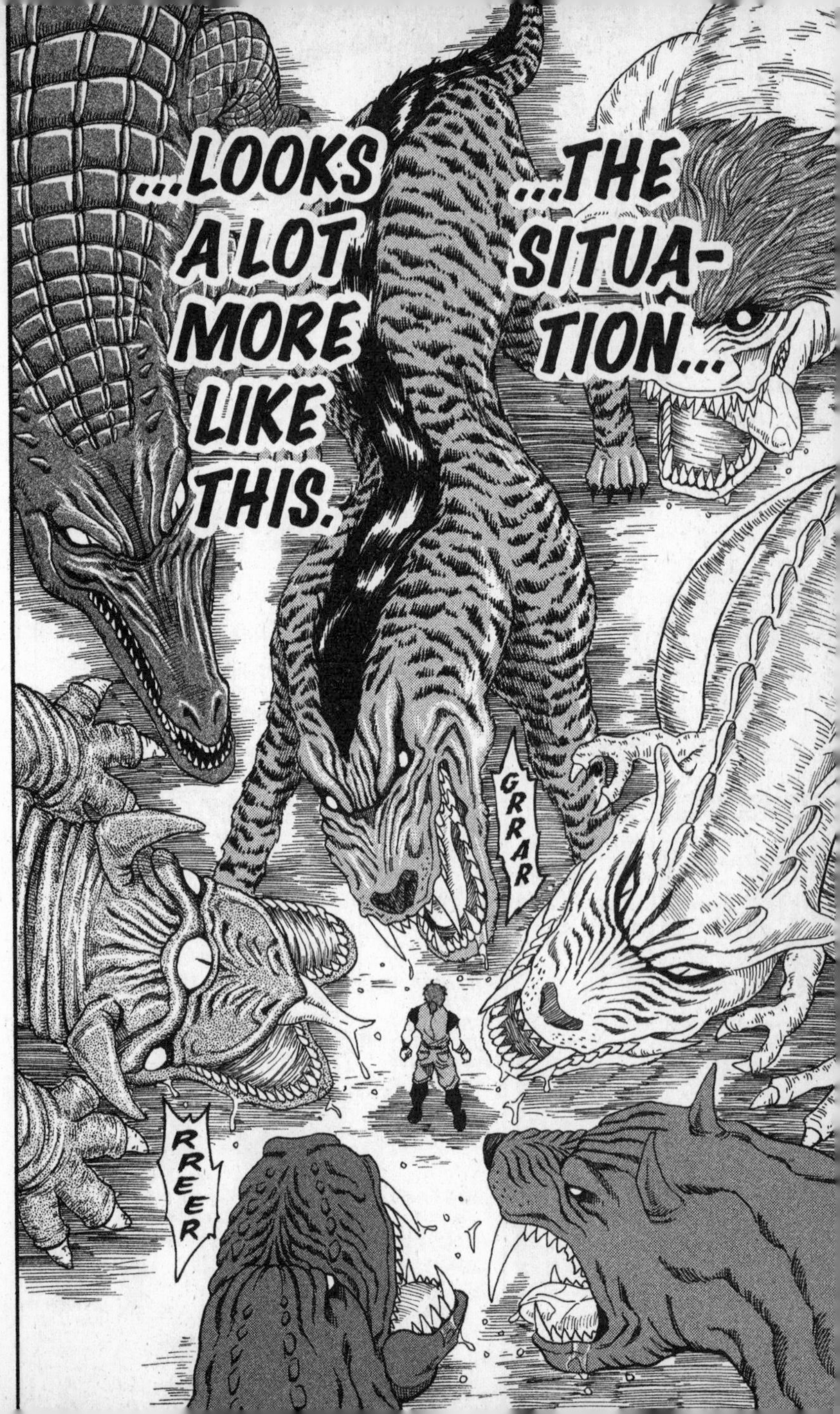
...THE SITUA-TION...
...LOOKS A LOT MORE LIKE THIS.
GRRRAR
RREER

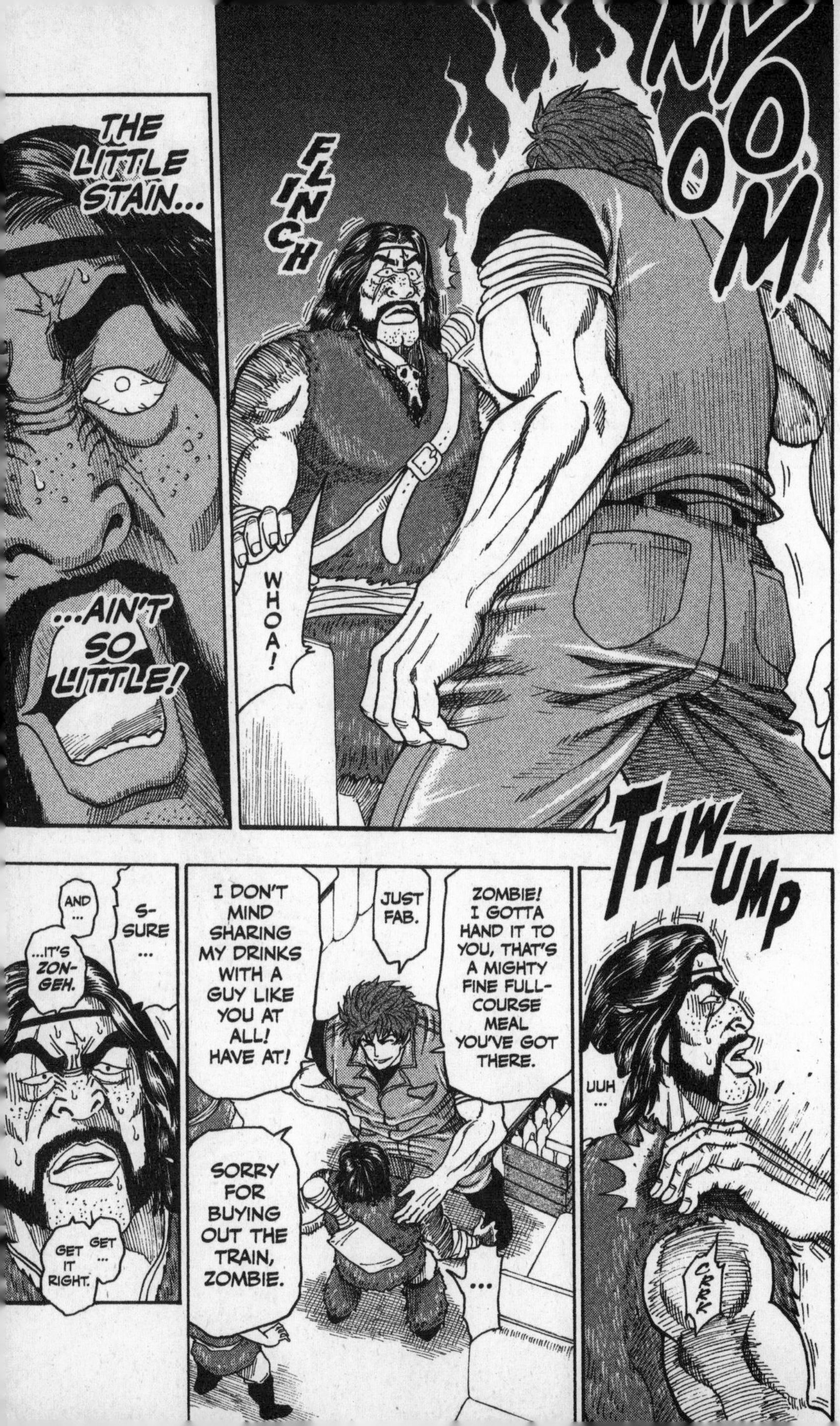
NYOOM
FLINCH
WHOA!
THE LITTLE STAIN...
...AIN'T SO LITTLE!
THWUMP
UUH...
CRRK
ZOMBIE! I GOTTA HAND IT TO YOU, THAT'S A MIGHTY FINE FULL-COURSE MEAL YOU'VE GOT THERE.
JUST FAB.
I DON'T MIND SHARING MY DRINKS WITH A GUY LIKE YOU AT ALL! HAVE AT!
SORRY FOR BUYING OUT THE TRAIN, ZOMBIE.
...
S-SURE...
AND...
...IT'S ZONGEH.
GET...
GET IT RIGHT.

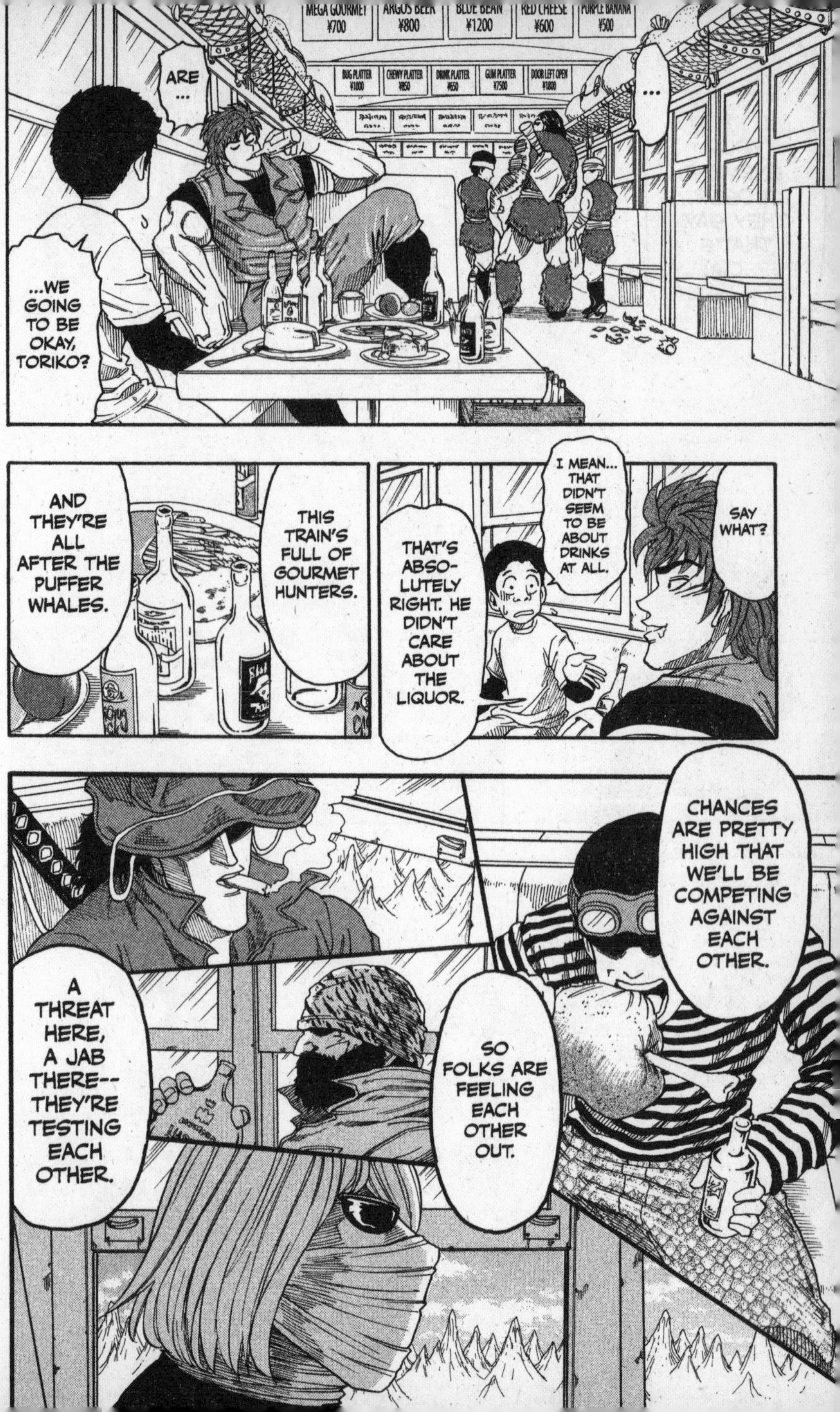
MEGA GOURMET ¥700
ARGUS BEER ¥800
BLUE BEAN ¥1200
RED CHEESE ¥600
PURPLE BANANA ¥500
BUG PLATTER ¥1000
CHEWY PLATTER ¥850
DRINK PLATTER ¥650
GUM PLATTER ¥7500
DOOR LEFT OPEN ¥1800
...
ARE ...
...WE GOING TO BE OKAY, TORIKO?
SAY WHAT?
I MEAN... THAT DIDN'T SEEM TO BE ABOUT DRINKS AT ALL.
THAT'S ABSOLUTELY RIGHT. HE DIDN'T CARE ABOUT THE LIQUOR.
THIS TRAIN'S FULL OF GOURMET HUNTERS.
AND THEY'RE ALL AFTER THE PUFFER WHALES.
CHANCES ARE PRETTY HIGH THAT WE'LL BE COMPETING AGAINST EACH OTHER.
SO FOLKS ARE FEELING EACH OTHER OUT.
A THREAT HERE, A JAB THERE--THEY'RE TESTING EACH OTHER.

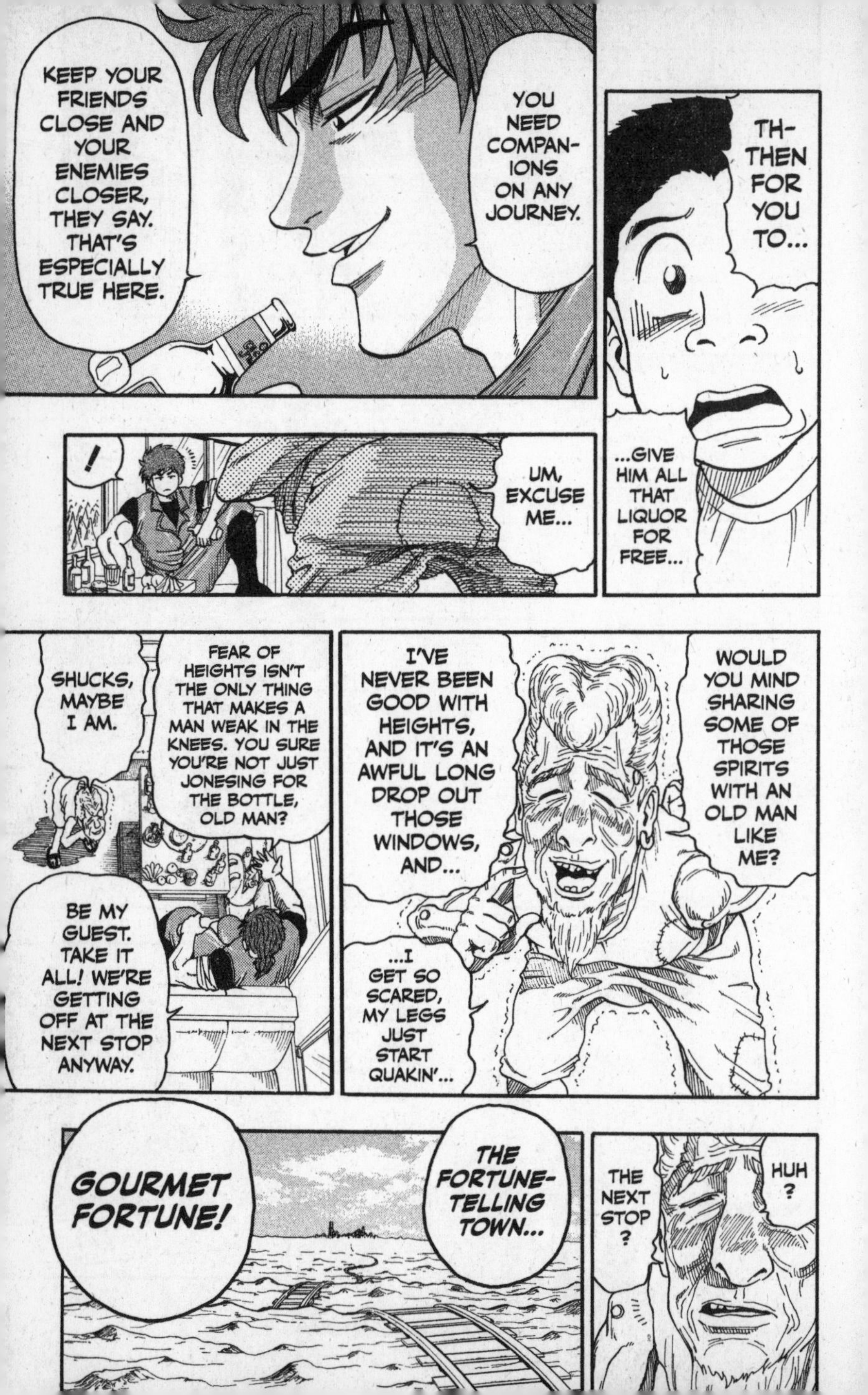
YOU NEED COMPANIONS ON ANY JOURNEY.
KEEP YOUR FRIENDS CLOSE AND YOUR ENEMIES CLOSER, THEY SAY. THAT'S ESPECIALLY TRUE HERE.
TH-THEN FOR YOU TO...
...GIVE HIM ALL THAT LIQUOR FOR FREE...
UM, EXCUSE ME...
!
WOULD YOU MIND SHARING SOME OF THOSE SPIRITS WITH AN OLD MAN LIKE ME?
I'VE NEVER BEEN GOOD WITH HEIGHTS, AND IT'S AN AWFUL LONG DROP OUT THOSE WINDOWS, AND...
...I GET SO SCARED, MY LEGS JUST START QUAKIN'...
FEAR OF HEIGHTS ISN'T THE ONLY THING THAT MAKES A MAN WEAK IN THE KNEES. YOU SURE YOU'RE NOT JUST JONESING FOR THE BOTTLE, OLD MAN?
SHUCKS, MAYBE I AM.
BE MY GUEST. TAKE IT ALL! WE'RE GETTING OFF AT THE NEXT STOP ANYWAY.
HUH?
THE NEXT STOP?
THE FORTUNE-TELLING TOWN...
GOURMET FORTUNE!

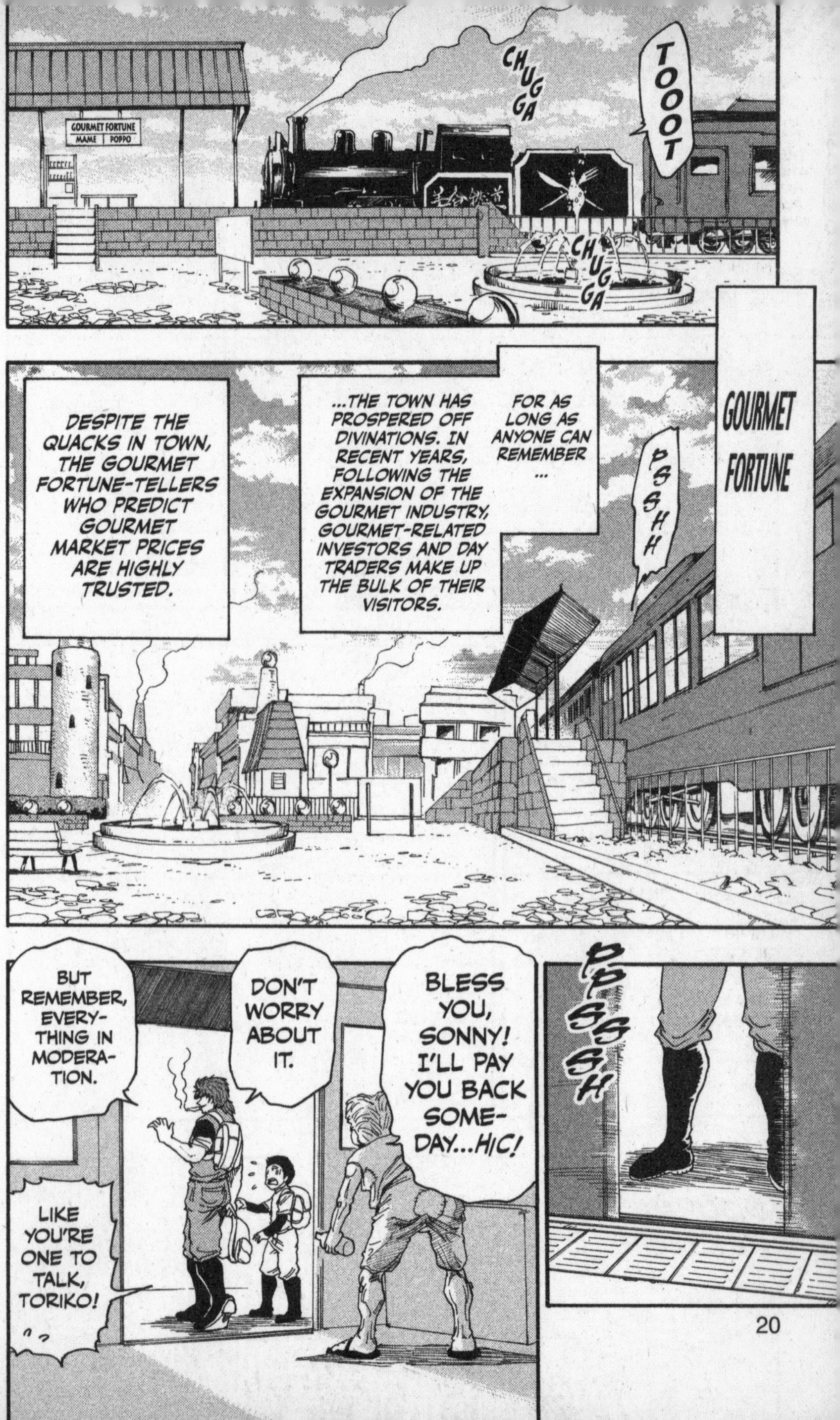
TOOOT
CHUGGA
GOURMET FORTUNE
MAME | POPPO
CHUGGA
GOURMET FORTUNE
PSSHH
FOR AS LONG AS ANYONE CAN REMEMBER...
...THE TOWN HAS PROSPERED OFF DIVINATIONS. IN RECENT YEARS, FOLLOWING THE EXPANSION OF THE GOURMET INDUSTRY, GOURMET-RELATED INVESTORS AND DAY TRADERS MAKE UP THE BULK OF THEIR VISITORS.
DESPITE THE QUACKS IN TOWN, THE GOURMET FORTUNE-TELLERS WHO PREDICT GOURMET MARKET PRICES ARE HIGHLY TRUSTED.
PPSSSH
BLESS YOU, SONNY! I'LL PAY YOU BACK SOME-DAY...HIC!
DON'T WORRY ABOUT IT.
BUT REMEMBER, EVERY-THING IN MODERA-TION.
LIKE YOU'RE ONE TO TALK, TORIKO!

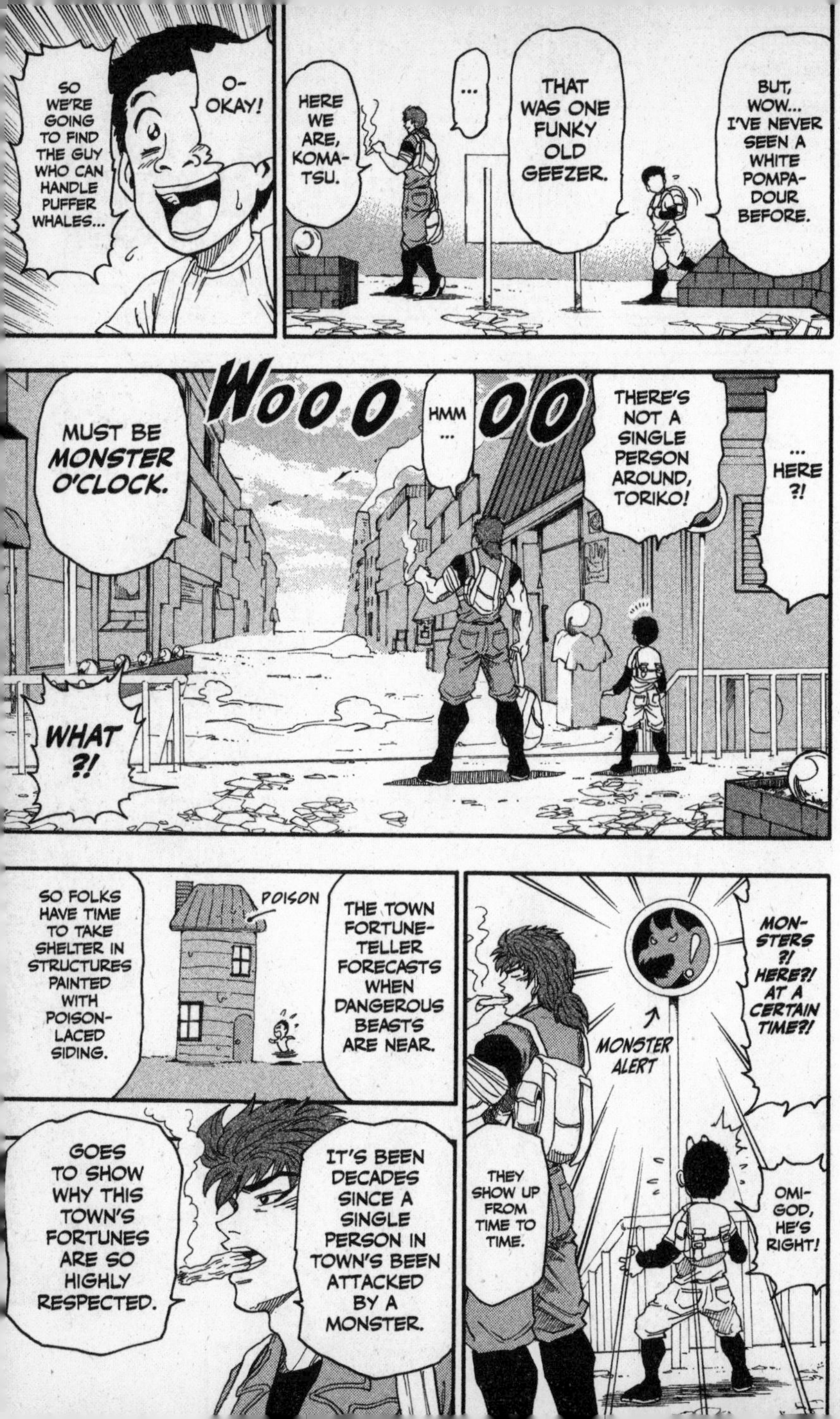
BUT, WOW... I'VE NEVER SEEN A WHITE POMPADOUR BEFORE.
THAT WAS ONE FUNKY OLD GEEZER.
...
HERE WE ARE, KOMATSU.
O-OKAY!
SO WE'RE GOING TO FIND THE GUY WHO CAN HANDLE PUFFER WHALES...
...HERE?!
THERE'S NOT A SINGLE PERSON AROUND, TORIKO!
HMM...
WOOOOO
MUST BE MONSTER O'CLOCK.
WHAT?!
MONSTERS?! HERE?! AT A CERTAIN TIME?!
MONSTER ALERT
OMIGOD, HE'S RIGHT!
THEY SHOW UP FROM TIME TO TIME.
THE TOWN FORTUNE-TELLER FORECASTS WHEN DANGEROUS BEASTS ARE NEAR.
POISON
SO FOLKS HAVE TIME TO TAKE SHELTER IN STRUCTURES PAINTED WITH POISON-LACED SIDING.
IT'S BEEN DECADES SINCE A SINGLE PERSON IN TOWN'S BEEN ATTACKED BY A MONSTER.
GOES TO SHOW WHY THIS TOWN'S FORTUNES ARE SO HIGHLY RESPECTED.

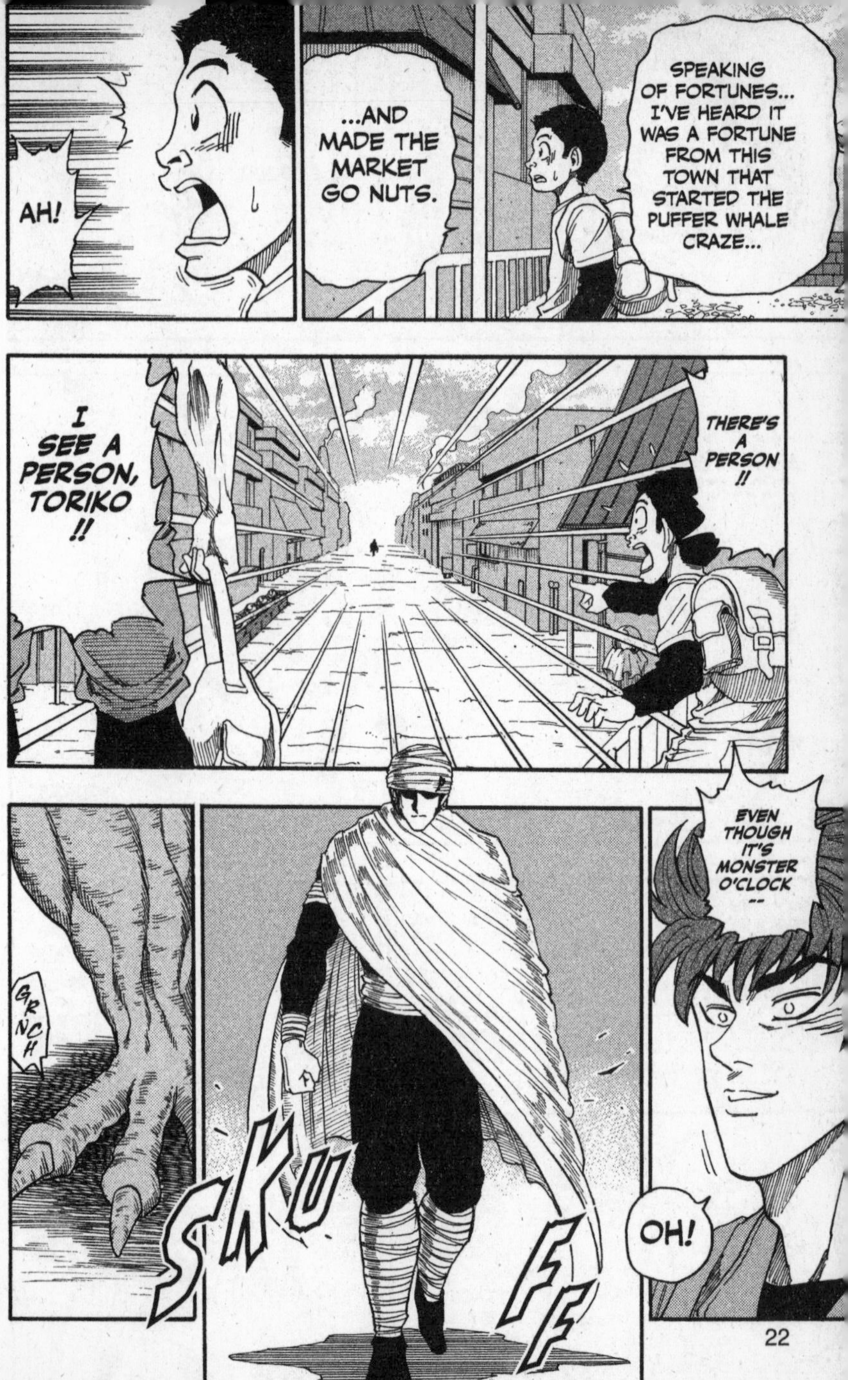

SPEAKING OF FORTUNES... I'VE HEARD IT WAS A FORTUNE FROM THIS TOWN THAT STARTED THE PUFFER WHALE CRAZE...
...AND MADE THE MARKET GO NUTS.
AH!
THERE'S A PERSON!!
I SEE A PERSON, TORIKO!!
EVEN THOUGH IT'S MONSTER O'CLOCK--
OH!
SKUFF
GRNCH

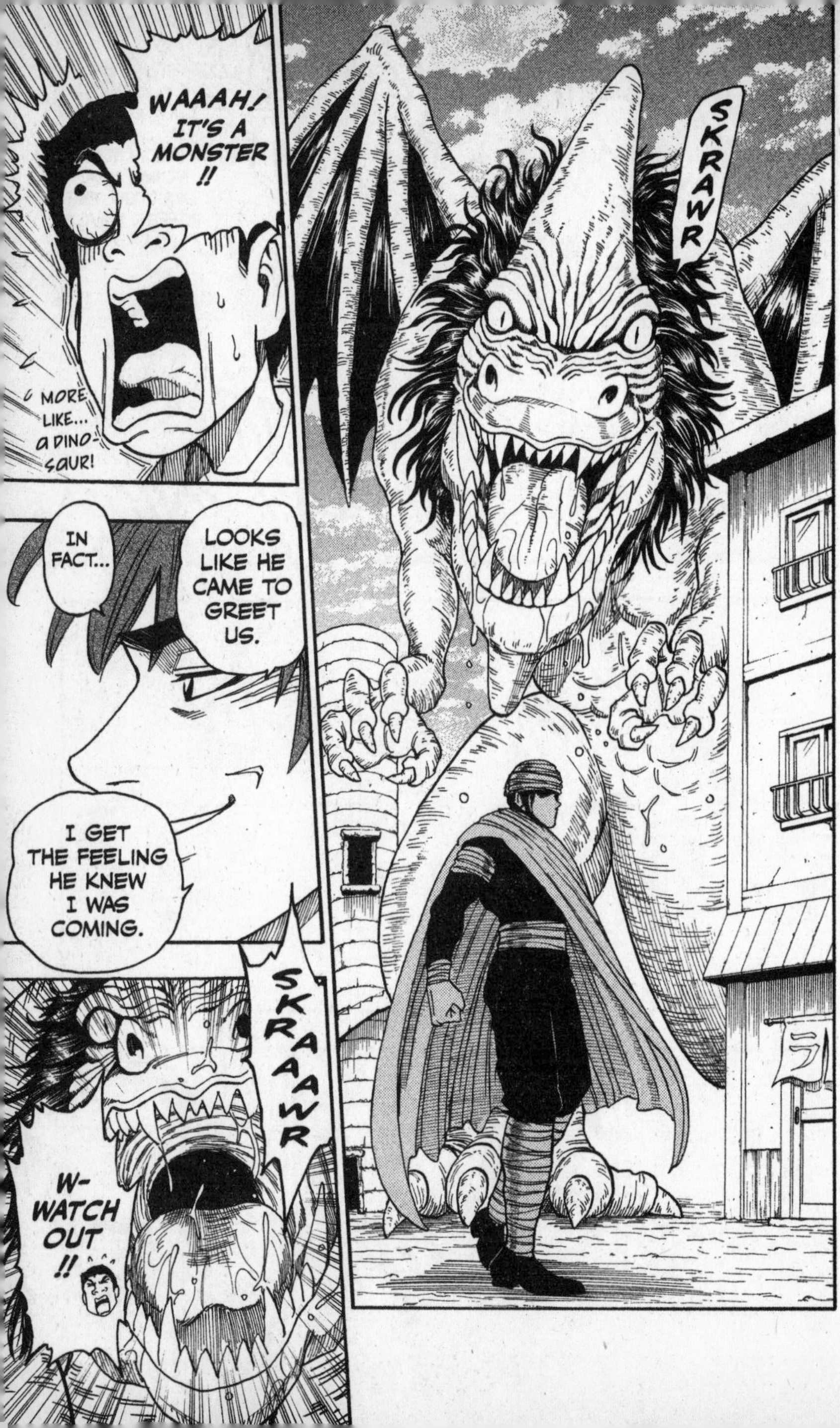
SKRAWR
WAAAH! IT'S A MONSTER!!
MORE LIKE... A DINO-SAUR!
LOOKS LIKE HE CAME TO GREET US.
IN FACT...
I GET THE FEELING HE KNEW I WAS COMING.
SKRAAAWR
W-WATCH OUT!!

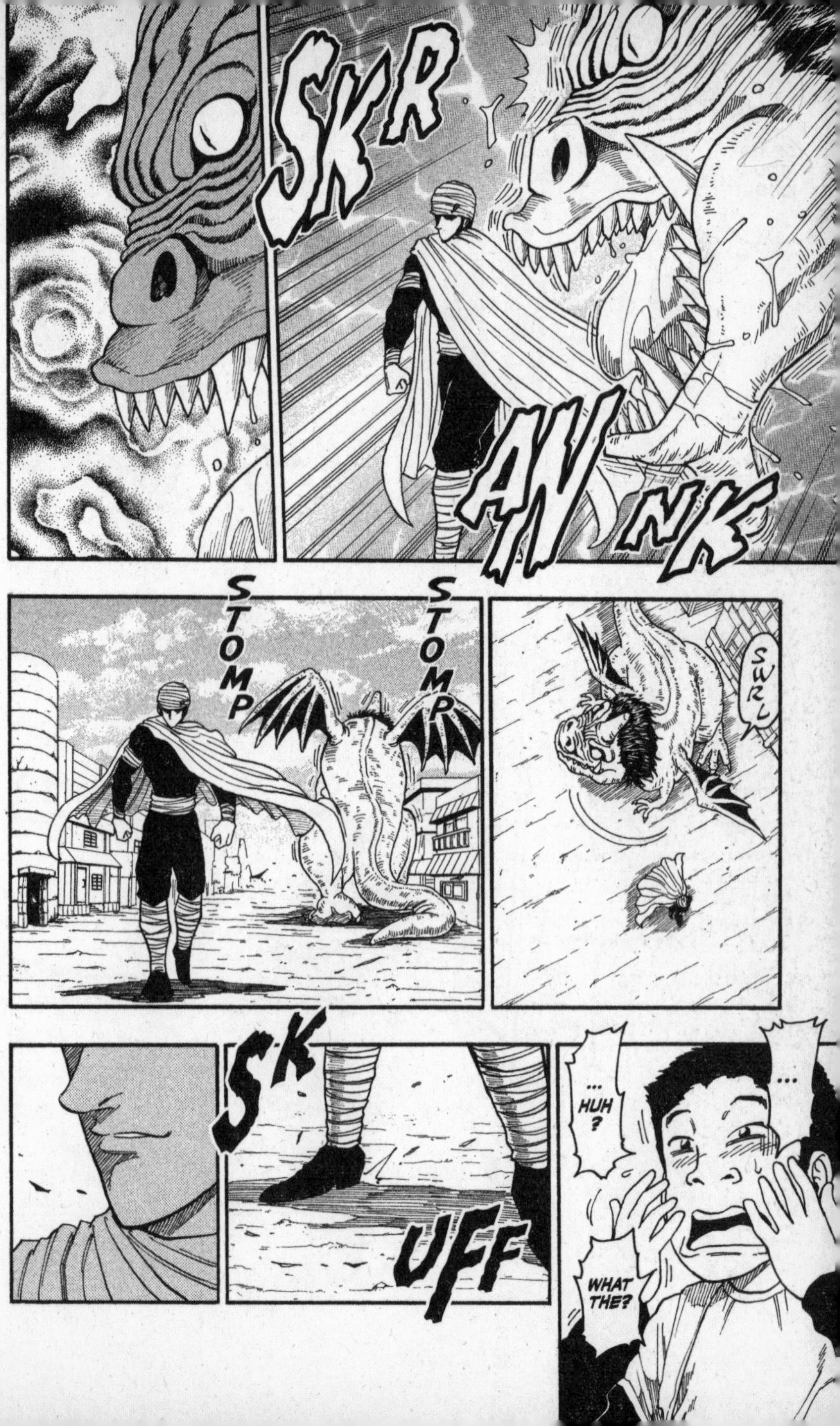
SKR
AN
NK
SWRL
STOMP
STOMP
...
... HUH?
WHAT THE?
SK
UFF

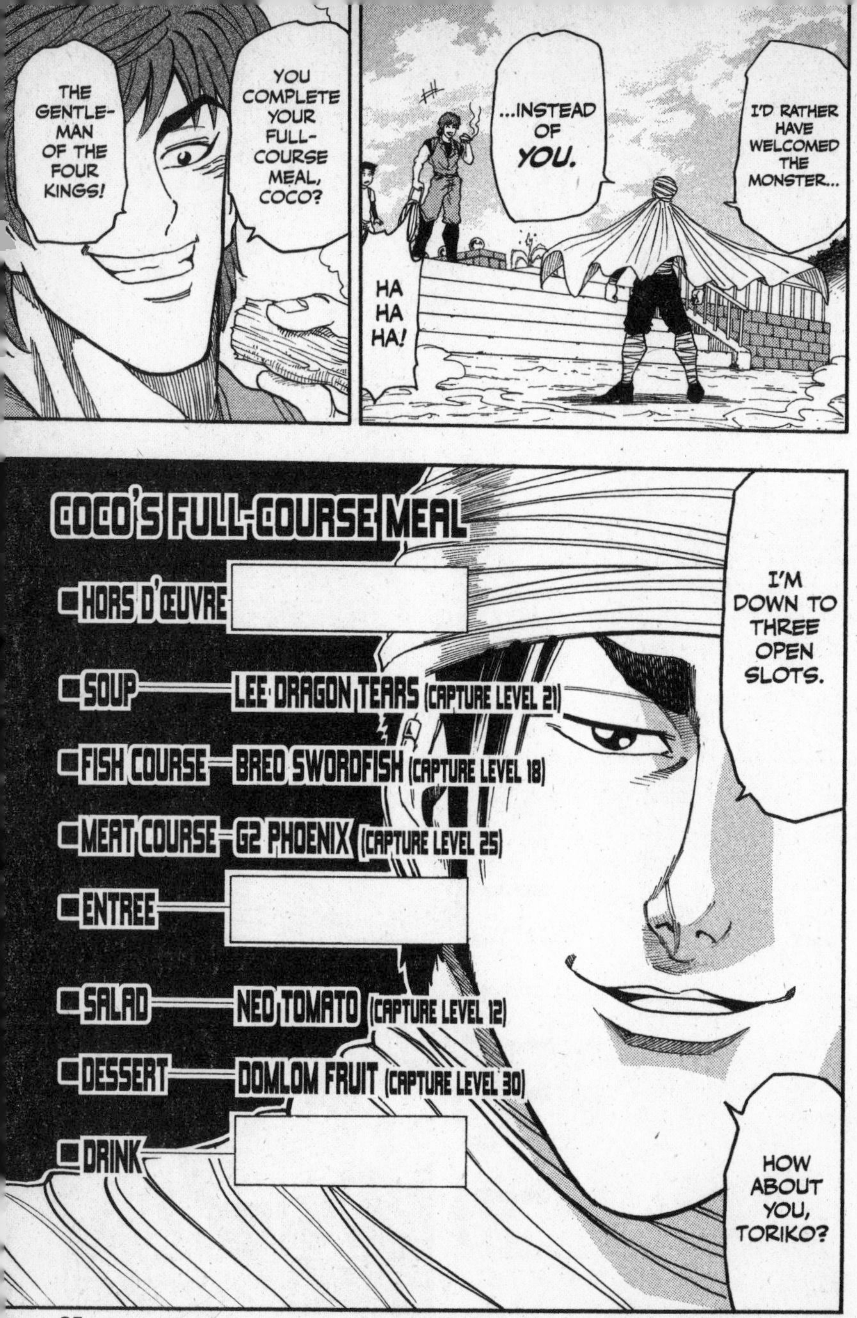
I'D RATHER HAVE WELCOMED THE MONSTER...
...INSTEAD OF YOU.
HA HA HA!
YOU COMPLETE YOUR FULL-COURSE MEAL, COCO?
THE GENTLEMAN OF THE FOUR KINGS!
I'M DOWN TO THREE OPEN SLOTS.
COCO'S FULL-COURSE MEAL
HORS D'ŒUVRE
SOUP LEE DRAGON TEARS (CAPTURE LEVEL 21)
FISH COURSE BREO SWORDFISH (CAPTURE LEVEL 18)
MEAT COURSE G2 PHOENIX (CAPTURE LEVEL 25)
ENTREE
SALAD NEO TOMATO (CAPTURE LEVEL 12)
DESSERT DOMLOM FRUIT (CAPTURE LEVEL 30)
DRINK
HOW ABOUT YOU, TORIKO?

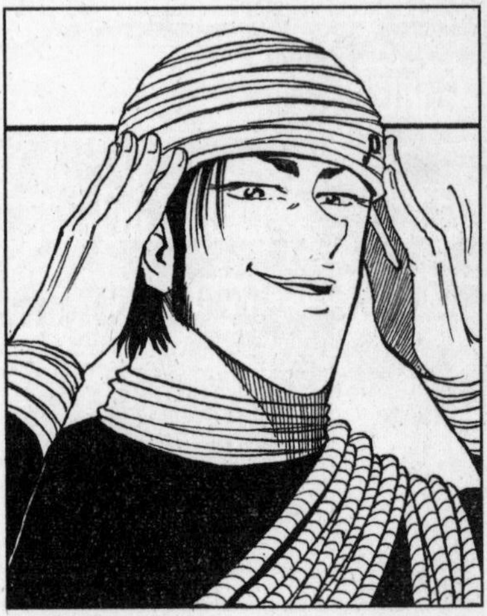

GOGO

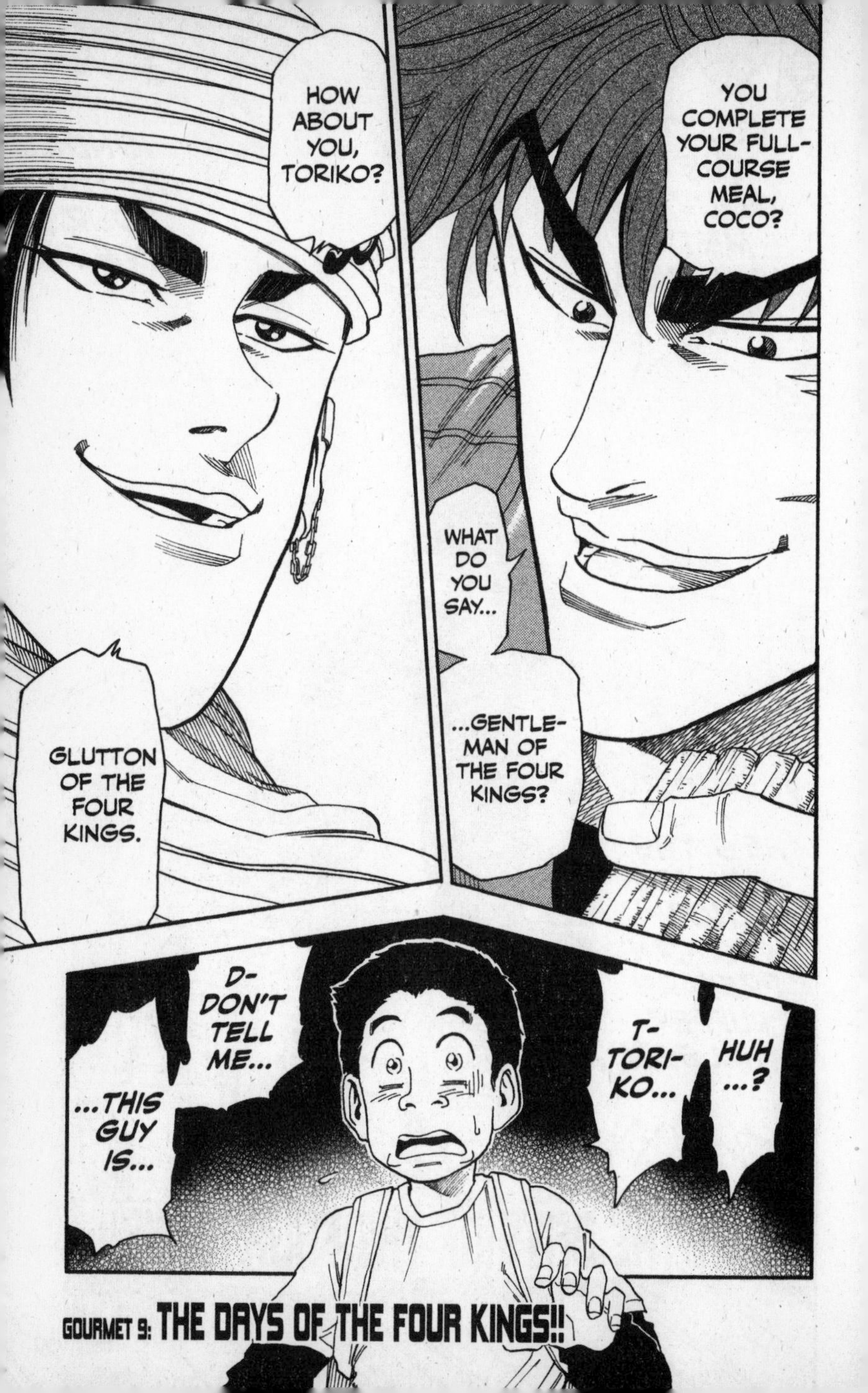
YOU COMPLETE YOUR FULL-COURSE MEAL, COCO?
WHAT DO YOU SAY...
...GENTLEMAN OF THE FOUR KINGS?
HOW ABOUT YOU, TORIKO?
GLUTTON OF THE FOUR KINGS.
HUH ...?
T-TORIKO...
D-DON'T TELL ME...
...THIS GUY IS...

GOURMET 9: THE DAYS OF THE FOUR KINGS!!

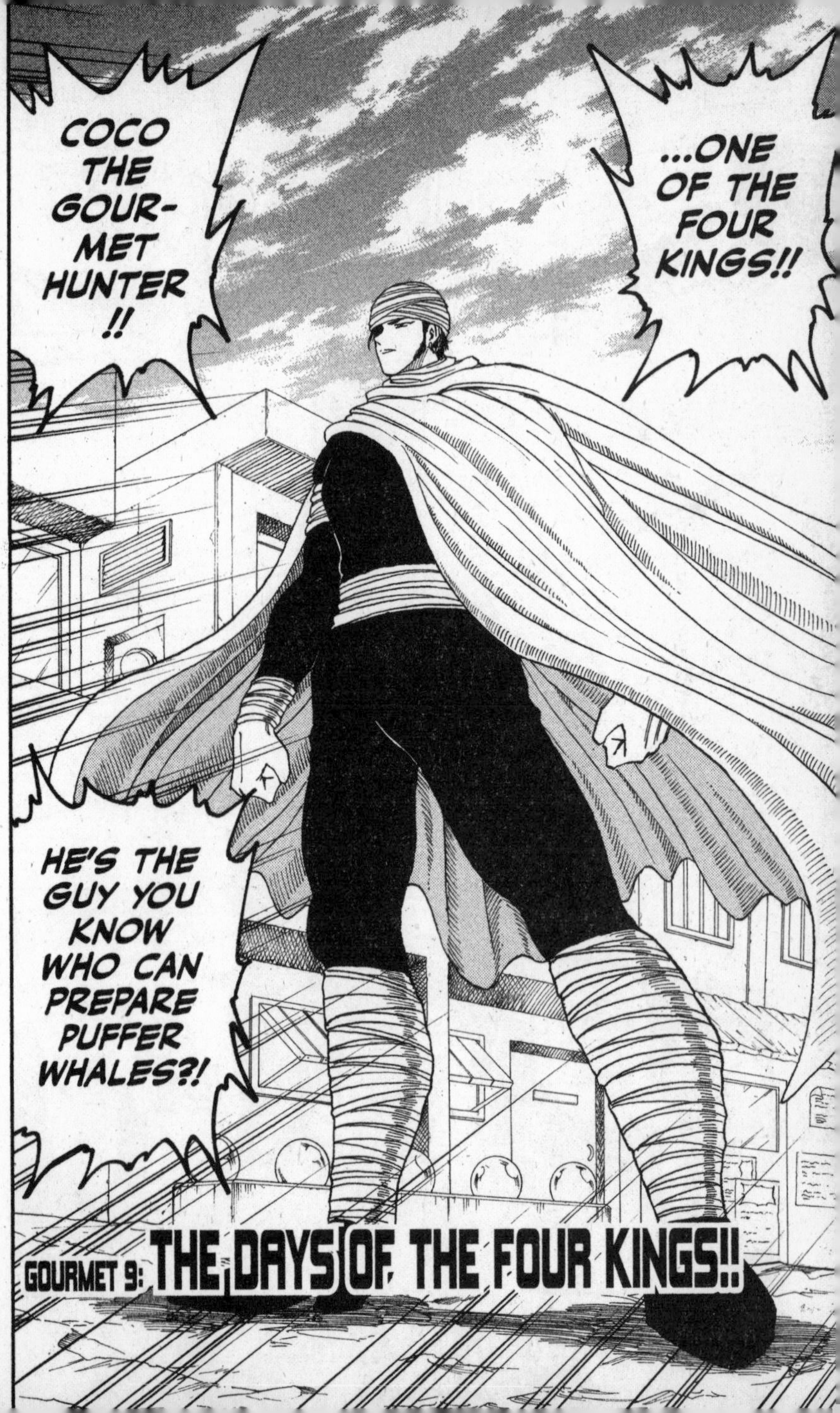
...ONE OF THE FOUR KINGS!!
COCO THE GOURMET HUNTER!!
HE'S THE GUY YOU KNOW WHO CAN PREPARE PUFFER WHALES?!
GOURMET 9: THE DAYS OF THE FOUR KINGS!!

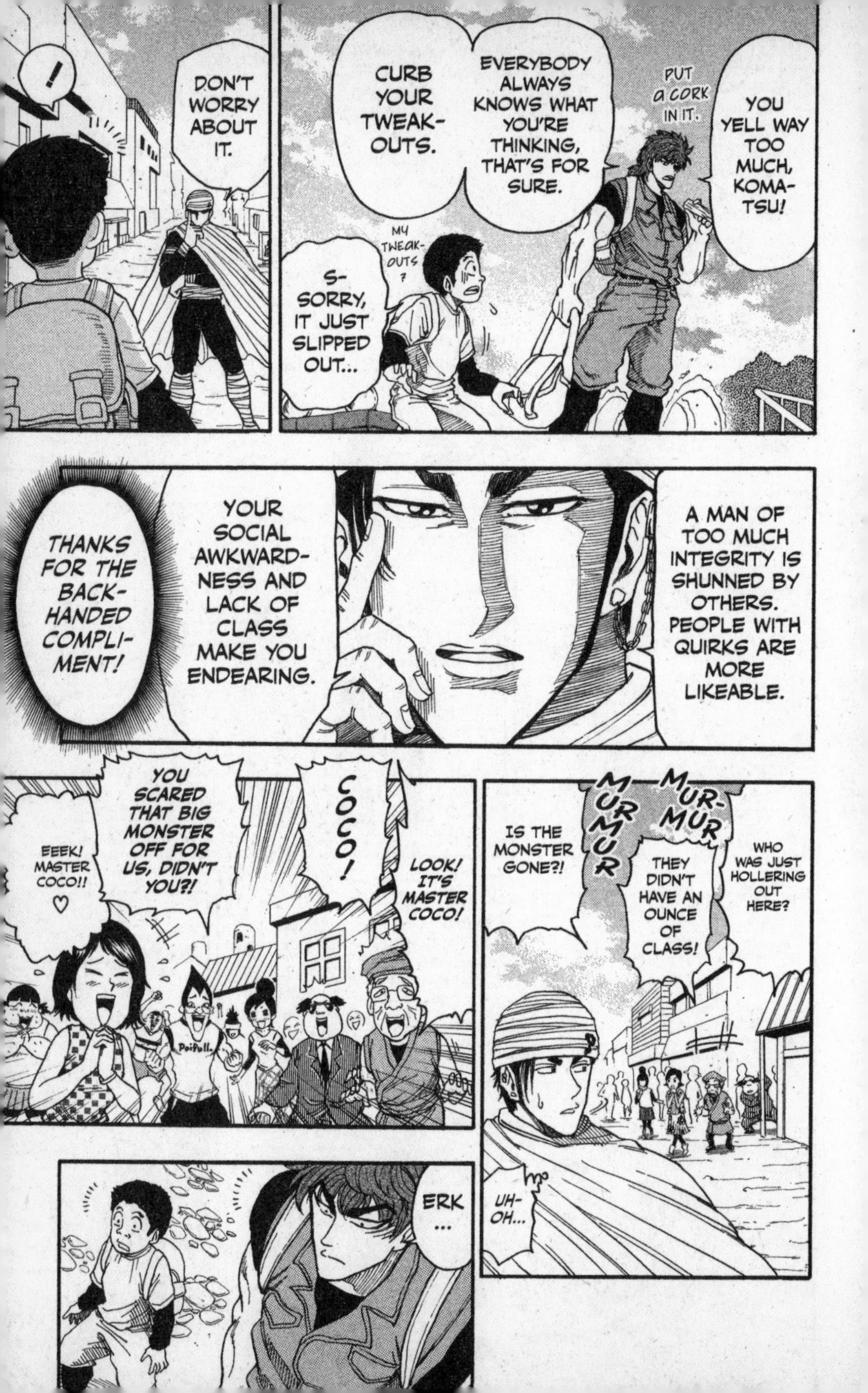
YOU YELL WAY TOO MUCH, KOMATSU!
PUT a CORK IN IT.
EVERYBODY ALWAYS KNOWS WHAT YOU'RE THINKING, THAT'S FOR SURE.
CURB YOUR TWEAK-OUTS.
MY TWEAK-OUTS?
S-SORRY, IT JUST SLIPPED OUT...
!
DON'T WORRY ABOUT IT.
A MAN OF TOO MUCH INTEGRITY IS SHUNNED BY OTHERS. PEOPLE WITH QUIRKS ARE MORE LIKEABLE.
YOUR SOCIAL AWKWARDNESS AND LACK OF CLASS MAKE YOU ENDEARING.
THANKS FOR THE BACK-HANDED COMPLIMENT!
MUR-MUR
MURMUR
WHO WAS JUST HOLLERING OUT HERE?
THEY DIDN'T HAVE AN OUNCE OF CLASS!
IS THE MONSTER GONE?!
UH-OH...
LOOK! IT'S MASTER COCO!
COCO!
YOU SCARED THAT BIG MONSTER OFF FOR US, DIDN'T YOU?!
EEEK! MASTER COCO!! ♡
ERK ...

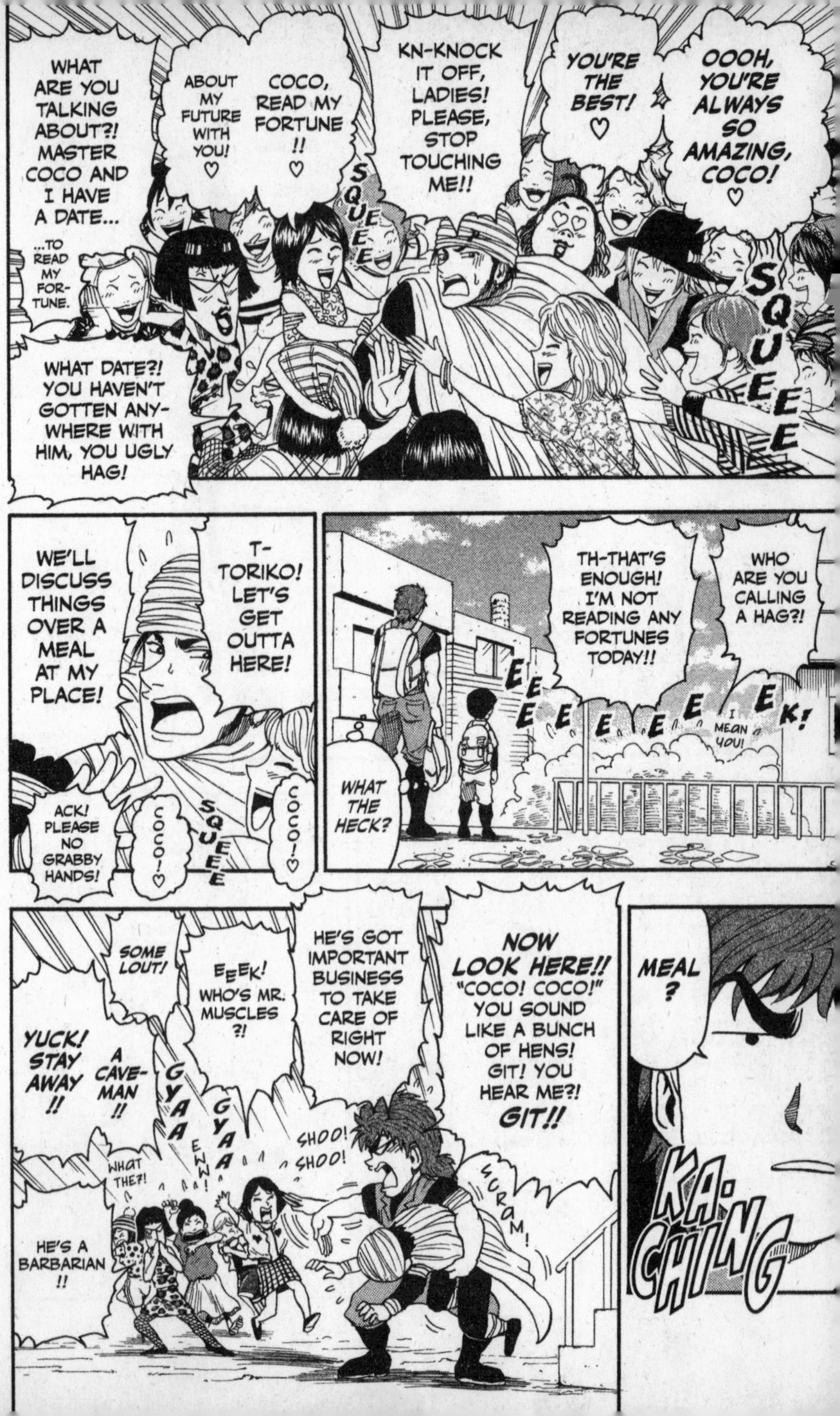
OOOH, YOU'RE ALWAYS SO AMAZING, COCO! ♡
YOU'RE THE BEST! ♡
KN-KNOCK IT OFF, LADIES! PLEASE, STOP TOUCHING ME!!
SQUEEE
COCO, READ MY FORTUNE!! ♡
SQUEEE
ABOUT MY FUTURE WITH YOU! ♡
WHAT ARE YOU TALKING ABOUT?! MASTER COCO AND I HAVE A DATE...
...TO READ MY FORTUNE.
WHAT DATE?! YOU HAVEN'T GOTTEN ANYWHERE WITH HIM, YOU UGLY HAG!
WHO ARE YOU CALLING A HAG?!
TH-THAT'S ENOUGH! I'M NOT READING ANY FORTUNES TODAY!!
EEEEEEEEEK!
I MEAN YOU!
WHAT THE HECK?
T-TORIKO! LET'S GET OUTTA HERE!
WE'LL DISCUSS THINGS OVER A MEAL AT MY PLACE!
COCO!♡
SQUEEE
COCO!♡
ACK! PLEASE NO GRABBY HANDS!
MEAL?
KA-CHING
NOW LOOK HERE!! "COCO! COCO!" YOU SOUND LIKE A BUNCH OF HENS! GIT! YOU HEAR ME?! GIT!!
HE'S GOT IMPORTANT BUSINESS TO TAKE CARE OF RIGHT NOW!
EEEK! WHO'S MR. MUSCLES?!
SOME LOUT!
A CAVEMAN!!
YUCK! STAY AWAY!!
GYAA
GYAA
SHOO! SHOO!
SCRAM!
EWW!
WHAT THE?!
HE'S A BARBARIAN!!

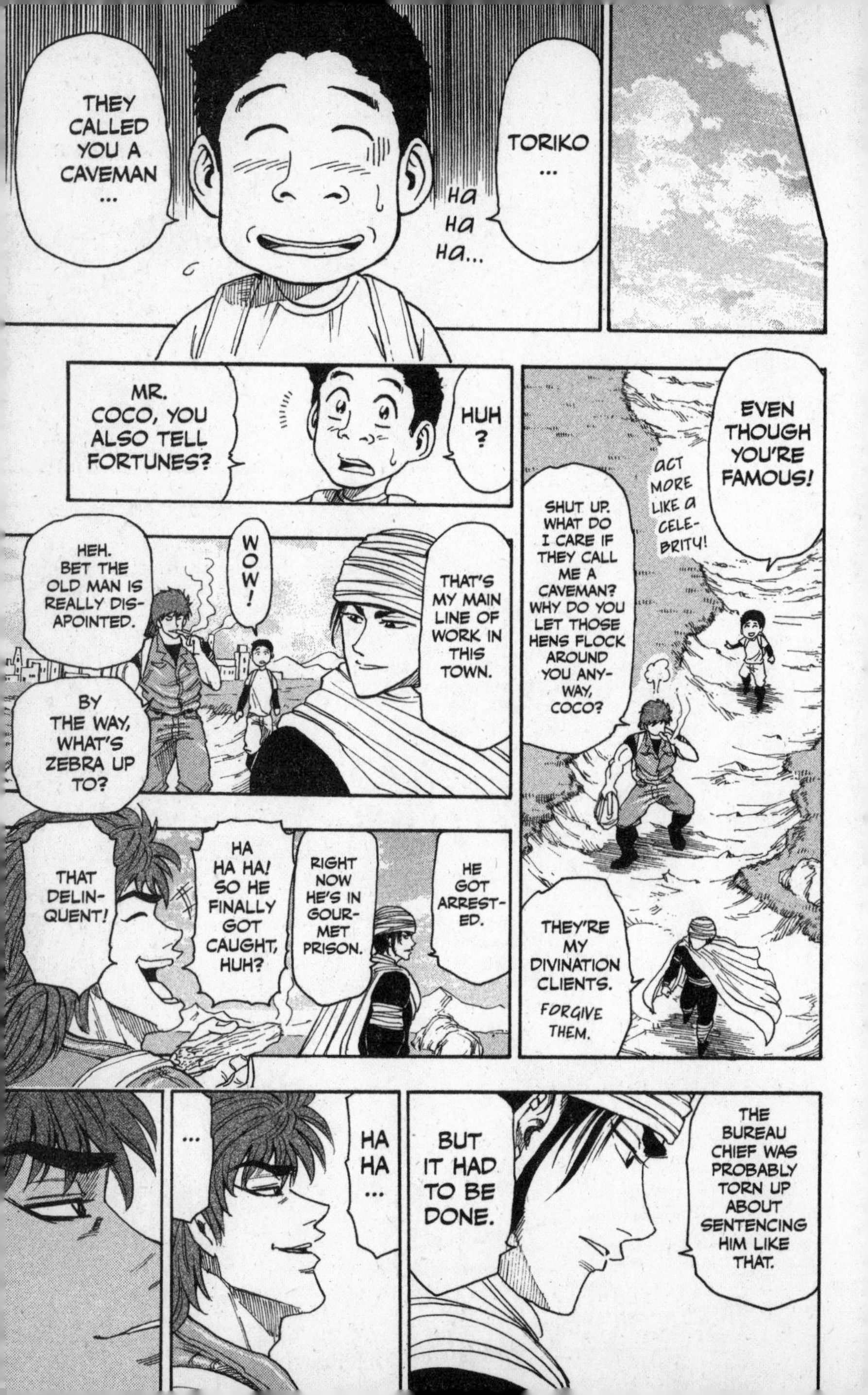
TORIKO ...
Ha Ha Ha...
THEY CALLED YOU A CAVEMAN ...
EVEN THOUGH YOU'RE FAMOUS!
ACT MORE LIKE A CELEBRITY!
SHUT UP. WHAT DO I CARE IF THEY CALL ME A CAVEMAN? WHY DO YOU LET THOSE HENS FLOCK AROUND YOU ANYWAY, COCO?
THEY'RE MY DIVINATION CLIENTS.
FORGIVE THEM.
HUH ?
MR. COCO, YOU ALSO TELL FORTUNES?
THAT'S MY MAIN LINE OF WORK IN THIS TOWN.
WOW!
HEH. BET THE OLD MAN IS REALLY DISAPOINTED.
BY THE WAY, WHAT'S ZEBRA UP TO?
HE GOT ARRESTED.
RIGHT NOW HE'S IN GOURMET PRISON.
HA HA HA! SO HE FINALLY GOT CAUGHT, HUH?
THAT DELINQUENT!
THE BUREAU CHIEF WAS PROBABLY TORN UP ABOUT SENTENCING HIM LIKE THAT.
BUT IT HAD TO BE DONE.
HA HA ...
...

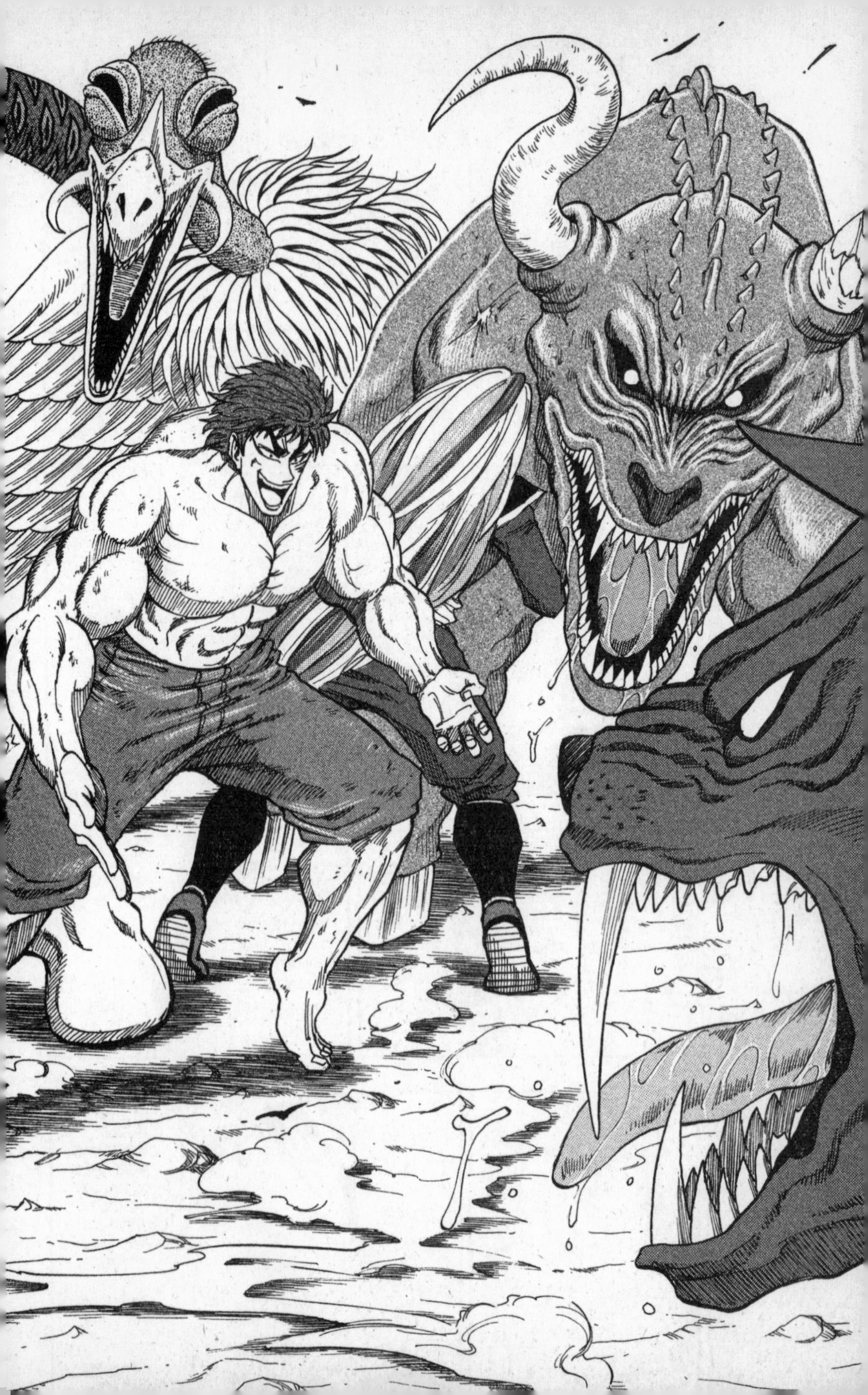

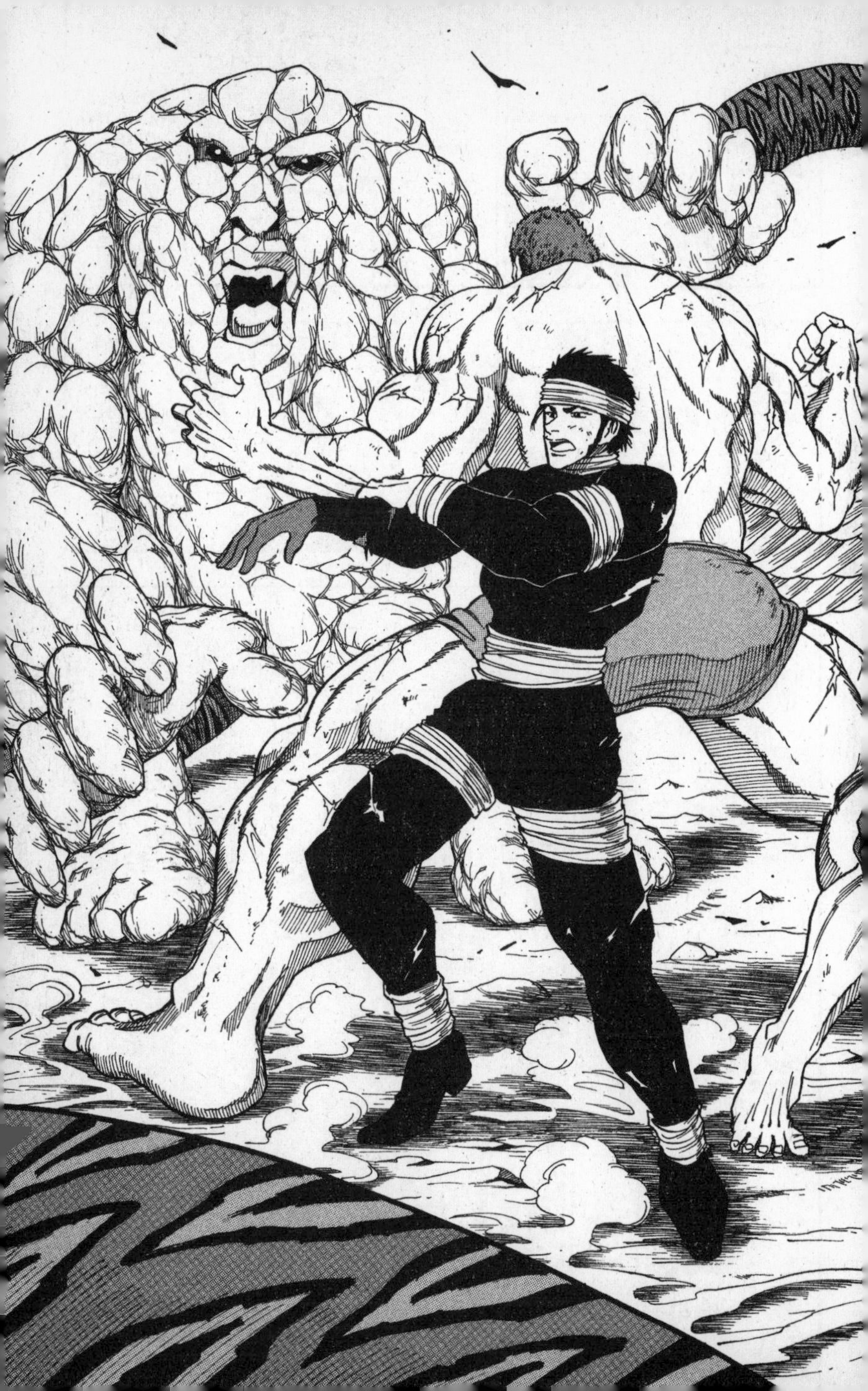

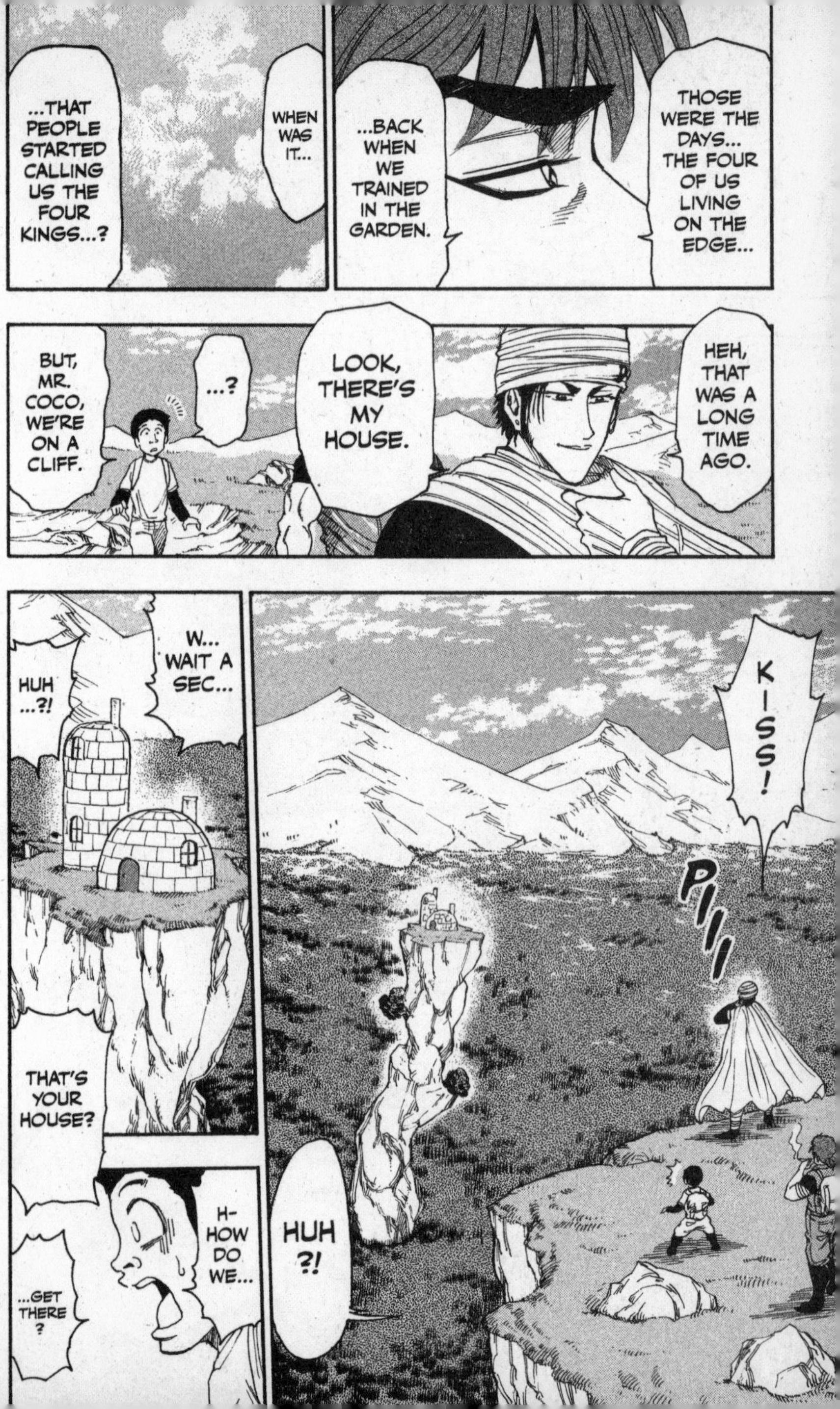
THOSE WERE THE DAYS... THE FOUR OF US LIVING ON THE EDGE...
...BACK WHEN WE TRAINED IN THE GARDEN.
WHEN WAS IT...
...THAT PEOPLE STARTED CALLING US THE FOUR KINGS...?
HEH, THAT WAS A LONG TIME AGO.
LOOK, THERE'S MY HOUSE.
...?
BUT, MR. COCO, WE'RE ON A CLIFF.
KISS!
PIII
HUH ?!
W... WAIT A SEC...
HUH ...?!
THAT'S YOUR HOUSE?
H-HOW DO WE...
...GET THERE ?

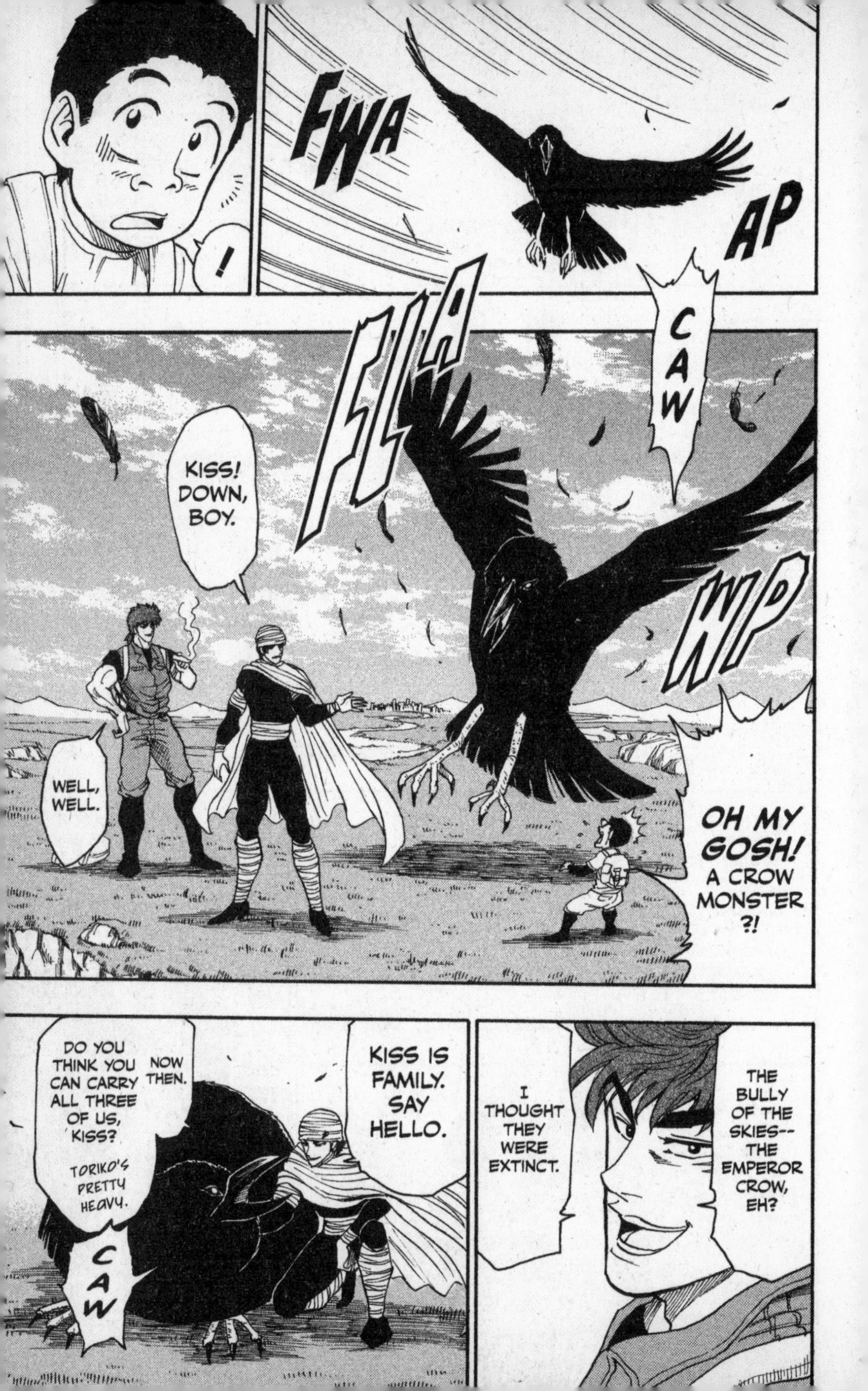
FWAP
!
CAW
OH MY GOSH! A CROW MONSTER ?!
KISS! DOWN, BOY.
WELL, WELL.
THE BULLY OF THE SKIES-- THE EMPEROR CROW, EH?
I THOUGHT THEY WERE EXTINCT.
KISS IS FAMILY. SAY HELLO.
NOW THEN.
DO YOU THINK YOU CAN CARRY ALL THREE OF US, KISS?
TORIKO'S PRETTY HEAVY.
CAW

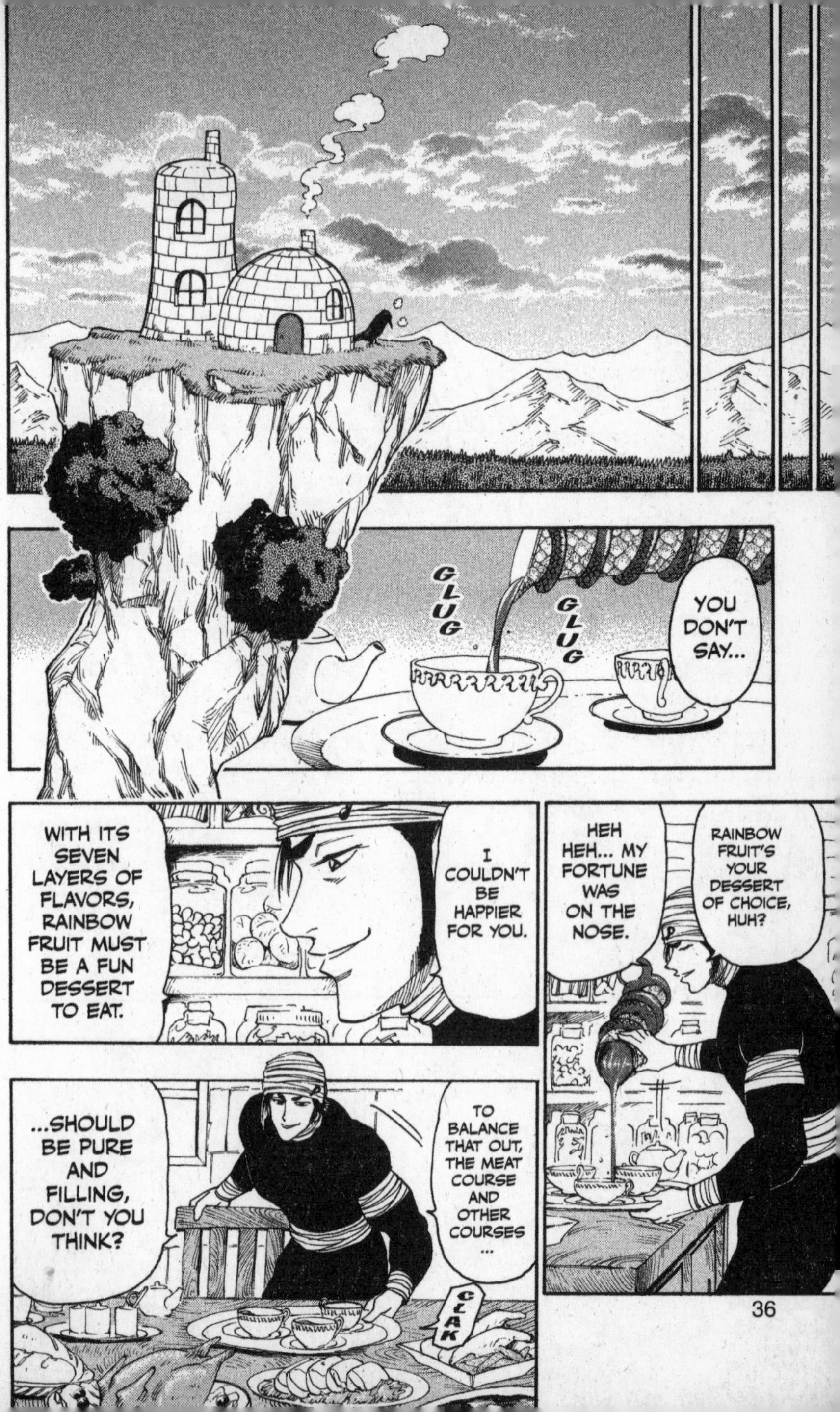
YOU DON'T SAY...
GLUG
GLUG
RAINBOW FRUIT'S YOUR DESSERT OF CHOICE, HUH?
HEH HEH... MY FORTUNE WAS ON THE NOSE.
I COULDN'T BE HAPPIER FOR YOU.
WITH ITS SEVEN LAYERS OF FLAVORS, RAINBOW FRUIT MUST BE A FUN DESSERT TO EAT.
TO BALANCE THAT OUT, THE MEAT COURSE AND OTHER COURSES ...
...SHOULD BE PURE AND FILLING, DON'T YOU THINK?
CLAK

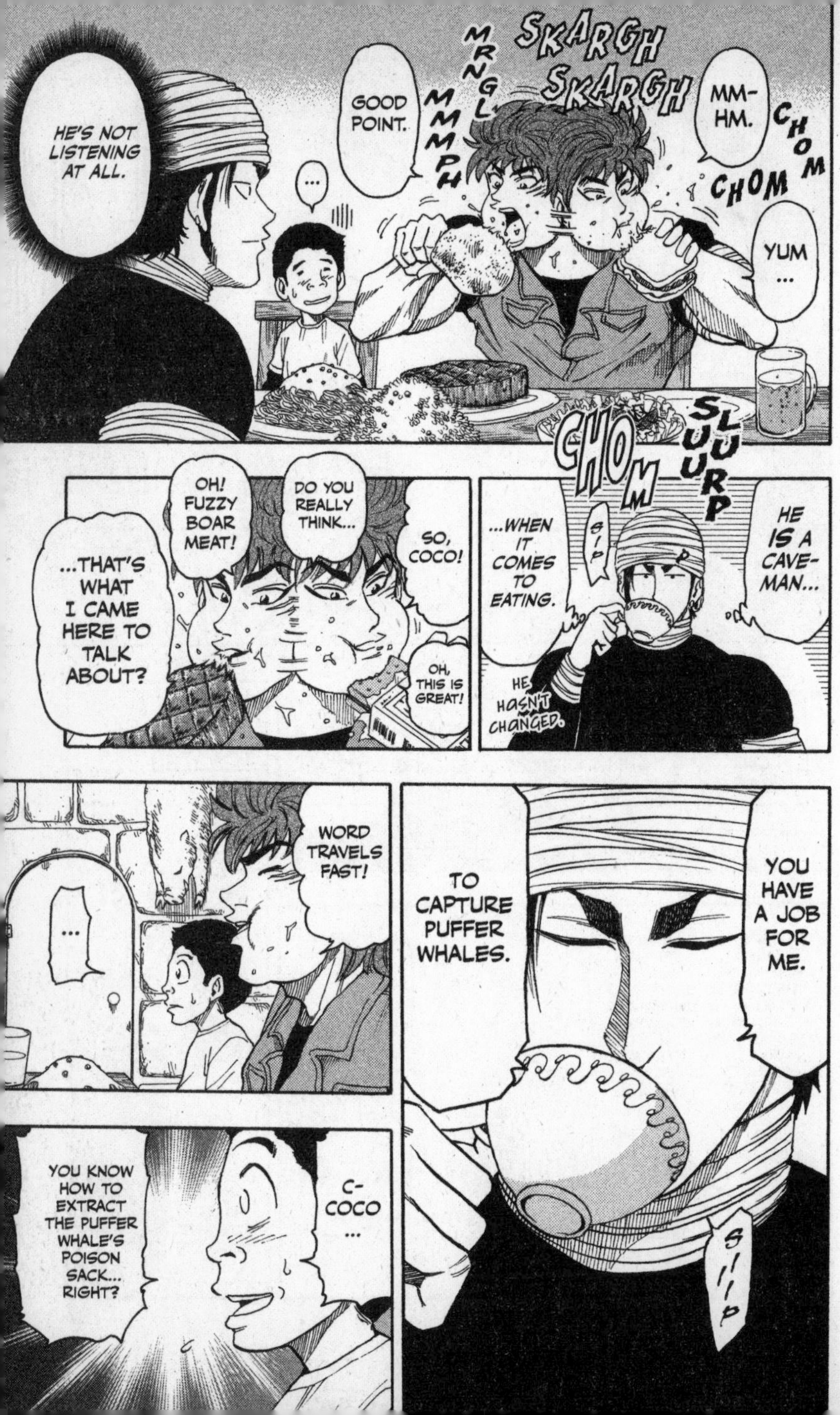
MM-HM.
CHOM CHOM
SKARGH SKARGH
MRNGL
YUM...
GOOD POINT.
MMMPH
...
HE'S NOT LISTENING AT ALL.
HE IS A CAVEMAN...
SLUURP
CHOM
SIP
...WHEN IT COMES TO EATING.
HE HASN'T CHANGED.
SO, COCO!
DO YOU REALLY THINK...
OH! FUZZY BOAR MEAT!
OH, THIS IS GREAT!
...THAT'S WHAT I CAME HERE TO TALK ABOUT?
YOU HAVE A JOB FOR ME.
TO CAPTURE PUFFER WHALES.
SIIP
WORD TRAVELS FAST!
...
C-COCO...
YOU KNOW HOW TO EXTRACT THE PUFFER WHALE'S POISON SACK... RIGHT?

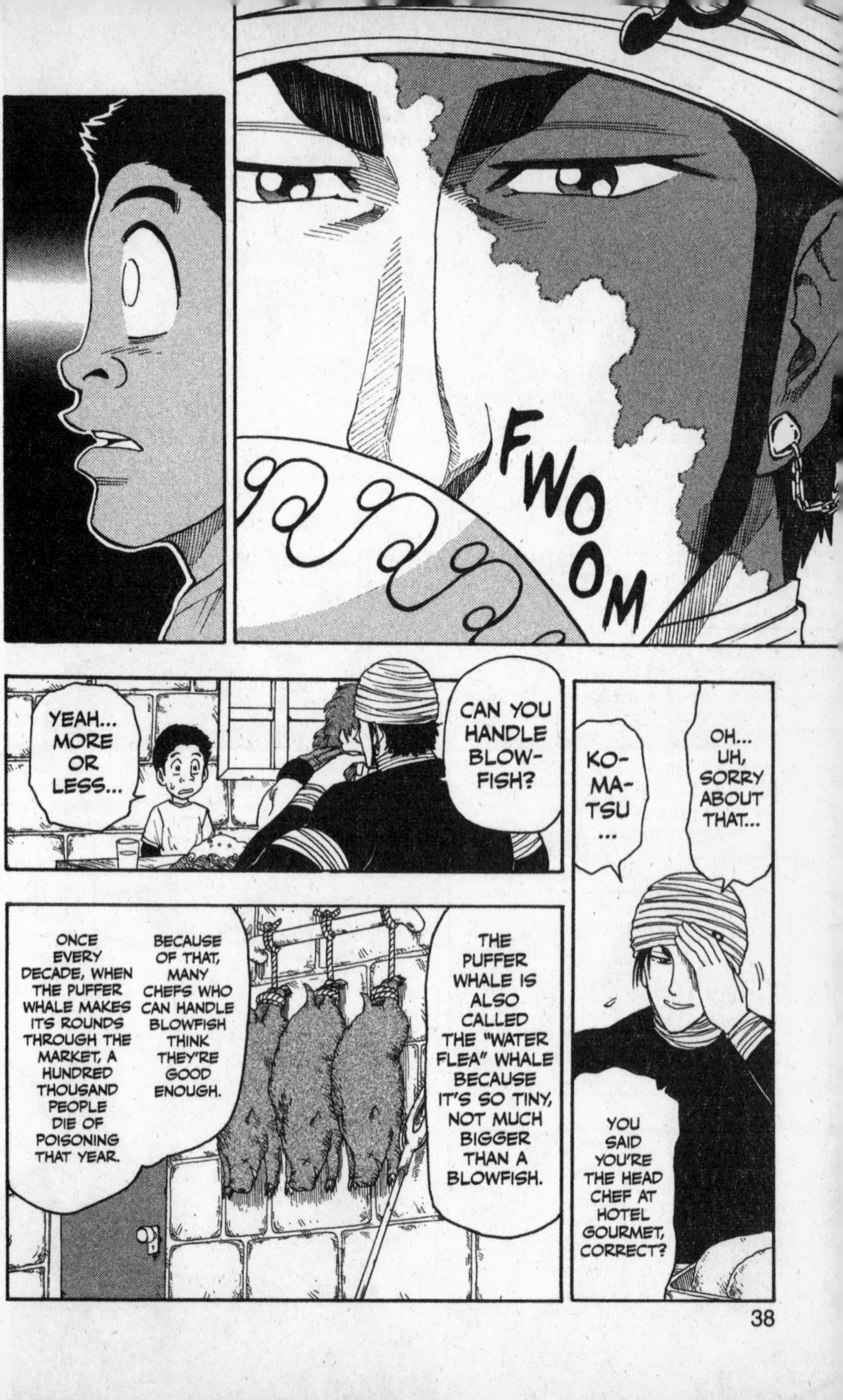
FWOOM
OH... UH, SORRY ABOUT THAT...
KO-MA-TSU...
YOU SAID YOU'RE THE HEAD CHEF AT HOTEL GOURMET, CORRECT?
CAN YOU HANDLE BLOW-FISH?
YEAH... MORE OR LESS...
THE PUFFER WHALE IS ALSO CALLED THE "WATER FLEA" WHALE BECAUSE IT'S SO TINY, NOT MUCH BIGGER THAN A BLOWFISH.
BECAUSE OF THAT, MANY CHEFS WHO CAN HANDLE BLOWFISH THINK THEY'RE GOOD ENOUGH.
ONCE EVERY DECADE, WHEN THE PUFFER WHALE MAKES ITS ROUNDS THROUGH THE MARKET, A HUNDRED THOUSAND PEOPLE DIE OF POISONING THAT YEAR.

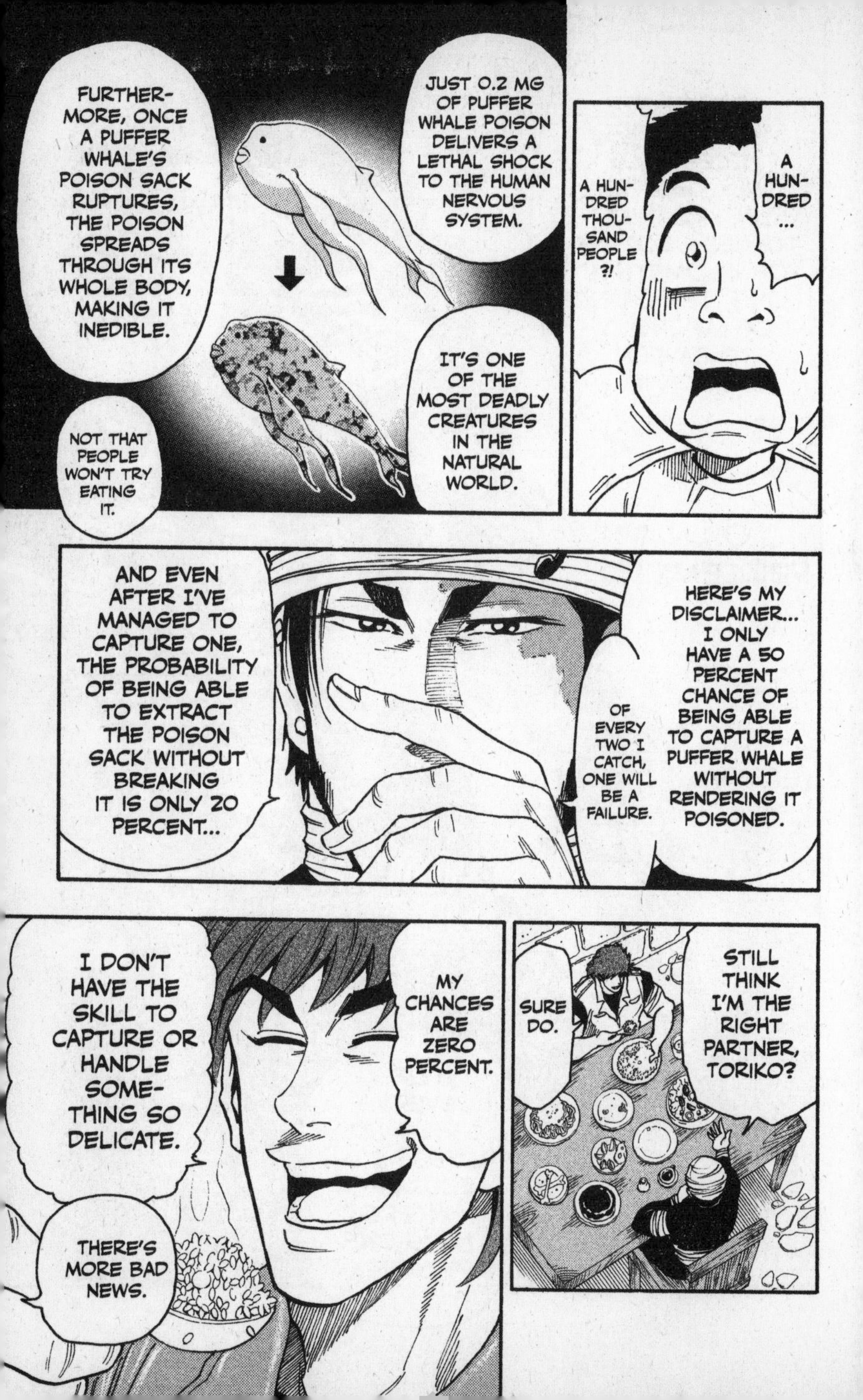
A HUNDRED...
A HUNDRED THOUSAND PEOPLE?!
JUST 0.2 MG OF PUFFER WHALE POISON DELIVERS A LETHAL SHOCK TO THE HUMAN NERVOUS SYSTEM.
FURTHERMORE, ONCE A PUFFER WHALE'S POISON SACK RUPTURES, THE POISON SPREADS THROUGH ITS WHOLE BODY, MAKING IT INEDIBLE.
IT'S ONE OF THE MOST DEADLY CREATURES IN THE NATURAL WORLD.
NOT THAT PEOPLE WON'T TRY EATING IT.
HERE'S MY DISCLAIMER... I ONLY HAVE A 50 PERCENT CHANCE OF BEING ABLE TO CAPTURE A PUFFER WHALE WITHOUT RENDERING IT POISONED.
OF EVERY TWO I CATCH, ONE WILL BE A FAILURE.
AND EVEN AFTER I'VE MANAGED TO CAPTURE ONE, THE PROBABILITY OF BEING ABLE TO EXTRACT THE POISON SACK WITHOUT BREAKING IT IS ONLY 20 PERCENT...
STILL THINK I'M THE RIGHT PARTNER, TORIKO?
SURE DO.
MY CHANCES ARE ZERO PERCENT.
I DON'T HAVE THE SKILL TO CAPTURE OR HANDLE SOMETHING SO DELICATE.
THERE'S MORE BAD NEWS.

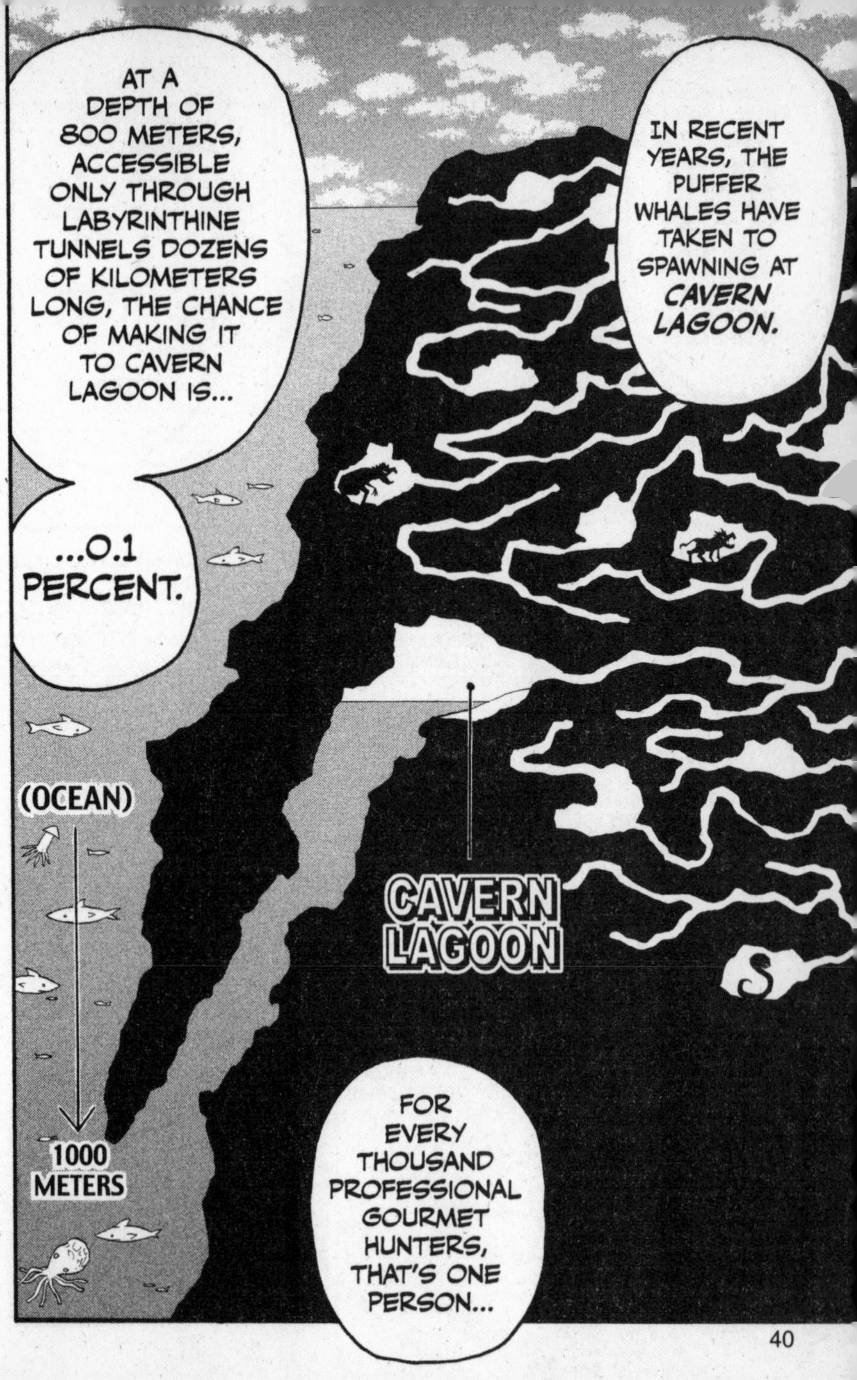
IN RECENT YEARS, THE PUFFER WHALES HAVE TAKEN TO SPAWNING AT *CAVERN LAGOON.*
AT A DEPTH OF 800 METERS, ACCESSIBLE ONLY THROUGH LABYRINTHINE TUNNELS DOZENS OF KILOMETERS LONG, THE CHANCE OF MAKING IT TO CAVERN LAGOON IS...
...0.1 PERCENT.
CAVERN LAGOON
(OCEAN)
1000 METERS
FOR EVERY THOUSAND PROFESSIONAL GOURMET HUNTERS, THAT'S ONE PERSON...

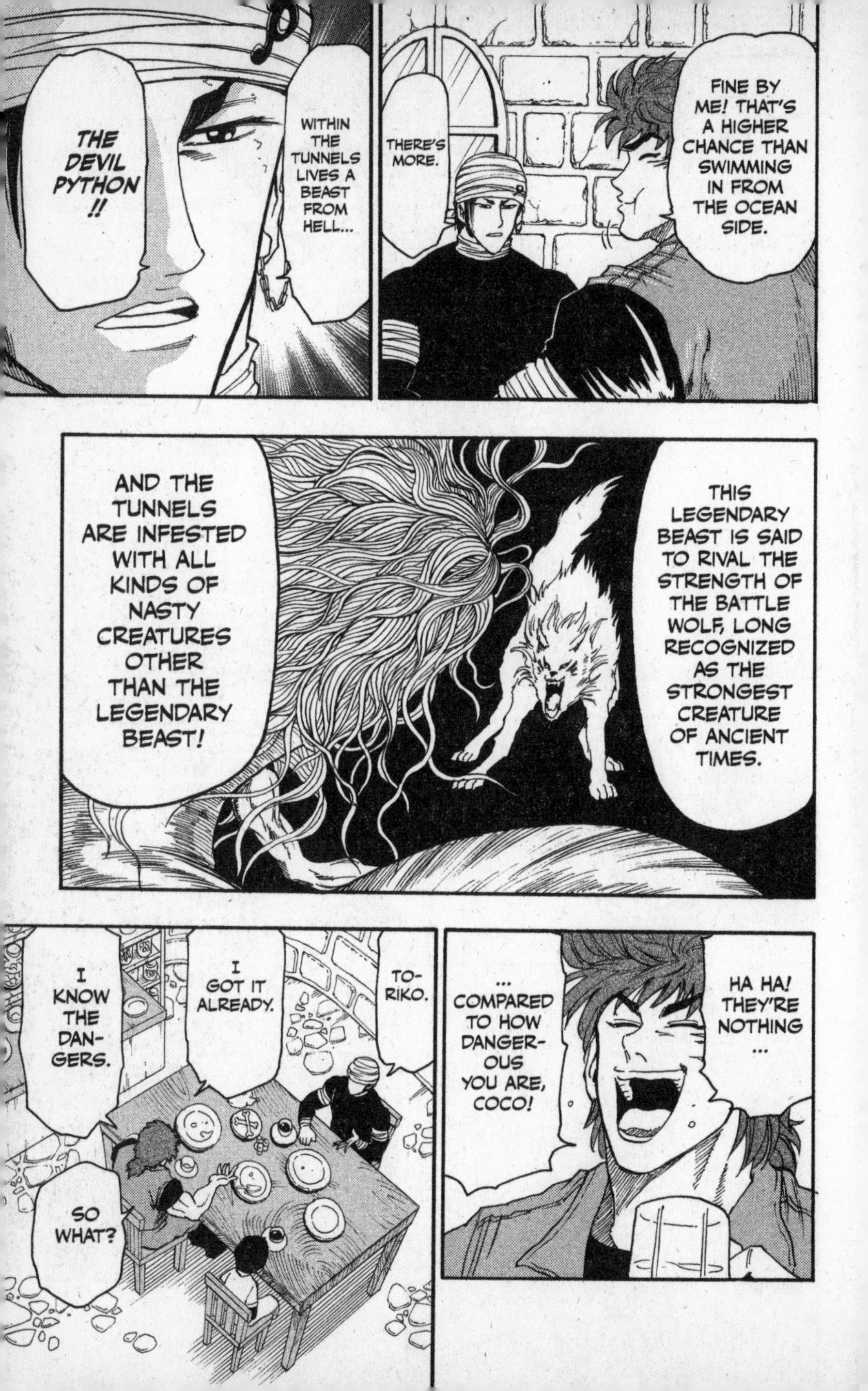
FINE BY ME! THAT'S A HIGHER CHANCE THAN SWIMMING IN FROM THE OCEAN SIDE.
THERE'S MORE.
WITHIN THE TUNNELS LIVES A BEAST FROM HELL...
THE DEVIL PYTHON!!
THIS LEGENDARY BEAST IS SAID TO RIVAL THE STRENGTH OF THE BATTLE WOLF, LONG RECOGNIZED AS THE STRONGEST CREATURE OF ANCIENT TIMES.
AND THE TUNNELS ARE INFESTED WITH ALL KINDS OF NASTY CREATURES OTHER THAN THE LEGENDARY BEAST!
HA HA! THEY'RE NOTHING...
...COMPARED TO HOW DANGER-OUS YOU ARE, COCO!
TO-RIKO.
I GOT IT ALREADY.
I KNOW THE DAN-GERS.
SO WHAT?

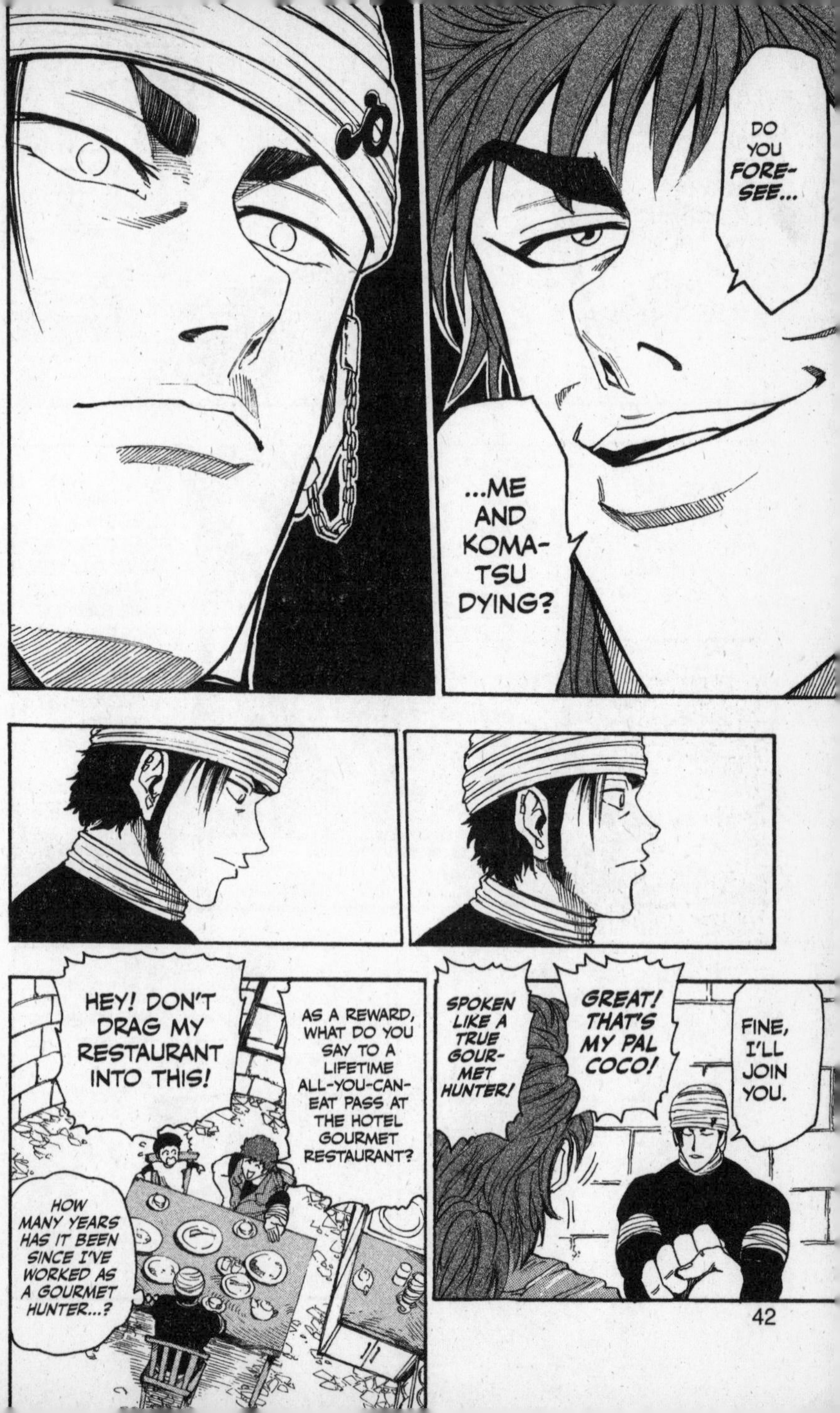

DO YOU FORE-SEE...
...ME AND KOMA-TSU DYING?
FINE, I'LL JOIN YOU.
GREAT! THAT'S MY PAL COCO!
SPOKEN LIKE A TRUE GOUR-MET HUNTER!
AS A REWARD, WHAT DO YOU SAY TO A LIFETIME ALL-YOU-CAN-EAT PASS AT THE HOTEL GOURMET RESTAURANT?
HEY! DON'T DRAG MY RESTAURANT INTO THIS!
HOW MANY YEARS HAS IT BEEN SINCE I'VE WORKED AS A GOURMET HUNTER...?

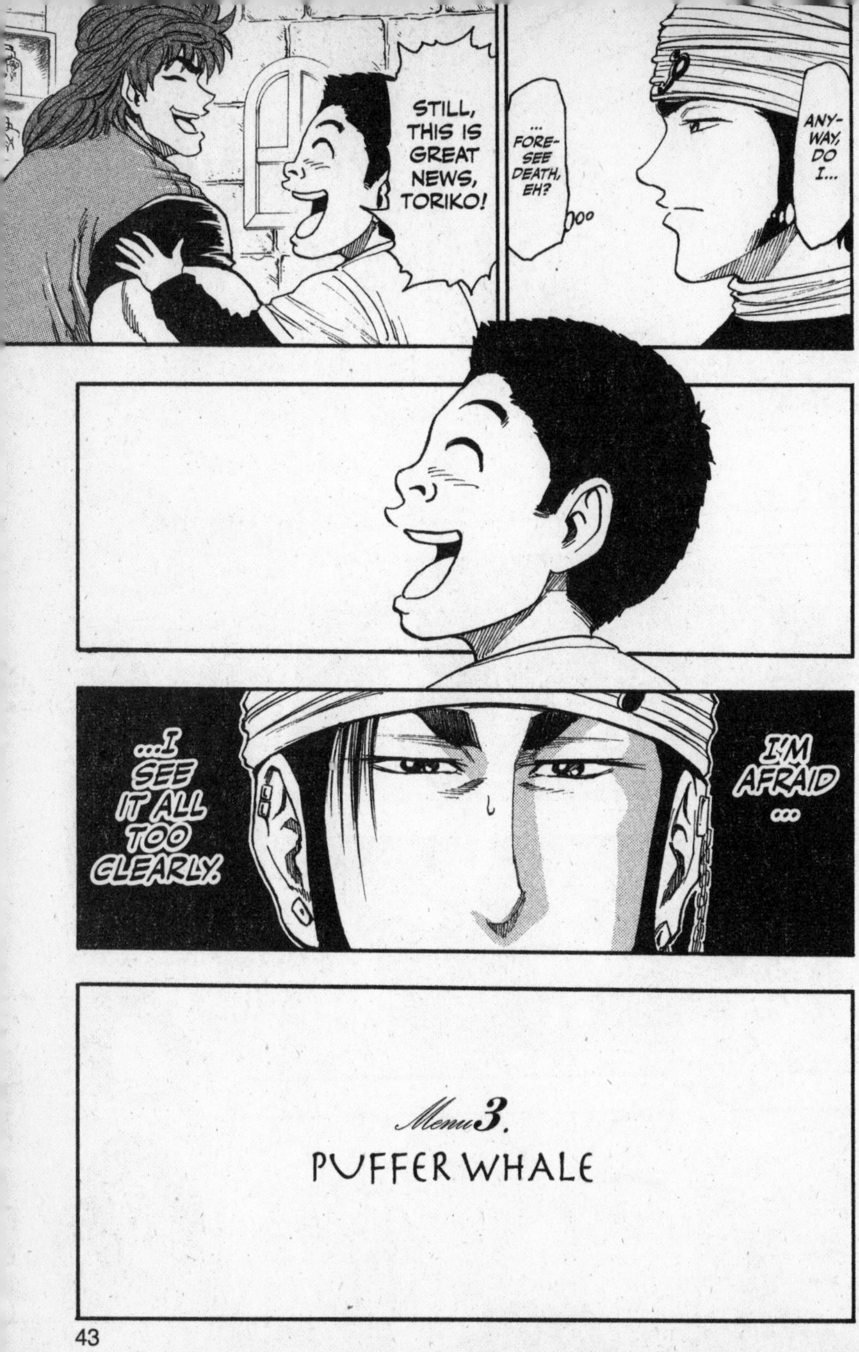
ANYWAY, DO I...
...FORESEE DEATH, EH?
STILL, THIS IS GREAT NEWS, TORIKO!
I'M AFRAID...
...I SEE IT ALL TOO CLEARLY.

Menu 3.
PUFFER WHALE

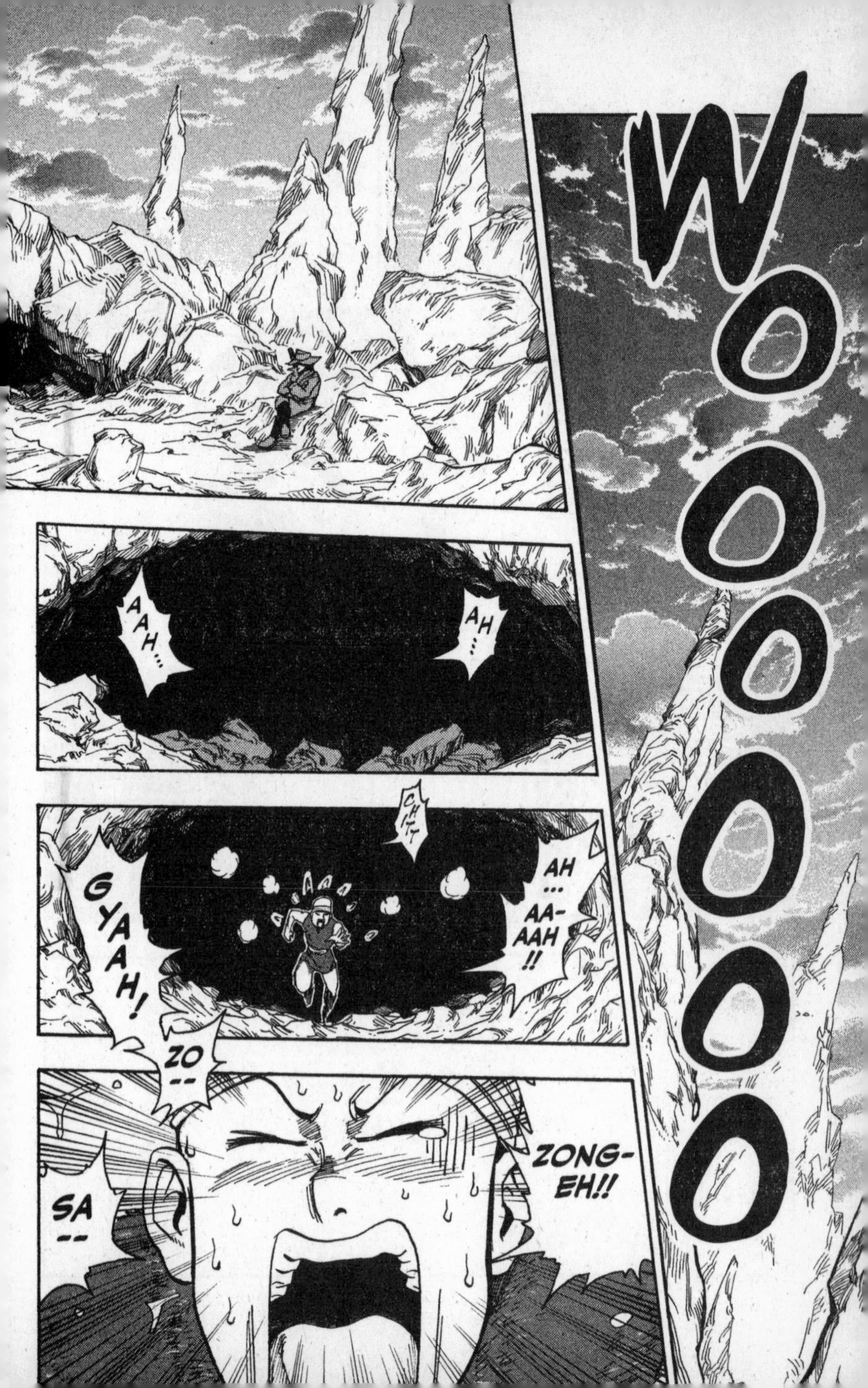
WOOOOOO
AH...
AAH...
CHITT
AH... AA-AAH!!
GYAAH!
ZONG-EH!!
ZO--
SA--

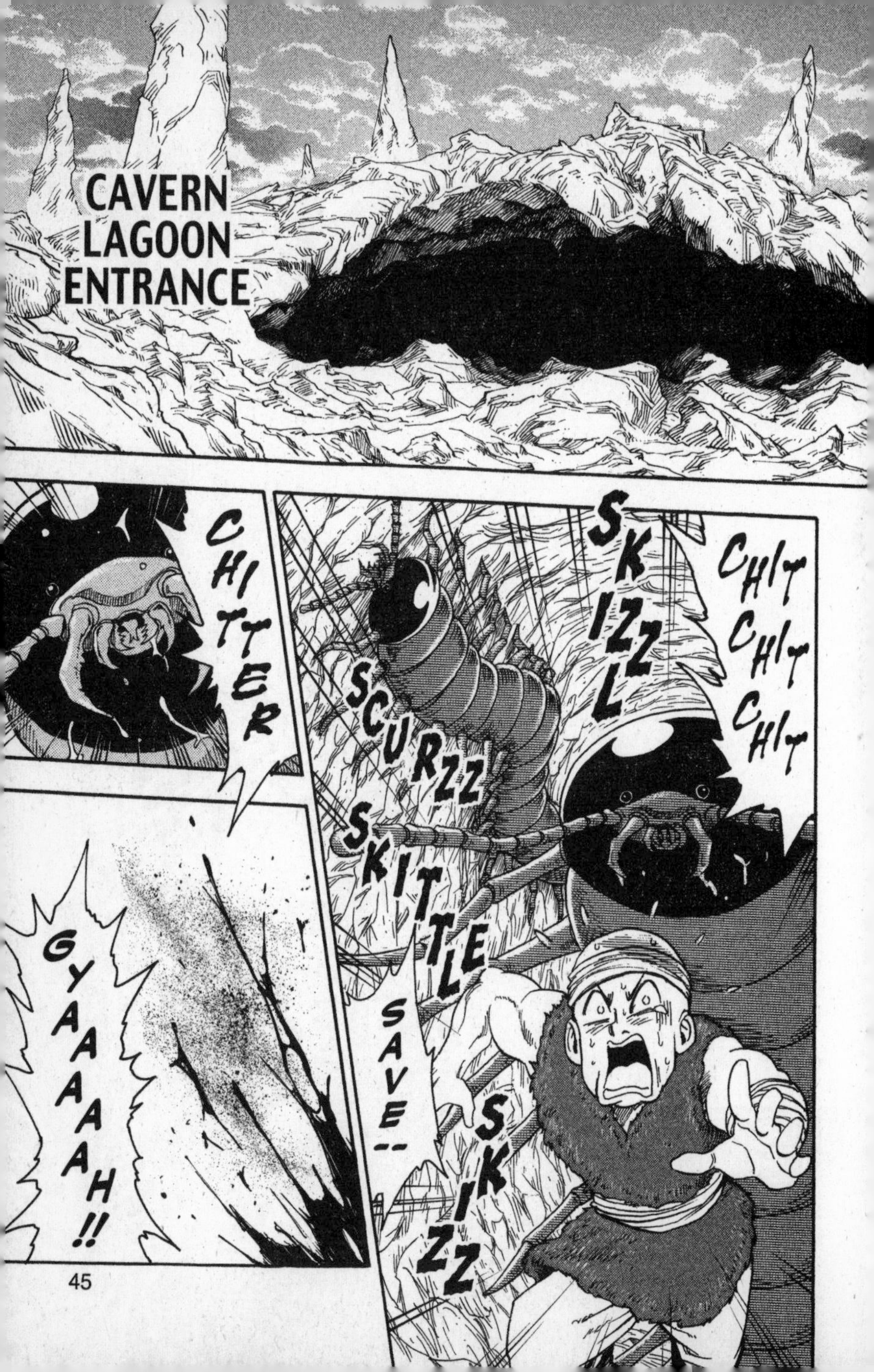
CAVERN LAGOON ENTRANCE
CHIT CHIT CHIT
SKIZZL
SCURZZZ
SKITTLE
SAVE--
SKIZZ
CHITTER
GYAAAAAH!!

TORIKO

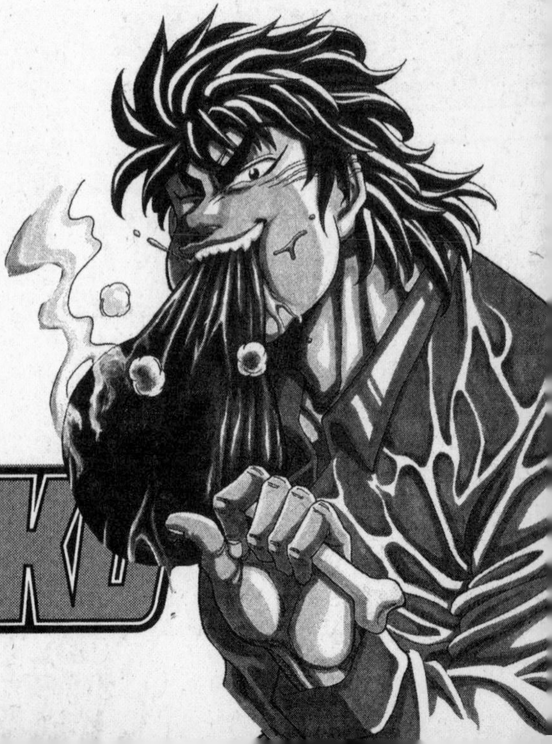

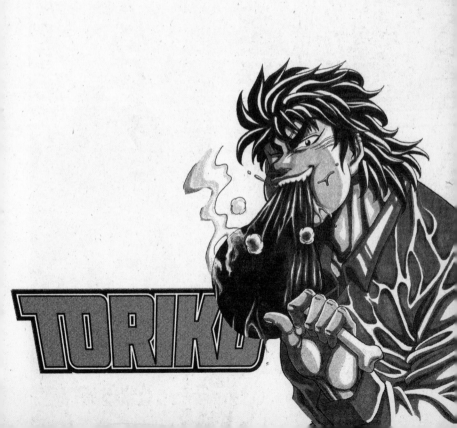

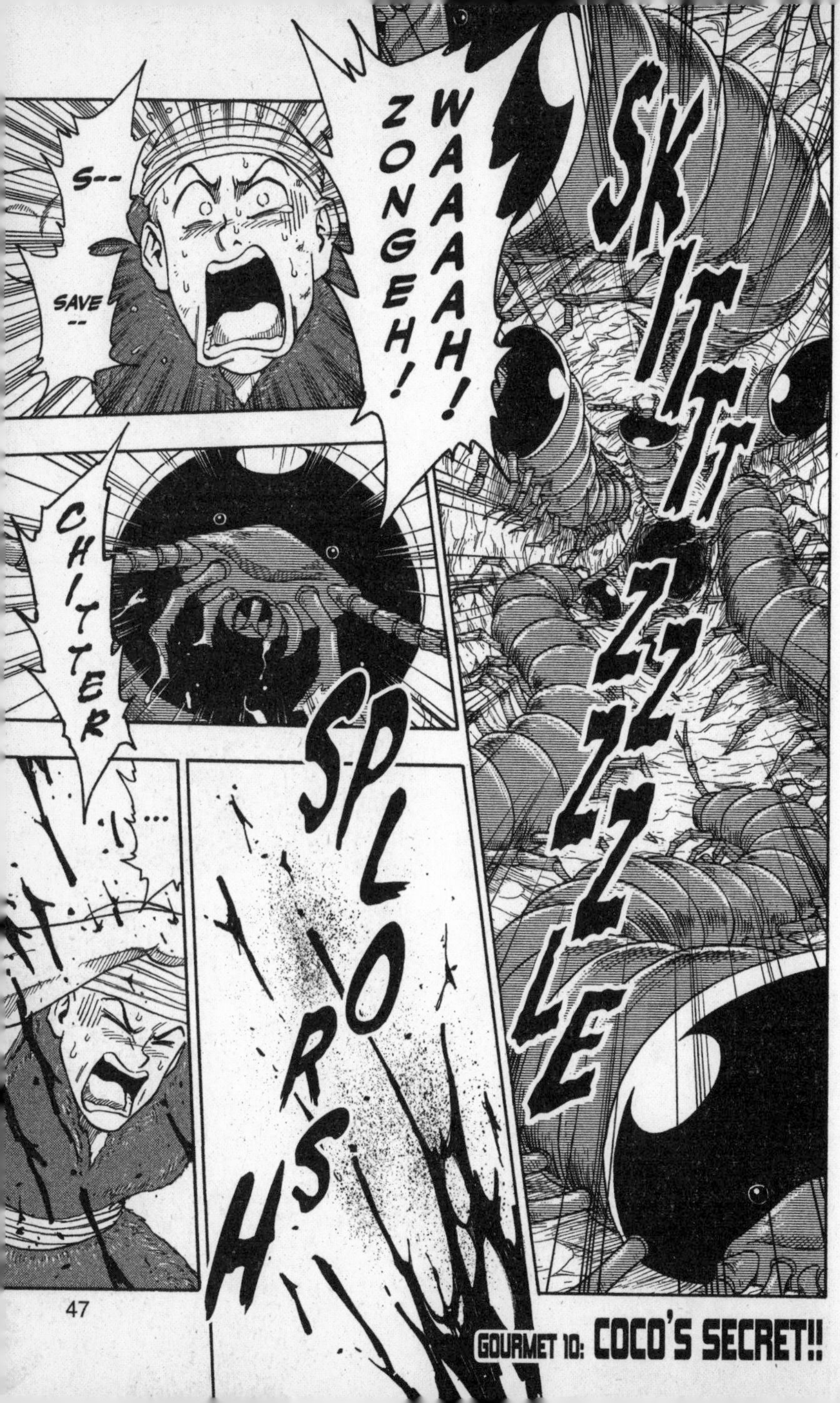
SKITTZZZLE
WAAAAH! ZONGEH!
S--
SAVE --
CHITTER
SPLORSH
...

GOURMET 10: COCO'S SECRET!!

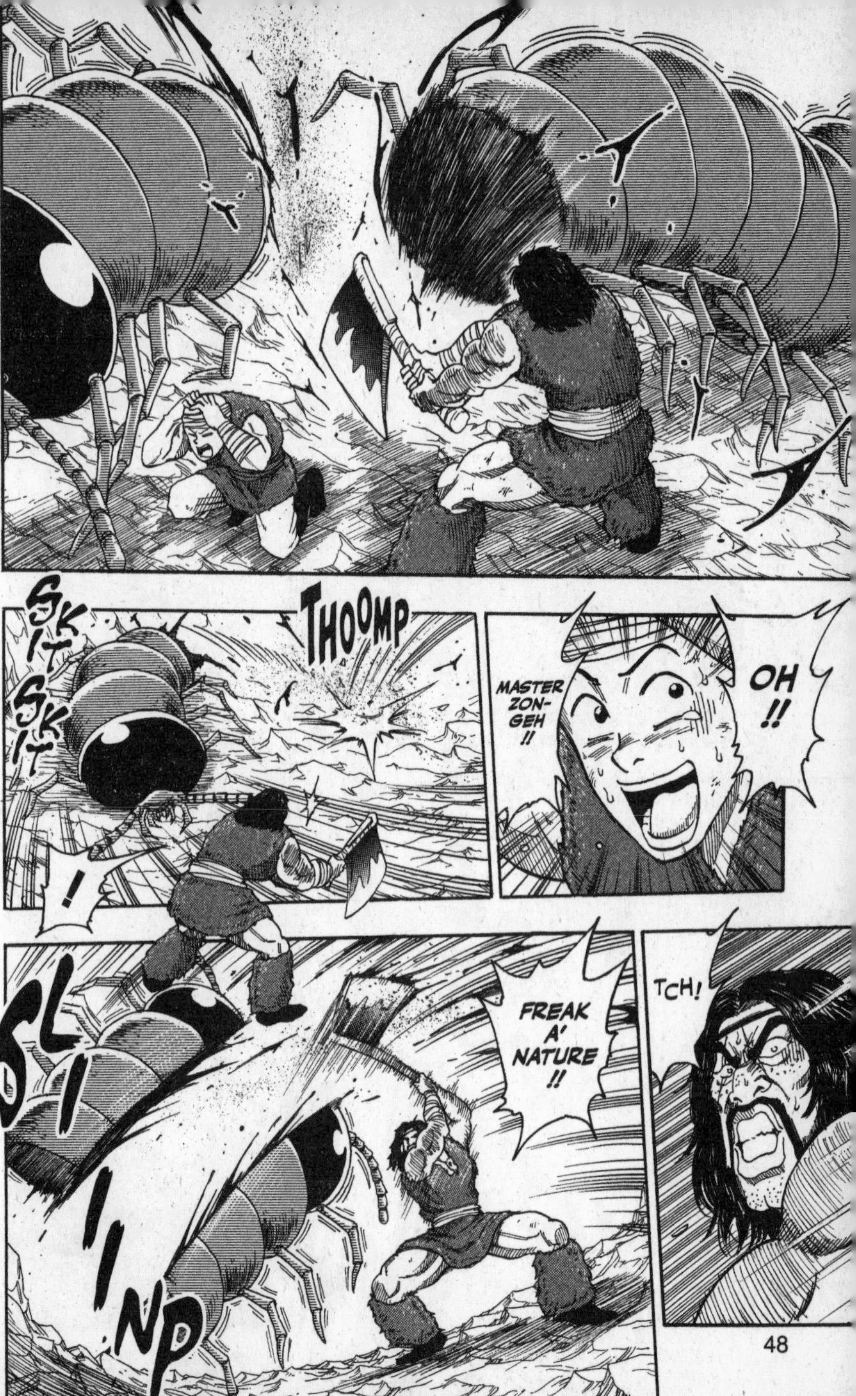
OH !!
MASTER ZONGEH !!
THOOMP
SKIT SKIT
!
TCH!
FREAK A' NATURE !!
SLIIINP

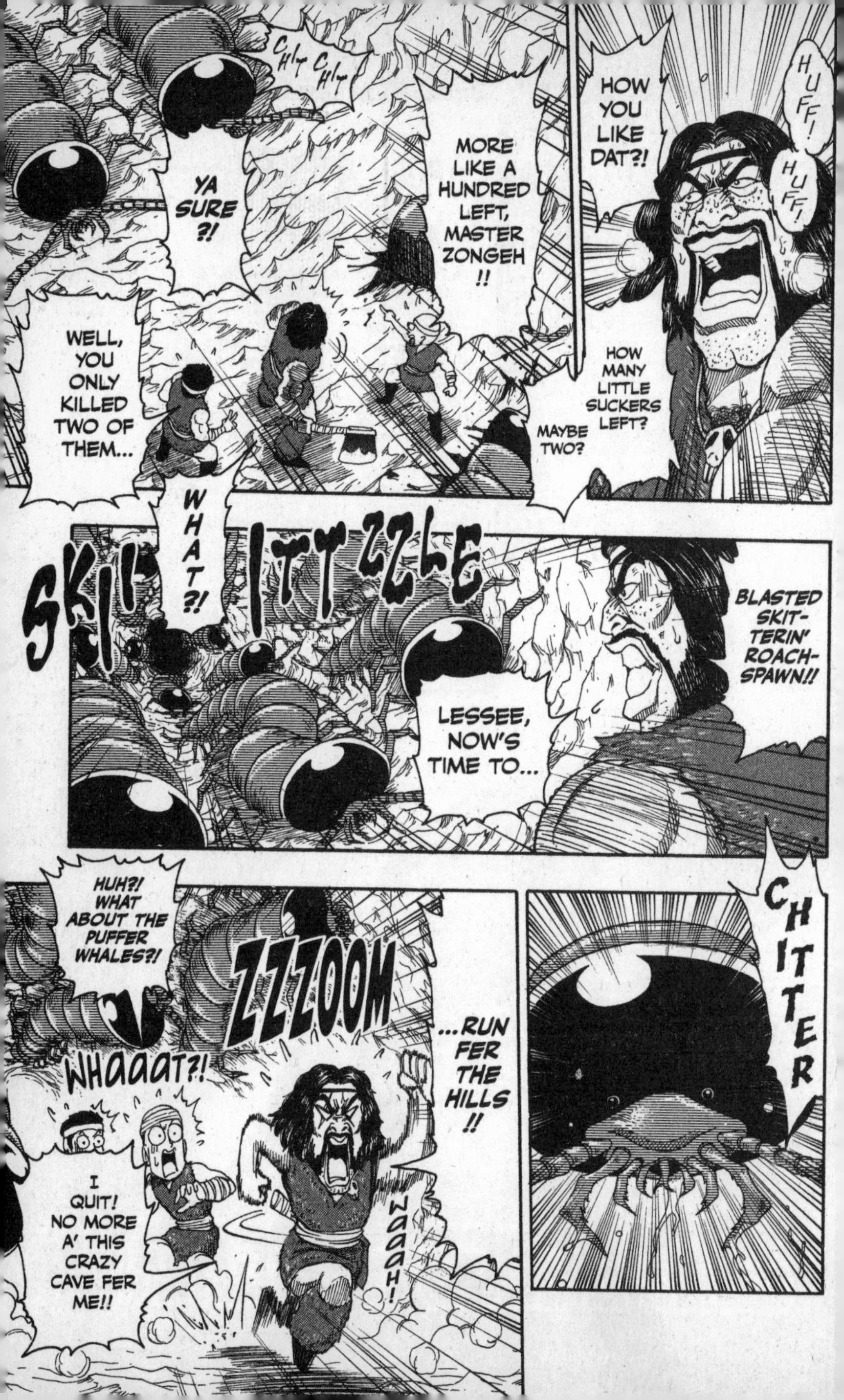
HUFF! HUFF!
HOW YOU LIKE DAT?!
HOW MANY LITTLE SUCKERS LEFT?
MAYBE TWO?
CHIT CHIT
MORE LIKE A HUNDRED LEFT, MASTER ZONGEH!!
YA SURE?!
WELL, YOU ONLY KILLED TWO OF THEM...
WHAT?!
BLASTED SKIT-TERIN' ROACH-SPAWN!!
LESSEE, NOW'S TIME TO...
SKITTZZLE
CHITTER
...RUN FER THE HILLS!!
ZZZOOM
HUH?! WHAT ABOUT THE PUFFER WHALES?!
WHAAAT?!
WAAAAH!
I QUIT! NO MORE A' THIS CRAZY CAVE FER ME!!

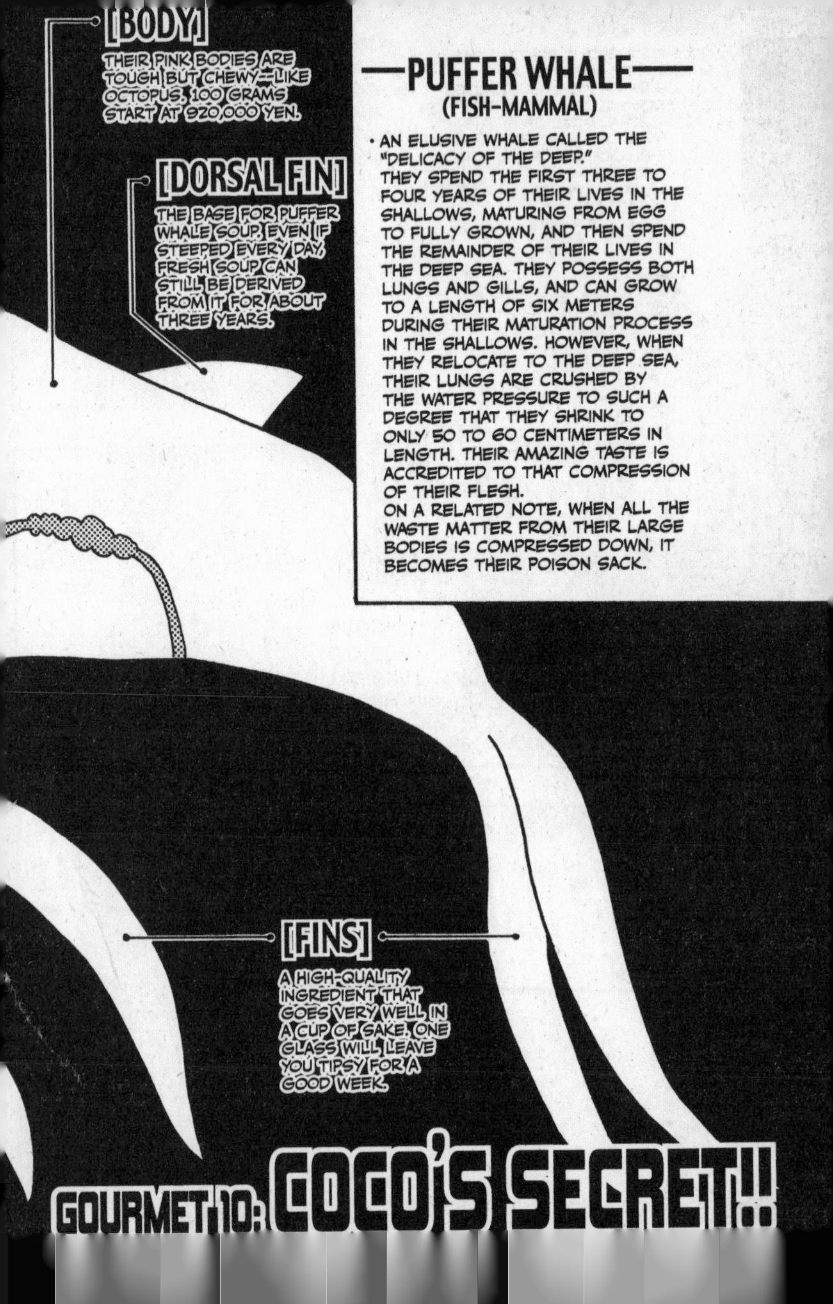
—PUFFER WHALE—
(FISH-MAMMAL)
• AN ELUSIVE WHALE CALLED THE "DELICACY OF THE DEEP." THEY SPEND THE FIRST THREE TO FOUR YEARS OF THEIR LIVES IN THE SHALLOWS, MATURING FROM EGG TO FULLY GROWN, AND THEN SPEND THE REMAINDER OF THEIR LIVES IN THE DEEP SEA. THEY POSSESS BOTH LUNGS AND GILLS, AND CAN GROW TO A LENGTH OF SIX METERS DURING THEIR MATURATION PROCESS IN THE SHALLOWS. HOWEVER, WHEN THEY RELOCATE TO THE DEEP SEA, THEIR LUNGS ARE CRUSHED BY THE WATER PRESSURE TO SUCH A DEGREE THAT THEY SHRINK TO ONLY 50 TO 60 CENTIMETERS IN LENGTH. THEIR AMAZING TASTE IS ACCREDITED TO THAT COMPRESSION OF THEIR FLESH.
ON A RELATED NOTE, WHEN ALL THE WASTE MATTER FROM THEIR LARGE BODIES IS COMPRESSED DOWN, IT BECOMES THEIR POISON SACK.
[BODY]
THEIR PINK BODIES ARE TOUGH BUT CHEWY—LIKE OCTOPUS. 100 GRAMS START AT 920,000 YEN.
[DORSAL FIN]
THE BASE FOR PUFFER WHALE SOUP. EVEN IF STEEPED EVERY DAY, FRESH SOUP CAN STILL BE DERIVED FROM IT FOR ABOUT THREE YEARS.
[FINS]
A HIGH-QUALITY INGREDIENT THAT GOES VERY WELL IN A CUP OF SAKE. ONE GLASS WILL LEAVE YOU TIPSY FOR A GOOD WEEK.
GOURMET 10: COCO'S SECRET!!

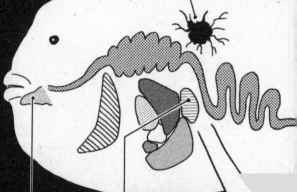

—POISON SACK—

ONCE RUPTURED, IT POISONS THE ENTIRE BODY INSTANTLY, AND CAUSES DEATH WITHIN 30 MINUTES TO 1 HOUR FOLLOWING CONSUMPTION. WITH A LETHAL DOSE OF 0.2 MG, IT COULD KILL ONE HUNDRED THOUSAND MICE. THE LOCATION OF THE POISON SACK VARIES FROM WHALE TO WHALE, MAKING ITS REMOVAL SO CHALLENGING IT'S SAID THAT ONLY TEN COOKS IN THE WHOLE WORLD CAN SUCCESSFULLY MANAGE IT.

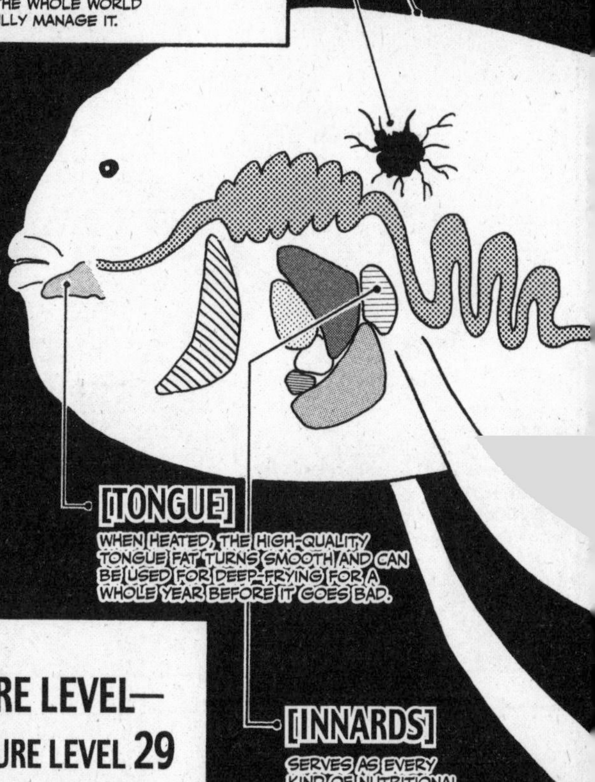

ACCORDING TO THE IGO'S "EIGHT RULES OF GOURMET," IT IS ILLEGAL TO SELL POISONED PUFFER WHALE. HOWEVER, SINCE THE POISON DOESN'T ALTER THE WHALE'S TASTE, PLENTY OF POISONED PUFFER WHALE CIRCULATES AROUND THE BLACK MARKET. PEOPLE RISK DEATH JUST TO TASTE IT, WHICH RESULTS IN A HUNDRED THOUSAND POISONING DEATHS ANNUALLY DURING HARVEST YEARS.

[SKIN]

IF DRIED, IT CAN REMAIN FRESH FOR OVER A CENTURY.

[TONGUE]

WHEN HEATED, THE HIGH-QUALITY TONGUE FAT TURNS SMOOTH AND CAN BE USED FOR DEEP-FRYING FOR A WHOLE YEAR BEFORE IT GOES BAD.

—CAPTURE LEVEL—

■ CAPTURE LEVEL 29

(THE CAPTURE LEVEL REFLECTS THE CHALLENGE OF CAPTURING ONE WITHOUT IT POISONING ITSELF. IF YOU IGNORE THE POISON, THE CAPTURE LEVEL DROPS BELOW ONE.)

[INNARDS]

SERVES AS EVERY KIND OF NUTRITIONAL SUPPLEMENT UNDER THE SUN. WHEN EATEN RAW, THEY PACK ENOUGH PUNCH TO KEEP YOU ACTIVE WITHOUT SLEEP OR REST FOR TEN DAYS STRAIGHT.

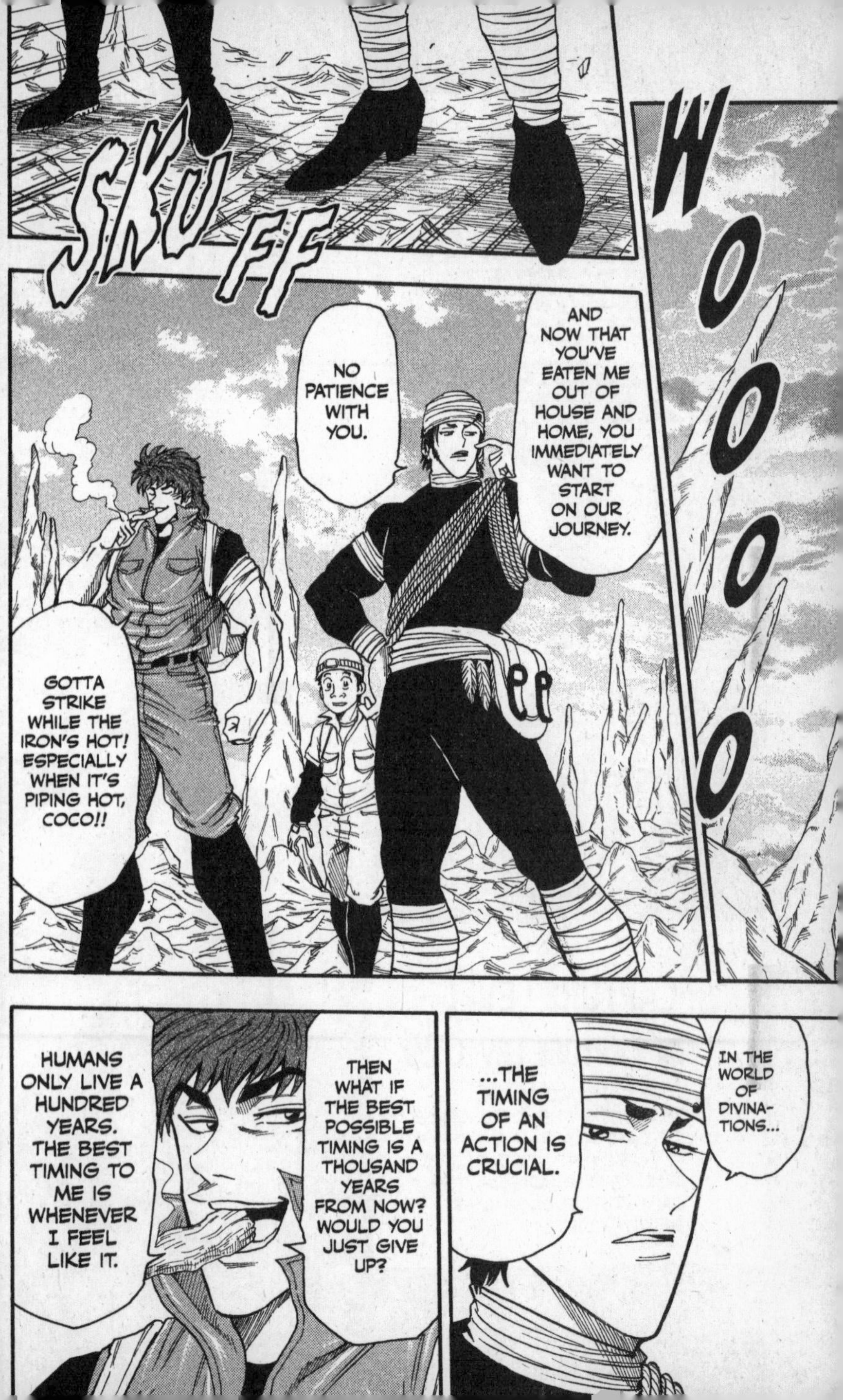
WOOOOO
SKUFF
AND NOW THAT YOU'VE EATEN ME OUT OF HOUSE AND HOME, YOU IMMEDIATELY WANT TO START ON OUR JOURNEY.
NO PATIENCE WITH YOU.
GOTTA STRIKE WHILE THE IRON'S HOT! ESPECIALLY WHEN IT'S PIPING HOT, COCO!!
IN THE WORLD OF DIVINATIONS...
...THE TIMING OF AN ACTION IS CRUCIAL.
THEN WHAT IF THE BEST POSSIBLE TIMING IS A THOUSAND YEARS FROM NOW? WOULD YOU JUST GIVE UP?
HUMANS ONLY LIVE A HUNDRED YEARS. THE BEST TIMING TO ME IS WHENEVER I FEEL LIKE IT.

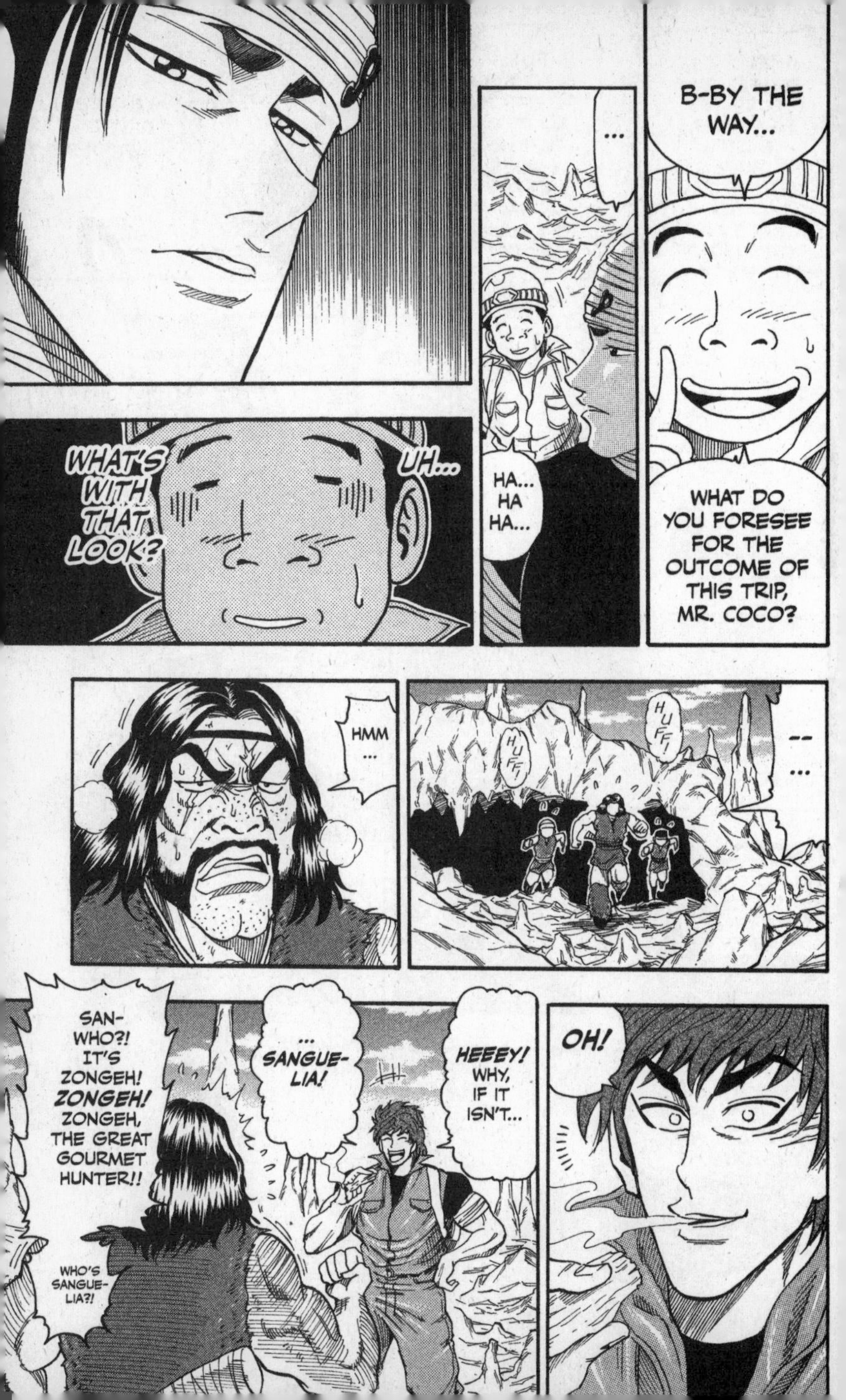
B-BY THE WAY...
WHAT DO YOU FORESEE FOR THE OUTCOME OF THIS TRIP, MR. COCO?
...
HA... HA HA...
UH...
WHAT'S WITH THAT LOOK?
HUFF! HUFF!
--...
HMM...
OH!
HEEEY! WHY, IF IT ISN'T...
... SANGUE-LIA!
SAN-WHO?! IT'S ZONGEH! ZONGEH! ZONGEH, THE GREAT GOURMET HUNTER!!
WHO'S SANGUE-LIA?!

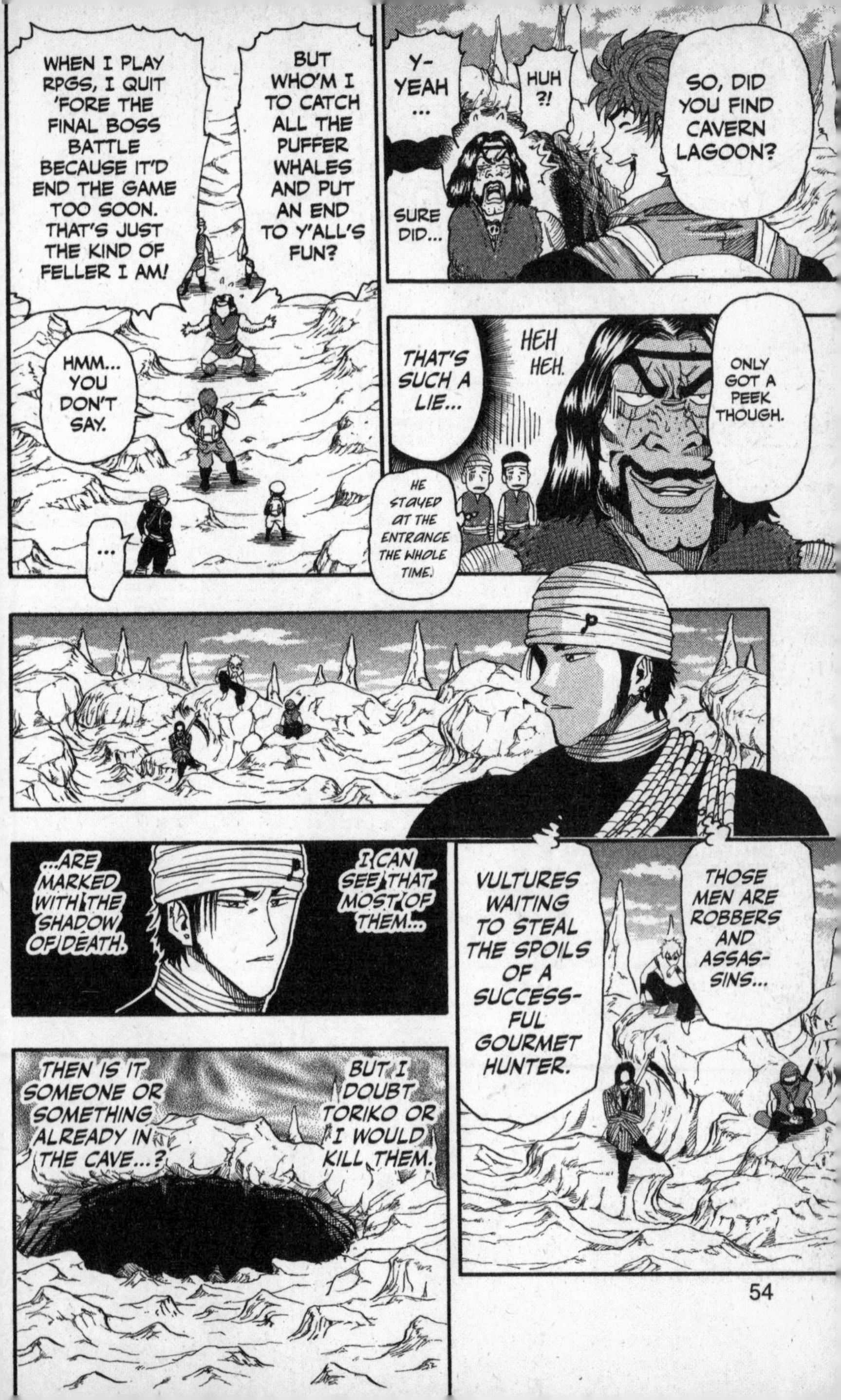
SO, DID YOU FIND CAVERN LAGOON?
HUH ?!
Y-YEAH ...
SURE DID...
ONLY GOT A PEEK THOUGH.
HEH HEH.
THAT'S SUCH A LIE...
HE STAYED AT THE ENTRANCE THE WHOLE TIME.
BUT WHO'M I TO CATCH ALL THE PUFFER WHALES AND PUT AN END TO Y'ALL'S FUN?
WHEN I PLAY RPGS, I QUIT 'FORE THE FINAL BOSS BATTLE BECAUSE IT'D END THE GAME TOO SOON. THAT'S JUST THE KIND OF FELLER I AM!
HMM... YOU DON'T SAY.
...
THOSE MEN ARE ROBBERS AND ASSAS-SINS...
VULTURES WAITING TO STEAL THE SPOILS OF A SUCCESS-FUL GOURMET HUNTER.
I CAN SEE THAT MOST OF THEM...
...ARE MARKED WITH THE SHADOW OF DEATH.
BUT I DOUBT TORIKO OR I WOULD KILL THEM.
THEN IS IT SOMEONE OR SOMETHING ALREADY IN THE CAVE...?

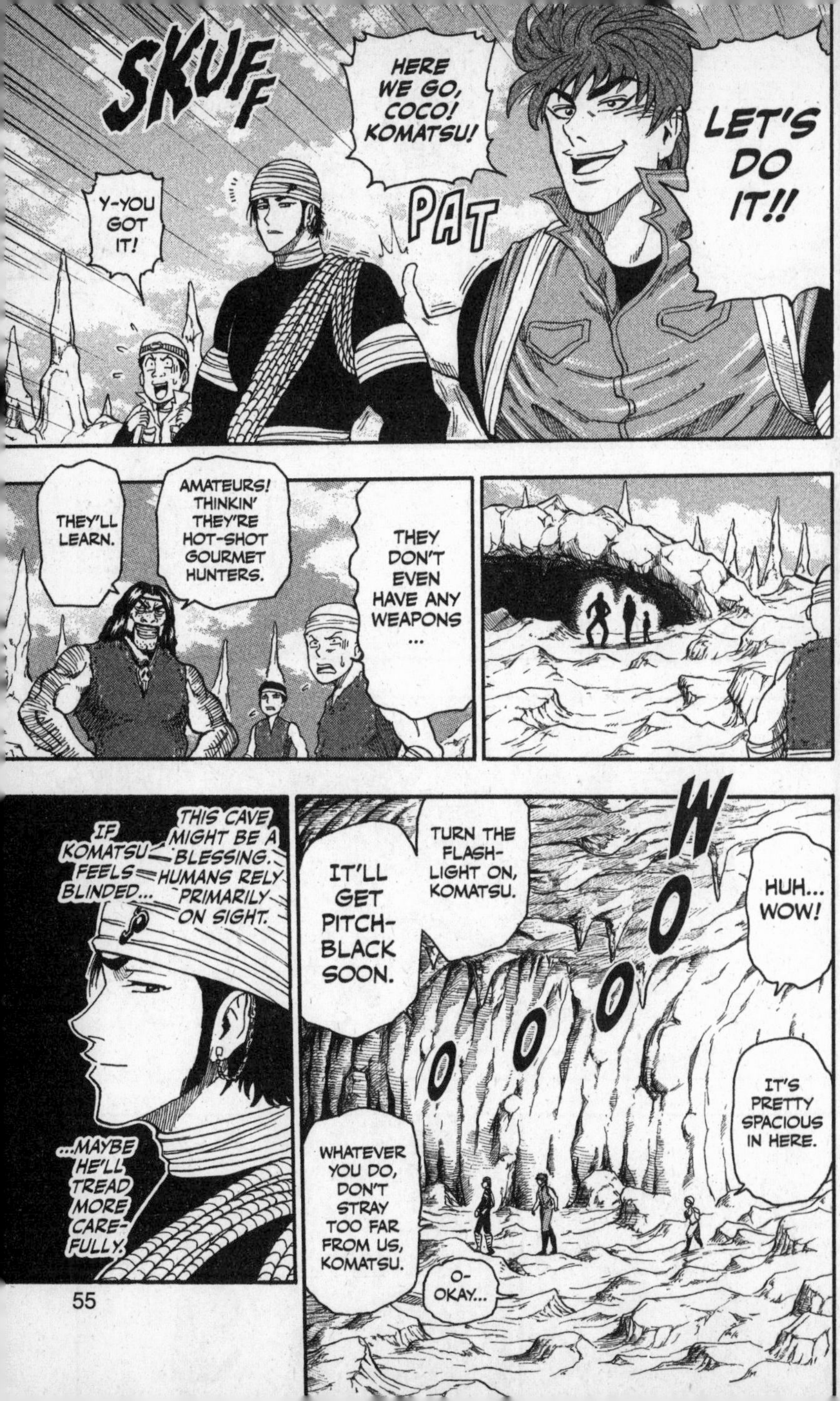
HERE WE GO, COCO! KOMATSU!
LET'S DO IT!!
SKUFF
PAT
Y-YOU GOT IT!
THEY DON'T EVEN HAVE ANY WEAPONS ...
AMATEURS! THINKIN' THEY'RE HOT-SHOT GOURMET HUNTERS.
THEY'LL LEARN.
HUH... WOW!
WOOOOOO
TURN THE FLASH-LIGHT ON, KOMATSU.
IT'LL GET PITCH-BLACK SOON.
IT'S PRETTY SPACIOUS IN HERE.
WHATEVER YOU DO, DON'T STRAY TOO FAR FROM US, KOMATSU.
O-OKAY...
THIS CAVE MIGHT BE A BLESSING. HUMANS RELY PRIMARILY ON SIGHT.
IF KOMATSU FEELS BLINDED...
...MAYBE HE'LL TREAD MORE CAREFULLY.

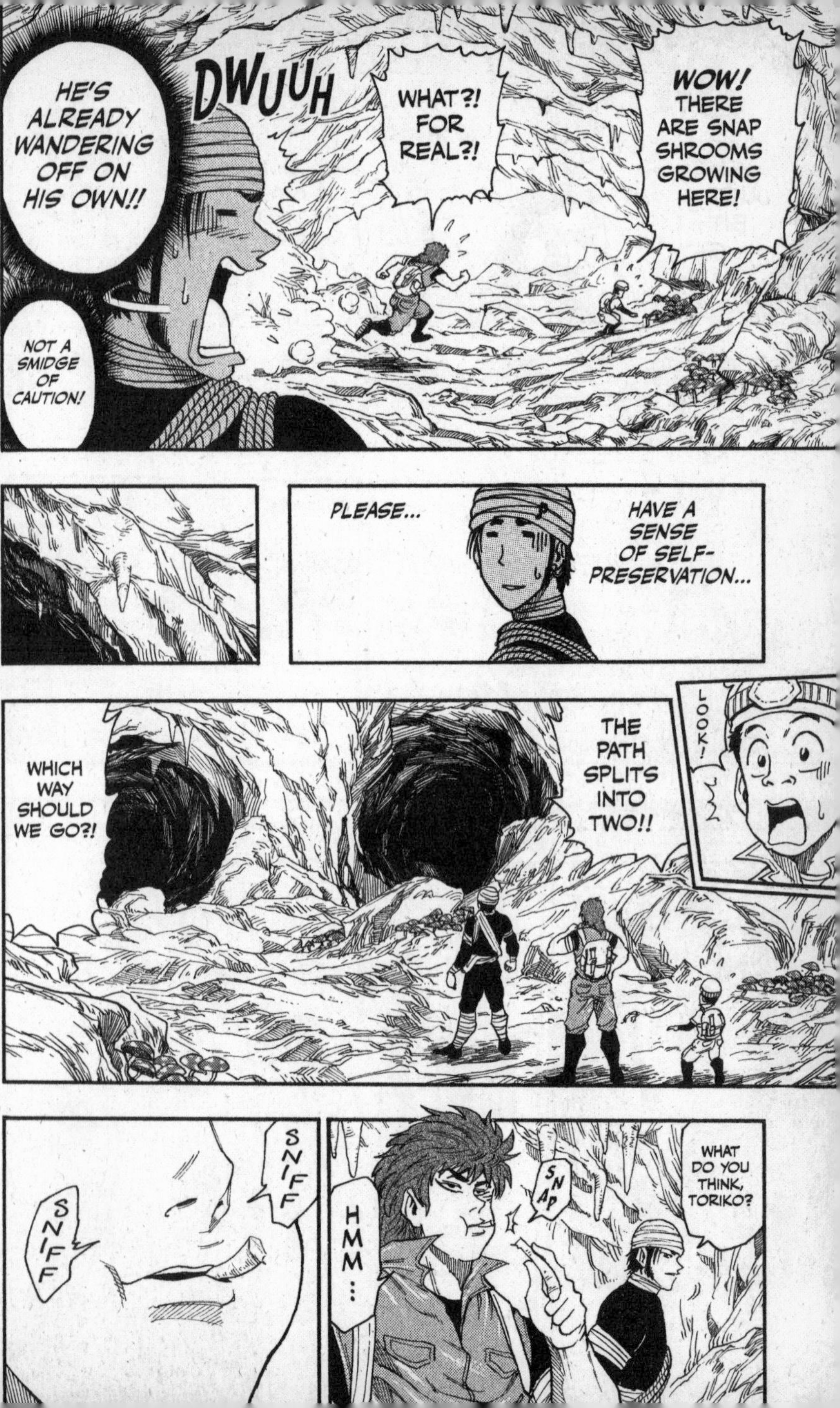
WOW! THERE ARE SNAP SHROOMS GROWING HERE!
WHAT?! FOR REAL?!
DWUUH
HE'S ALREADY WANDERING OFF ON HIS OWN!!
NOT A SMIDGE OF CAUTION!
PLEASE...
HAVE A SENSE OF SELF-PRESERVATION...
LOOK!
THE PATH SPLITS INTO TWO!!
WHICH WAY SHOULD WE GO?!
WHAT DO YOU THINK, TORIKO?
SNAP
HMM...
SNIFF
SNIFF

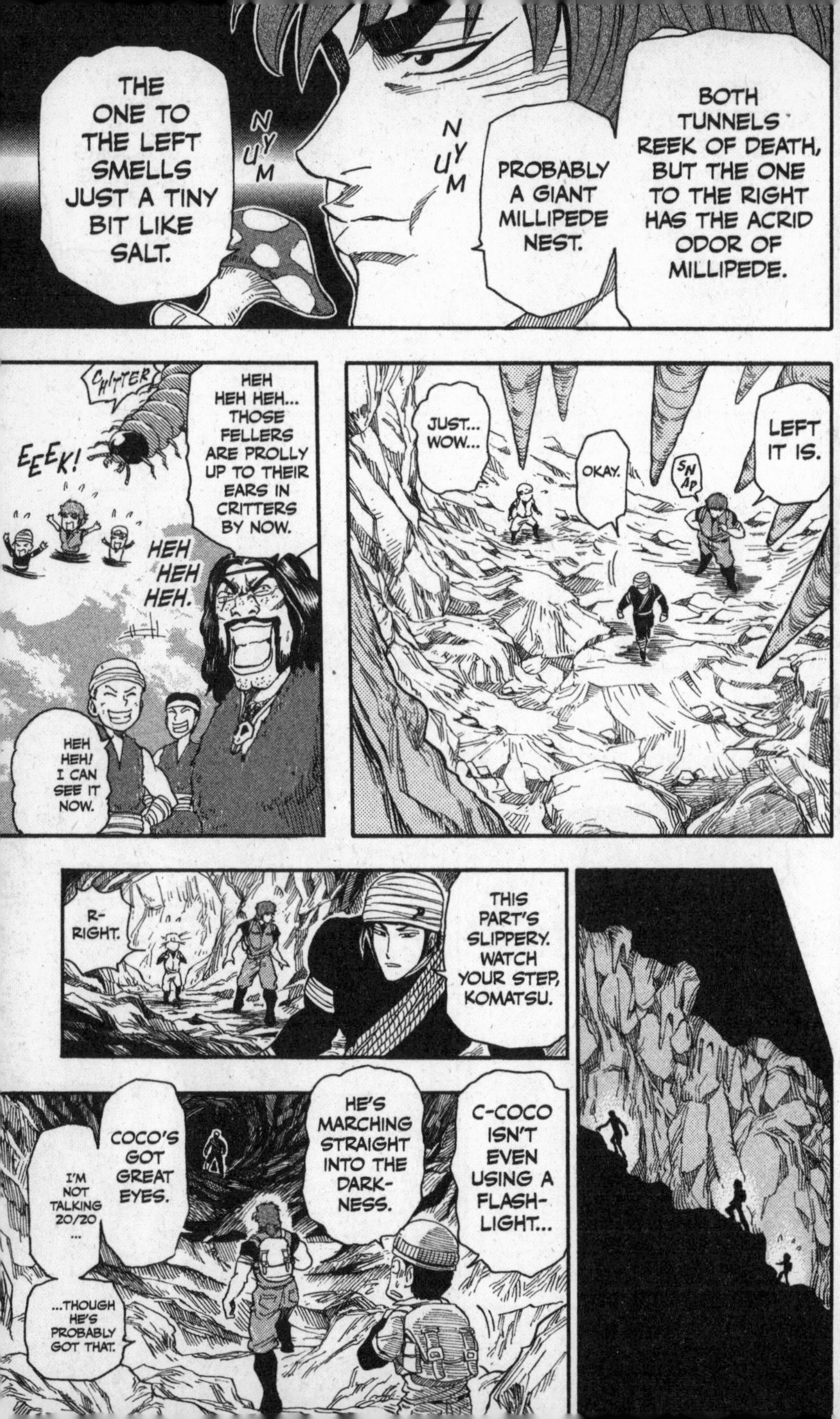
BOTH TUNNELS REEK OF DEATH, BUT THE ONE TO THE RIGHT HAS THE ACRID ODOR OF MILLIPEDE.
PROBABLY A GIANT MILLIPEDE NEST.
NYUM
NYUM
THE ONE TO THE LEFT SMELLS JUST A TINY BIT LIKE SALT.
LEFT IT IS.
SNAP
OKAY.
JUST... WOW...
HEH HEH HEH... THOSE FELLERS ARE PROLLY UP TO THEIR EARS IN CRITTERS BY NOW.
CHITTER
EEEK!
HEH HEH HEH.
HEH HEH! I CAN SEE IT NOW.
THIS PART'S SLIPPERY. WATCH YOUR STEP, KOMATSU.
R-RIGHT.
C-COCO ISN'T EVEN USING A FLASH-LIGHT...
HE'S MARCHING STRAIGHT INTO THE DARK-NESS.
COCO'S GOT GREAT EYES.
I'M NOT TALKING 20/20 ...
...THOUGH HE'S PROBABLY GOT THAT.

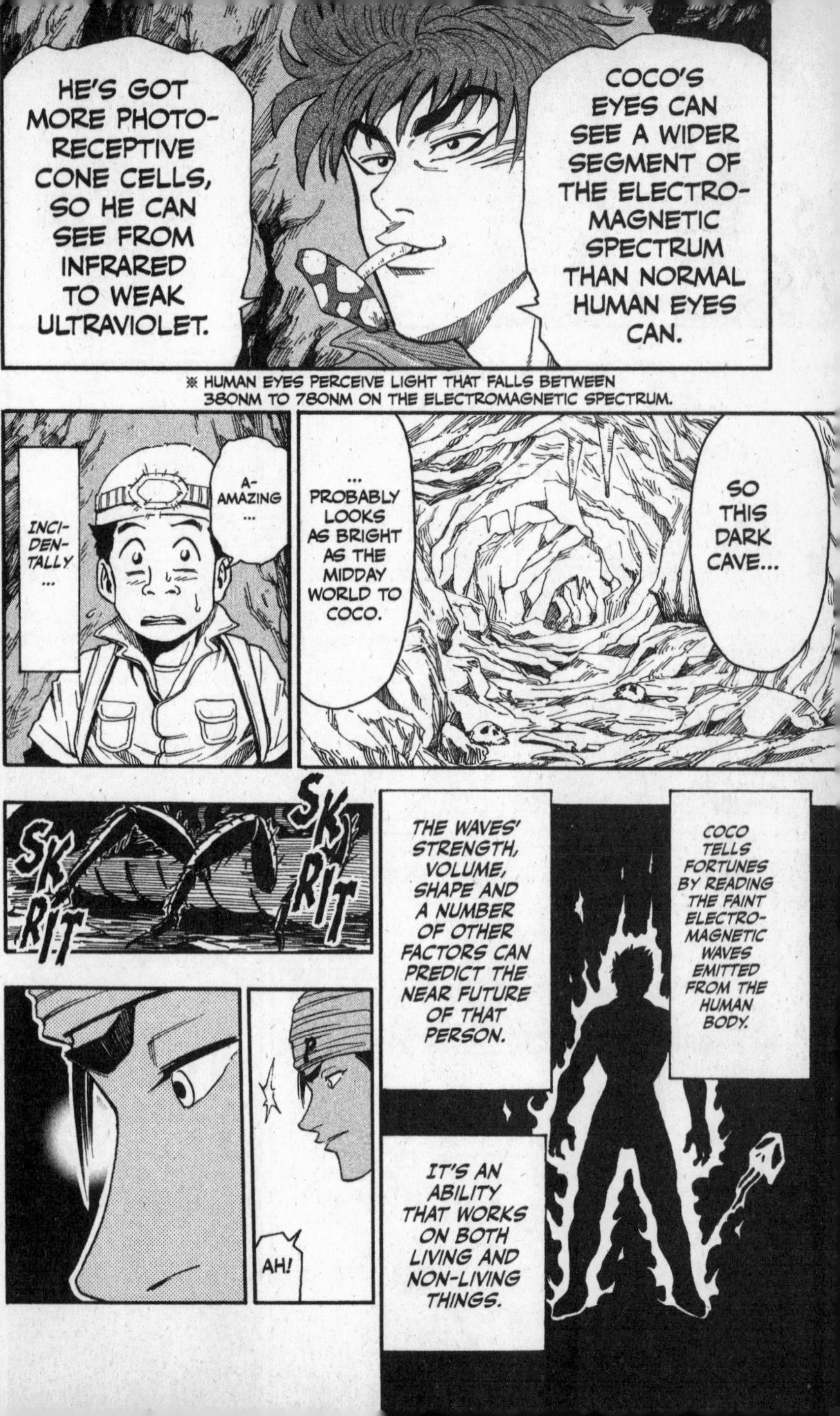
COCO'S EYES CAN SEE A WIDER SEGMENT OF THE ELECTRO-MAGNETIC SPECTRUM THAN NORMAL HUMAN EYES CAN.
HE'S GOT MORE PHOTO-RECEPTIVE CONE CELLS, SO HE CAN SEE FROM INFRARED TO WEAK ULTRAVIOLET.
※ HUMAN EYES PERCEIVE LIGHT THAT FALLS BETWEEN 380NM TO 780NM ON THE ELECTROMAGNETIC SPECTRUM.
SO THIS DARK CAVE...
... PROBABLY LOOKS AS BRIGHT AS THE MIDDAY WORLD TO COCO.
A-AMAZING ...
INCIDENTALLY ...
COCO TELLS FORTUNES BY READING THE FAINT ELECTRO-MAGNETIC WAVES EMITTED FROM THE HUMAN BODY.
THE WAVES' STRENGTH, VOLUME, SHAPE AND A NUMBER OF OTHER FACTORS CAN PREDICT THE NEAR FUTURE OF THAT PERSON.
IT'S AN ABILITY THAT WORKS ON BOTH LIVING AND NON-LIVING THINGS.
SKRIT
SKRIT
AH!

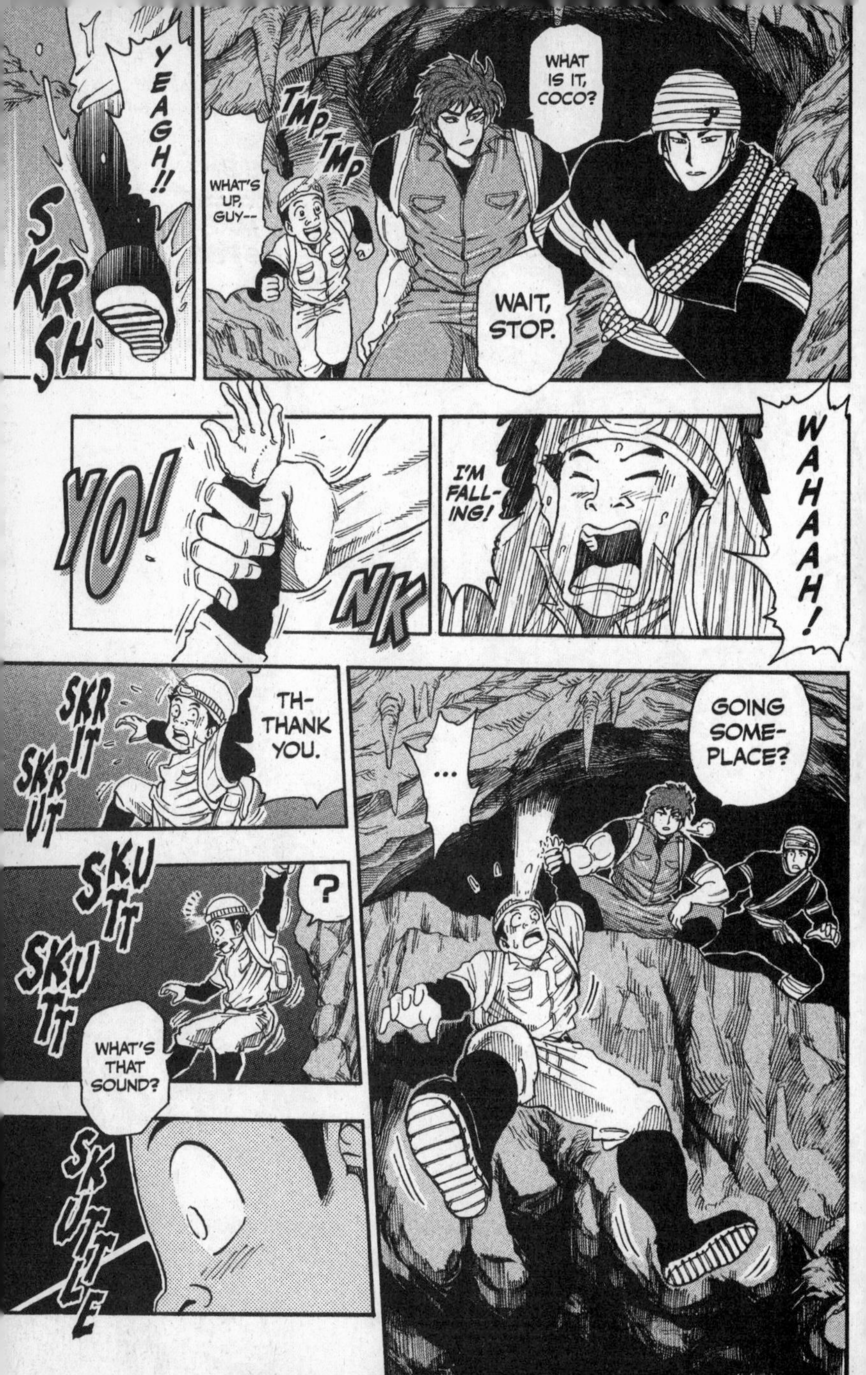
WHAT IS IT, COCO?
TMP TMP
WHAT'S UP, GUY--
WAIT, STOP.
YEAGH!!
SKRSH
WAHAAAH!
I'M FALL-ING!
YOINK
GOING SOME-PLACE?
...
TH-THANK YOU.
SKRIT SKRUT
?
SKUTT SKUTT
WHAT'S THAT SOUND?
SKUTTLE

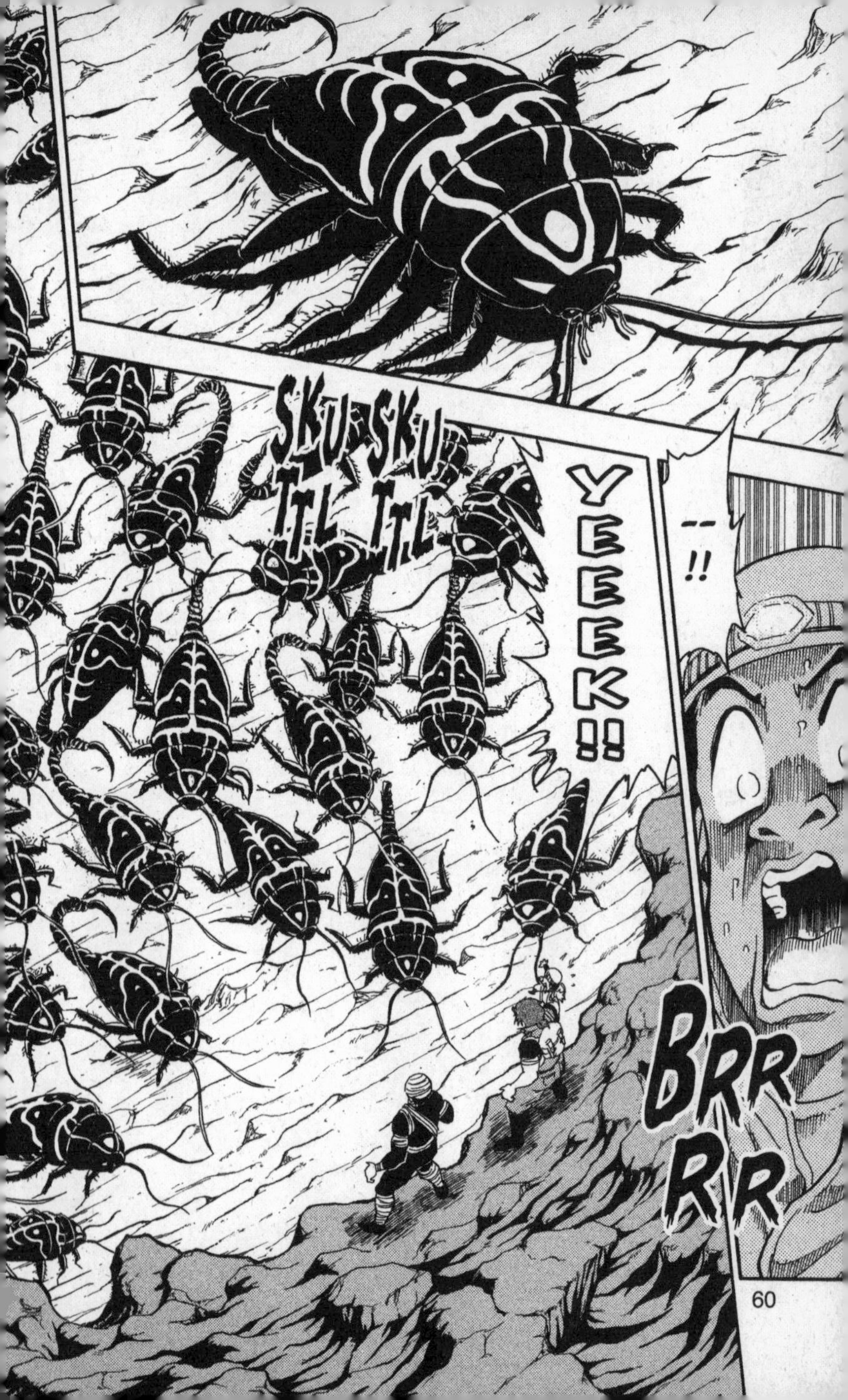
--!!
BRRRR
YEEEK!!
SKUSKU ITL ITL

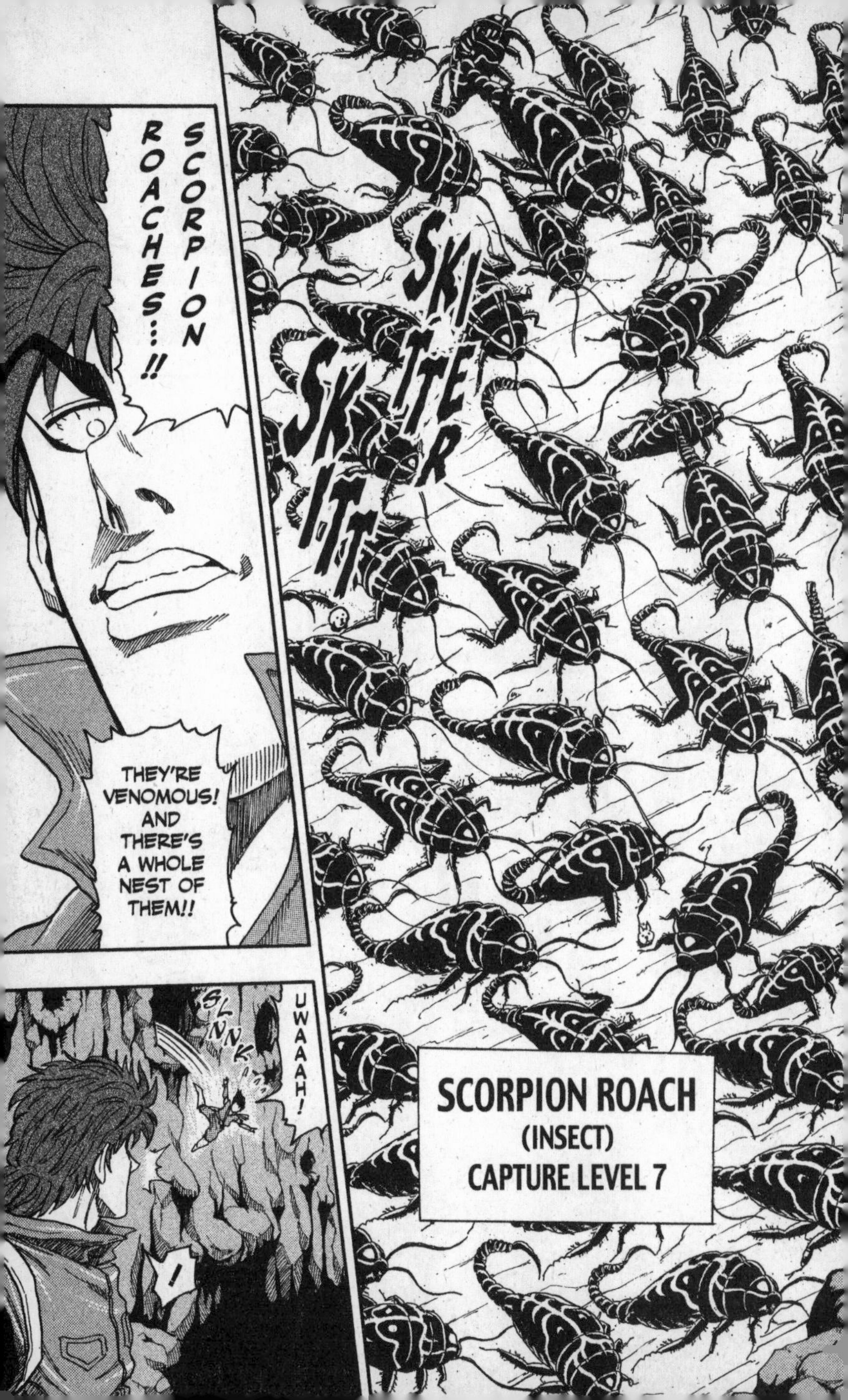
SKITTER
SKITT
SCORPION ROACH
(INSECT)
CAPTURE LEVEL 7
SCORPION ROACHES...!!
THEY'RE VENOMOUS! AND THERE'S A WHOLE NEST OF THEM!!
UWAAAAH!
SLNNK
!

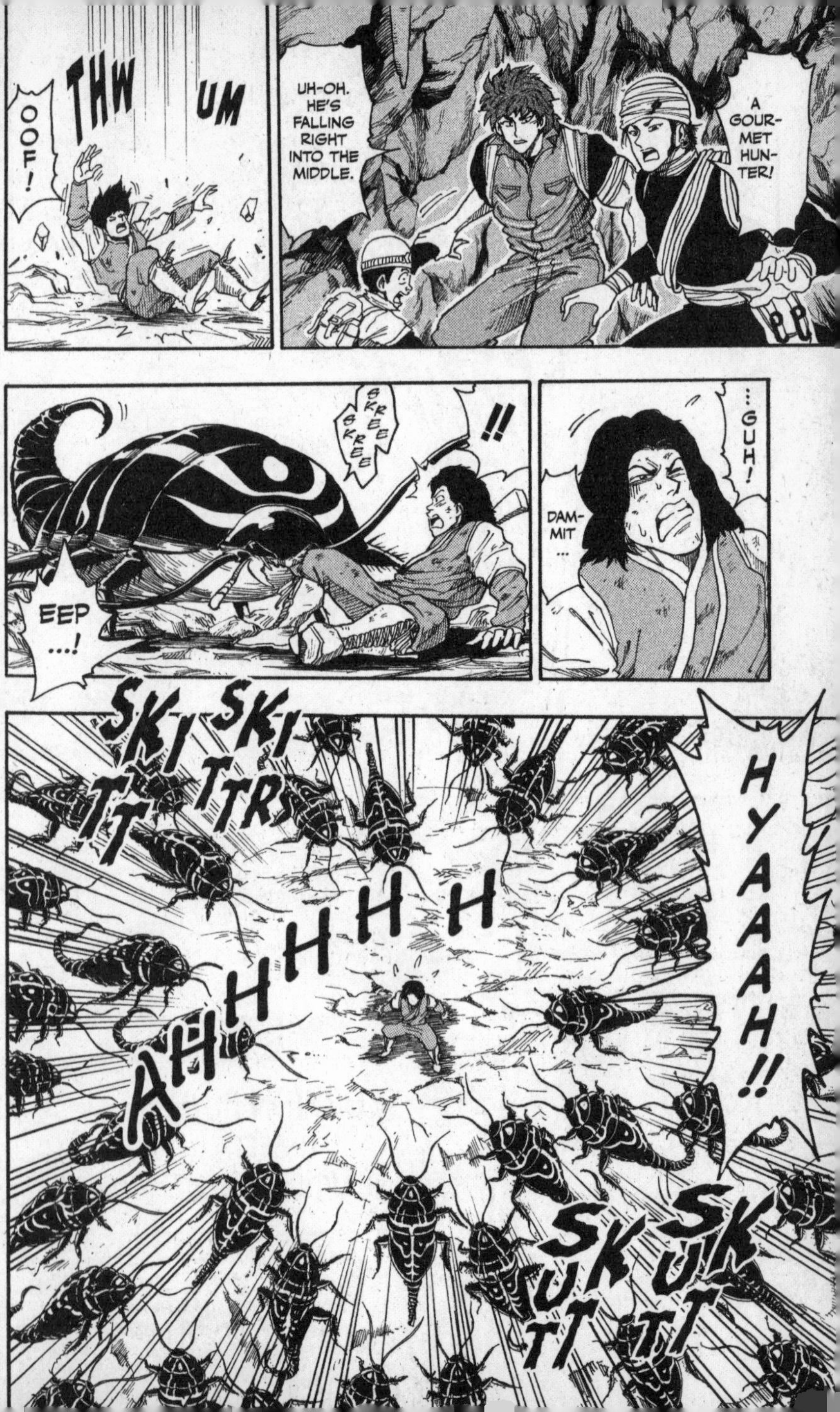
A GOURMET HUNTER!
UH-OH. HE'S FALLING RIGHT INTO THE MIDDLE.
THWUM
OOF!
...GUH!
DAMMIT...
!!
SKREE SKREE
EEP...!
HYAAAAH!!
AHHHHHH
SKI-TTRS
SKITTT
SKUKTTT
SKUKTTT

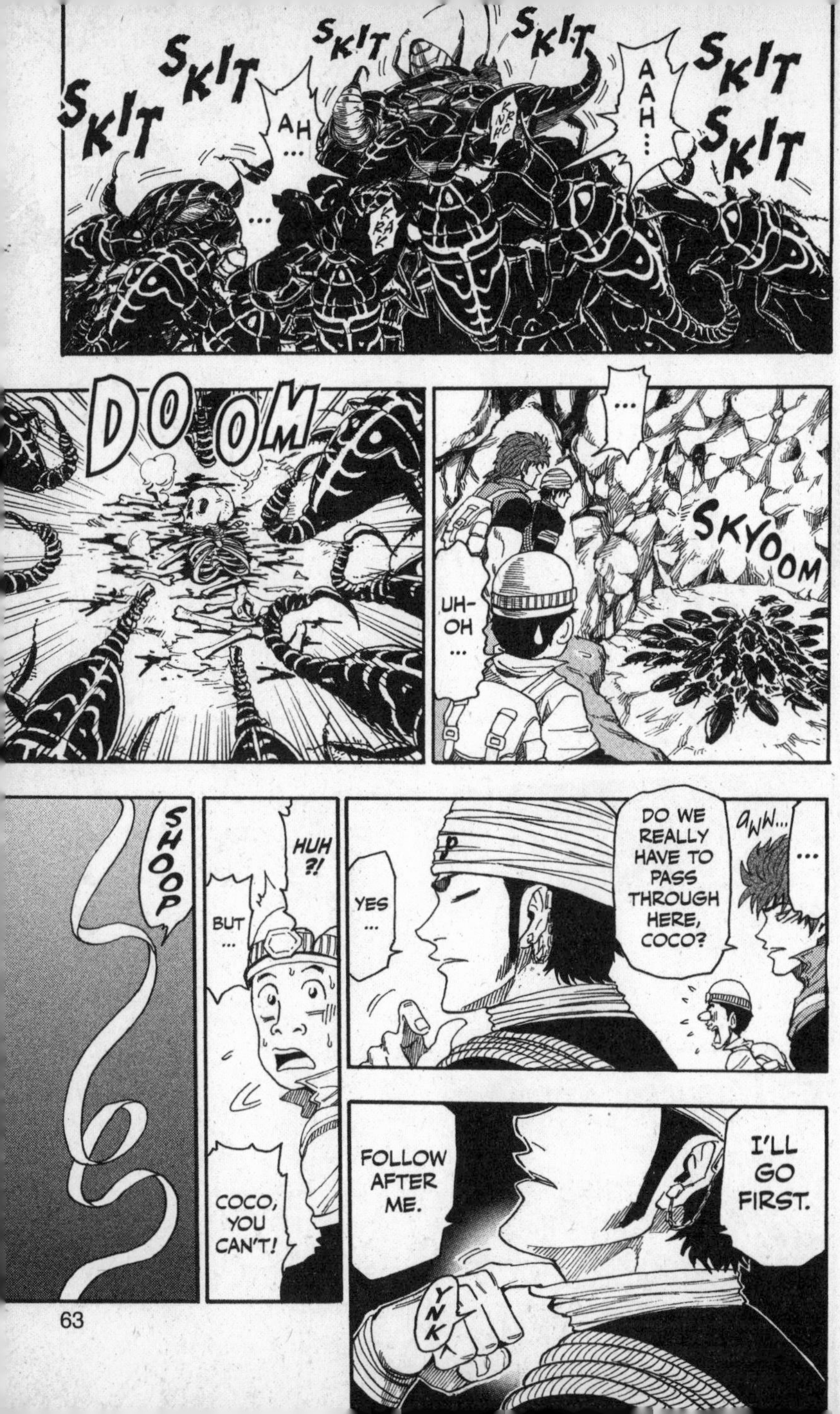
SKIT
SKIT
AAH...
SKIT
KNRHC
SKIT
AH...
SKIT
SKIT
KRAK
...
...
SKYOOM
UH-OH...
DOOM
AWW... ...
DO WE REALLY HAVE TO PASS THROUGH HERE, COCO?
YES...
I'LL GO FIRST.
FOLLOW AFTER ME.
YNK
HUH?!
BUT...
COCO, YOU CAN'T!
SHOOP

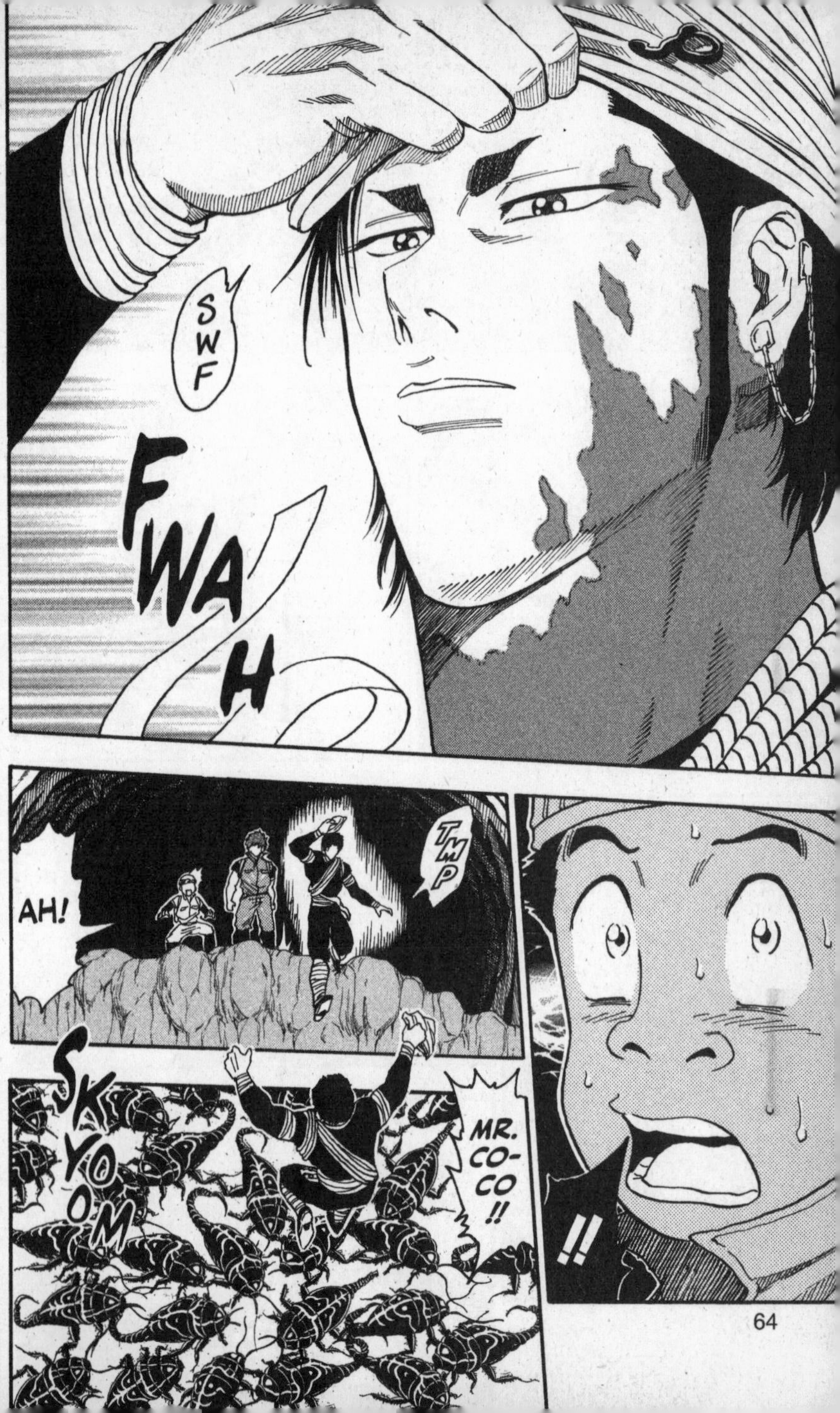
SWF
FWAH
MR. CO-CO!!
!!
TMP
AH!
SKYOOM

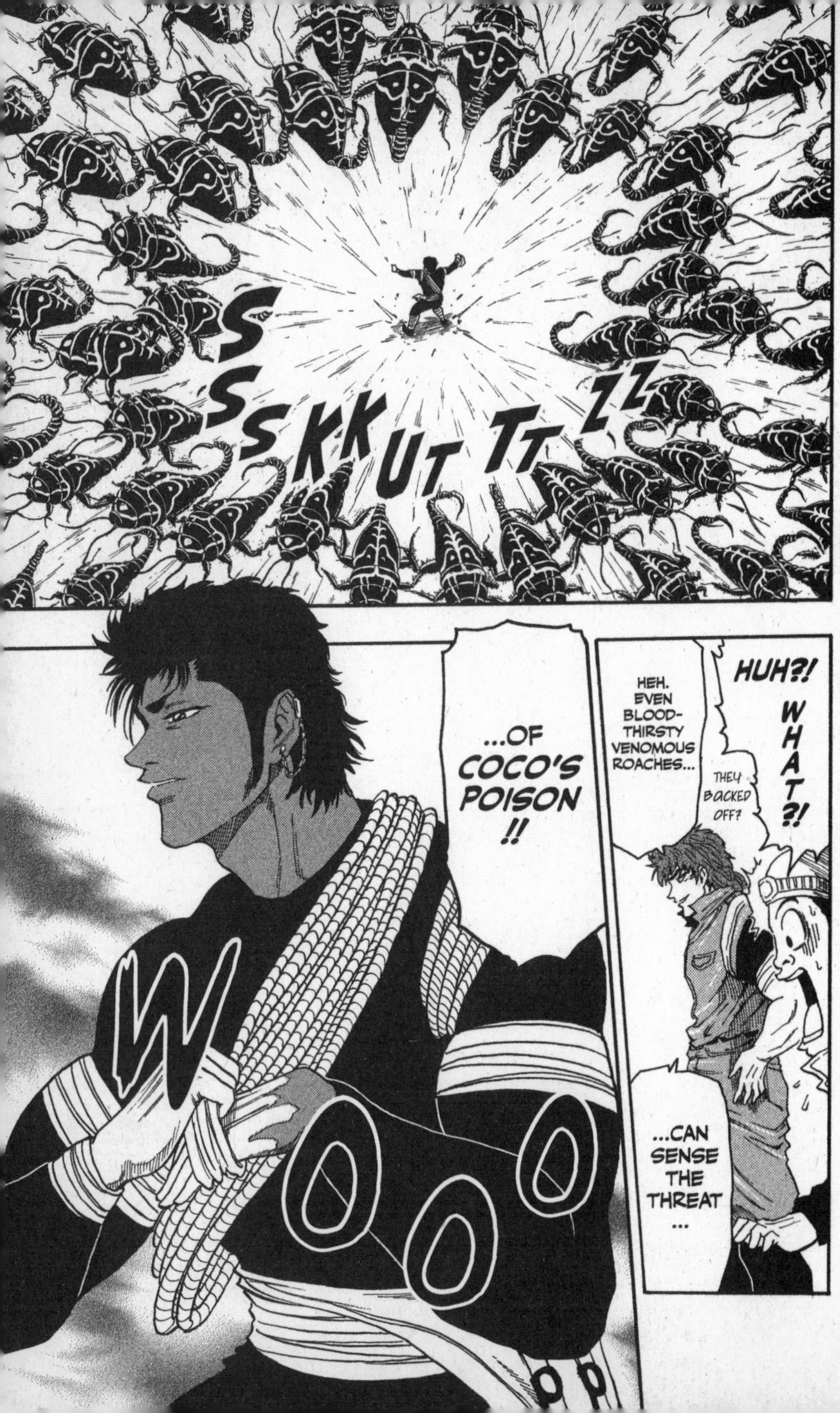
SSSKKUTTTZZ
HUH?!
WHAT?!
THEY BACKED OFF?
HEH. EVEN BLOOD-THIRSTY VENOMOUS ROACHES...
...CAN SENSE THE THREAT...
...OF COCO'S POISON!!
WOOOO

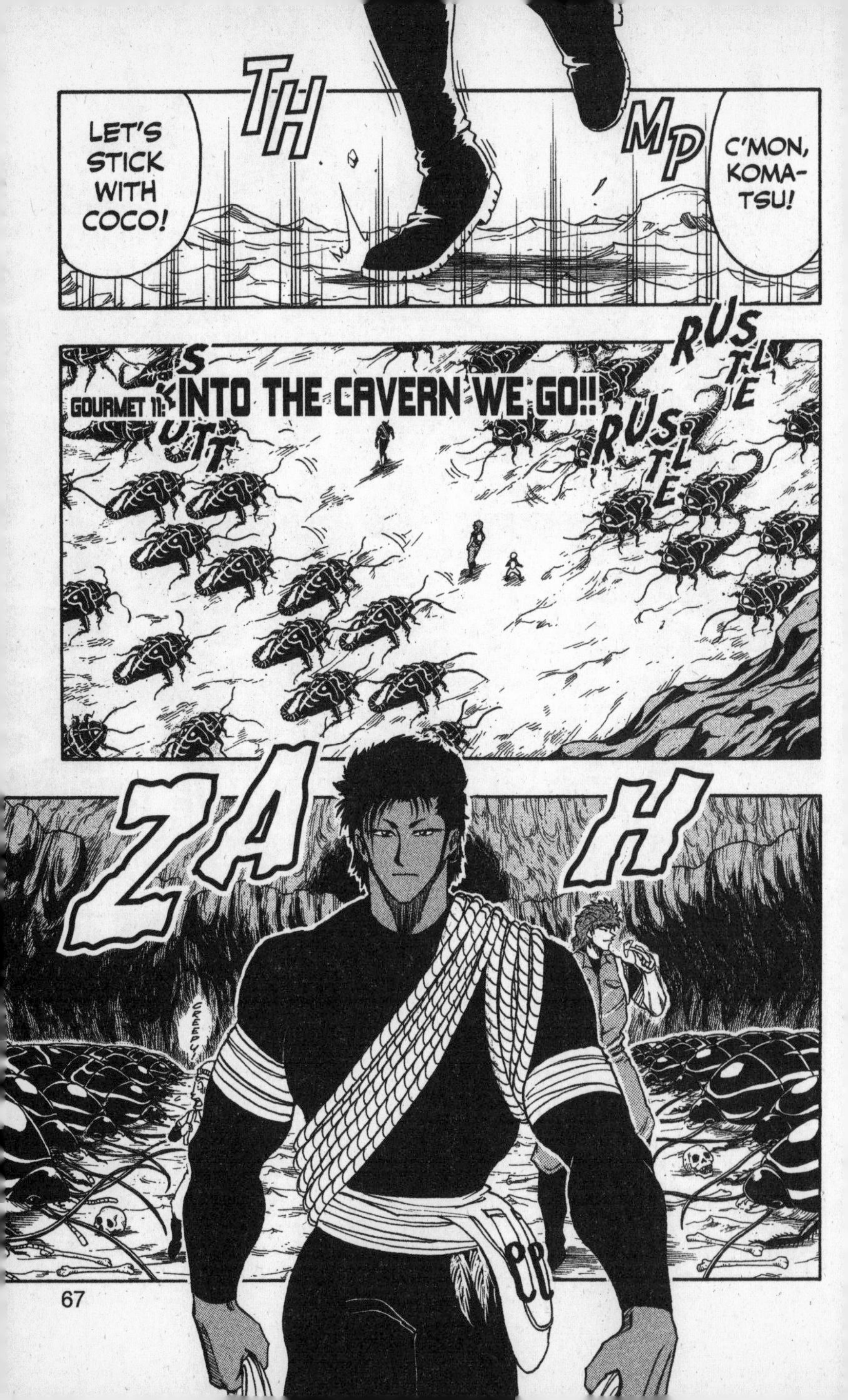

C'MON, KOMATSU!
THMP
LET'S STICK WITH COCO!
GOURMET 11: INTO THE CAVERN WE GO!!
RUSTLE
RUSTLE
ZAH
CREEPY!

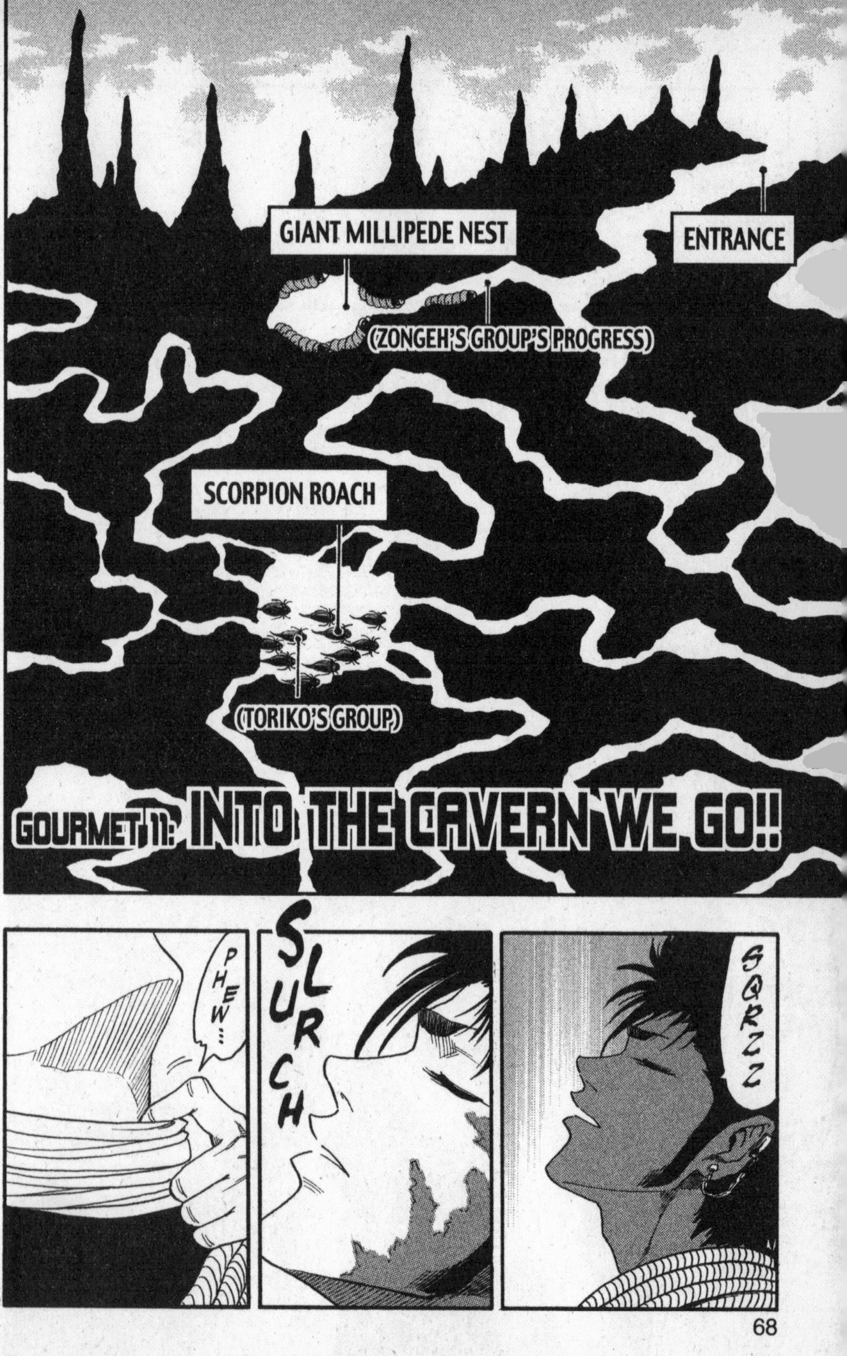
ENTRANCE
GIANT MILLIPEDE NEST
(ZONGEH'S GROUP'S PROGRESS)
SCORPION ROACH
(TORIKO'S GROUP)
GOURMET 11: INTO THE CAVERN WE GO!!
SQRZZ
SLURCH
PHEW...

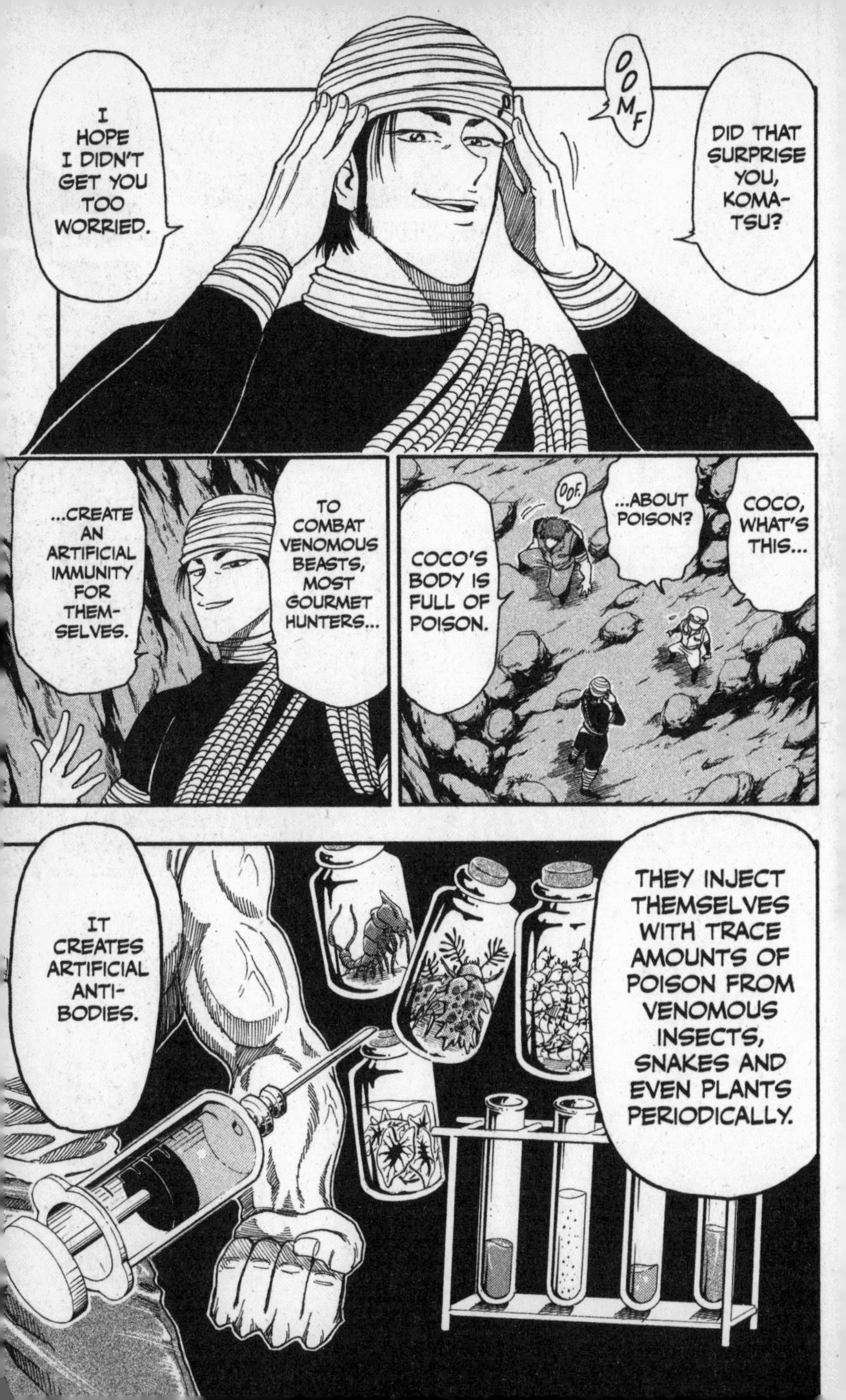

DID THAT SURPRISE YOU, KOMATSU?
OOMF
I HOPE I DIDN'T GET YOU TOO WORRIED.
COCO, WHAT'S THIS...
...ABOUT POISON?
OOF.
COCO'S BODY IS FULL OF POISON.
TO COMBAT VENOMOUS BEASTS, MOST GOURMET HUNTERS...
...CREATE AN ARTIFICIAL IMMUNITY FOR THEMSELVES.
THEY INJECT THEMSELVES WITH TRACE AMOUNTS OF POISON FROM VENOMOUS INSECTS, SNAKES AND EVEN PLANTS PERIODICALLY.
IT CREATES ARTIFICIAL ANTIBODIES.

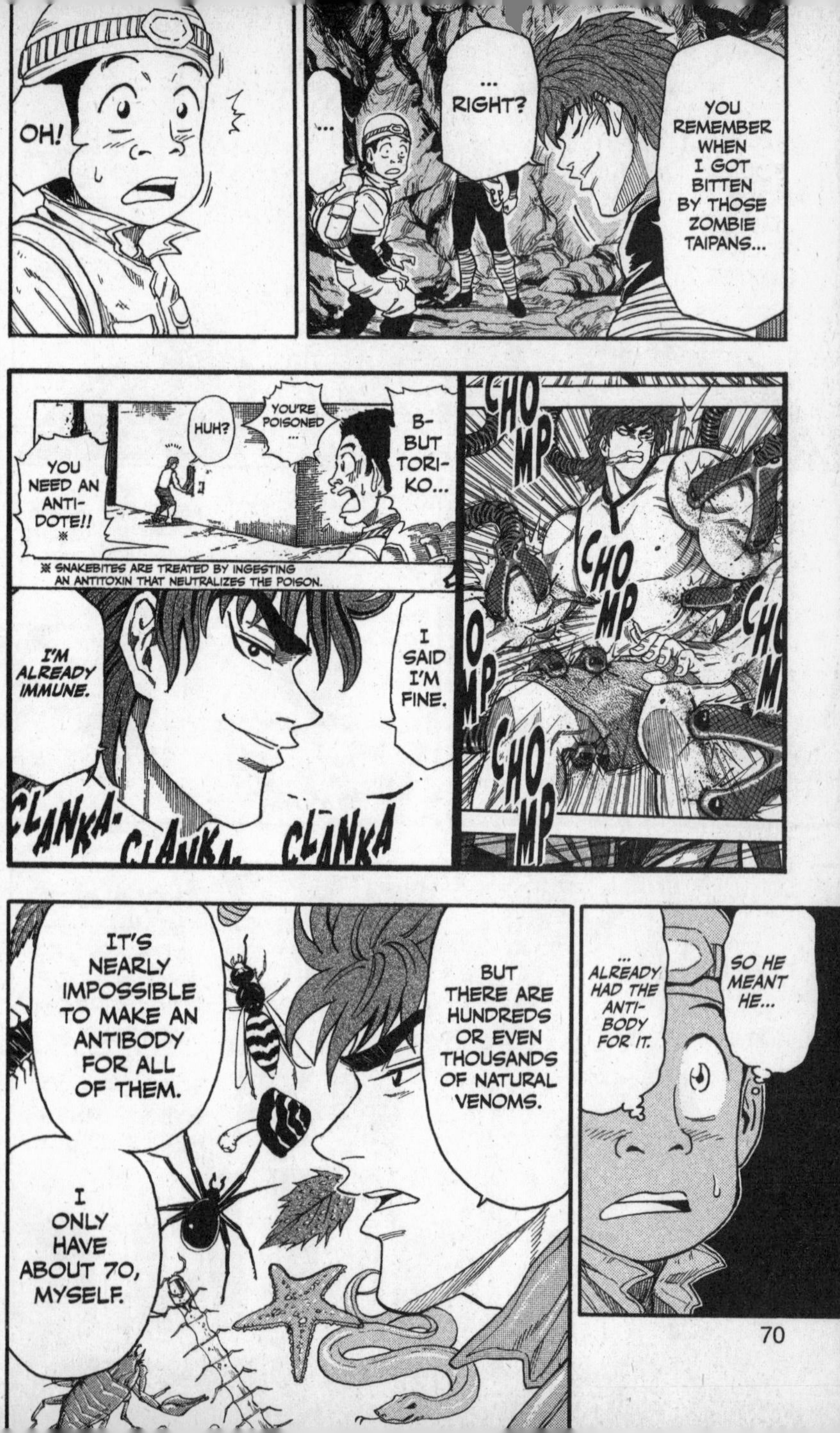
YOU REMEMBER WHEN I GOT BITTEN BY THOSE ZOMBIE TAIPANS...
... RIGHT?
...
OH!
CHOMP CHOMP CHOMP CHOMP CHOMP
B-BUT TORIKO...
YOU'RE POISONED ...
HUH?
YOU NEED AN ANTI-DOTE!! ※
※ SNAKEBITES ARE TREATED BY INGESTING AN ANTITOXIN THAT NEUTRALIZES THE POISON.
I SAID I'M FINE.
I'M ALREADY IMMUNE.
CLANKA-CLANKA-CLANKA
SO HE MEANT HE...
...ALREADY HAD THE ANTI-BODY FOR IT.
BUT THERE ARE HUNDREDS OR EVEN THOUSANDS OF NATURAL VENOMS.
IT'S NEARLY IMPOSSIBLE TO MAKE AN ANTIBODY FOR ALL OF THEM.
I ONLY HAVE ABOUT 70, MYSELF.

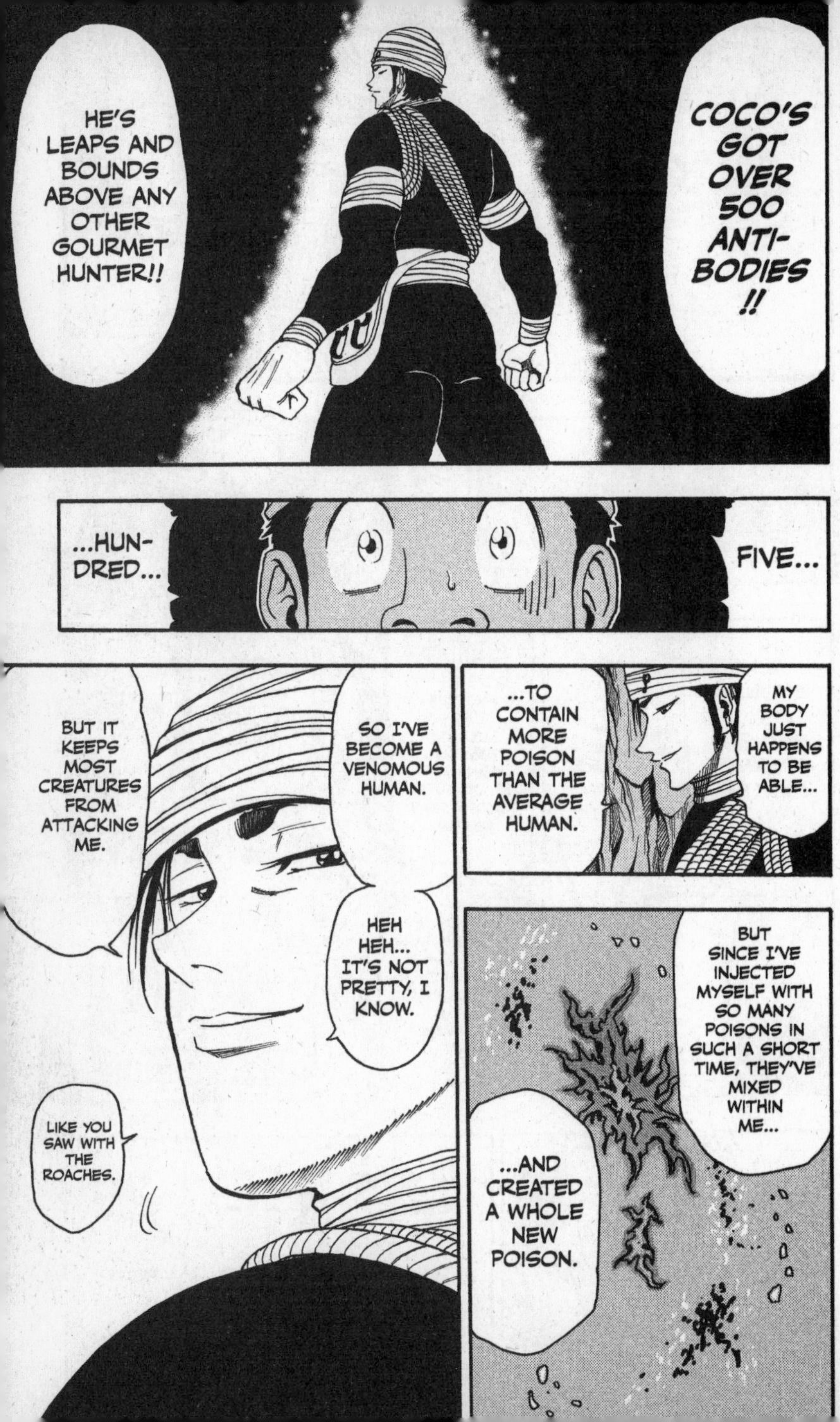
COCO'S GOT OVER 500 ANTI-BODIES!!
HE'S LEAPS AND BOUNDS ABOVE ANY OTHER GOURMET HUNTER!!
FIVE...
...HUN-DRED...
MY BODY JUST HAPPENS TO BE ABLE...
...TO CONTAIN MORE POISON THAN THE AVERAGE HUMAN.
BUT SINCE I'VE INJECTED MYSELF WITH SO MANY POISONS IN SUCH A SHORT TIME, THEY'VE MIXED WITHIN ME...
...AND CREATED A WHOLE NEW POISON.
SO I'VE BECOME A VENOMOUS HUMAN.
BUT IT KEEPS MOST CREATURES FROM ATTACKING ME.
HEH HEH... IT'S NOT PRETTY, I KNOW.
LIKE YOU SAW WITH THE ROACHES.

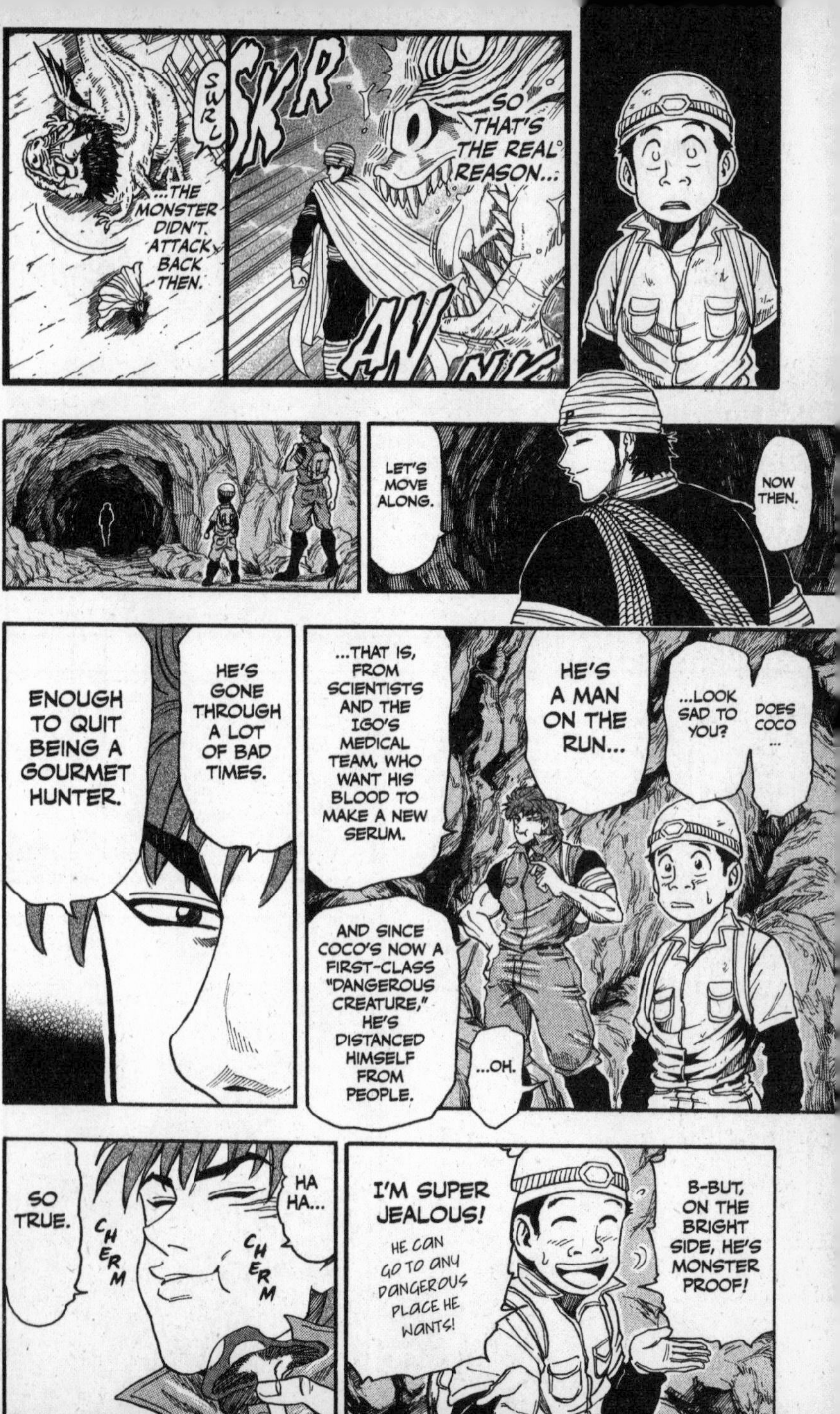
SO THAT'S THE REAL REASON...
SKR
AN
SWRL
...THE MONSTER DIDN'T ATTACK BACK THEN.
NOW THEN.
LET'S MOVE ALONG.
DOES COCO...
...LOOK SAD TO YOU?
HE'S A MAN ON THE RUN...
...THAT IS, FROM SCIENTISTS AND THE IGO'S MEDICAL TEAM, WHO WANT HIS BLOOD TO MAKE A NEW SERUM.
...OH.
AND SINCE COCO'S NOW A FIRST-CLASS "DANGEROUS CREATURE," HE'S DISTANCED HIMSELF FROM PEOPLE.
HE'S GONE THROUGH A LOT OF BAD TIMES.
ENOUGH TO QUIT BEING A GOURMET HUNTER.
B-BUT, ON THE BRIGHT SIDE, HE'S MONSTER PROOF!
I'M SUPER JEALOUS!
HE CAN GO TO ANY DANGEROUS PLACE HE WANTS!
HA HA...
CHERM
CHERM
SO TRUE.

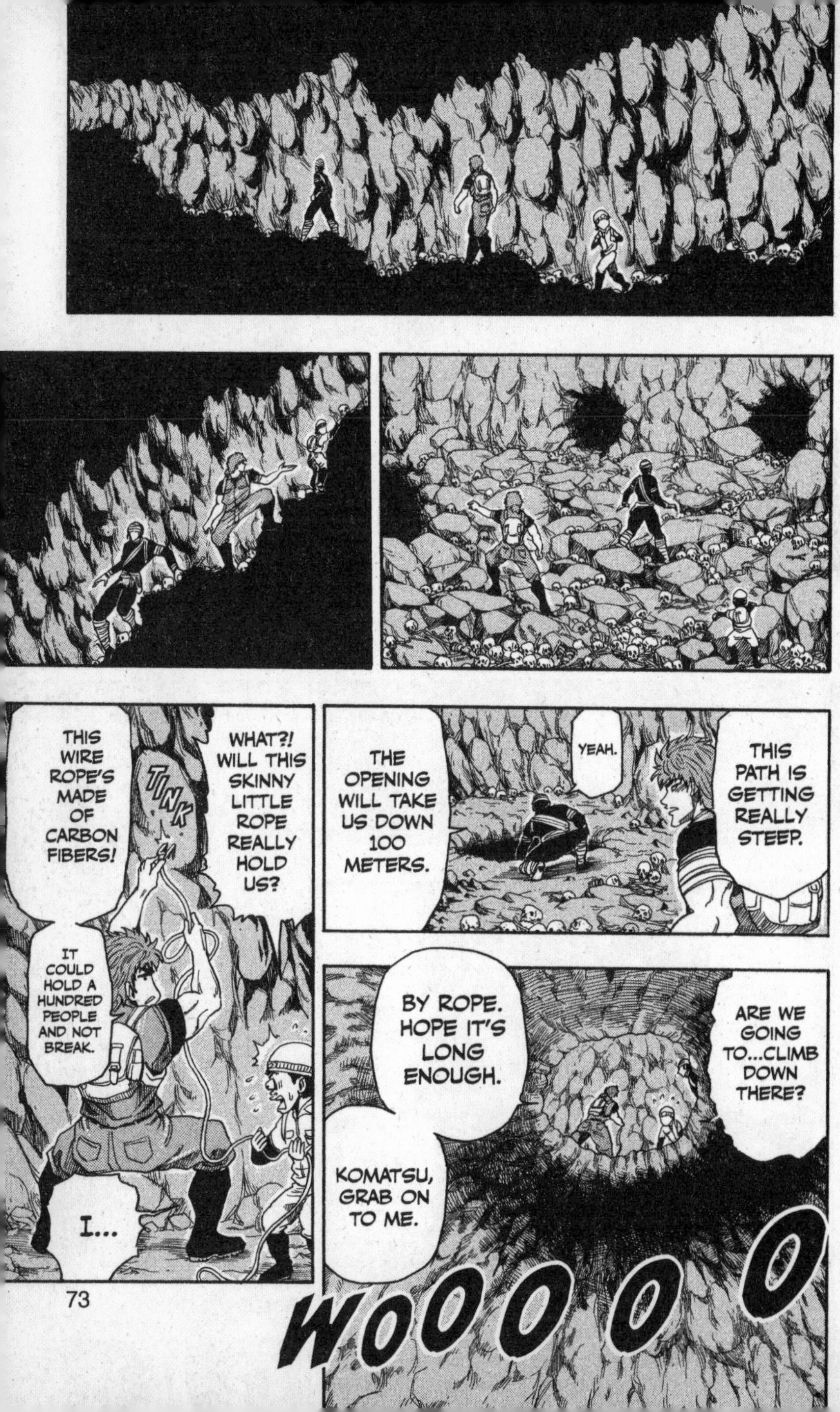
THIS PATH IS GETTING REALLY STEEP.
YEAH.
THE OPENING WILL TAKE US DOWN 100 METERS.
ARE WE GOING TO...CLIMB DOWN THERE?
BY ROPE. HOPE IT'S LONG ENOUGH.
KOMATSU, GRAB ON TO ME.
WOOOOOO
WHAT?! WILL THIS SKINNY LITTLE ROPE REALLY HOLD US?
TINK
THIS WIRE ROPE'S MADE OF CARBON FIBERS!
IT COULD HOLD A HUNDRED PEOPLE AND NOT BREAK.
I...

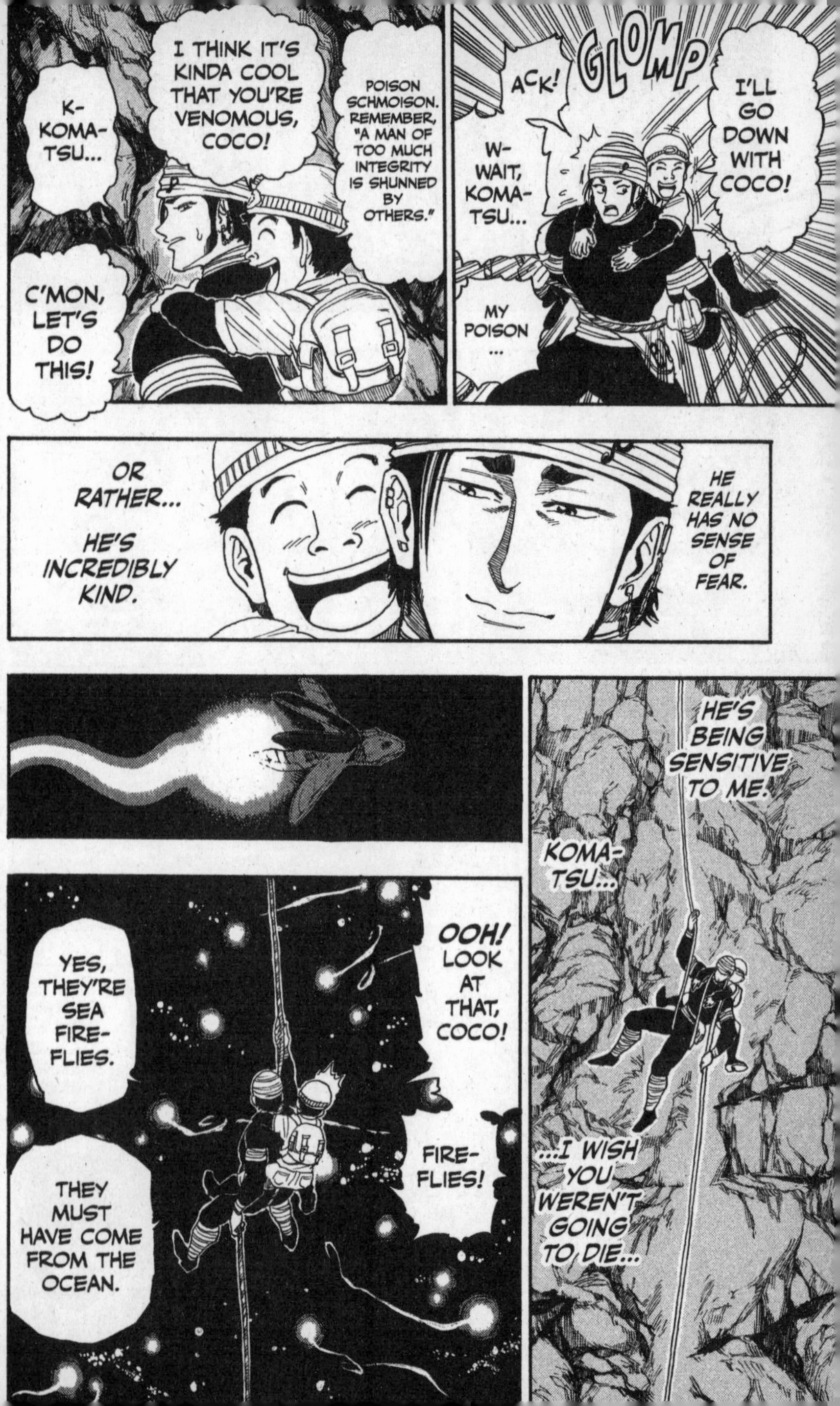
I'LL GO DOWN WITH COCO!
GLOMP
ACK!
W-WAIT, KOMATSU...
MY POISON...
POISON SCHMOISON. REMEMBER, "A MAN OF TOO MUCH INTEGRITY IS SHUNNED BY OTHERS."
I THINK IT'S KINDA COOL THAT YOU'RE VENOMOUS, COCO!
K-KOMATSU...
C'MON, LET'S DO THIS!
HE REALLY HAS NO SENSE OF FEAR.
OR RATHER...
HE'S INCREDIBLY KIND.
HE'S BEING SENSITIVE TO ME.
KOMATSU...
...I WISH YOU WEREN'T GOING TO DIE...
OOH! LOOK AT THAT, COCO!
FIREFLIES!
YES, THEY'RE SEA FIREFLIES.
THEY MUST HAVE COME FROM THE OCEAN.

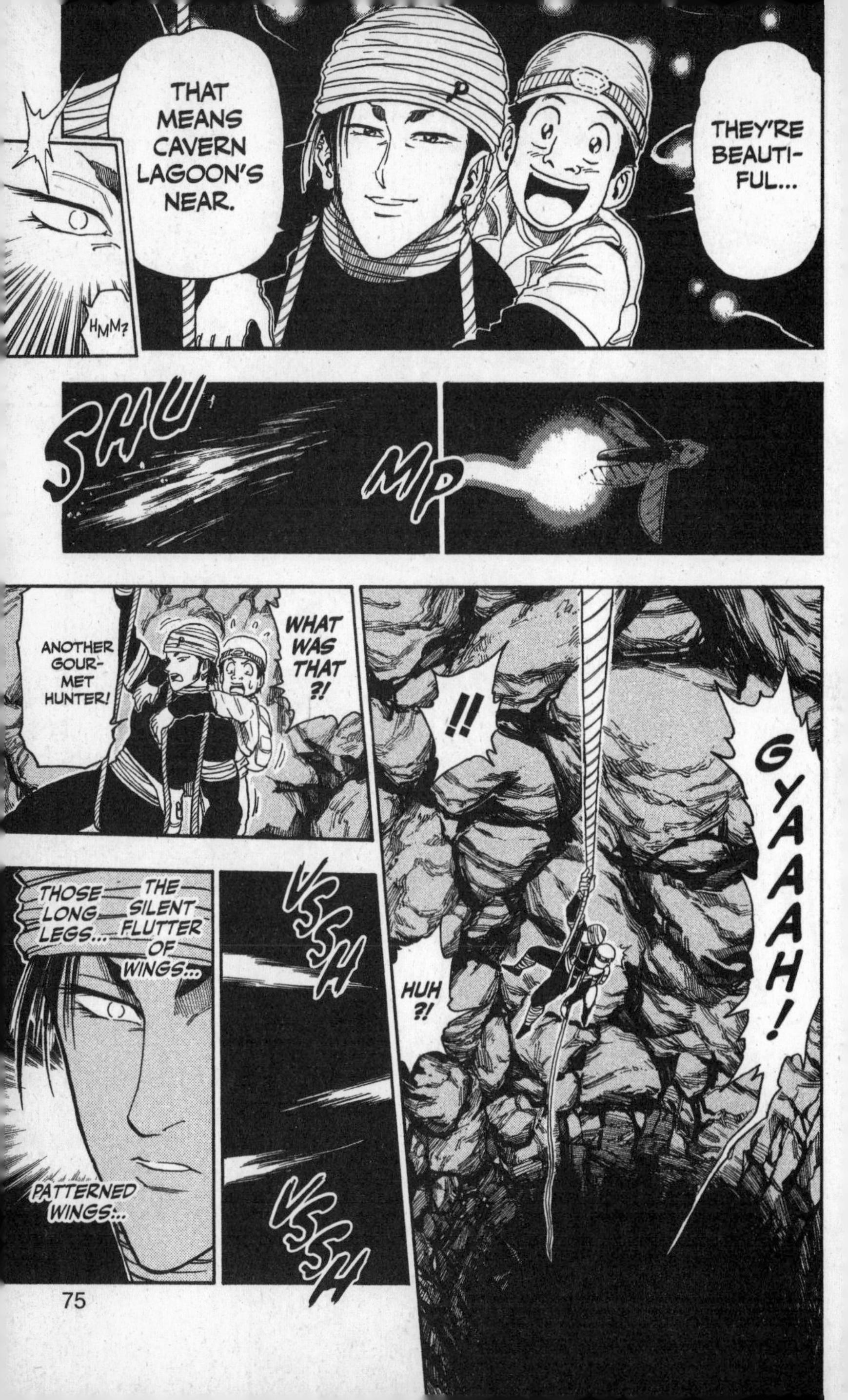
THEY'RE BEAUTIFUL...
THAT MEANS CAVERN LAGOON'S NEAR.
HMM?
SHU
MP
GYAAAAH!
!!
HUH?!
WHAT WAS THAT?!
ANOTHER GOURMET HUNTER!
VSSH
VSSH
THE SILENT FLUTTER OF WINGS...
THOSE LONG LEGS...
PATTERNED WINGS...

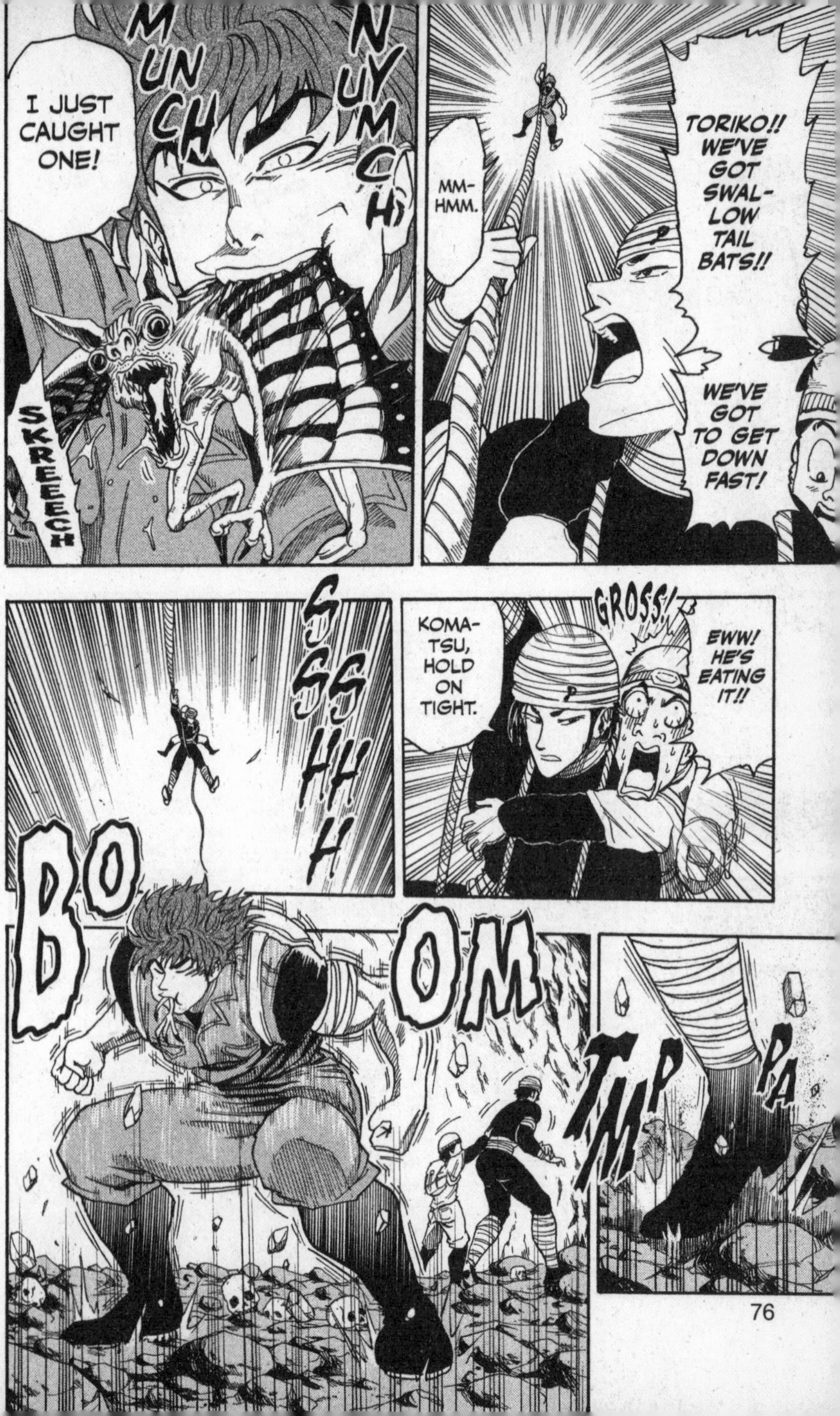
TORIKO!! WE'VE GOT SWALLOW TAIL BATS!!
MM-HMM.
WE'VE GOT TO GET DOWN FAST!
NYUMCHI
I JUST CAUGHT ONE!
MUNCH
SKREEEECH
GROSS!
EWW! HE'S EATING IT!!
KOMATSU, HOLD ON TIGHT.
SSSHHHH
BOOM
PA
TMP

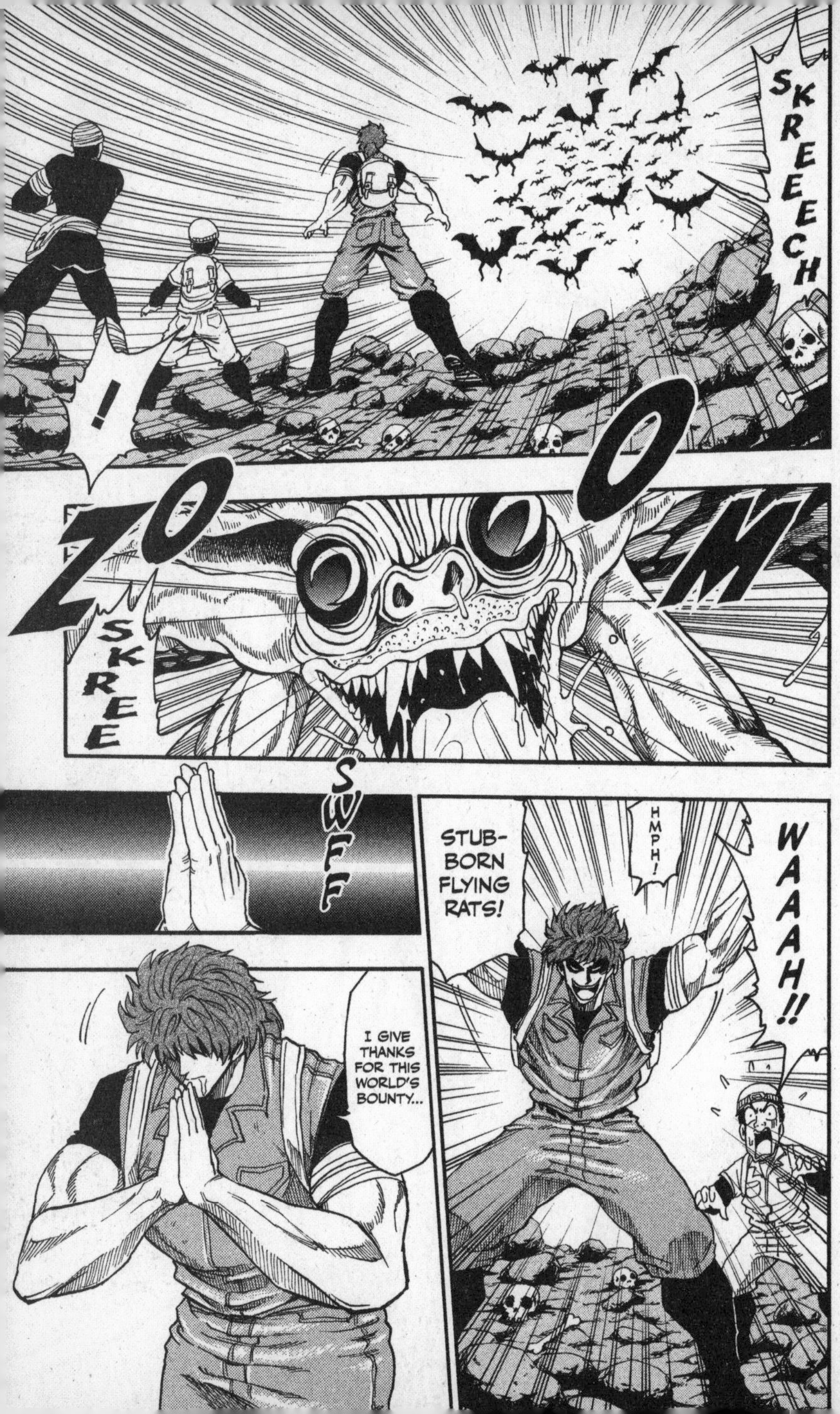
SKREEECH
!
ZOOOM
SKREE
WAAAAH!!
HMPH!
STUB-BORN FLYING RATS!
SWFF
I GIVE THANKS FOR THIS WORLD'S BOUNTY...

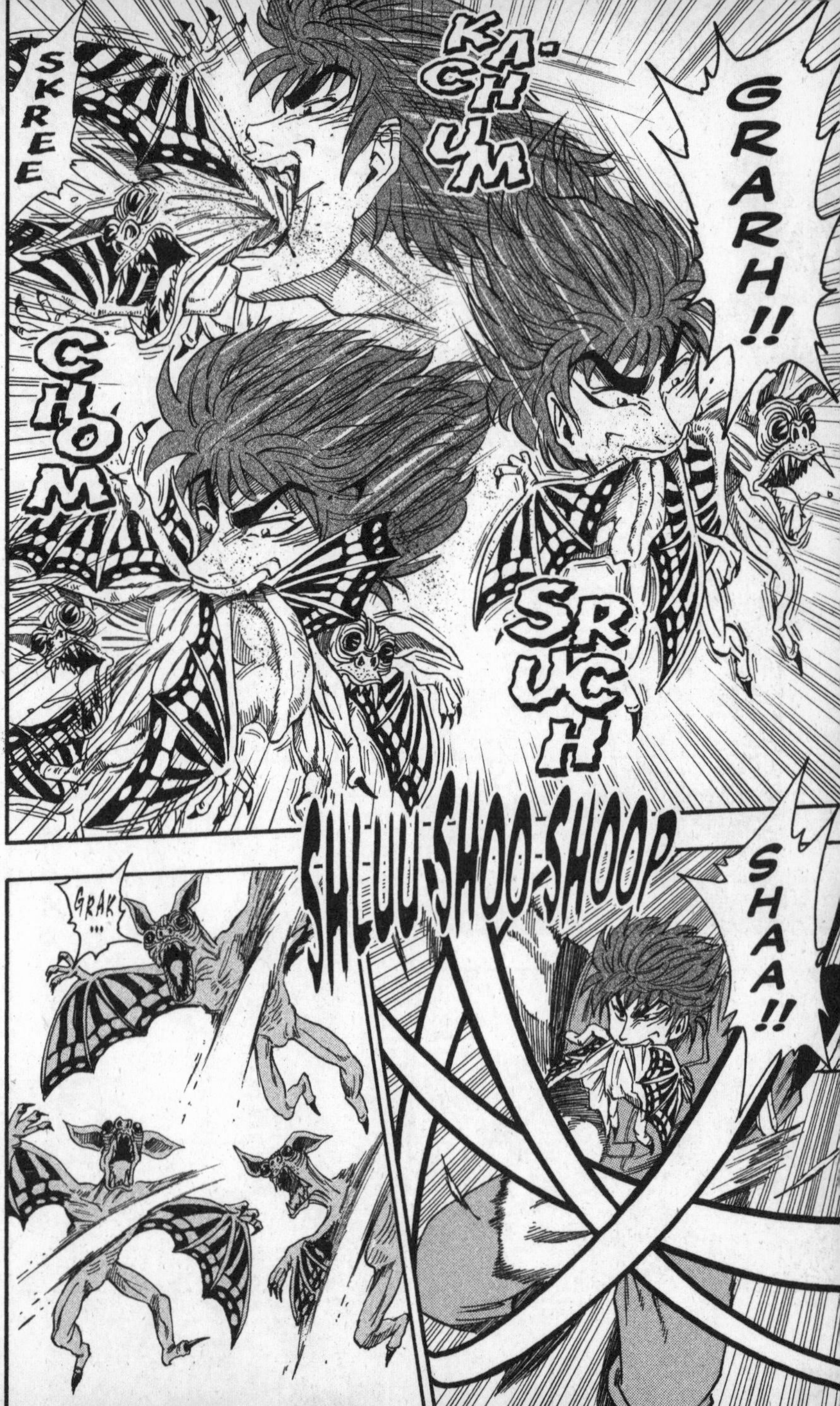
GRARH!!
KA-CHUM
SRUCH
SKREE
CHOM
SHAA!!
SHUU-SHOO-SHOOP
GRAK...

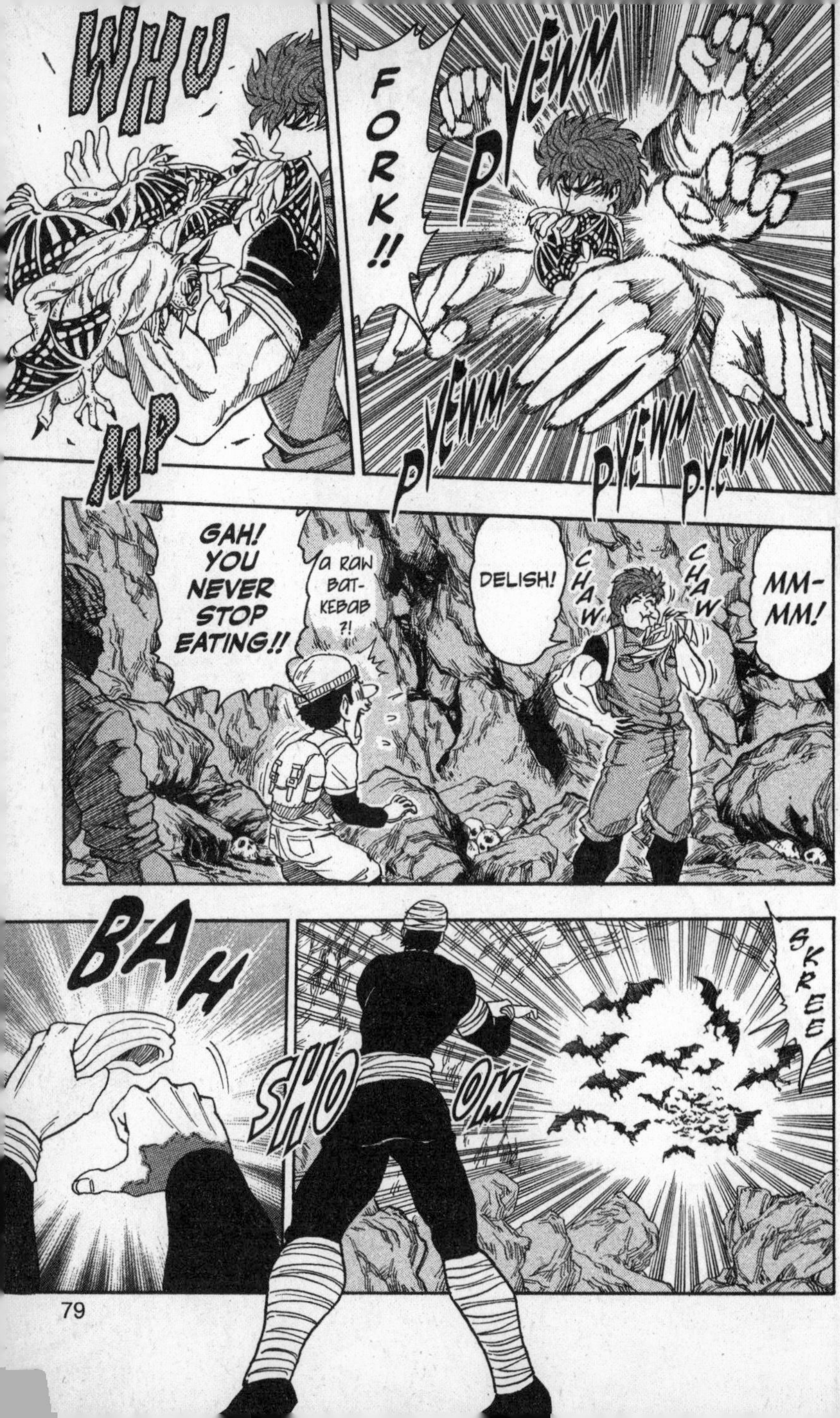
FORK!!
PYEWM
PYEWM
PYEWM
PYEWM
PYEWM
WHU
MP
MM-MM!
CHAW
CHAW
DELISH!
a RAW BAT-KEBAB?!
GAH! YOU NEVER STOP EATING!!
SKREE
SHOOM
BAH

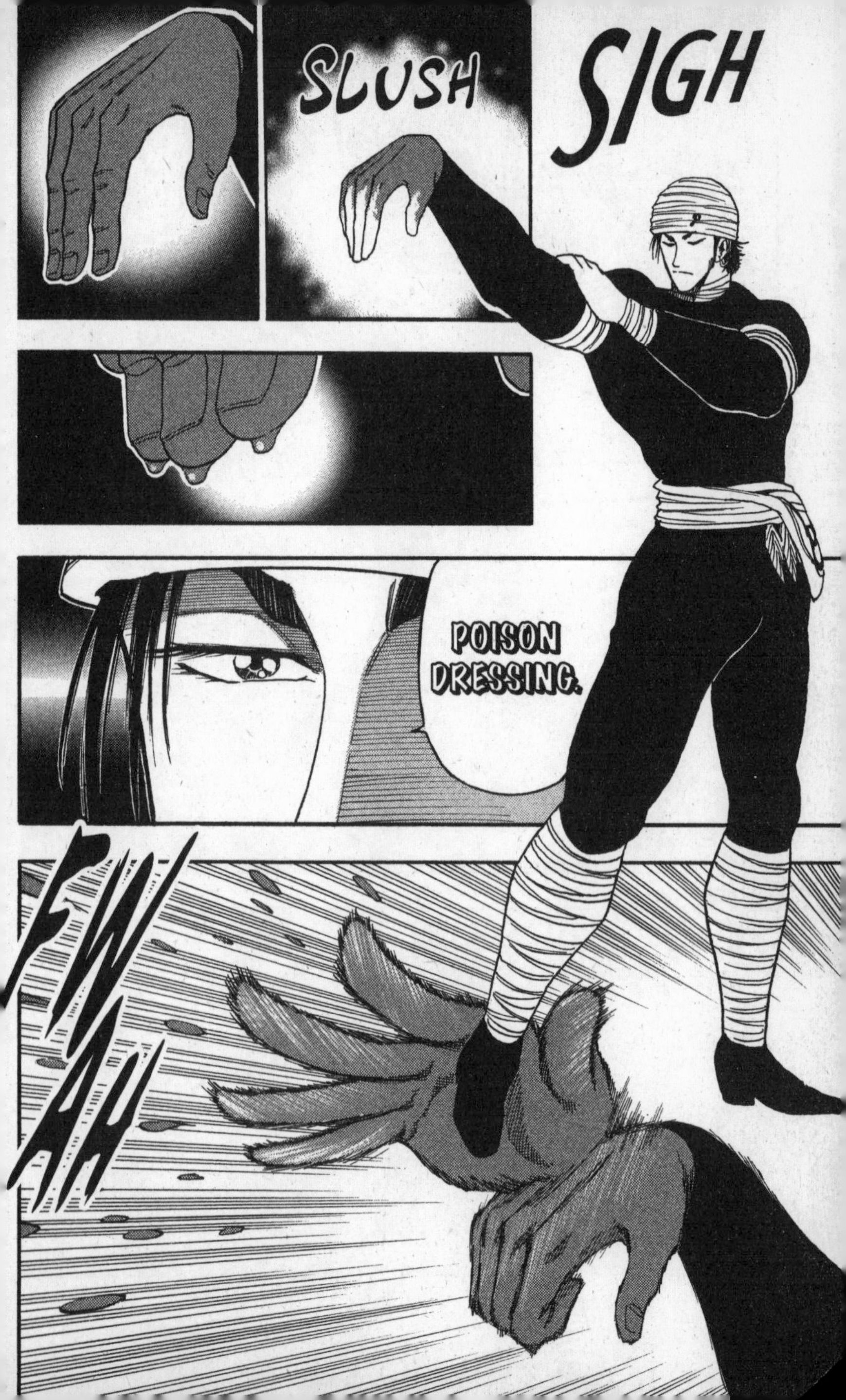
SIGH
SLUSH
POISON DRESSING.
FWAH

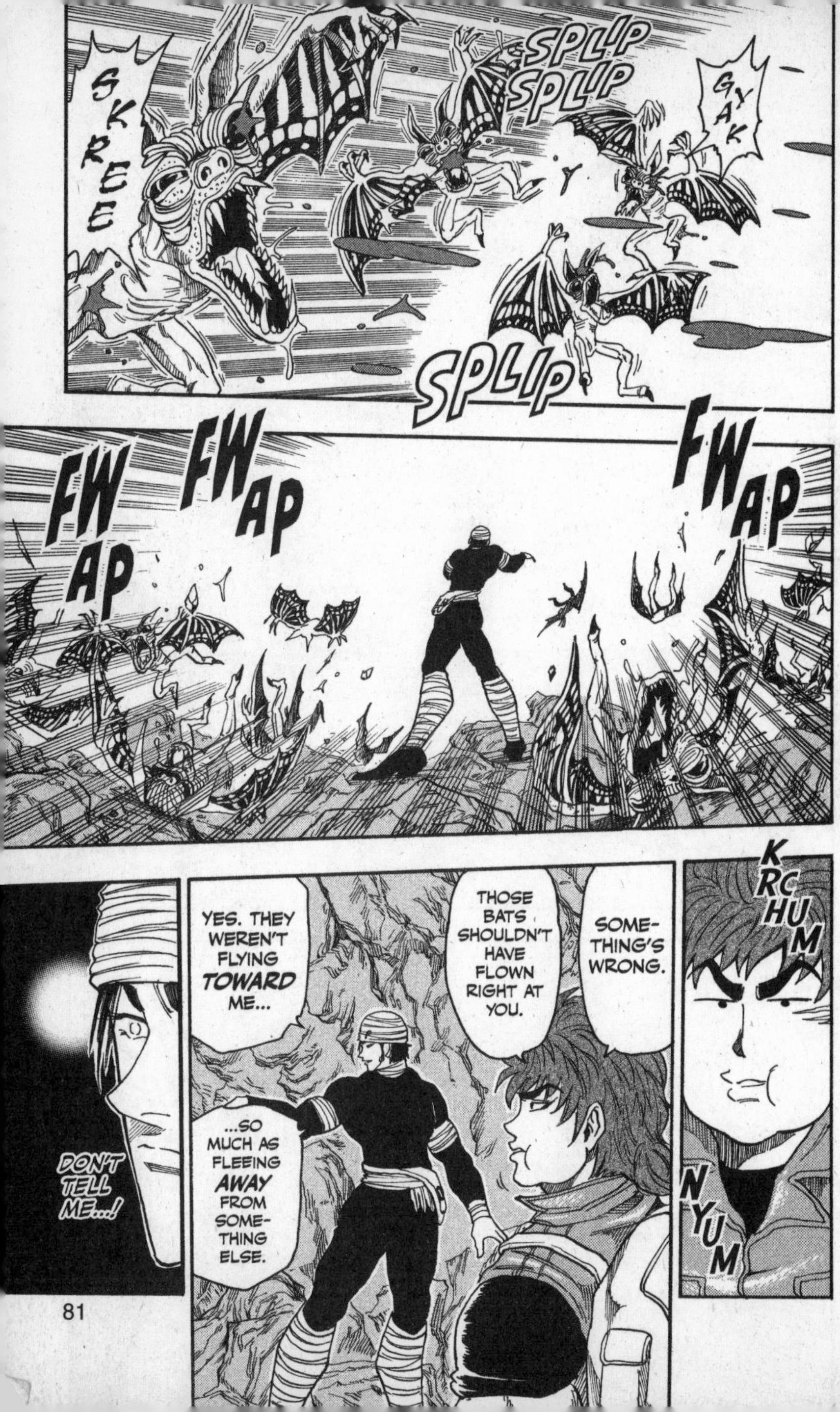
GYAK
SPLIP SPLIP
SKREE
SPLIP
FWAP
FWAP
FWAP
KRCHUM
NYUM
SOMETHING'S WRONG.
THOSE BATS SHOULDN'T HAVE FLOWN RIGHT AT YOU.
YES. THEY WEREN'T FLYING **TOWARD** ME...
...SO MUCH AS FLEEING **AWAY** FROM SOMETHING ELSE.
DON'T TELL ME...!

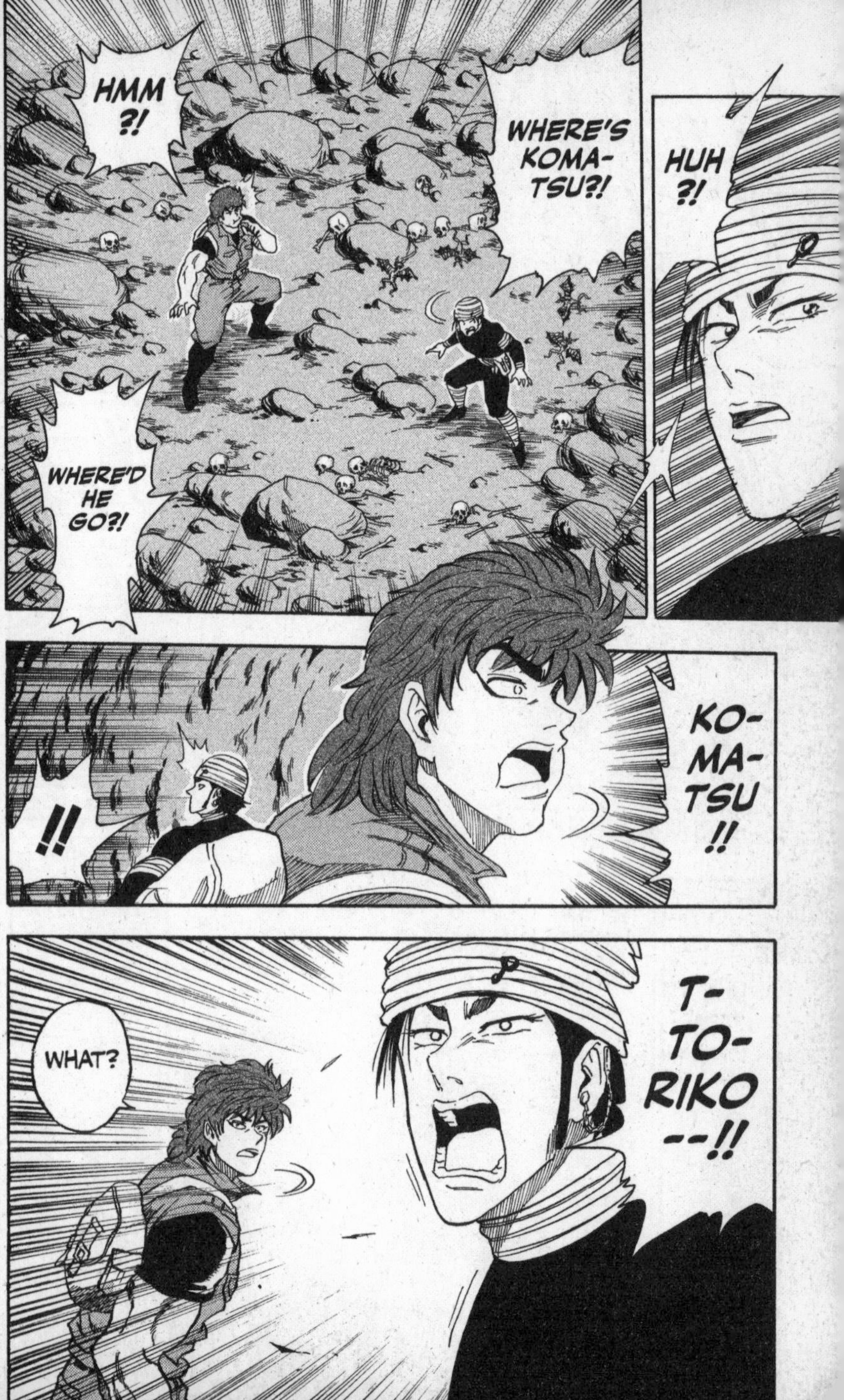
HUH ?!
HMM ?!
WHERE'S KOMA-TSU?!
WHERE'D HE GO?!
KO-MA-TSU !!
!!
T-TO-RIKO --!!
WHAT?

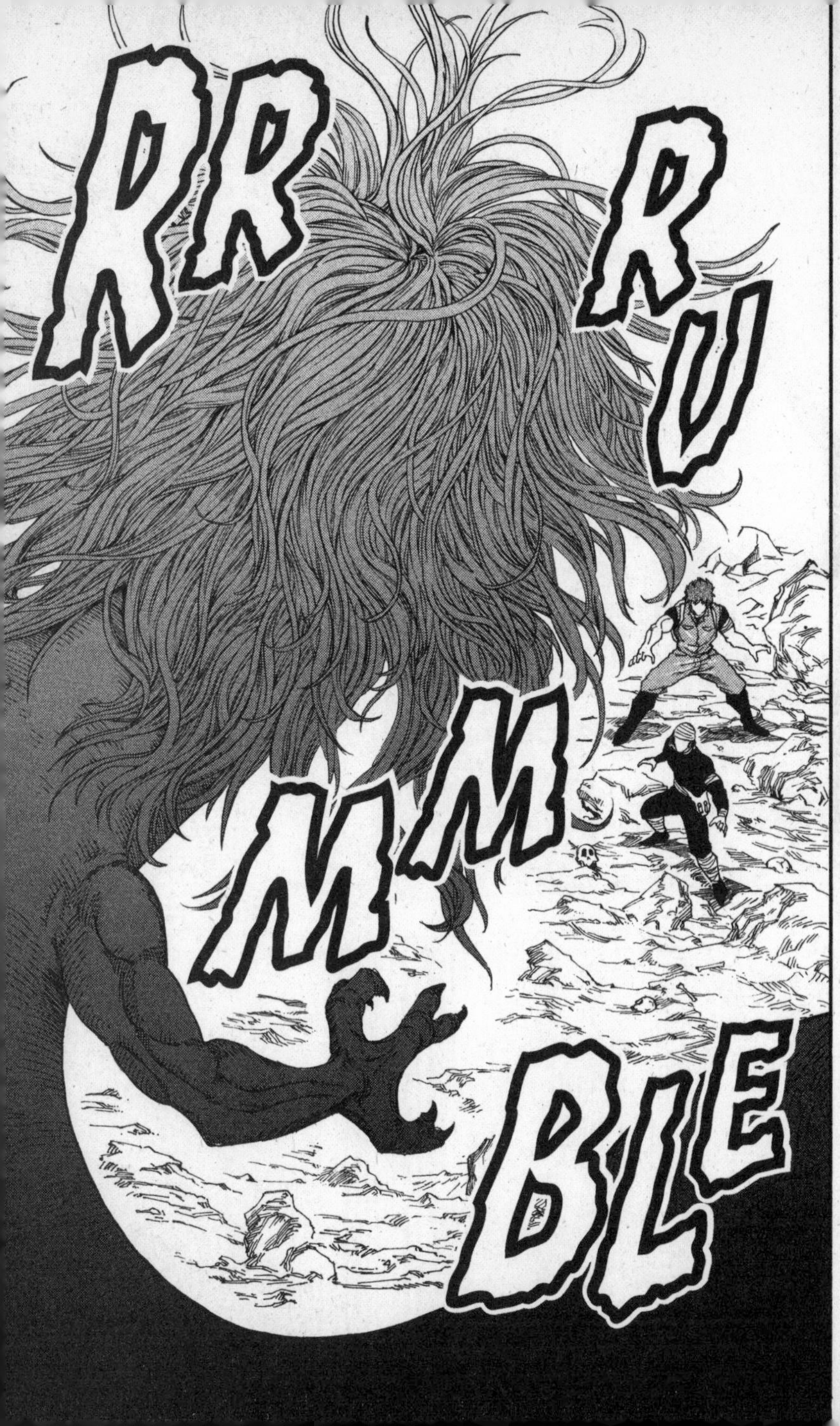
RRRUMMBLE

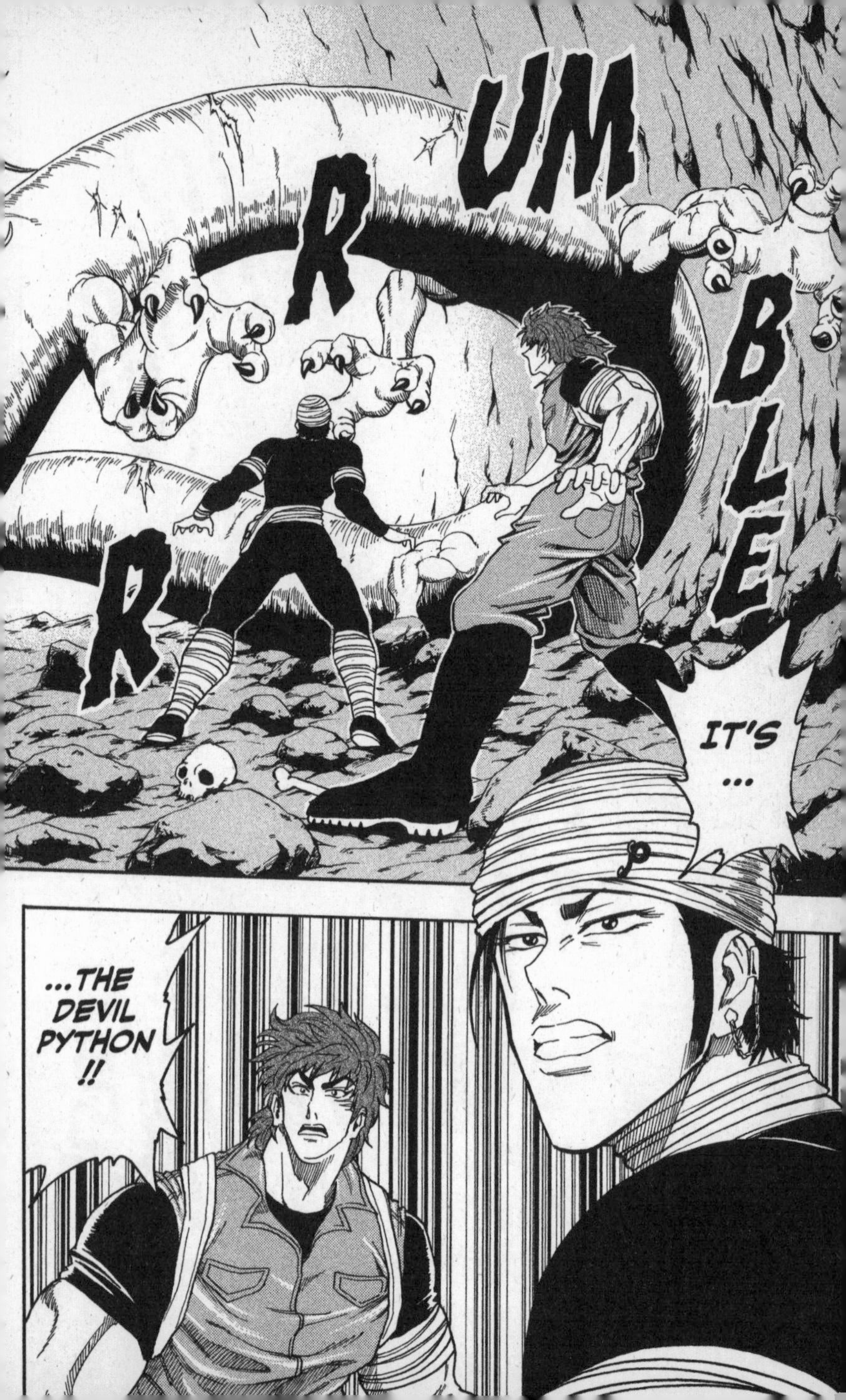
RUMBLE
RR
IT'S ...
...THE DEVIL PYTHON !!

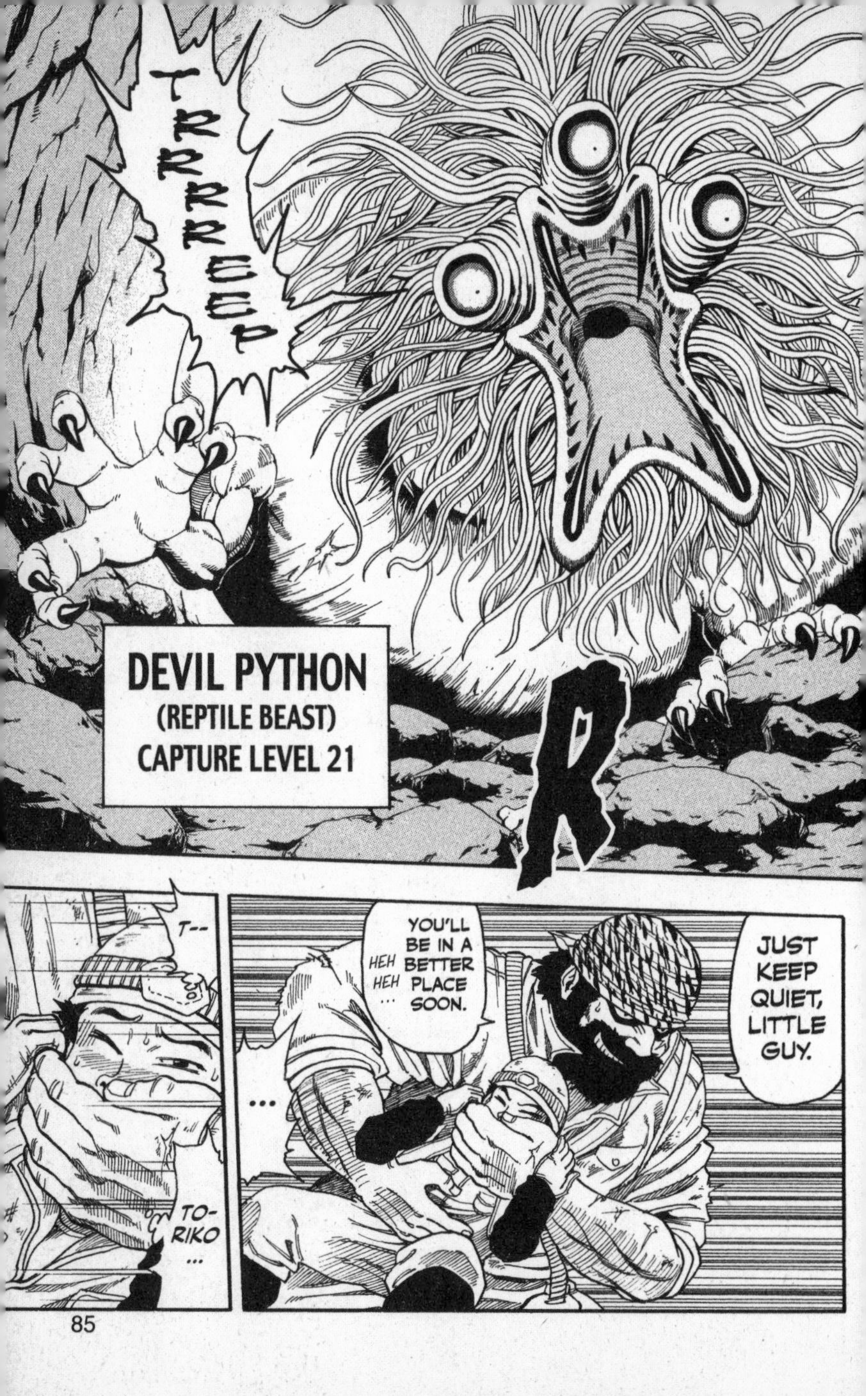
TRRRREEP
DEVIL PYTHON
(REPTILE BEAST)
CAPTURE LEVEL 21
R
JUST KEEP QUIET, LITTLE GUY.
YOU'LL BE IN A BETTER PLACE SOON.
HEH HEH ...
...
T--
TO-RIKO ...

KOMATSU

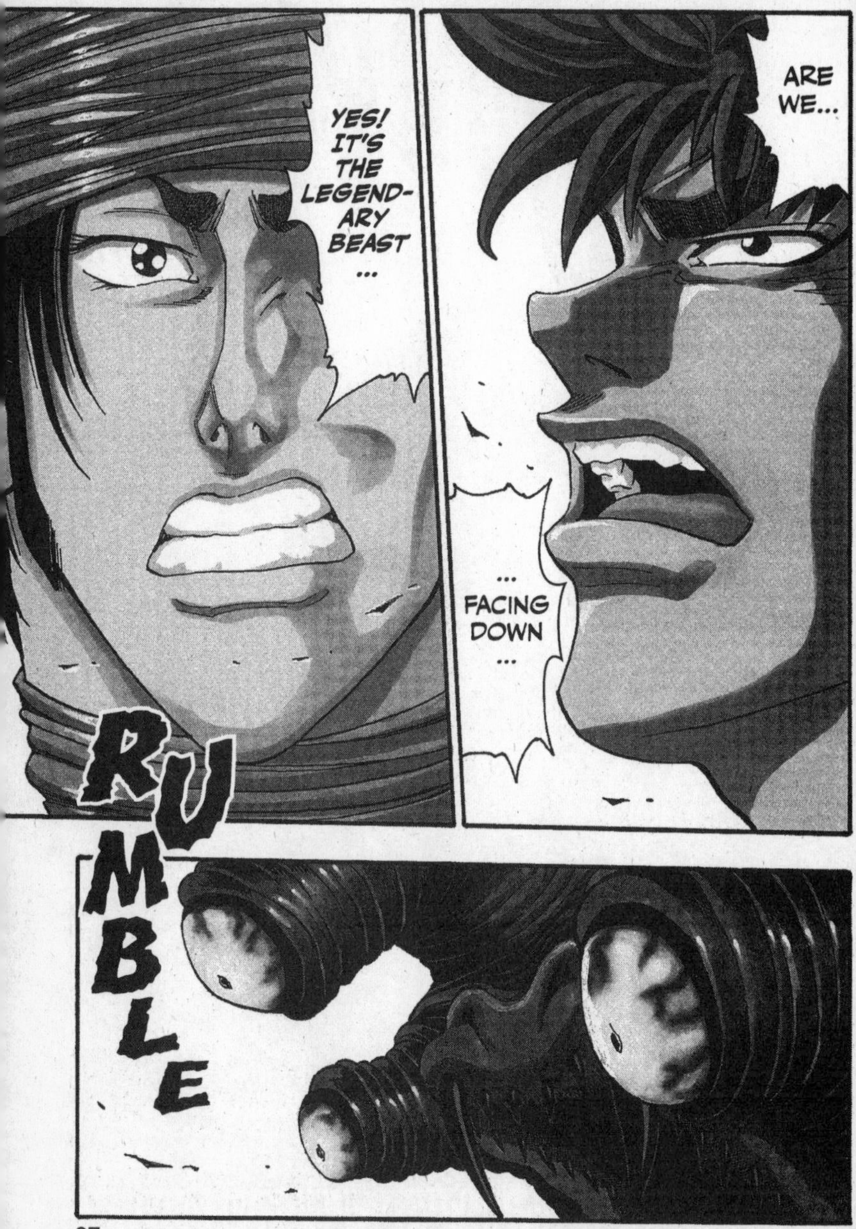
ARE WE...
... FACING DOWN ...
YES! IT'S THE LEGENDARY BEAST ...
RUMBLE

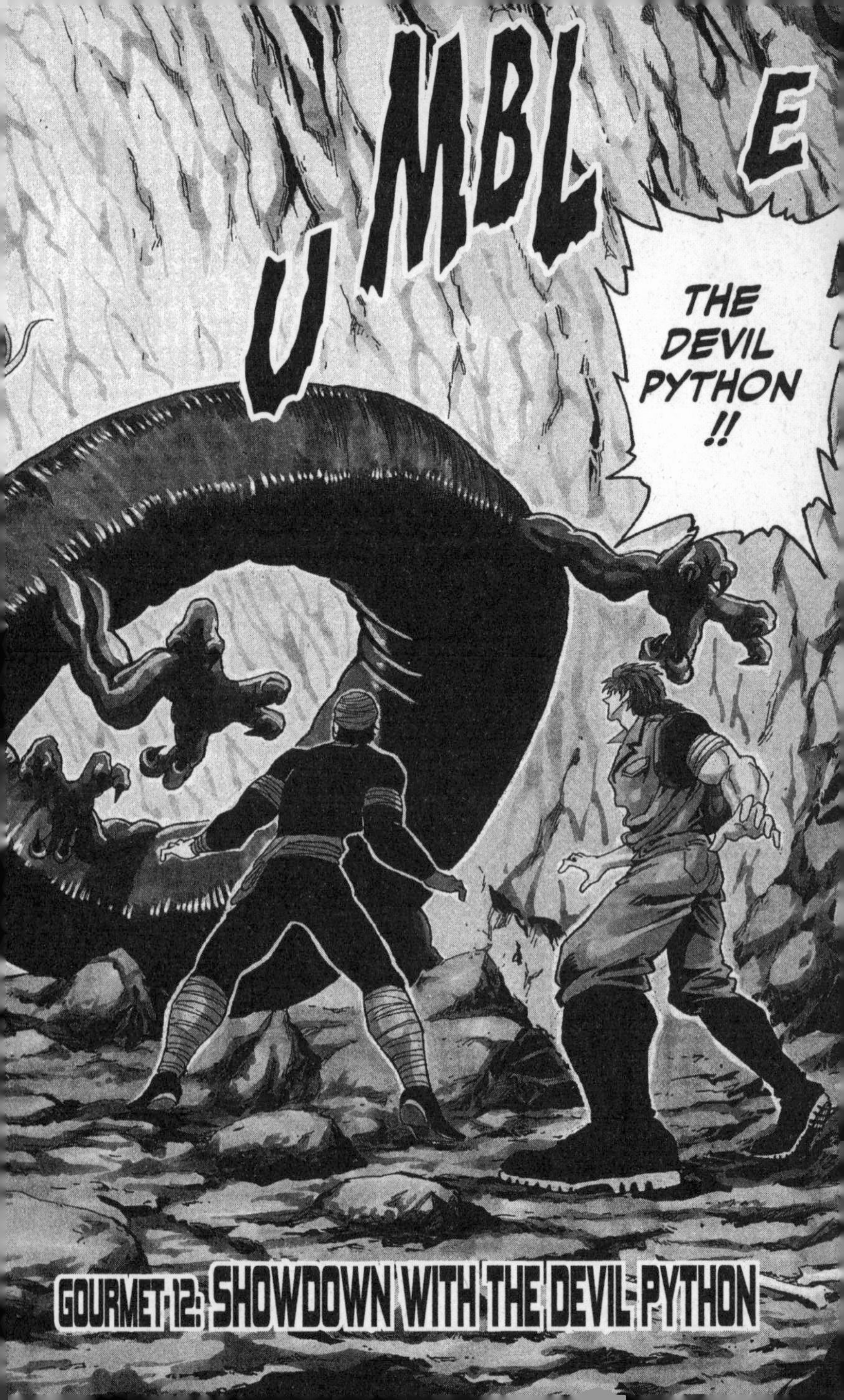
THE DEVIL PYTHON !!
UMBLE
GOURMET 12: SHOWDOWN WITH THE DEVIL PYTHON

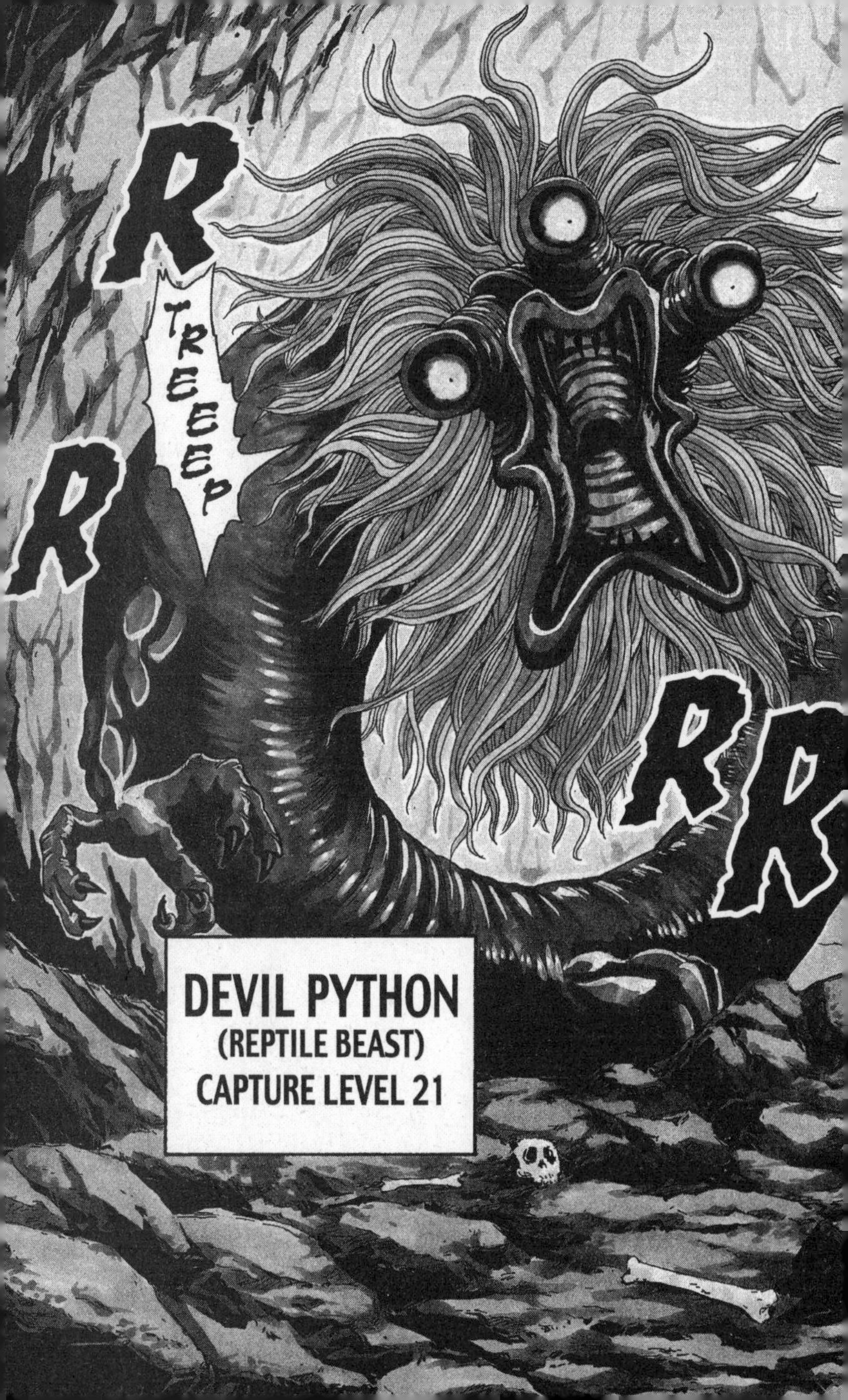

R
R
TREEEEP
R
R
DEVIL PYTHON
(REPTILE BEAST)
CAPTURE LEVEL 21

TORIKO

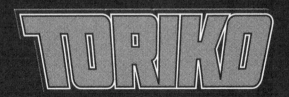

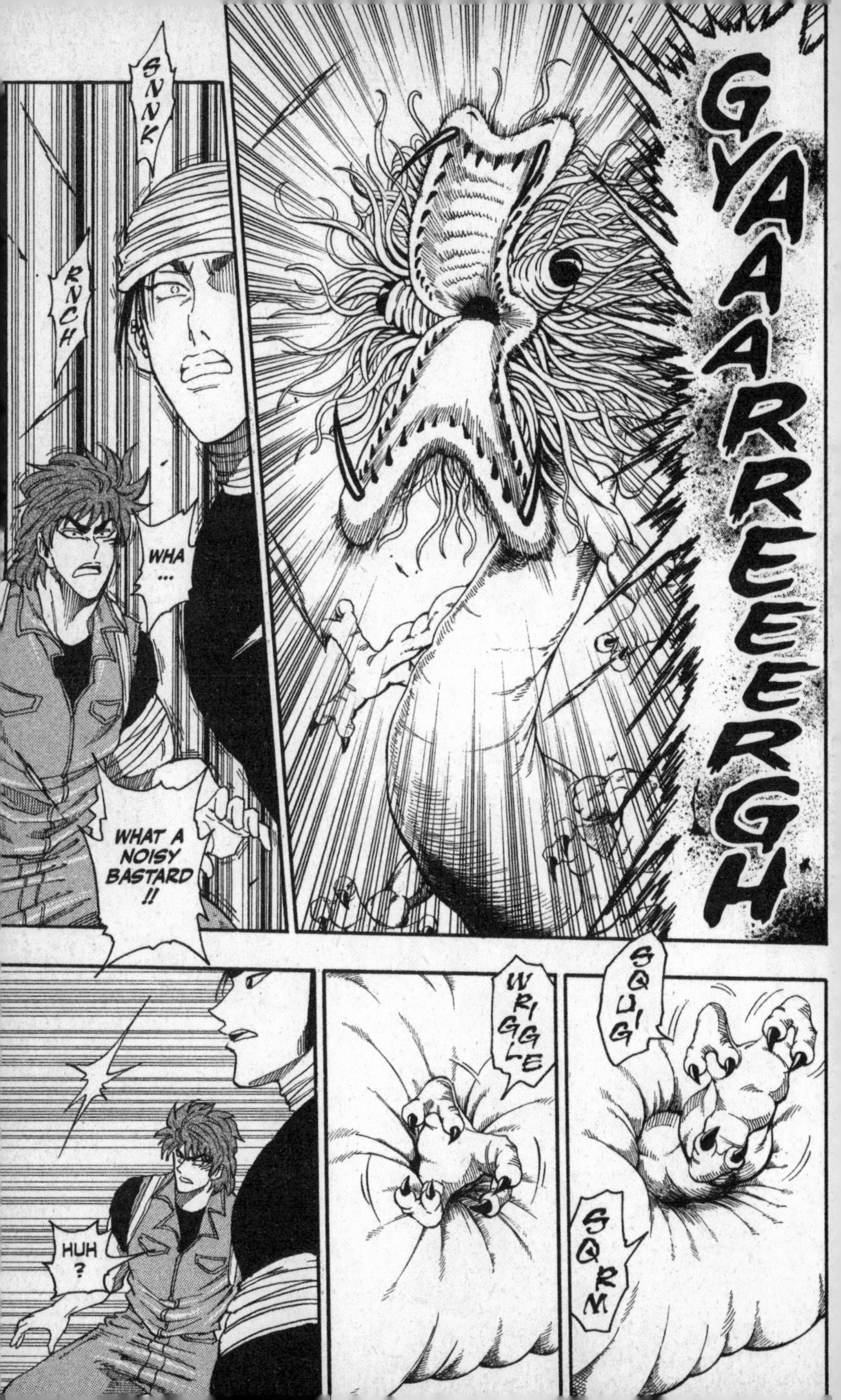
GYAAARREEERGH
SNNK
RNCH
WHA ...
WHAT A NOISY BASTARD !!
SQUG
SQRM
WRIGGLE
HUH ?

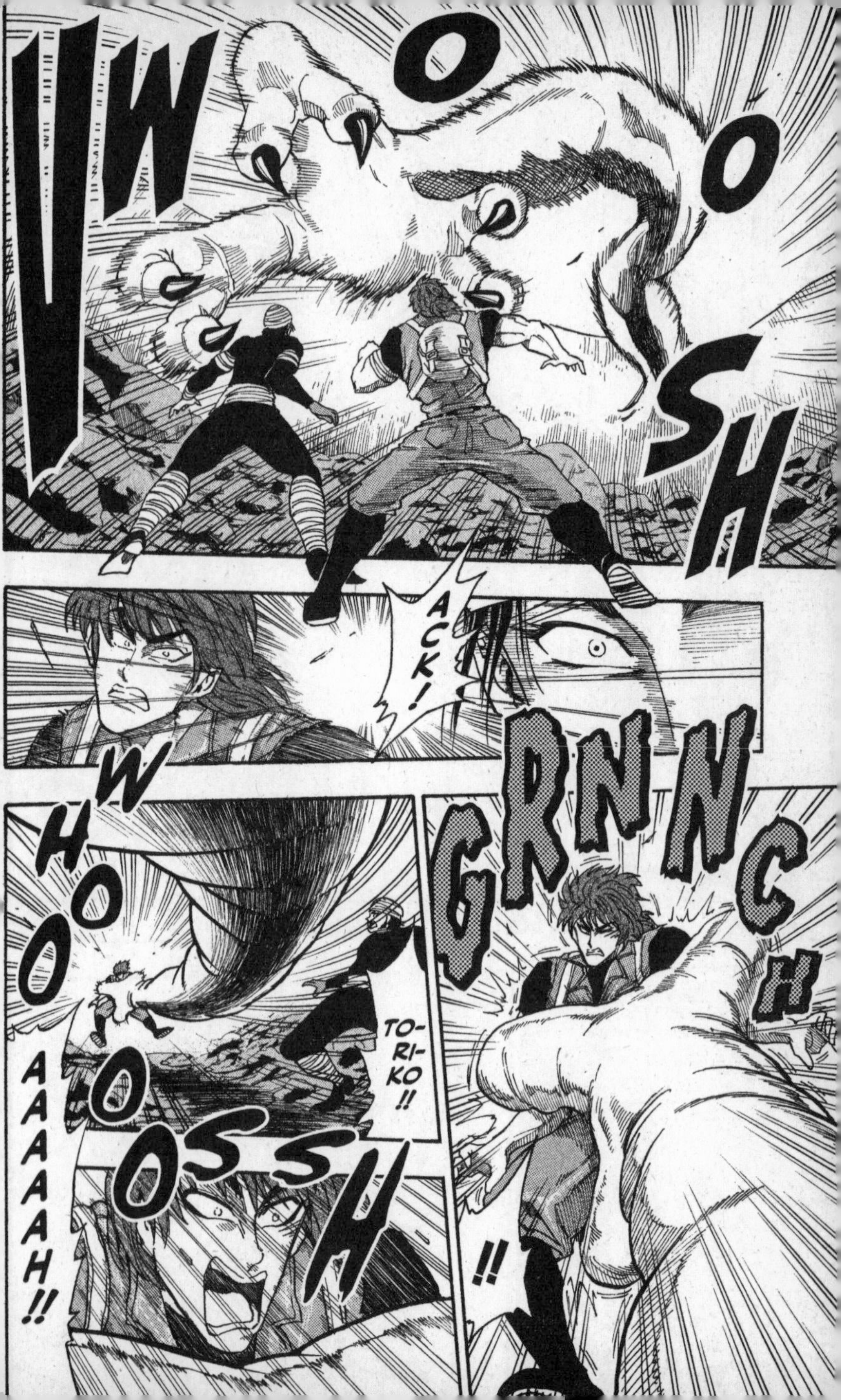
VWOOSH
ACK!
GRNNCH
!!
WHOOOOSSH
TO-RI-KO!!
AAAAAAAH!!

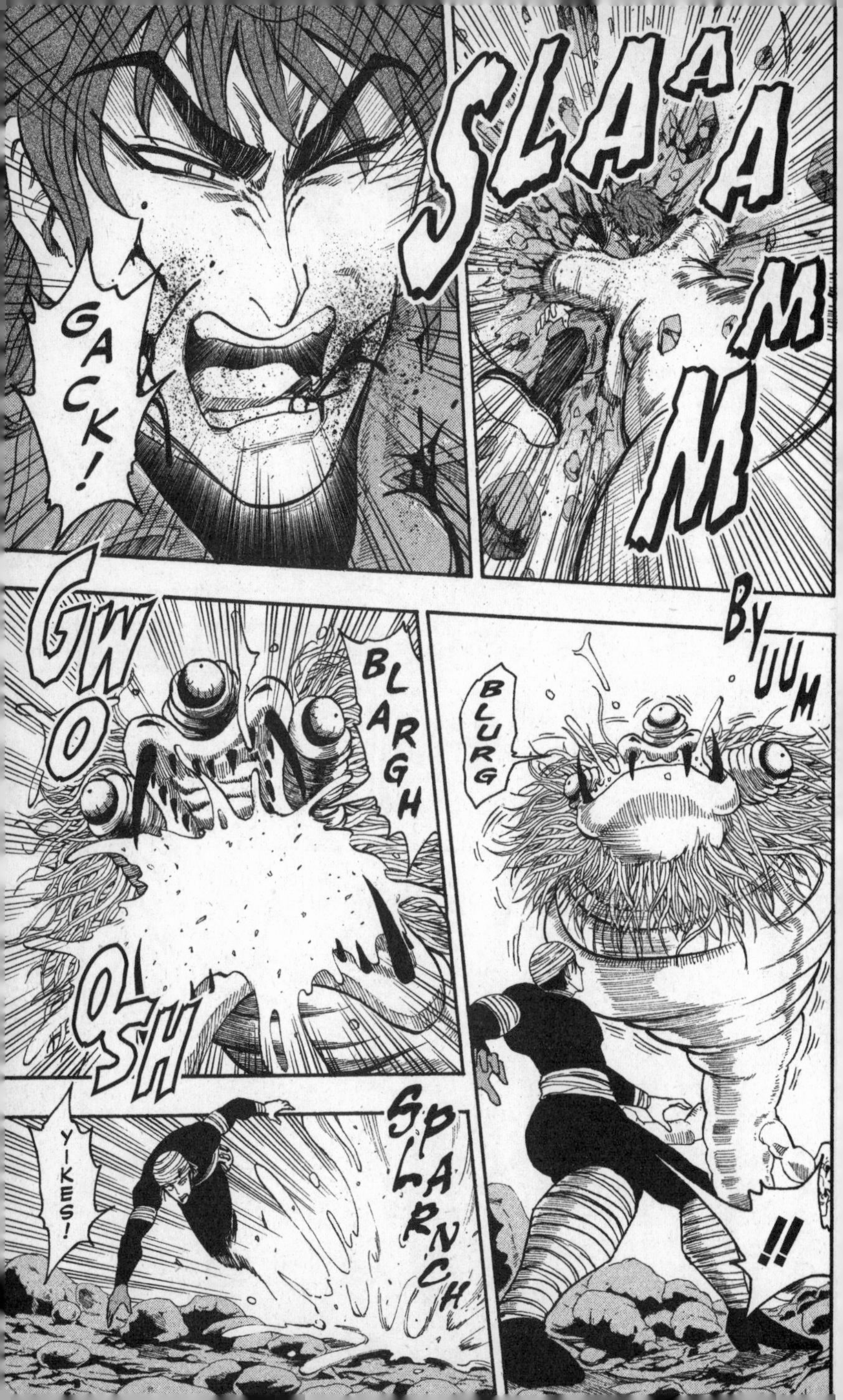
SLAAAMM
GACK!
BYUUM
BLURG
!!
GWOOSH
BLARGH
SPLARNCH
YIKES!

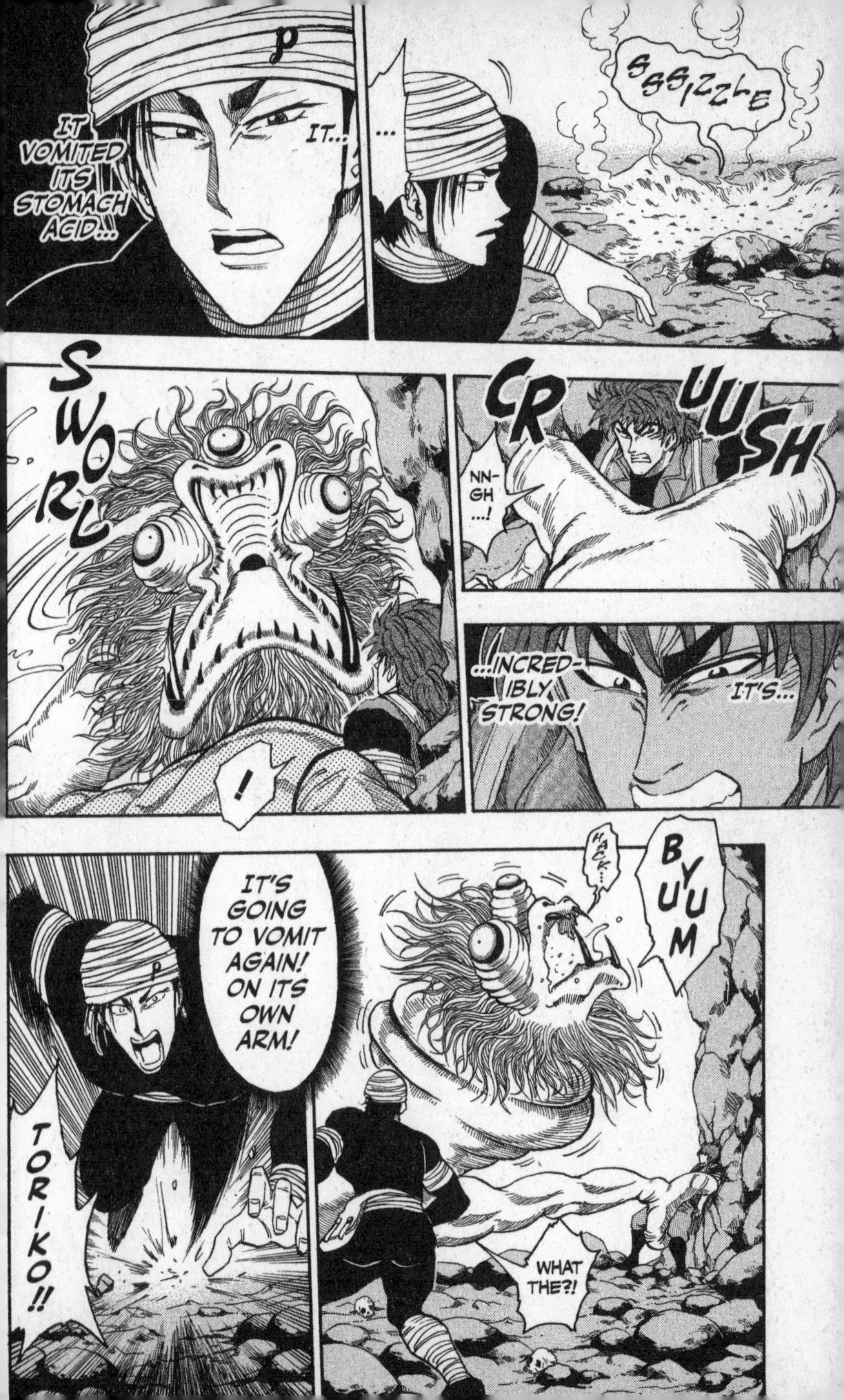
SSSIZZLE
IT...
...
IT VOMITED ITS STOMACH ACID...!
CRUUSH
NNGH...!
IT'S...
...INCREDIBLY STRONG!
SWORL
!
BYUUM
HACK...
WHAT THE?!
IT'S GOING TO VOMIT AGAIN! ON ITS OWN ARM!
TORIKO!!

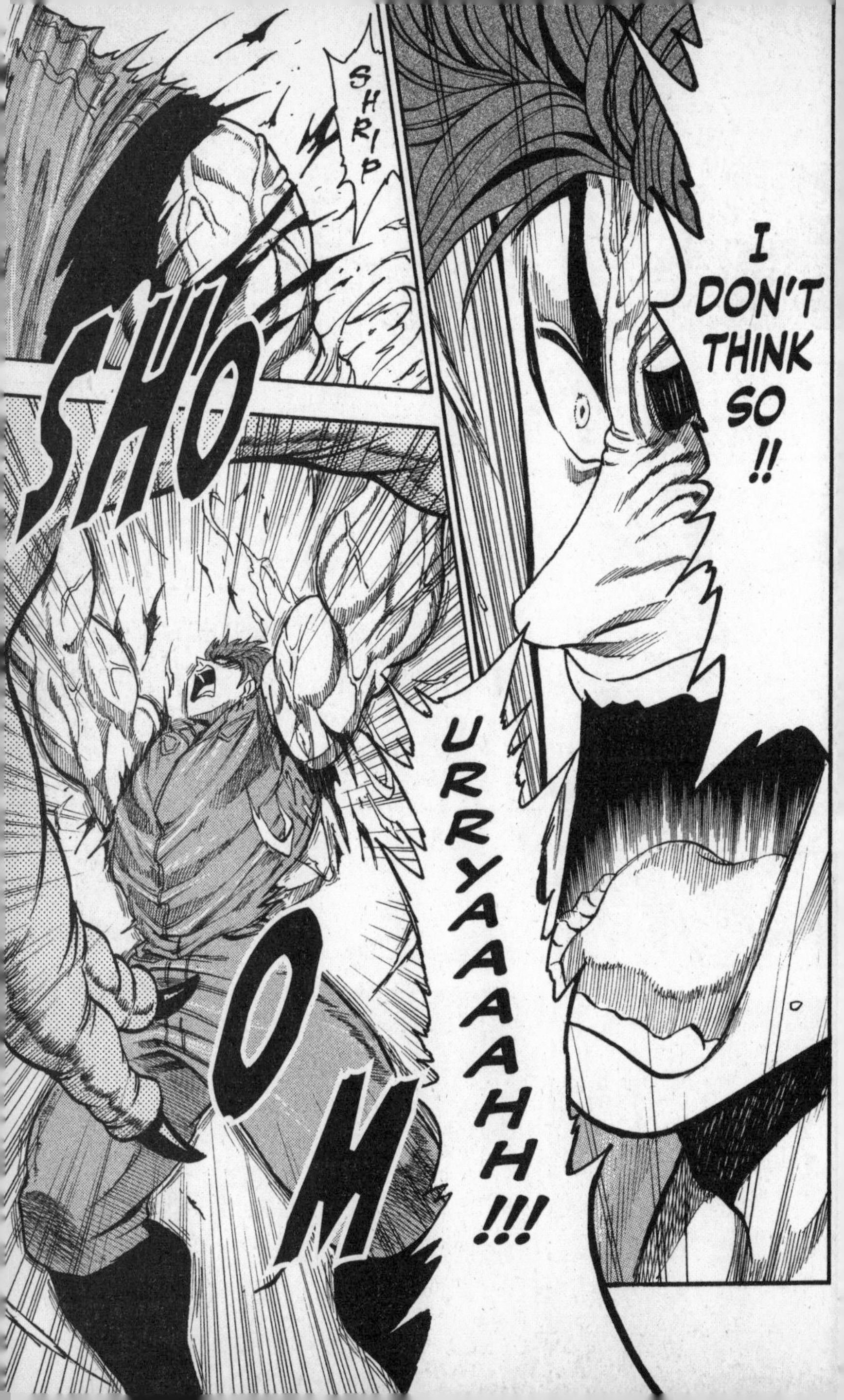
I DON'T THINK SO!!
URRYAAAAHH!!!
SHRIP
SHOOMM

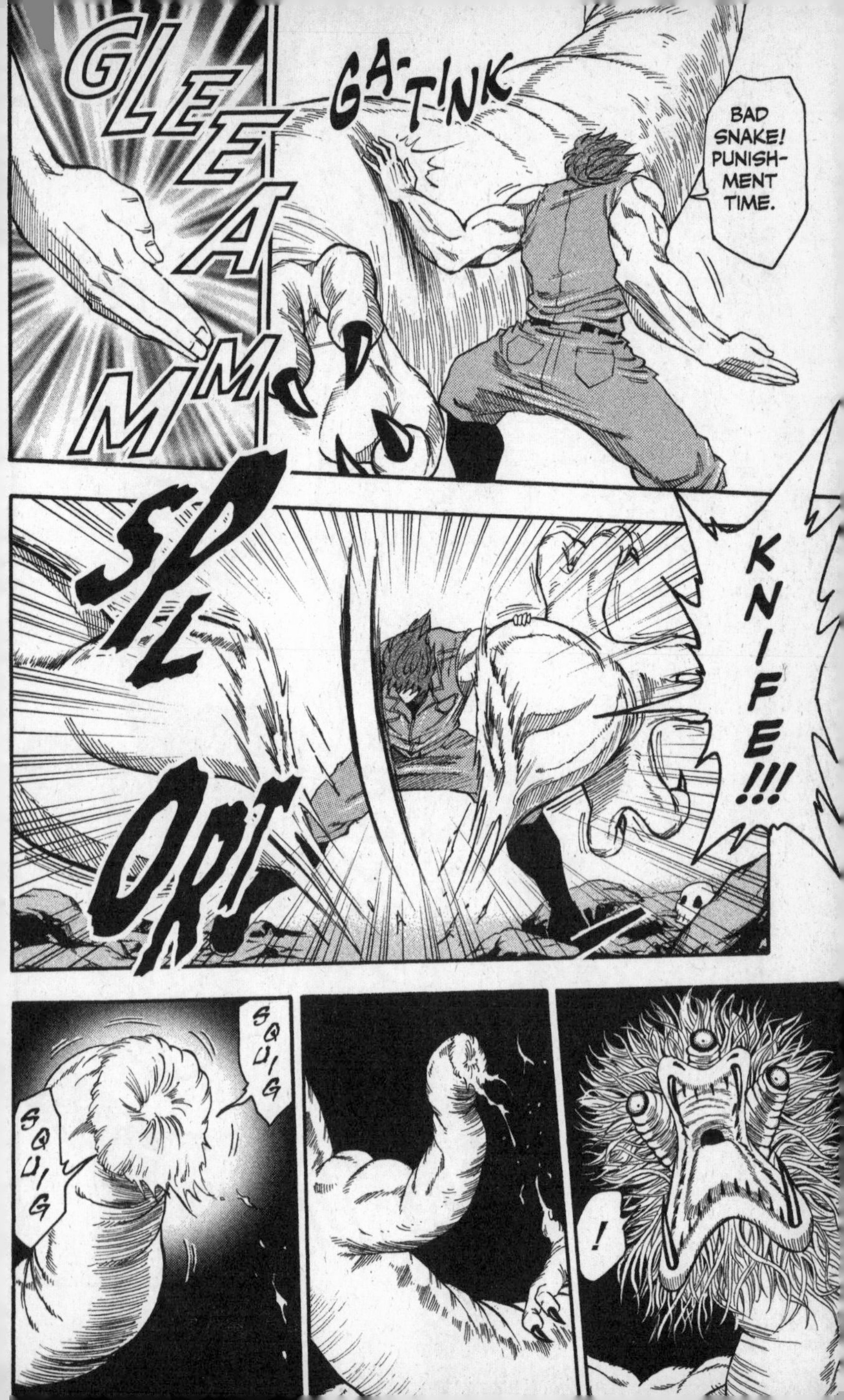
BAD SNAKE! PUNISHMENT TIME.
GA-TINK
GLEEAMM
KNIFE!!!
SPLORT!
!
SQUIG
SQUIG

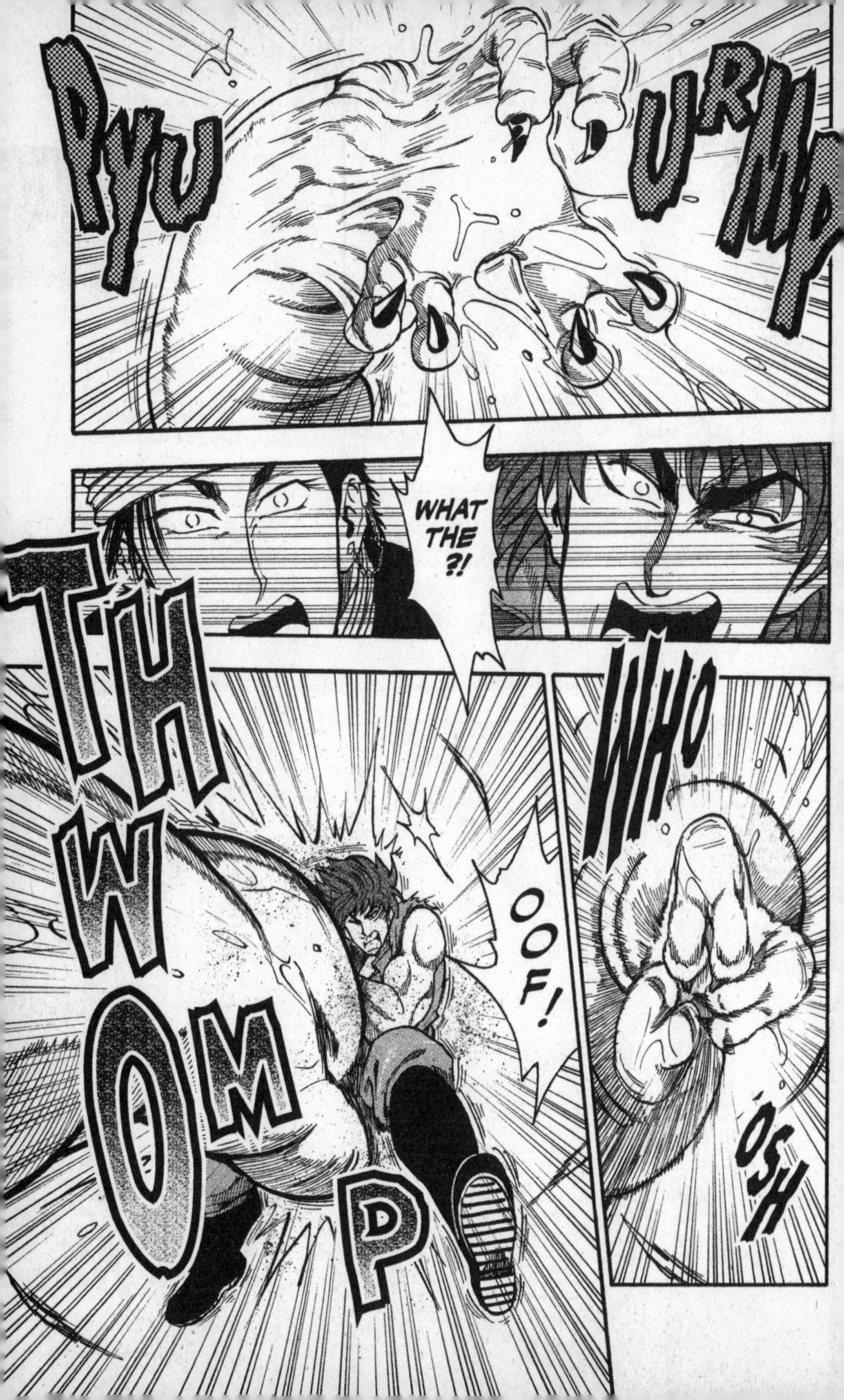
PYU
URMP
WHAT THE ?!
WHO
OSH
THWOMP
OOF!

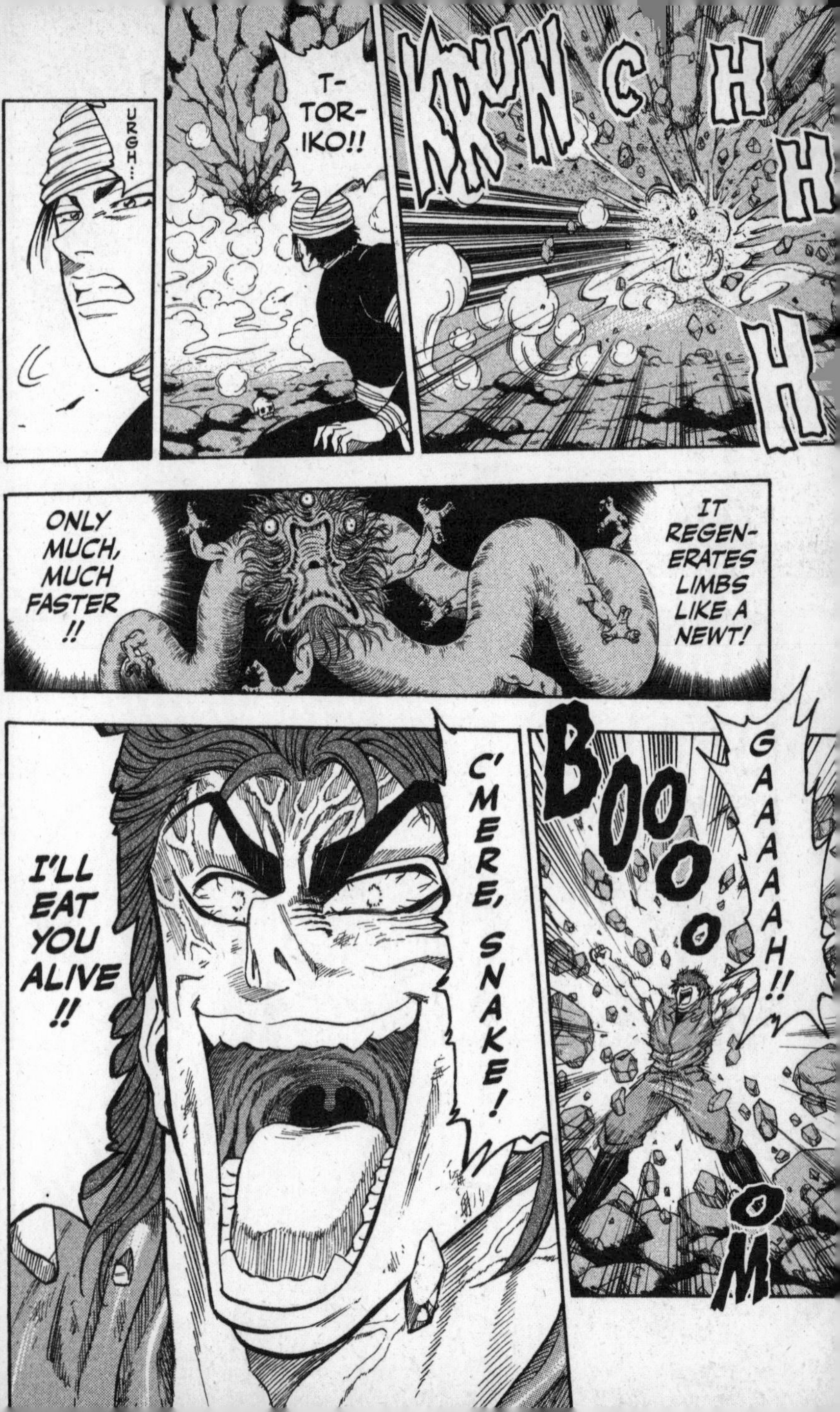
KRUNCHHH
T-TORIKO!!
URGH...
IT REGENERATES LIMBS LIKE A NEWT!
ONLY MUCH, MUCH FASTER!!
GAAAAAH!!
BOOOOOOM
C'MERE, SNAKE!
I'LL EAT YOU ALIVE!!

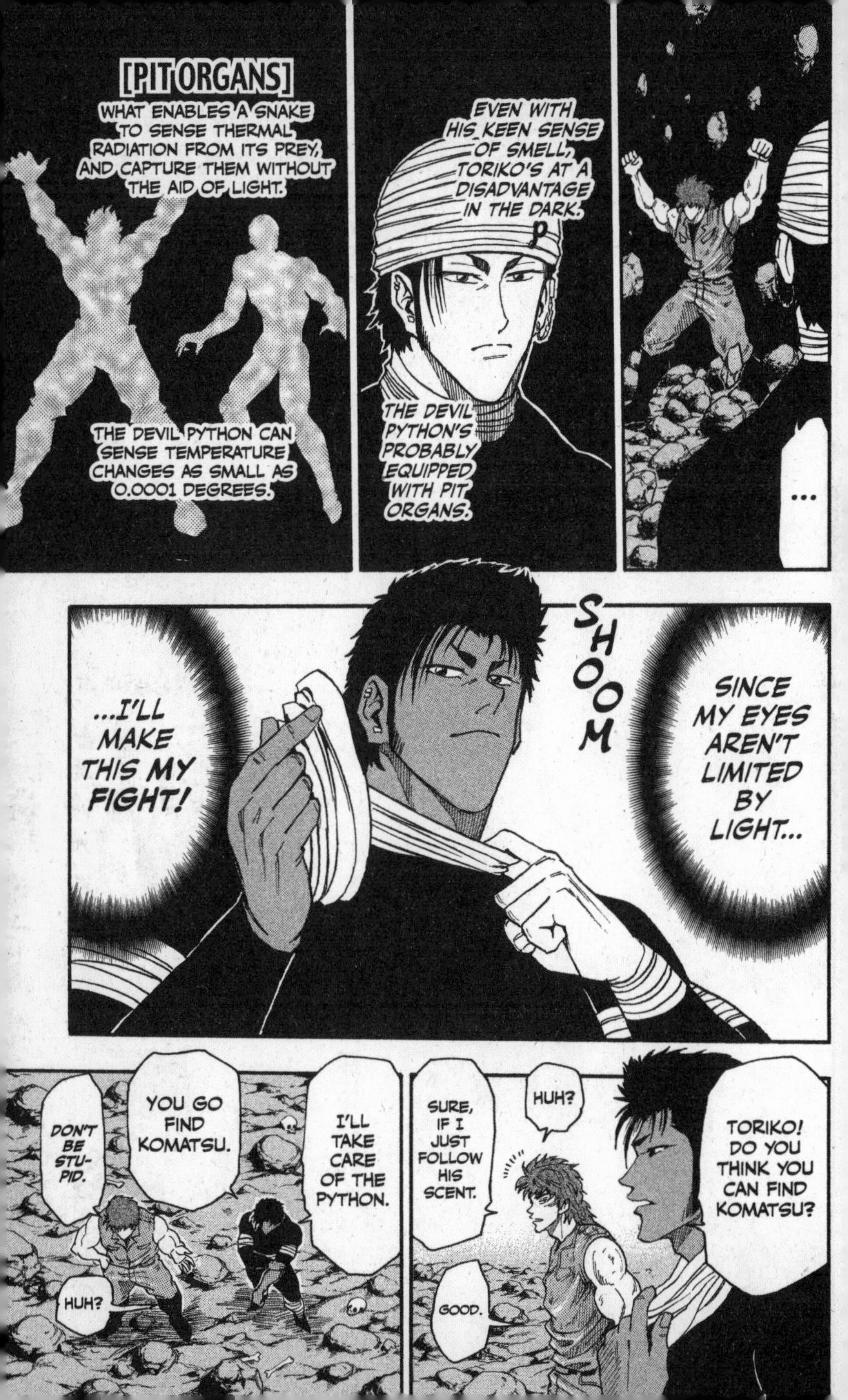
...
EVEN WITH HIS KEEN SENSE OF SMELL, TORIKO'S AT A DISADVANTAGE IN THE DARK.
THE DEVIL PYTHON'S PROBABLY EQUIPPED WITH PIT ORGANS.
[PIT ORGANS]
WHAT ENABLES A SNAKE TO SENSE THERMAL RADIATION FROM ITS PREY, AND CAPTURE THEM WITHOUT THE AID OF LIGHT.
THE DEVIL PYTHON CAN SENSE TEMPERATURE CHANGES AS SMALL AS 0.0001 DEGREES.
SHOOM
SINCE MY EYES AREN'T LIMITED BY LIGHT...
...I'LL MAKE THIS MY FIGHT!
TORIKO! DO YOU THINK YOU CAN FIND KOMATSU?
HUH?
SURE, IF I JUST FOLLOW HIS SCENT.
GOOD.
I'LL TAKE CARE OF THE PYTHON.
YOU GO FIND KOMATSU.
DON'T BE STU-PID.
HUH?

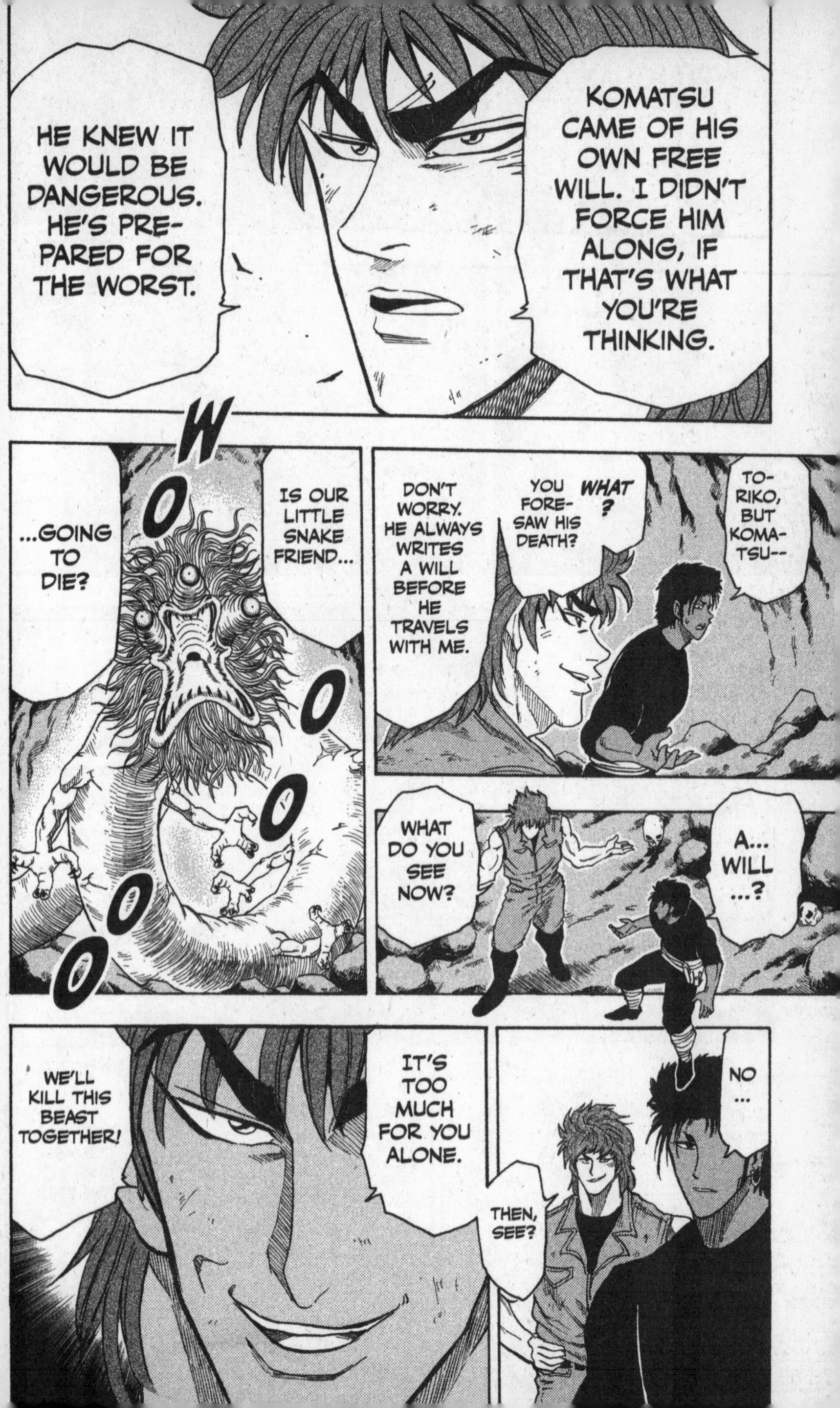
KOMATSU CAME OF HIS OWN FREE WILL. I DIDN'T FORCE HIM ALONG, IF THAT'S WHAT YOU'RE THINKING.
HE KNEW IT WOULD BE DANGEROUS. HE'S PREPARED FOR THE WORST.
TORIKO, BUT KOMATSU--
YOU FORESAW HIS DEATH? WHAT?
DON'T WORRY. HE ALWAYS WRITES A WILL BEFORE HE TRAVELS WITH ME.
A... WILL...?
WHAT DO YOU SEE NOW?
IS OUR LITTLE SNAKE FRIEND...
...GOING TO DIE?
WOOOOOO
NO...
THEN, SEE?
IT'S TOO MUCH FOR YOU ALONE.
WE'LL KILL THIS BEAST TOGETHER!

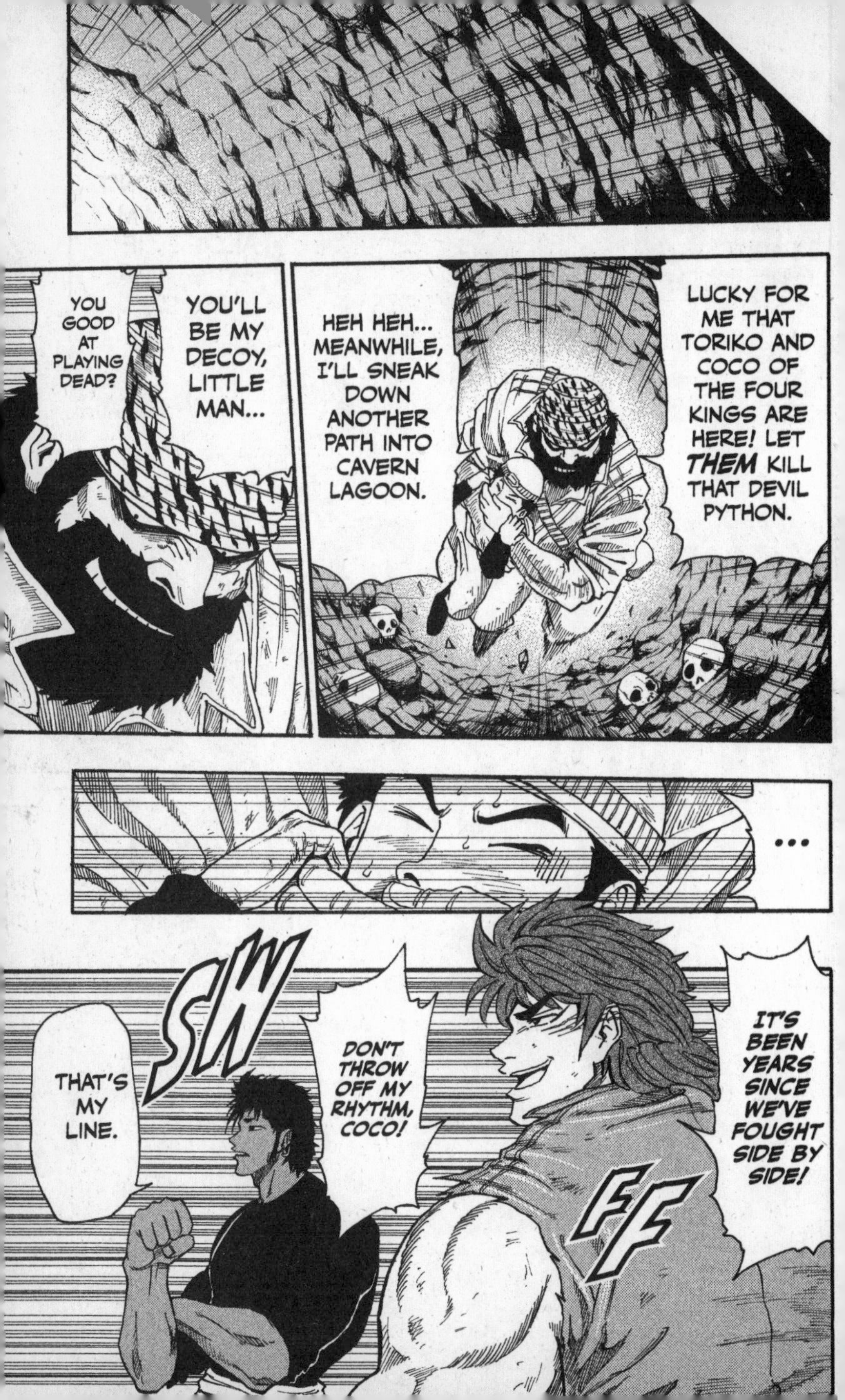
LUCKY FOR ME THAT TORIKO AND COCO OF THE FOUR KINGS ARE HERE! LET THEM KILL THAT DEVIL PYTHON.
HEH HEH... MEANWHILE, I'LL SNEAK DOWN ANOTHER PATH INTO CAVERN LAGOON.
YOU'LL BE MY DECOY, LITTLE MAN...
YOU GOOD AT PLAYING DEAD?
...
IT'S BEEN YEARS SINCE WE'VE FOUGHT SIDE BY SIDE!
FF
DON'T THROW OFF MY RHYTHM, COCO!
SH
THAT'S MY LINE.

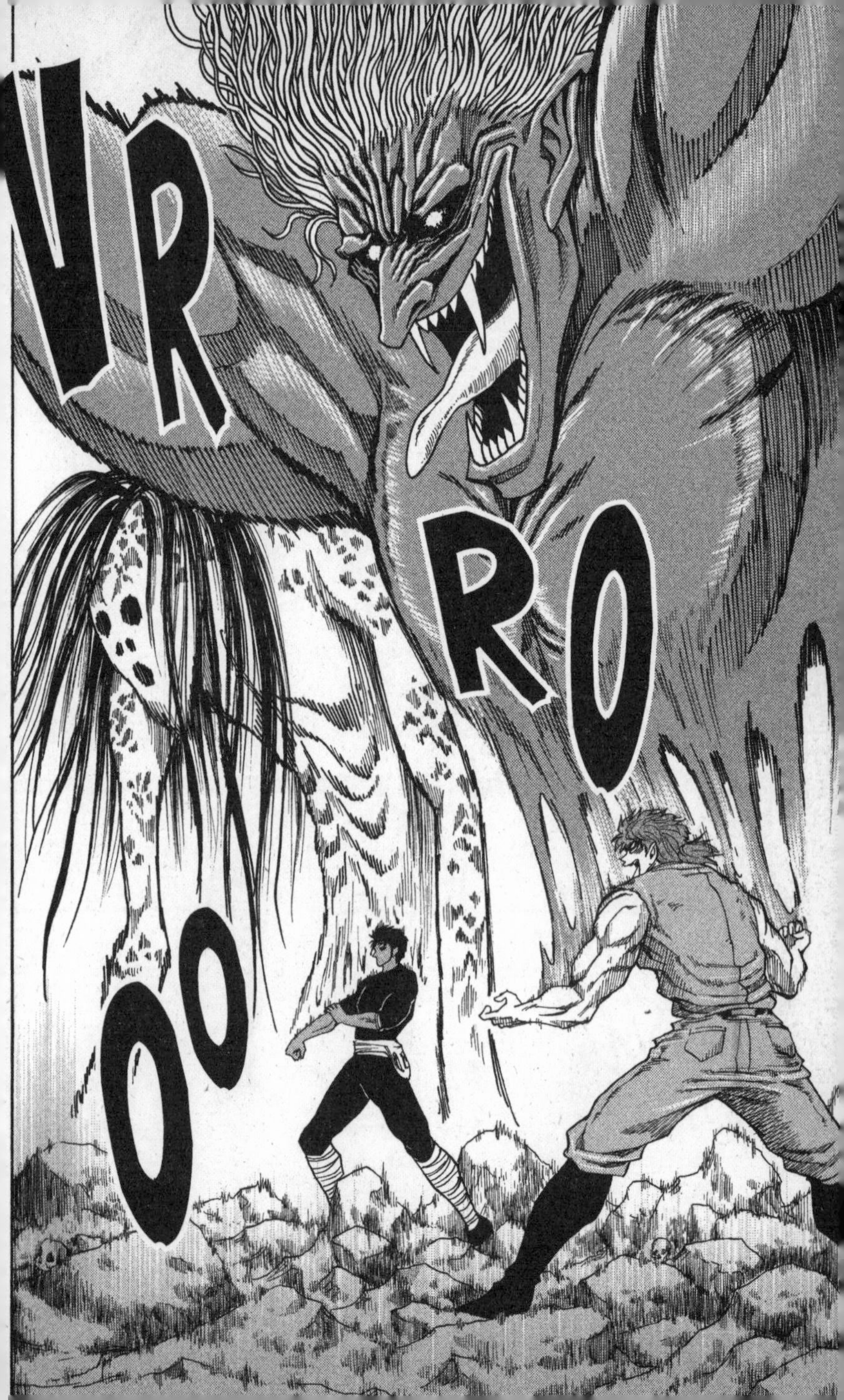
VRROOO

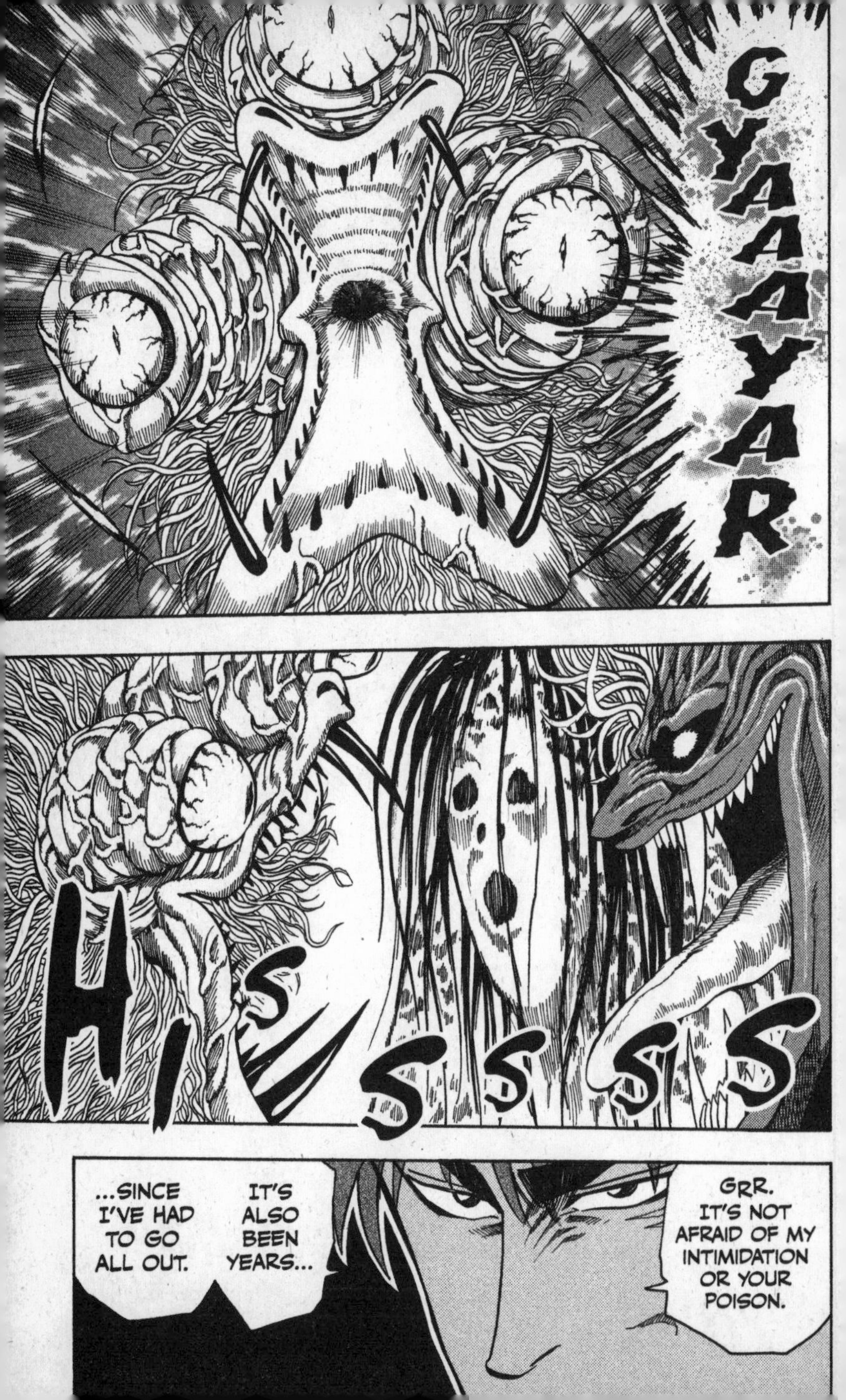
GYAAYAR
HISSSSS
GRR. IT'S NOT AFRAID OF MY INTIMIDATION OR YOUR POISON.
IT'S ALSO BEEN YEARS...
...SINCE I'VE HAD TO GO ALL OUT.

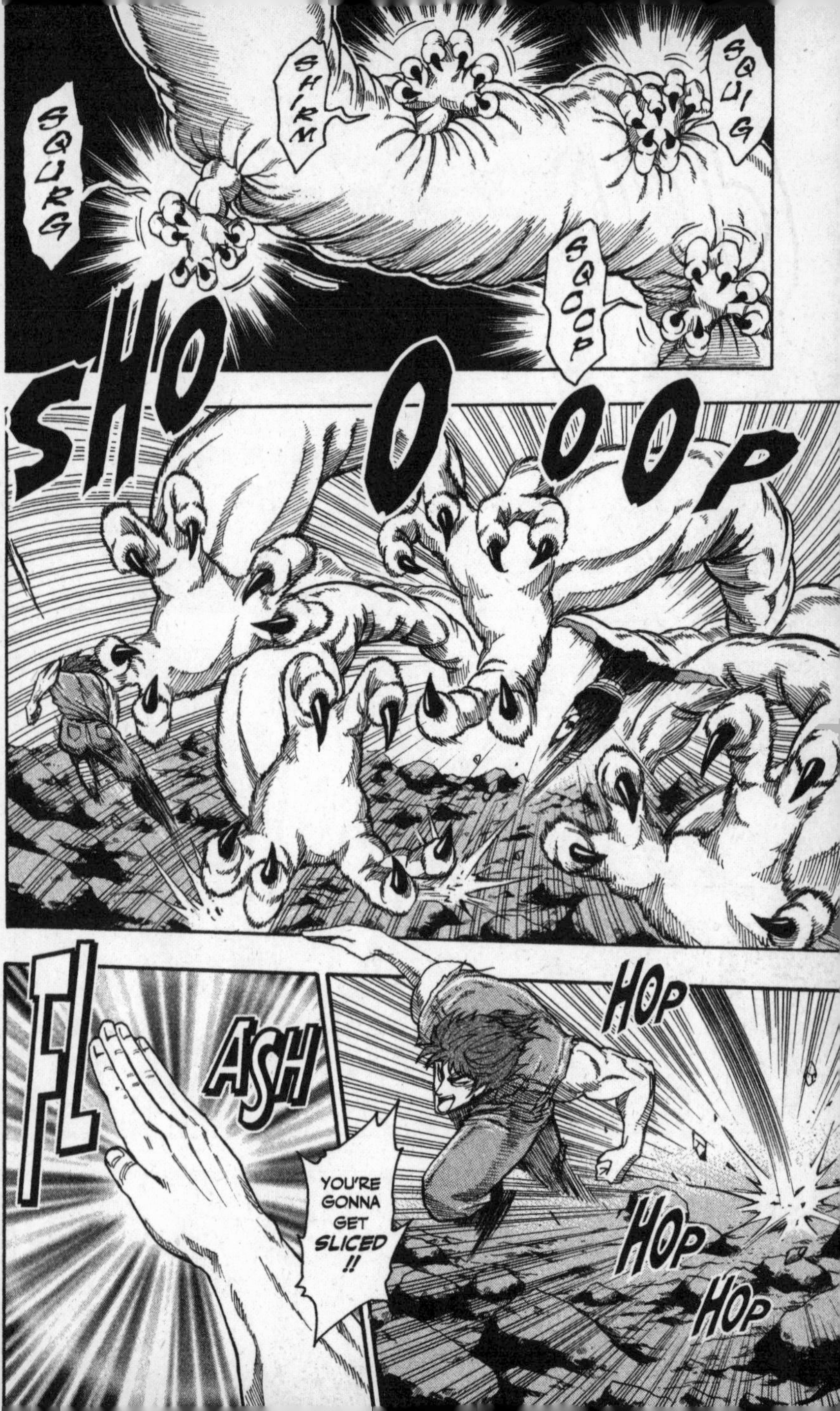
SQUIG
SHIRM
SQOOP
SQURG
SHOOOOP
HOP
HOP
HOP
YOU'RE GONNA GET SLICED!!
FLASH

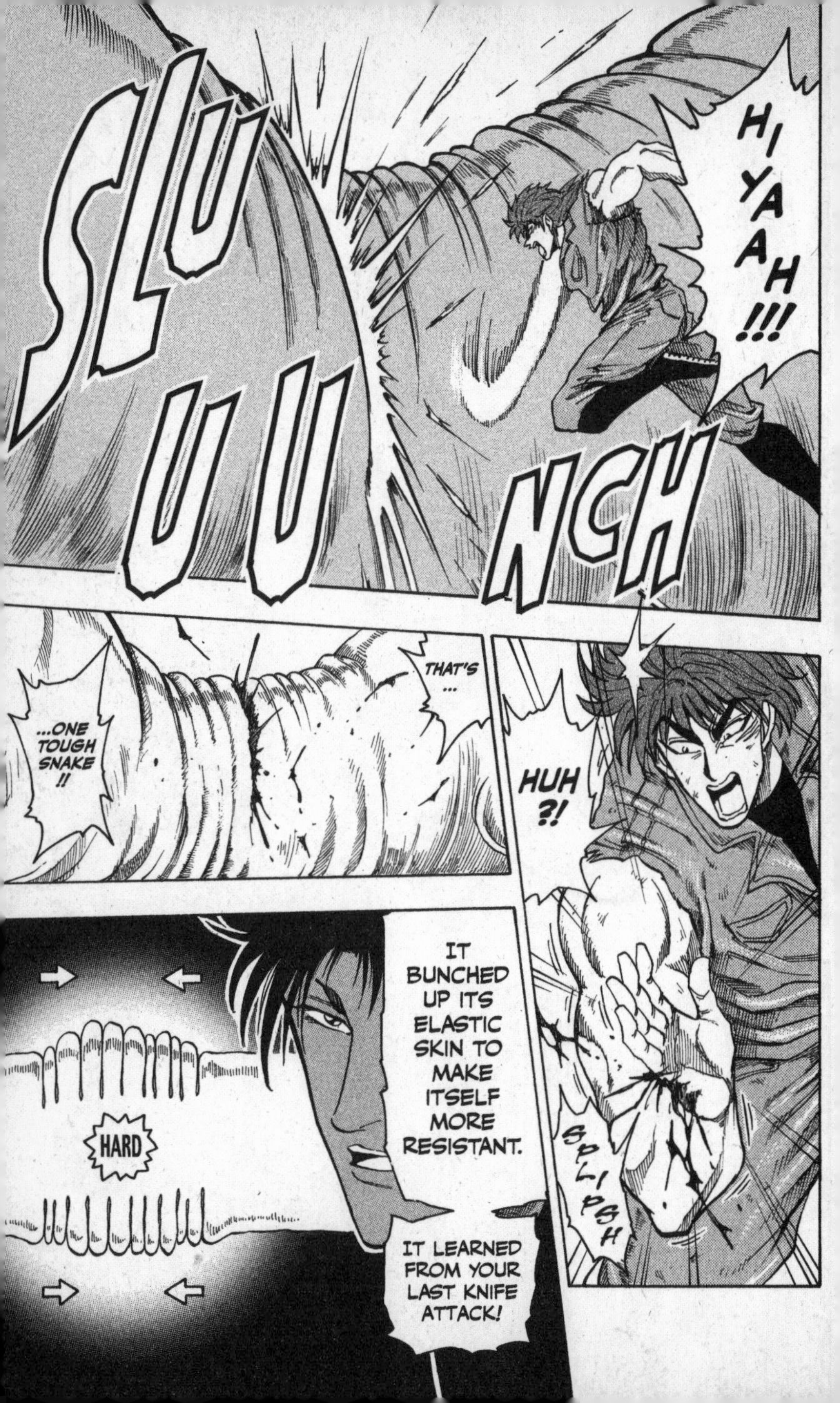
HI YAAH!!!
SLUUUUNCH
HUH ?!
SPLISH
THAT'S ...
...ONE TOUGH SNAKE !!
IT BUNCHED UP ITS ELASTIC SKIN TO MAKE ITSELF MORE RESISTANT.
IT LEARNED FROM YOUR LAST KNIFE ATTACK!
HARD

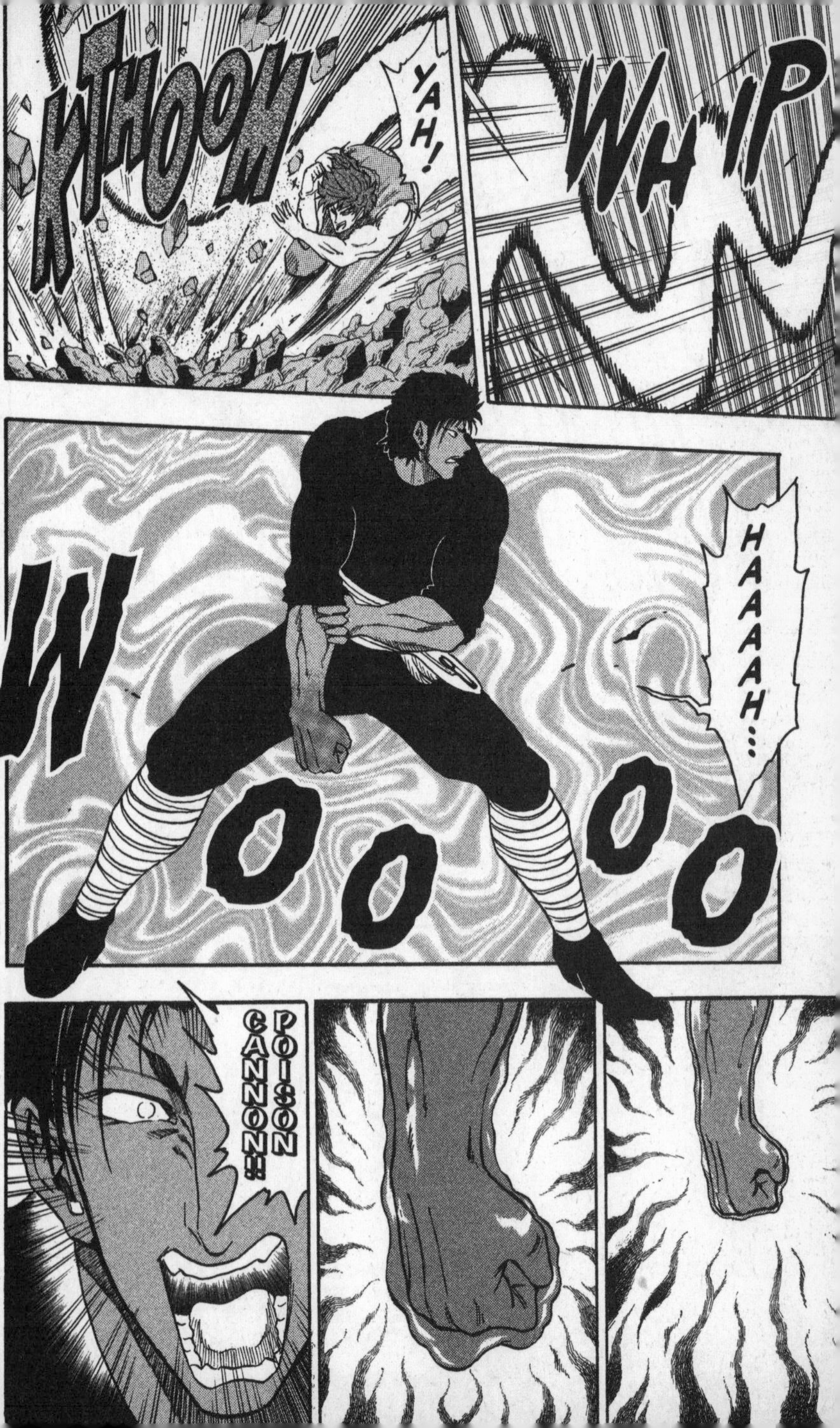

WHIP
YAH!
K'THOOM
HAAAAAH...
WOOOOOO
POISON CANNON!!

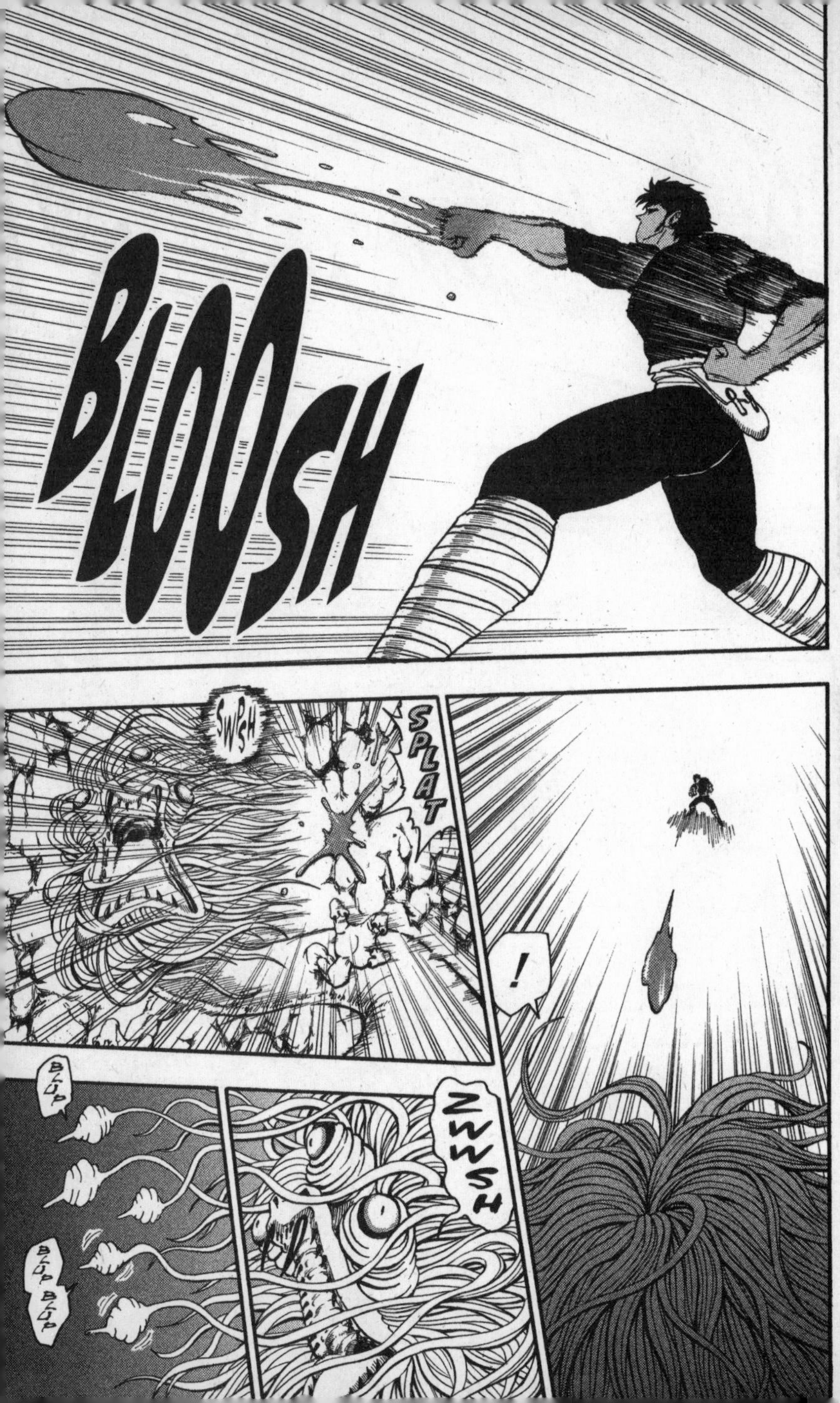
BLOOSH
!
SWPSH
SPLAT
ZWWSH
BLUP
BLUP BLUP

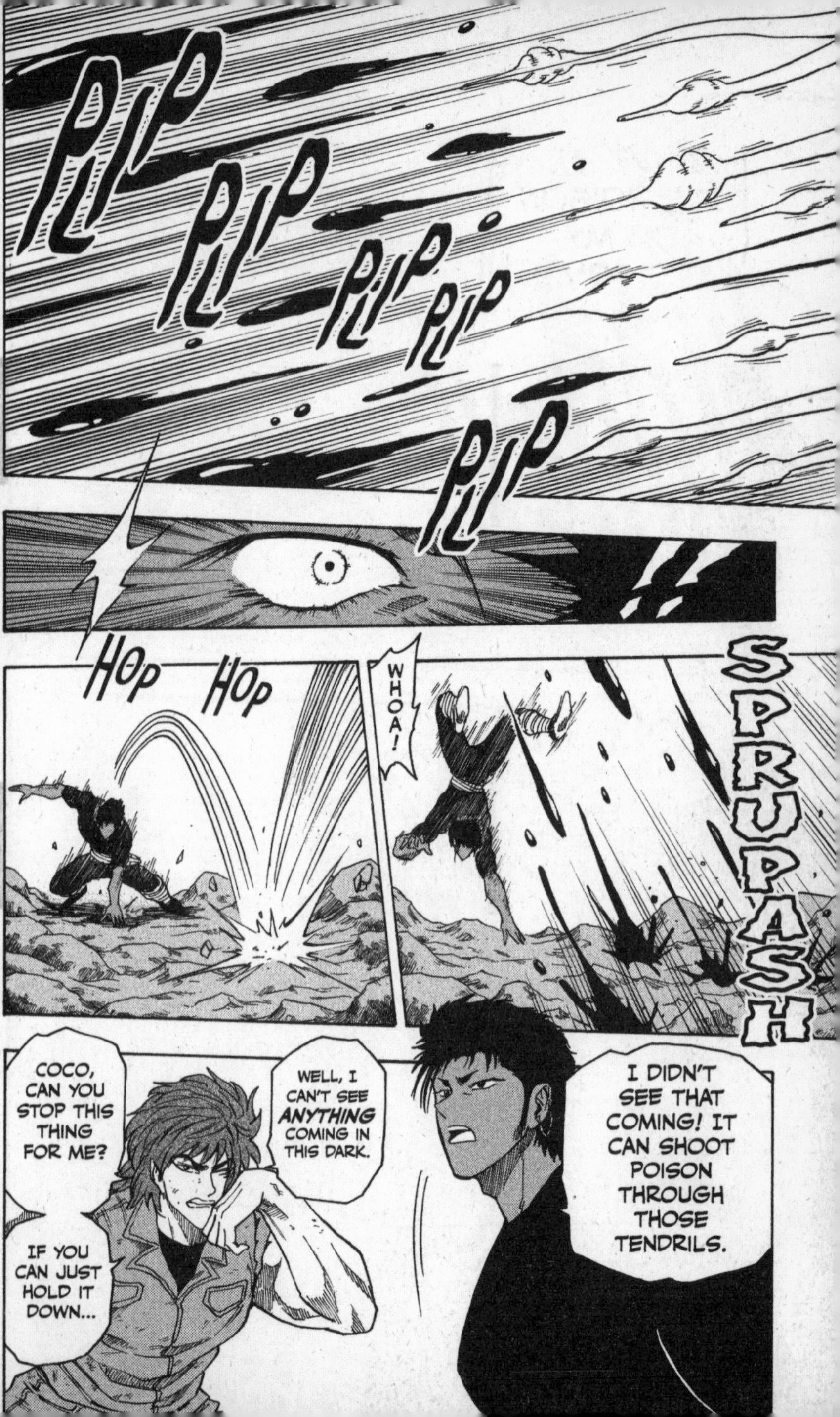
PLIP
PLIP
PLIP
PLIP
PLIP
SPRUPASH
WHOA!
HOP
HOP
I DIDN'T SEE THAT COMING! IT CAN SHOOT POISON THROUGH THOSE TENDRILS.
WELL, I CAN'T SEE *ANYTHING* COMING IN THIS DARK.
COCO, CAN YOU STOP THIS THING FOR ME?
IF YOU CAN JUST HOLD IT DOWN...

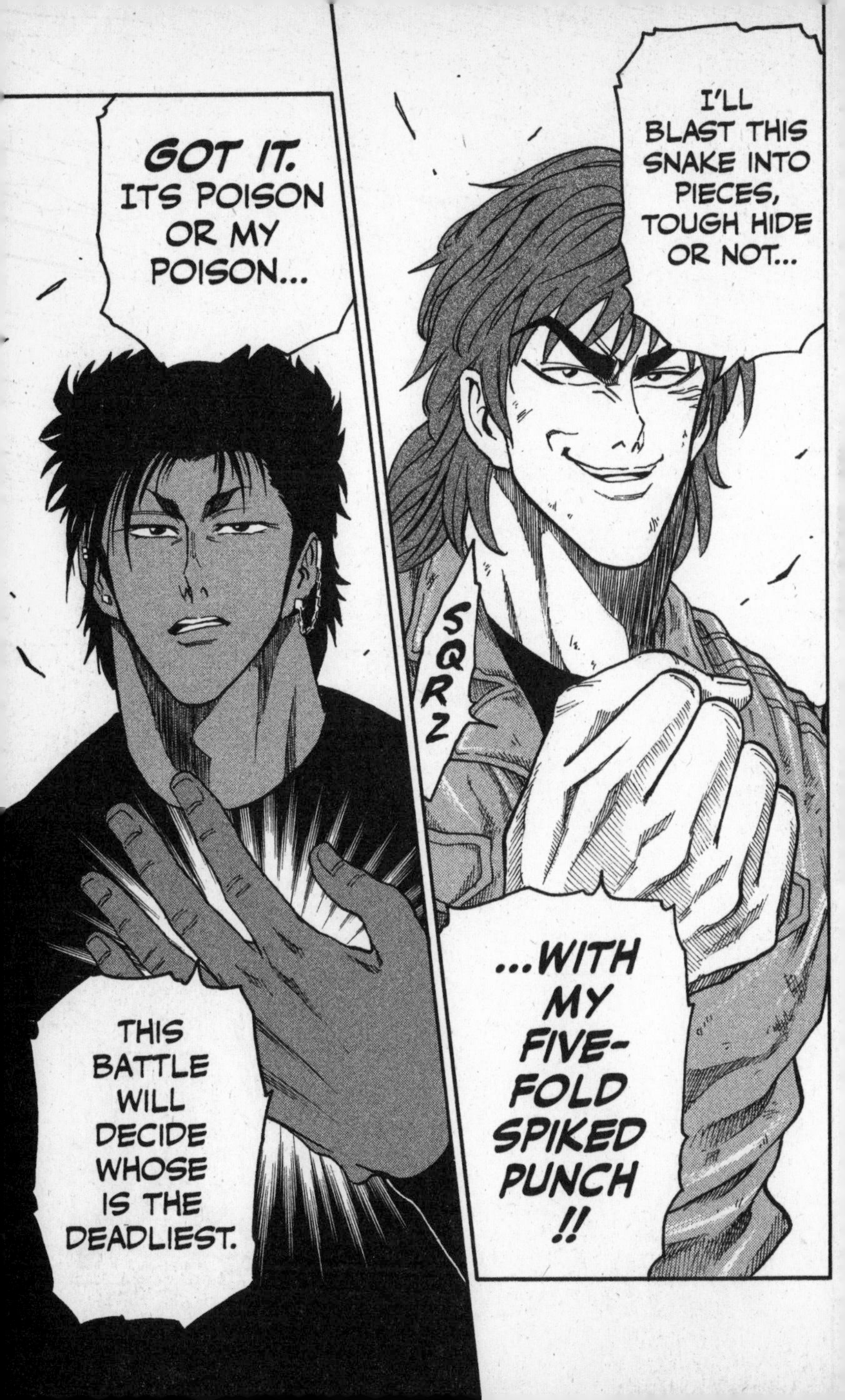
I'LL BLAST THIS SNAKE INTO PIECES, TOUGH HIDE OR NOT...
SQRZ
...WITH MY FIVE-FOLD SPIKED PUNCH!!
GOT IT. ITS POISON OR MY POISON...
THIS BATTLE WILL DECIDE WHOSE IS THE DEADLIEST.

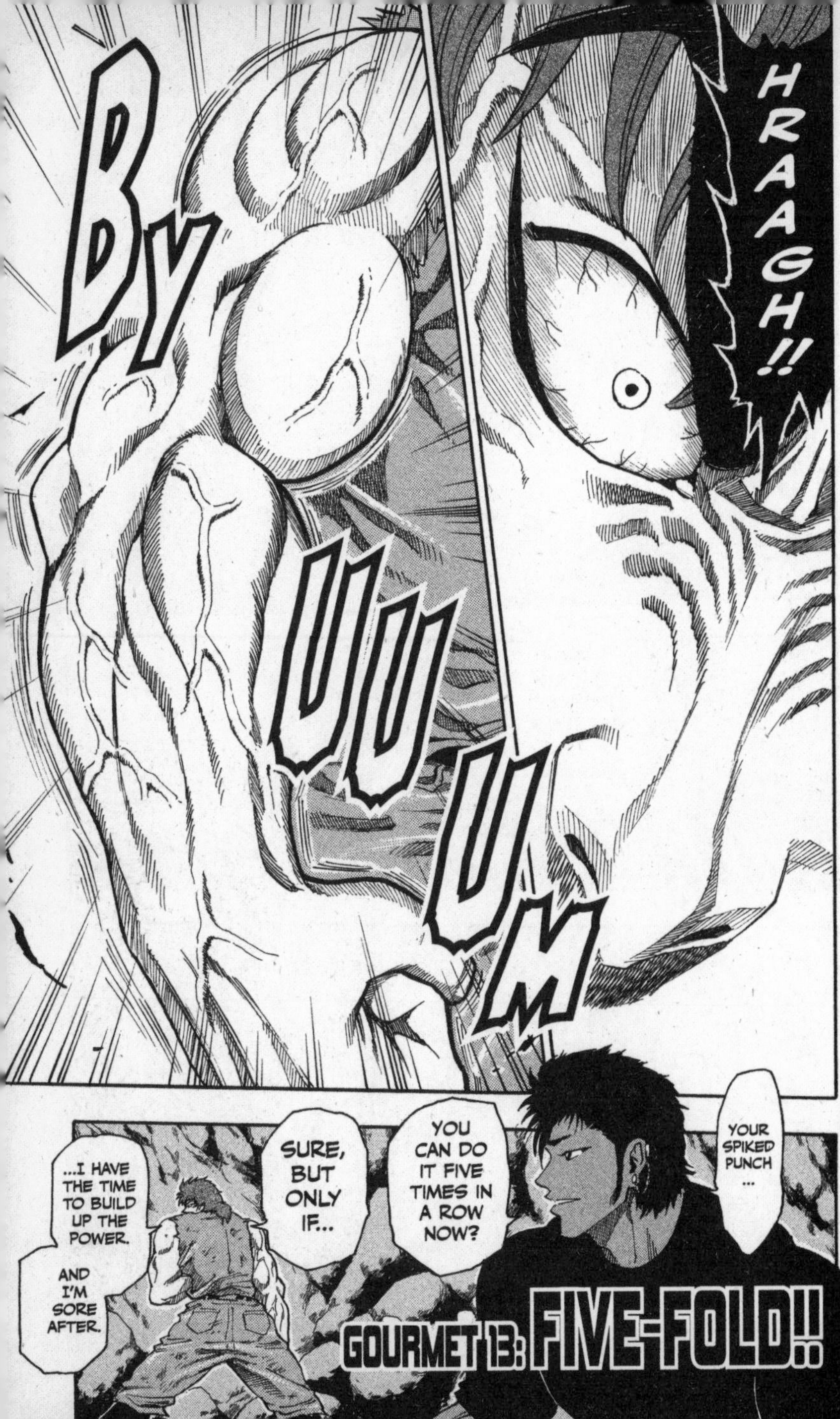
HRAAGH!!
BYUUUM
YOUR SPIKED PUNCH ...
YOU CAN DO IT FIVE TIMES IN A ROW NOW?
SURE, BUT ONLY IF...
...I HAVE THE TIME TO BUILD UP THE POWER.
AND I'M SORE AFTER.
GOURMET 13: FIVE-FOLD!!

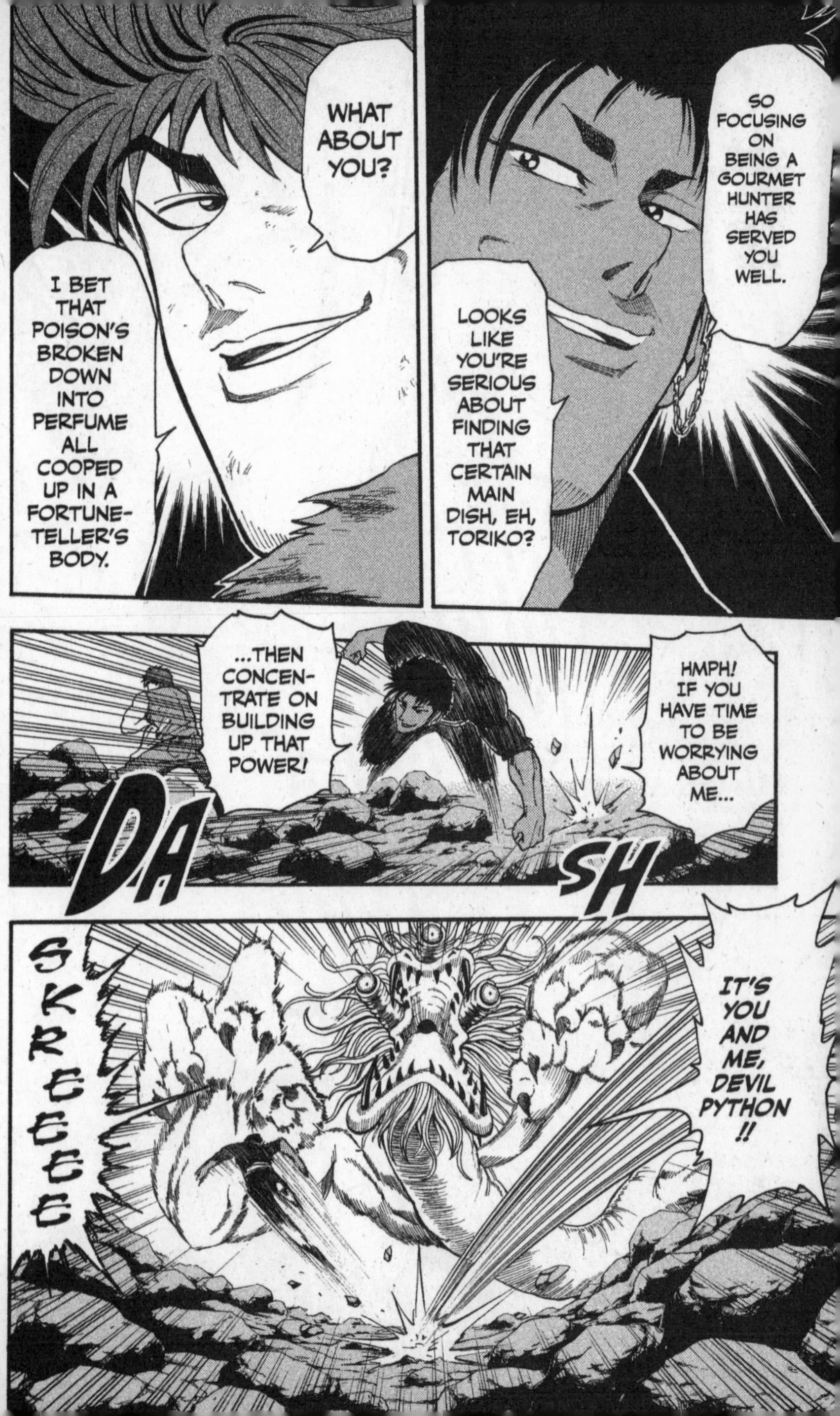
SO FOCUSING ON BEING A GOURMET HUNTER HAS SERVED YOU WELL.
LOOKS LIKE YOU'RE SERIOUS ABOUT FINDING THAT CERTAIN MAIN DISH, EH, TORIKO?
WHAT ABOUT YOU?
I BET THAT POISON'S BROKEN DOWN INTO PERFUME ALL COOPED UP IN A FORTUNE-TELLER'S BODY.
HMPH! IF YOU HAVE TIME TO BE WORRYING ABOUT ME...
...THEN CONCENTRATE ON BUILDING UP THAT POWER!
DASH
IT'S YOU AND ME, DEVIL PYTHON!!
SKREEEE

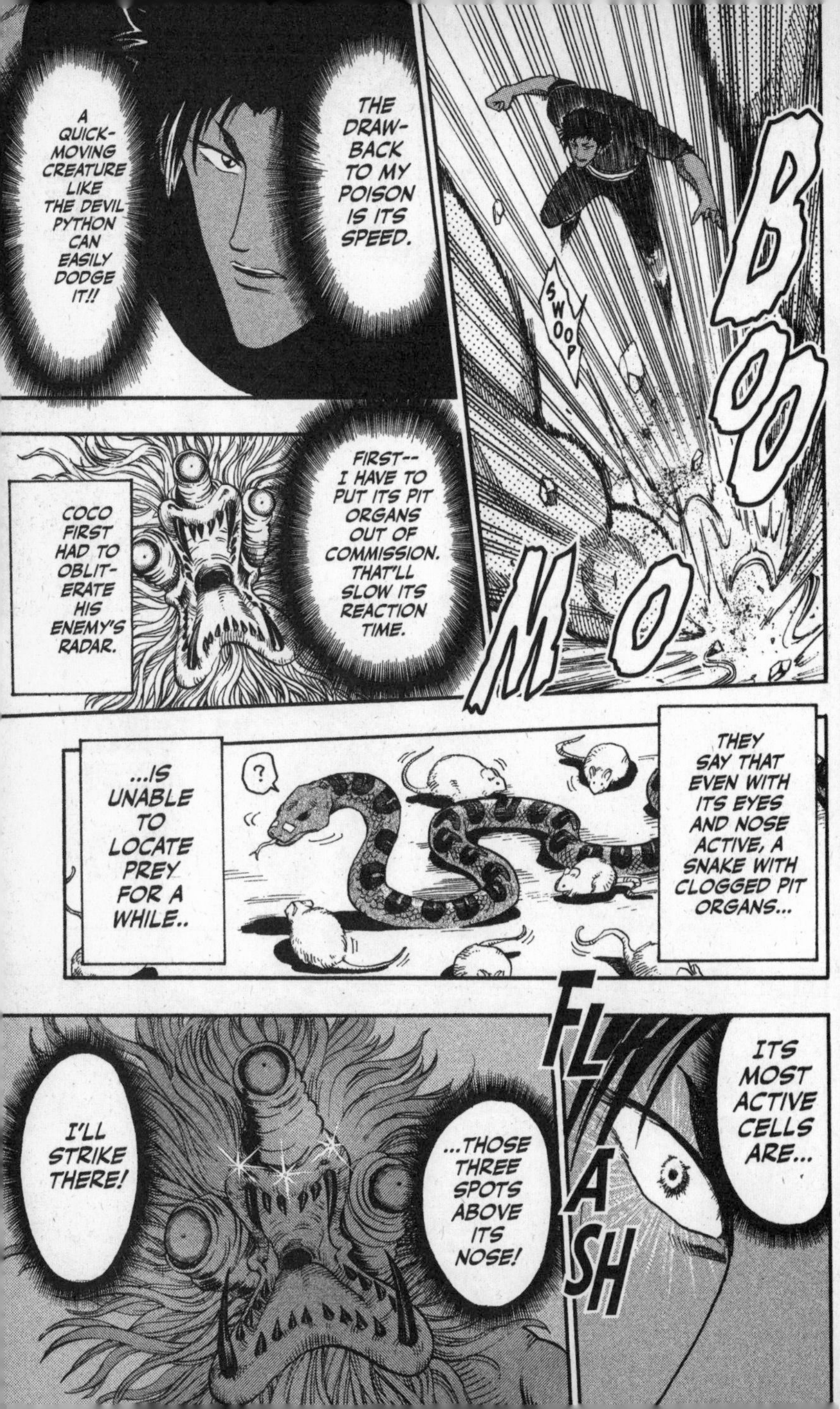
SWOOP
BOOOOM
THE DRAW-BACK TO MY POISON IS ITS SPEED.
A QUICK-MOVING CREATURE LIKE THE DEVIL PYTHON CAN EASILY DODGE IT!!
FIRST-- I HAVE TO PUT ITS PIT ORGANS OUT OF COMMISSION. THAT'LL SLOW ITS REACTION TIME.
COCO FIRST HAD TO OBLIT-ERATE HIS ENEMY'S RADAR.
THEY SAY THAT EVEN WITH ITS EYES AND NOSE ACTIVE, A SNAKE WITH CLOGGED PIT ORGANS...
?
...IS UNABLE TO LOCATE PREY FOR A WHILE..
ITS MOST ACTIVE CELLS ARE...
FLASH
...THOSE THREE SPOTS ABOVE ITS NOSE!
I'LL STRIKE THERE!

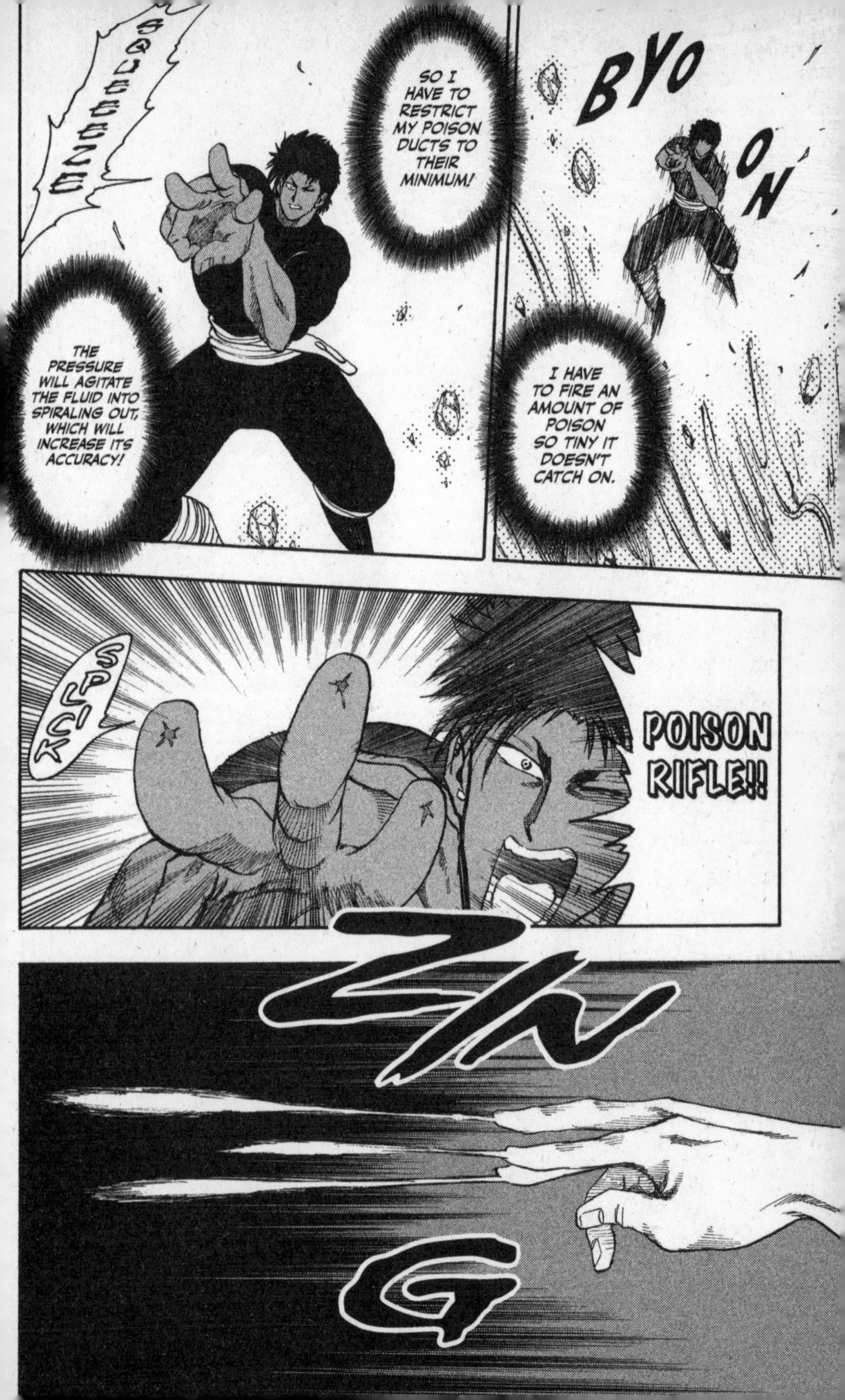

BYO ON
I HAVE TO FIRE AN AMOUNT OF POISON SO TINY IT DOESN'T CATCH ON.
SO I HAVE TO RESTRICT MY POISON DUCTS TO THEIR MINIMUM!
SQUEEEEZE
THE PRESSURE WILL AGITATE THE FLUID INTO SPIRALING OUT, WHICH WILL INCREASE ITS ACCURACY!
POISON RIFLE!!
SPLICK
ZHN
G

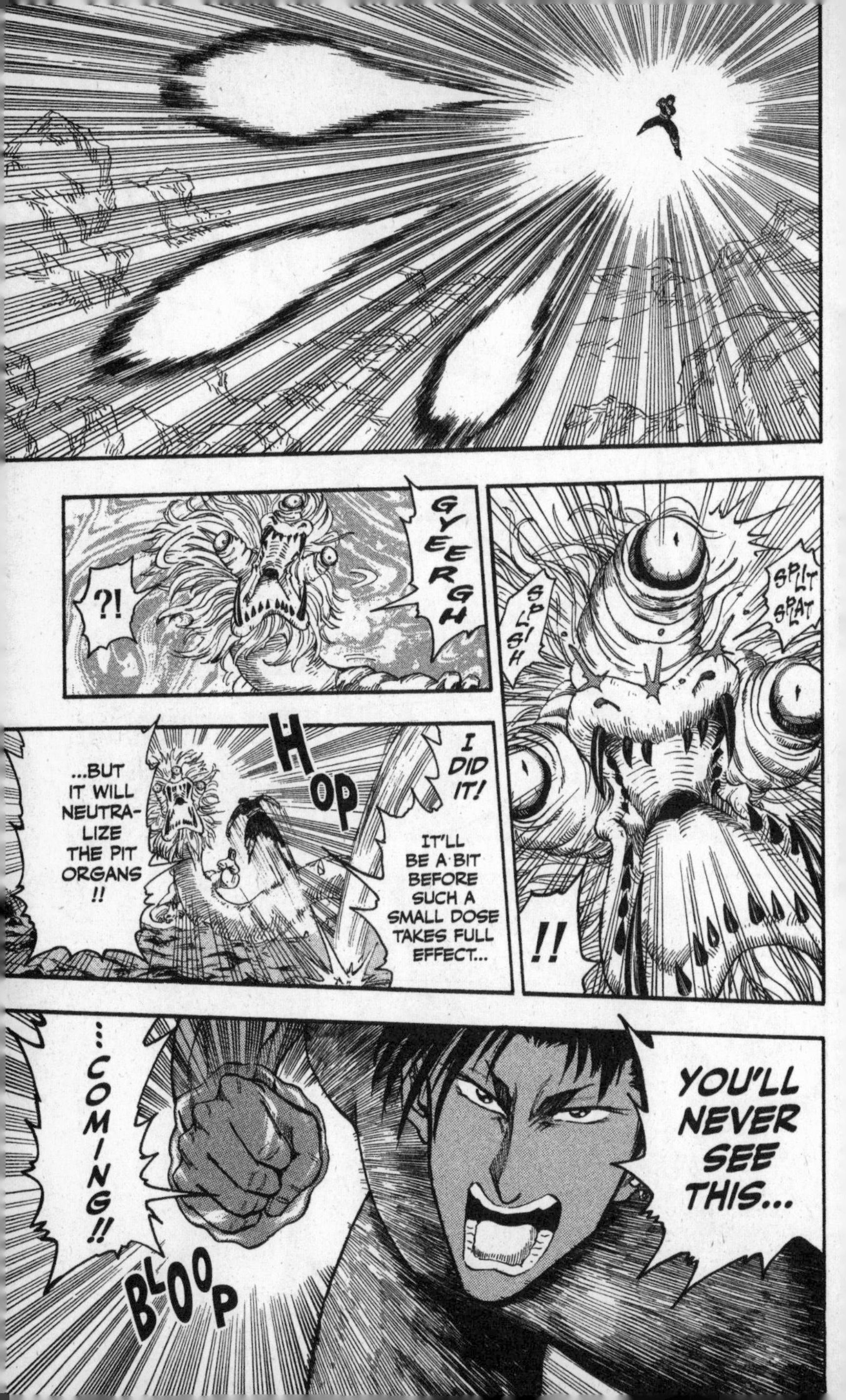
SPLIT SPLAT
SPLISH
!!
GYEERGH
?!
I DID IT!
IT'LL BE A BIT BEFORE SUCH A SMALL DOSE TAKES FULL EFFECT...
HOP
...BUT IT WILL NEUTRALIZE THE PIT ORGANS!!
YOU'LL NEVER SEE THIS...
...COMING!!
BLOOP

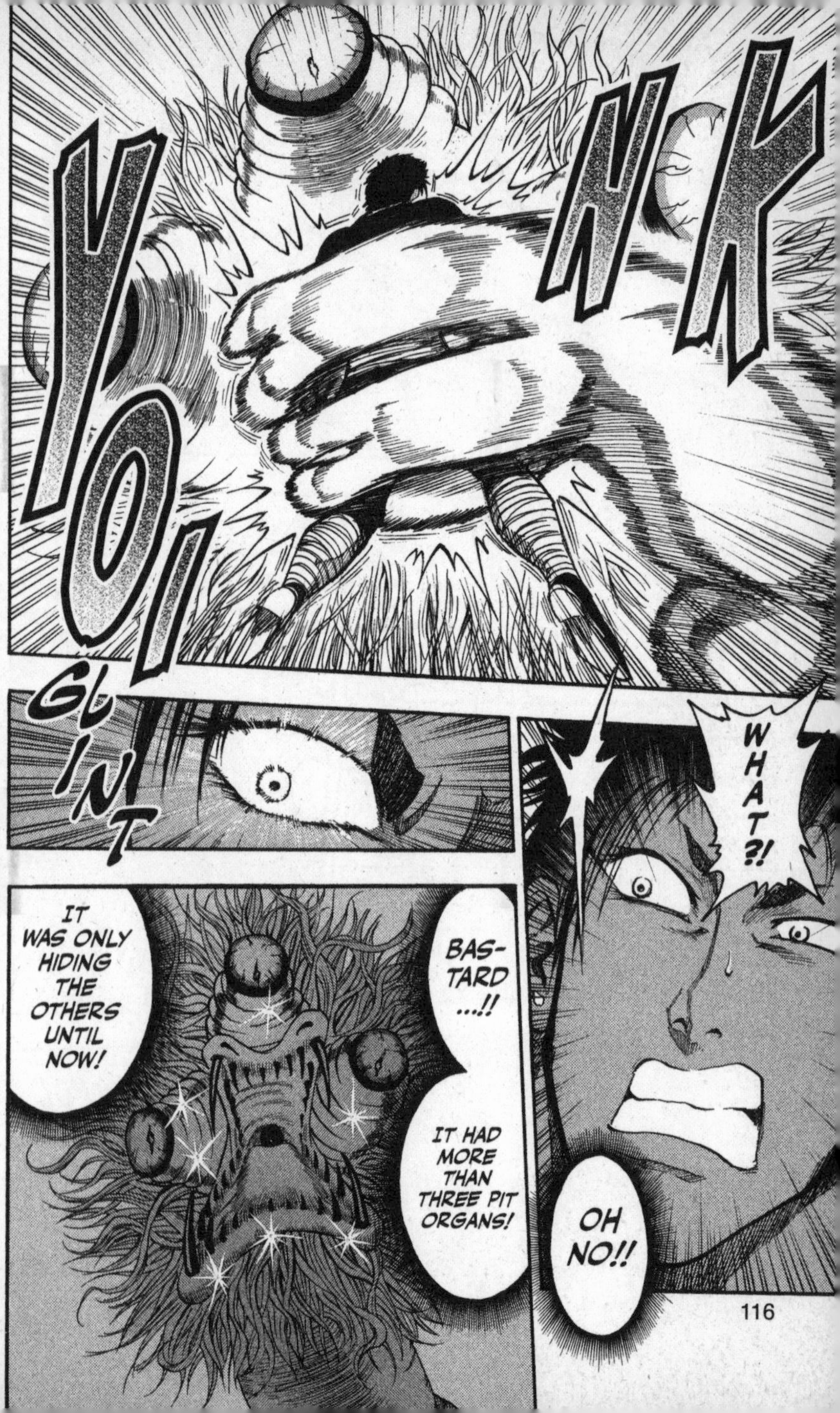
YOINK
WHAT?!
OH NO!!
GLINT
BAS-TARD ...!!
IT HAD MORE THAN THREE PIT ORGANS!
IT WAS ONLY HIDING THE OTHERS UNTIL NOW!

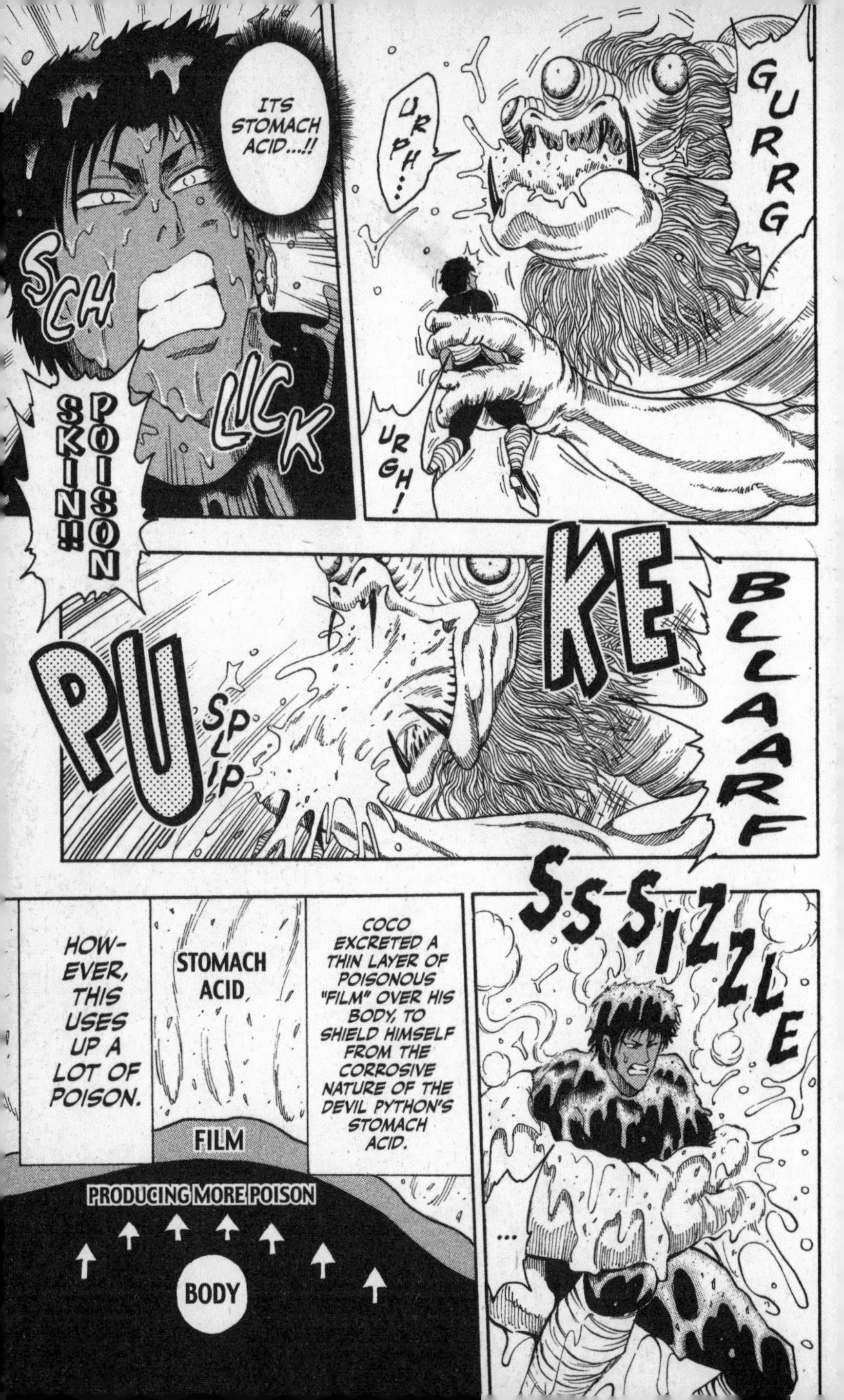
GURRG
URPH...
URGH!
ITS STOMACH ACID...!!
SCHLICK
POISON SKIN!!
BLLAARF
KE
PU
SPLIP
SSSIZZLE
...
COCO EXCRETED A THIN LAYER OF POISONOUS "FILM" OVER HIS BODY, TO SHIELD HIMSELF FROM THE CORROSIVE NATURE OF THE DEVIL PYTHON'S STOMACH ACID.
STOMACH ACID
FILM
PRODUCING MORE POISON
BODY
HOW-EVER, THIS USES UP A LOT OF POISON.

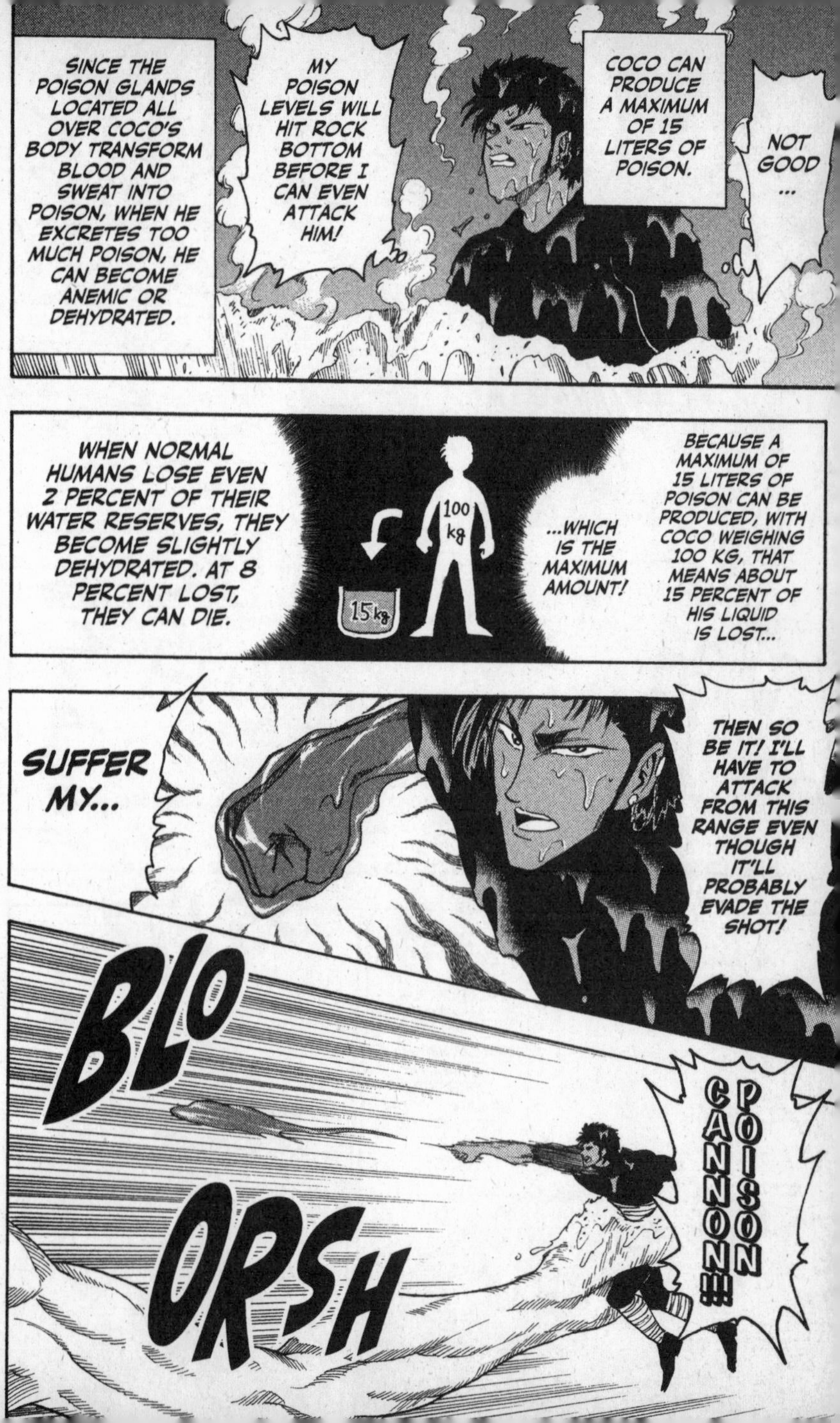
NOT GOOD ...
COCO CAN PRODUCE A MAXIMUM OF 15 LITERS OF POISON.
MY POISON LEVELS WILL HIT ROCK BOTTOM BEFORE I CAN EVEN ATTACK HIM!
SINCE THE POISON GLANDS LOCATED ALL OVER COCO'S BODY TRANSFORM BLOOD AND SWEAT INTO POISON, WHEN HE EXCRETES TOO MUCH POISON, HE CAN BECOME ANEMIC OR DEHYDRATED.
BECAUSE A MAXIMUM OF 15 LITERS OF POISON CAN BE PRODUCED, WITH COCO WEIGHING 100 KG, THAT MEANS ABOUT 15 PERCENT OF HIS LIQUID IS LOST...
...WHICH IS THE MAXIMUM AMOUNT!
100 kg
15 kg
WHEN NORMAL HUMANS LOSE EVEN 2 PERCENT OF THEIR WATER RESERVES, THEY BECOME SLIGHTLY DEHYDRATED. AT 8 PERCENT LOST, THEY CAN DIE.
THEN SO BE IT! I'LL HAVE TO ATTACK FROM THIS RANGE EVEN THOUGH IT'LL PROBABLY EVADE THE SHOT!
SUFFER MY...
POISON CANNON!!!
BLO
ORSH

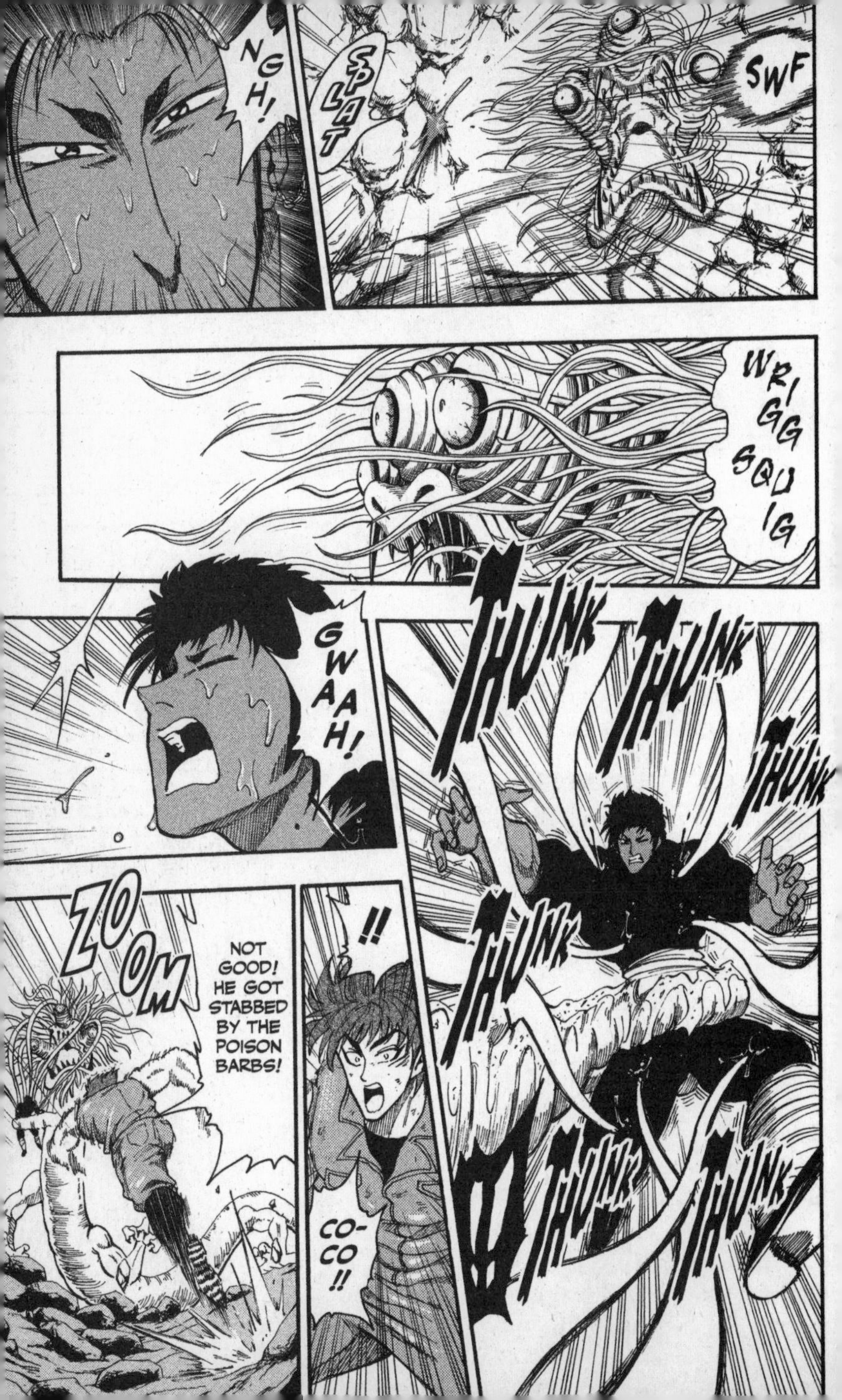
SWF
SPLAT
NGH!
WRIGG SQUIG
THUNK
THUNK
THUNK
THUNK
THUNK
THUNK
GWAAH!
!!
CO-CO!!
ZOOM
NOT GOOD! HE GOT STABBED BY THE POISON BARBS!

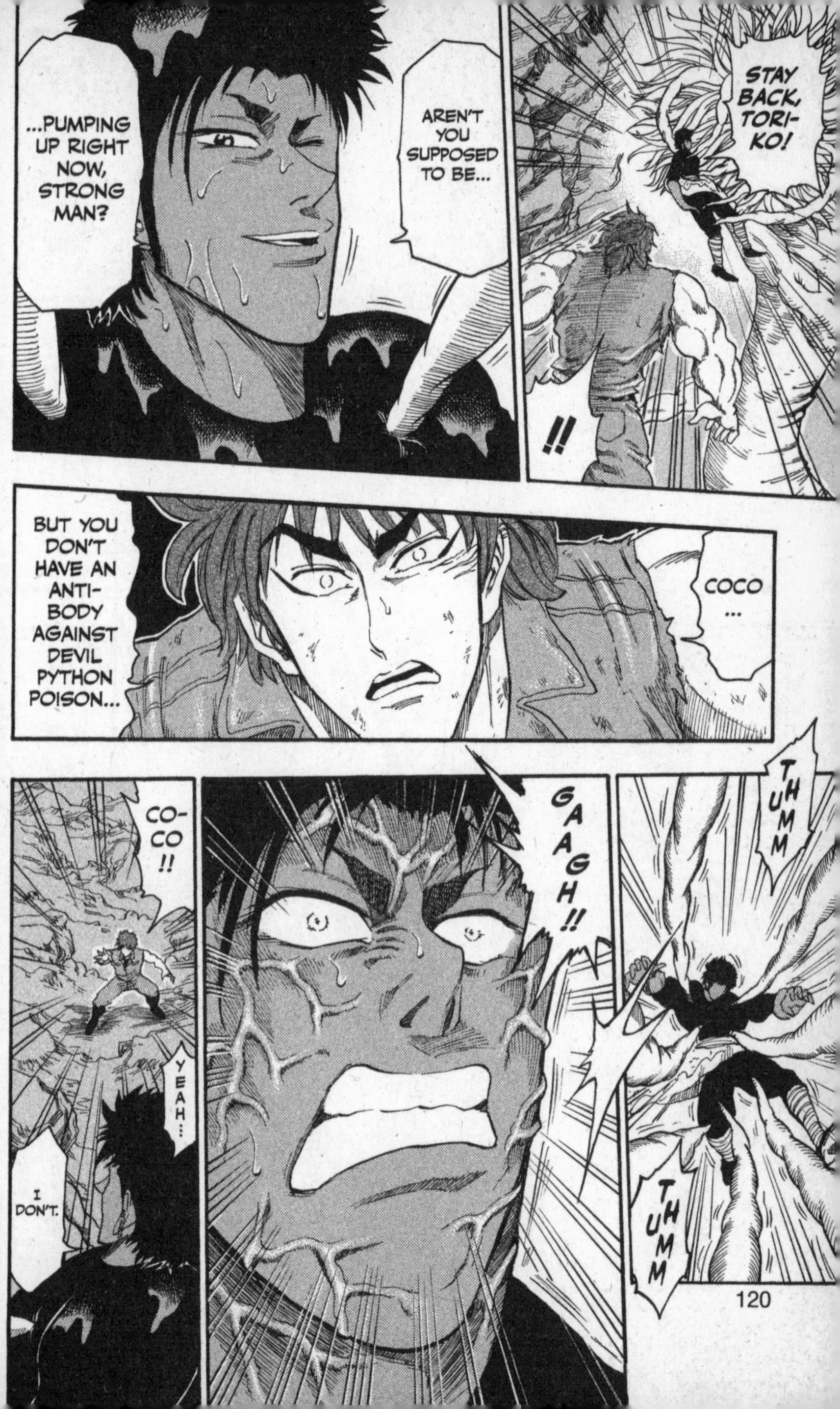
STAY BACK, TORI-KO!
!!
AREN'T YOU SUPPOSED TO BE...
...PUMPING UP RIGHT NOW, STRONG MAN?
COCO...
BUT YOU DON'T HAVE AN ANTI-BODY AGAINST DEVIL PYTHON POISON...
THUMM
THUMM
GAAGH!!
CO-CO!!
YEAH...
I DON'T.

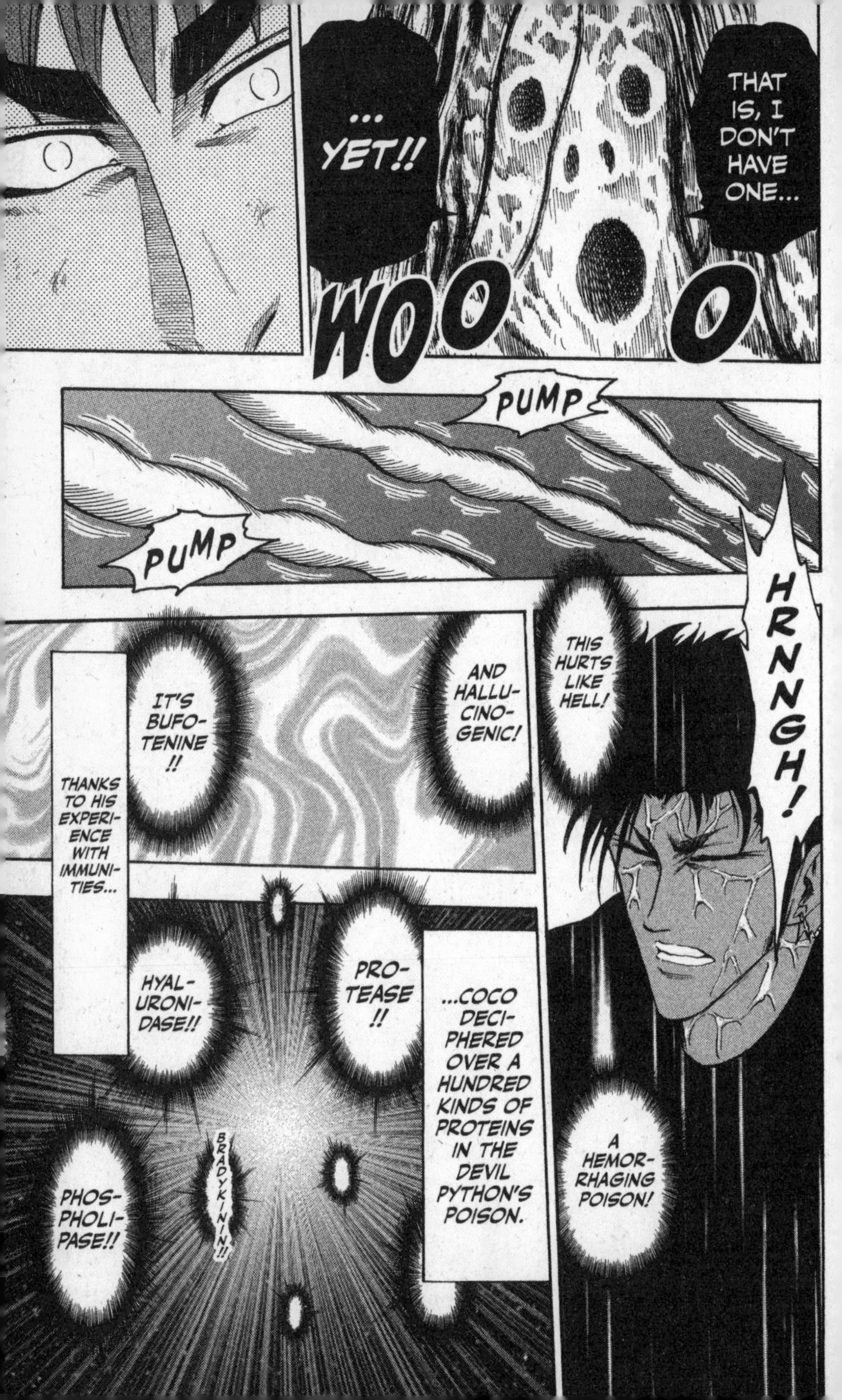
THAT IS, I DON'T HAVE ONE...
...YET!!
WOOO
PUMP
PUMP
HRNNGH!
THIS HURTS LIKE HELL!
A HEMORRHAGING POISON!
AND HALLUCINOGENIC!
IT'S BUFOTENINE!!
THANKS TO HIS EXPERIENCE WITH IMMUNITIES...
...COCO DECIPHERED OVER A HUNDRED KINDS OF PROTEINS IN THE DEVIL PYTHON'S POISON.
PROTEASE!!
HYALURONIDASE!!
BRADYKININ!!
PHOSPHOLIPASE!!

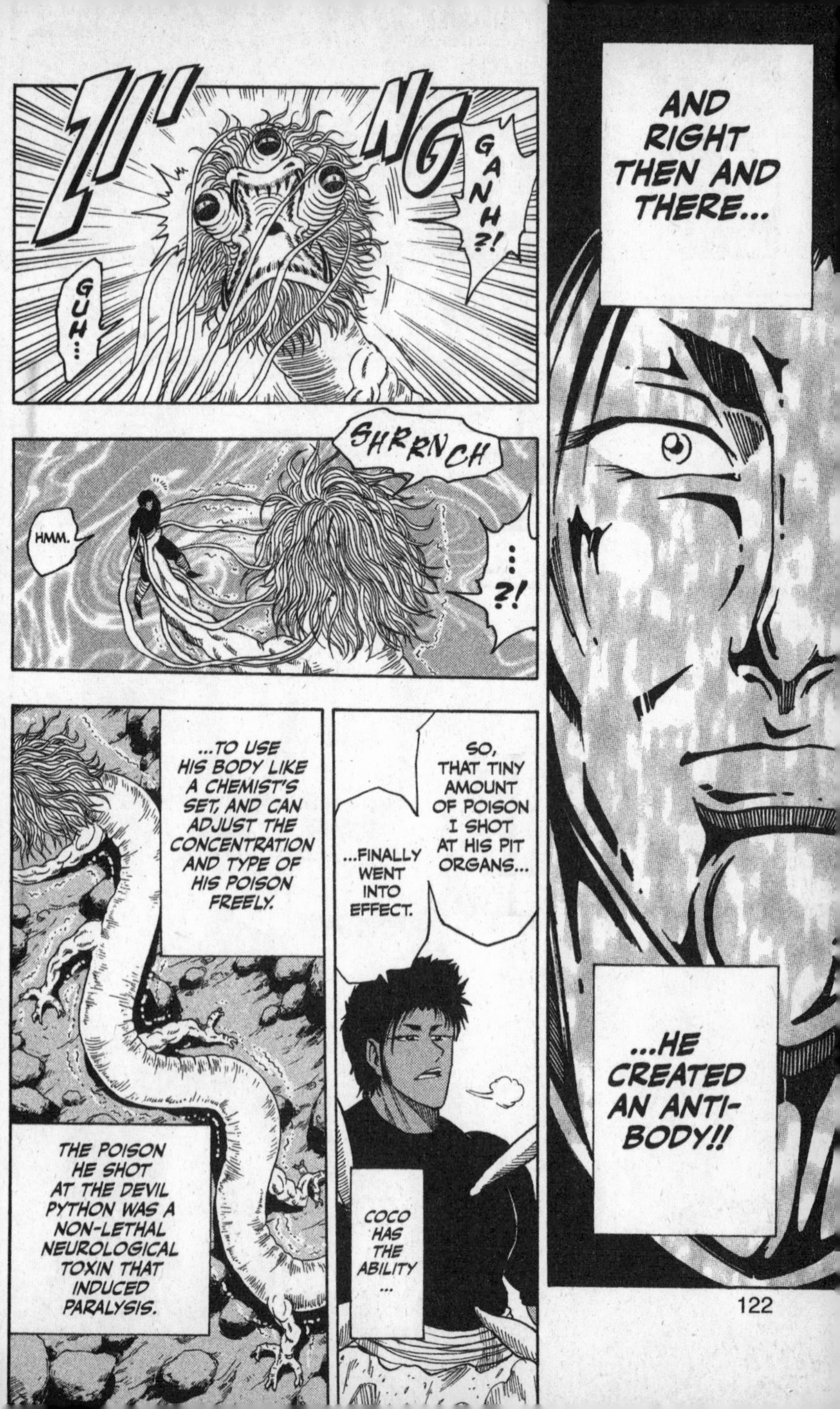
AND RIGHT THEN AND THERE...
...HE CREATED AN ANTI-BODY!!
ZU'NG
GANH?!
GUH...
SHRRNCH
...?!
HMM.
SO, THAT TINY AMOUNT OF POISON I SHOT AT HIS PIT ORGANS...
...FINALLY WENT INTO EFFECT.
COCO HAS THE ABILITY...
...TO USE HIS BODY LIKE A CHEMIST'S SET, AND CAN ADJUST THE CONCENTRATION AND TYPE OF HIS POISON FREELY.
THE POISON HE SHOT AT THE DEVIL PYTHON WAS A NON-LETHAL NEUROLOGICAL TOXIN THAT INDUCED PARALYSIS.

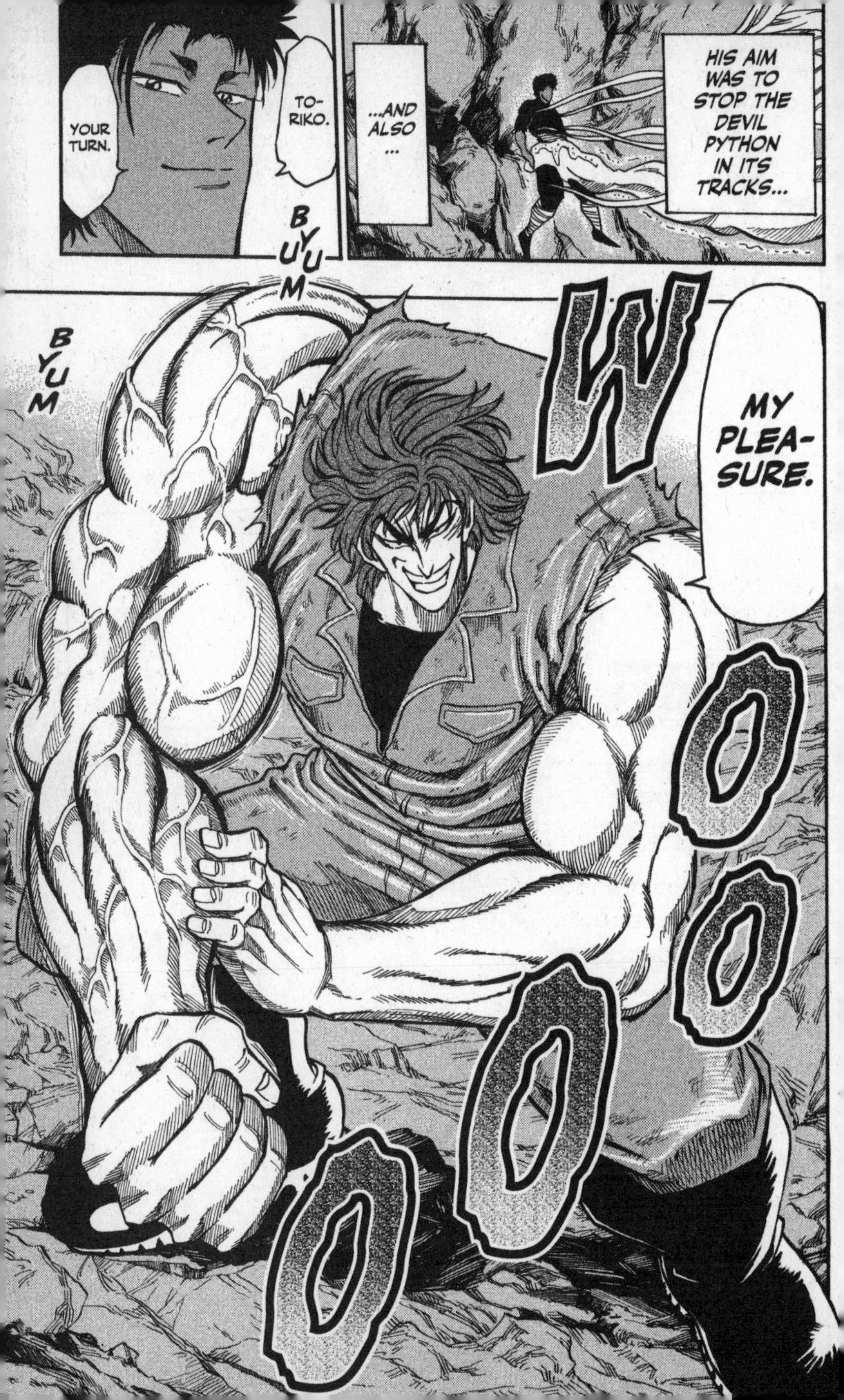
HIS AIM WAS TO STOP THE DEVIL PYTHON IN ITS TRACKS...
...AND ALSO ...
TO-RIKO.
YOUR TURN.
BYUUM
BYUM
MY PLEA-SURE.
WOOOOO

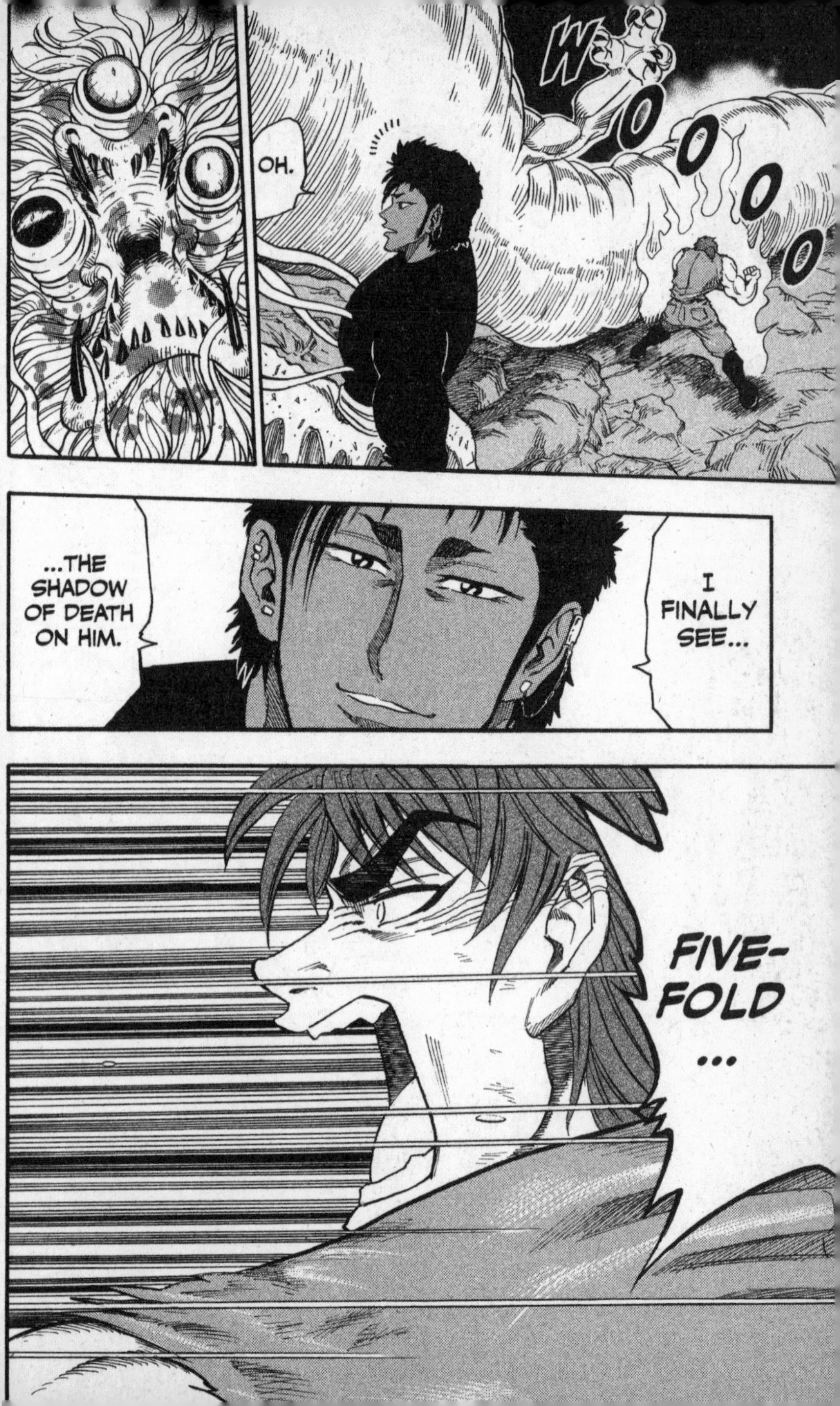
WOOOO
OH.
I FINALLY SEE...
...THE SHADOW OF DEATH ON HIM.
FIVE-FOLD...

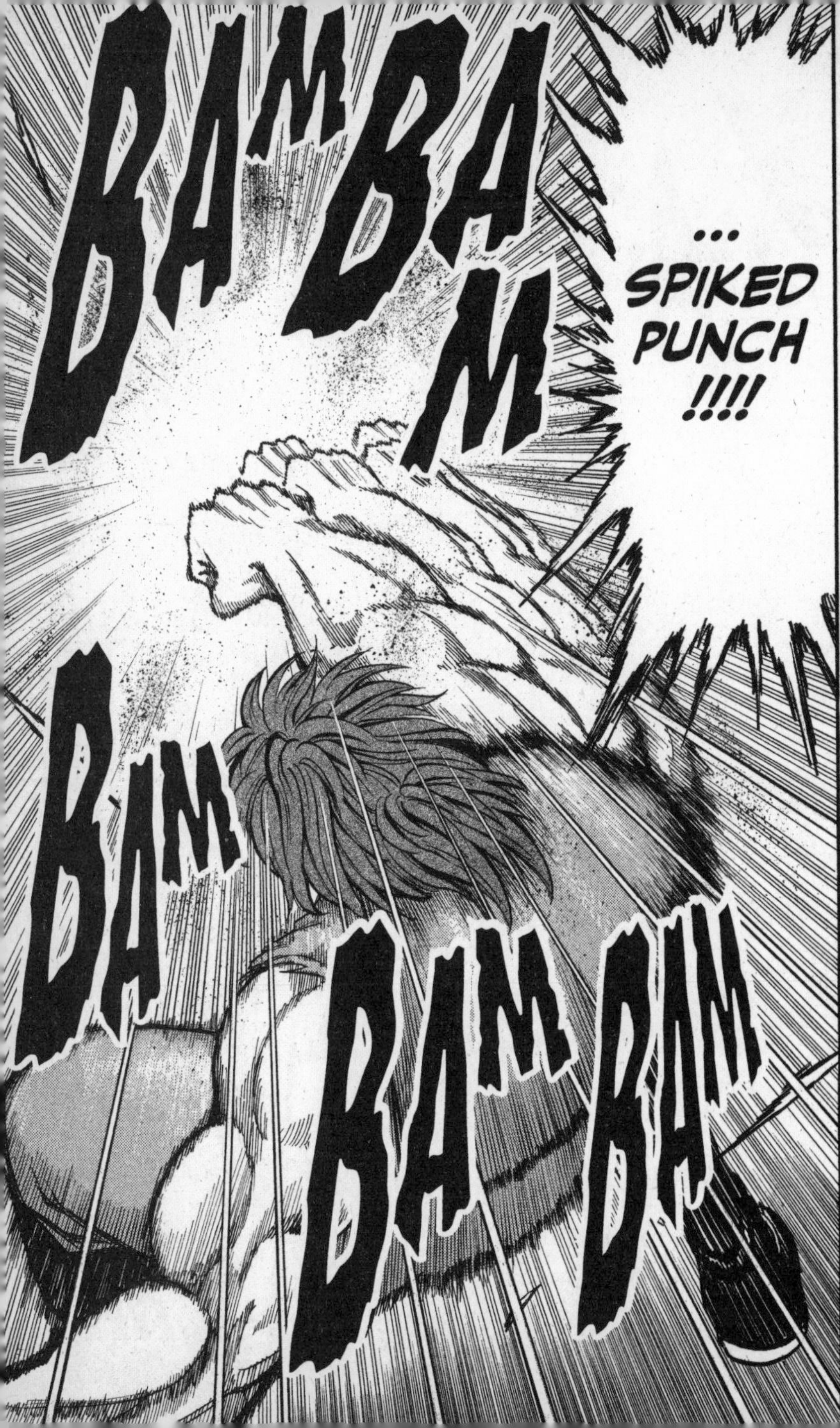
... SPIKED PUNCH !!!!
BAMBAM
BAM
BAM
BAM

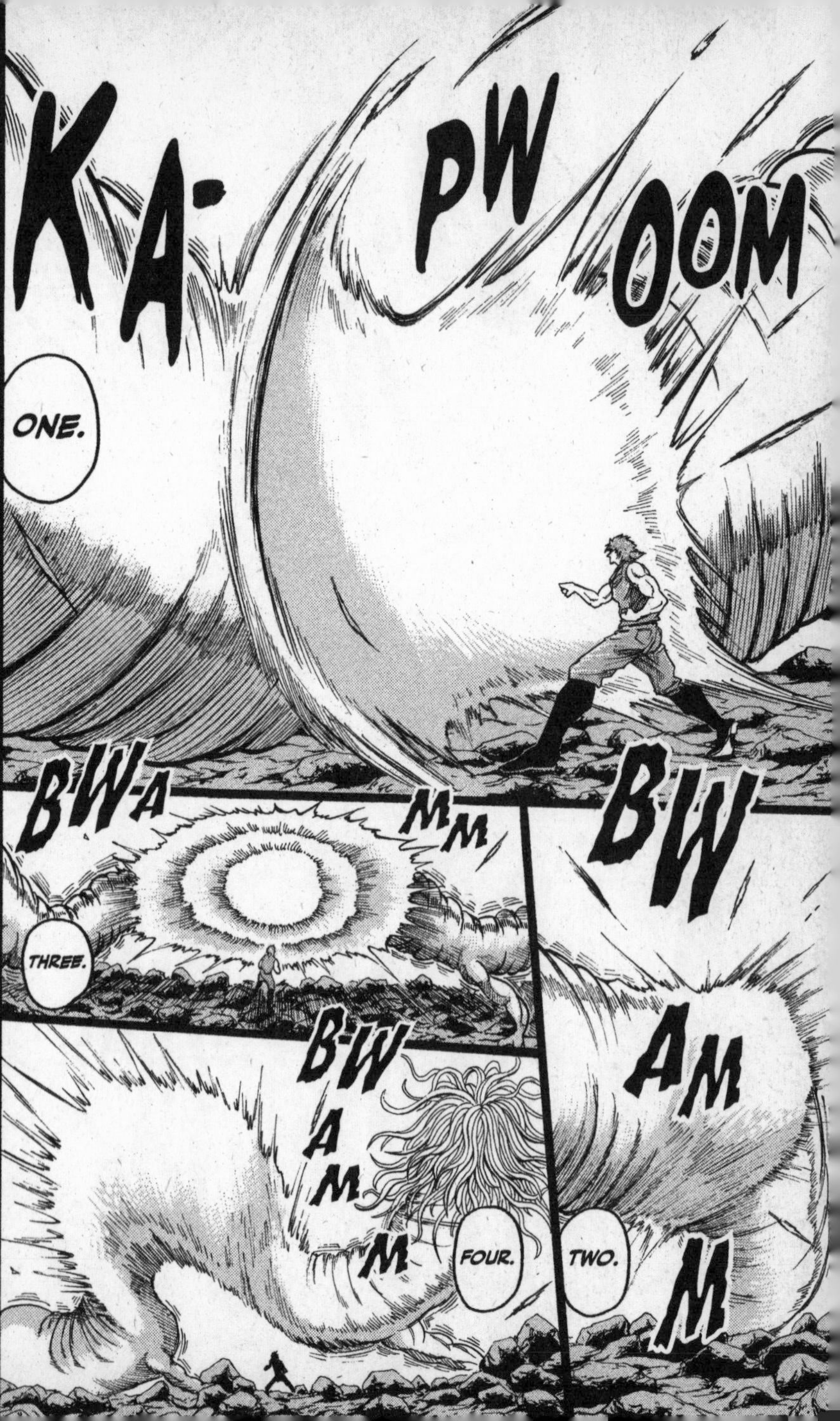
KA-PWOOM
ONE.
BWAMM
TWO.
BW-AMM
THREE.
B-WAMM
FOUR.

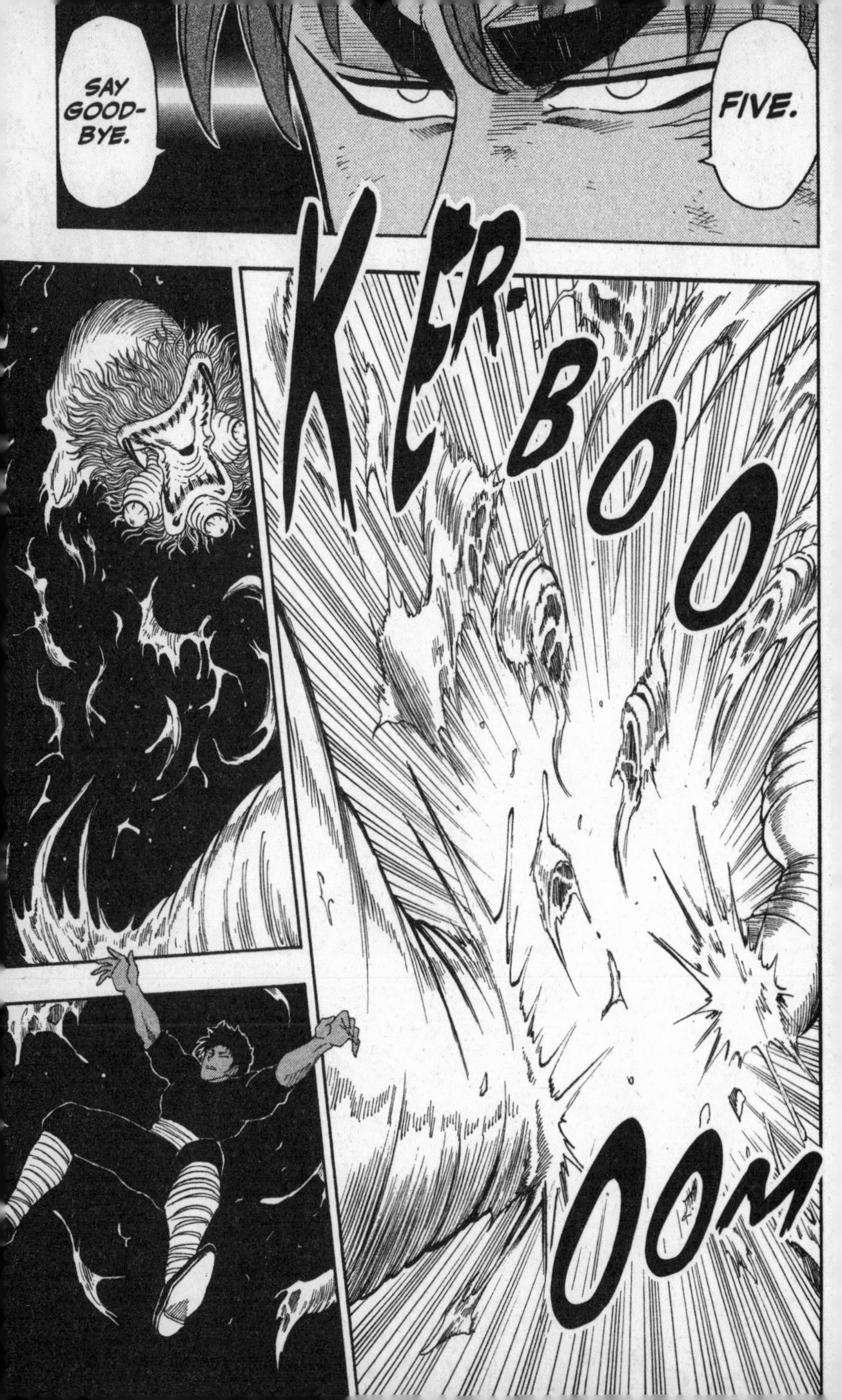
FIVE.
SAY GOOD-BYE.
KER-BOOOOOM

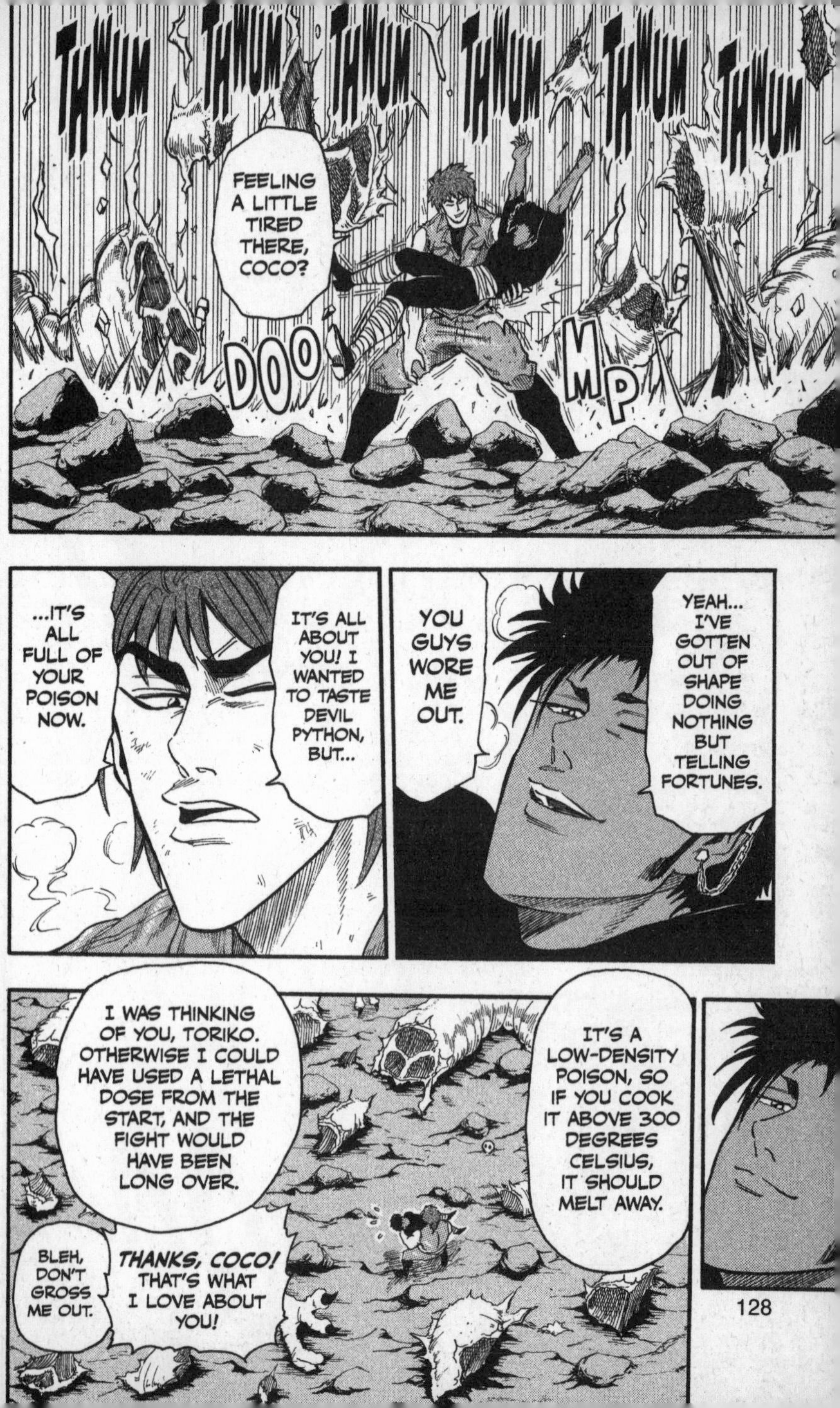
THNUM THNUM THNUM THNUM THNUM THNUM
FEELING A LITTLE TIRED THERE, COCO?
DOOMP
YEAH... I'VE GOTTEN OUT OF SHAPE DOING NOTHING BUT TELLING FORTUNES.
YOU GUYS WORE ME OUT.
IT'S ALL ABOUT YOU! I WANTED TO TASTE DEVIL PYTHON, BUT...
...IT'S ALL FULL OF YOUR POISON NOW.
IT'S A LOW-DENSITY POISON, SO IF YOU COOK IT ABOVE 300 DEGREES CELSIUS, IT SHOULD MELT AWAY.
I WAS THINKING OF YOU, TORIKO. OTHERWISE I COULD HAVE USED A LETHAL DOSE FROM THE START, AND THE FIGHT WOULD HAVE BEEN LONG OVER.
THANKS, COCO! THAT'S WHAT I LOVE ABOUT YOU!
BLEH, DON'T GROSS ME OUT.

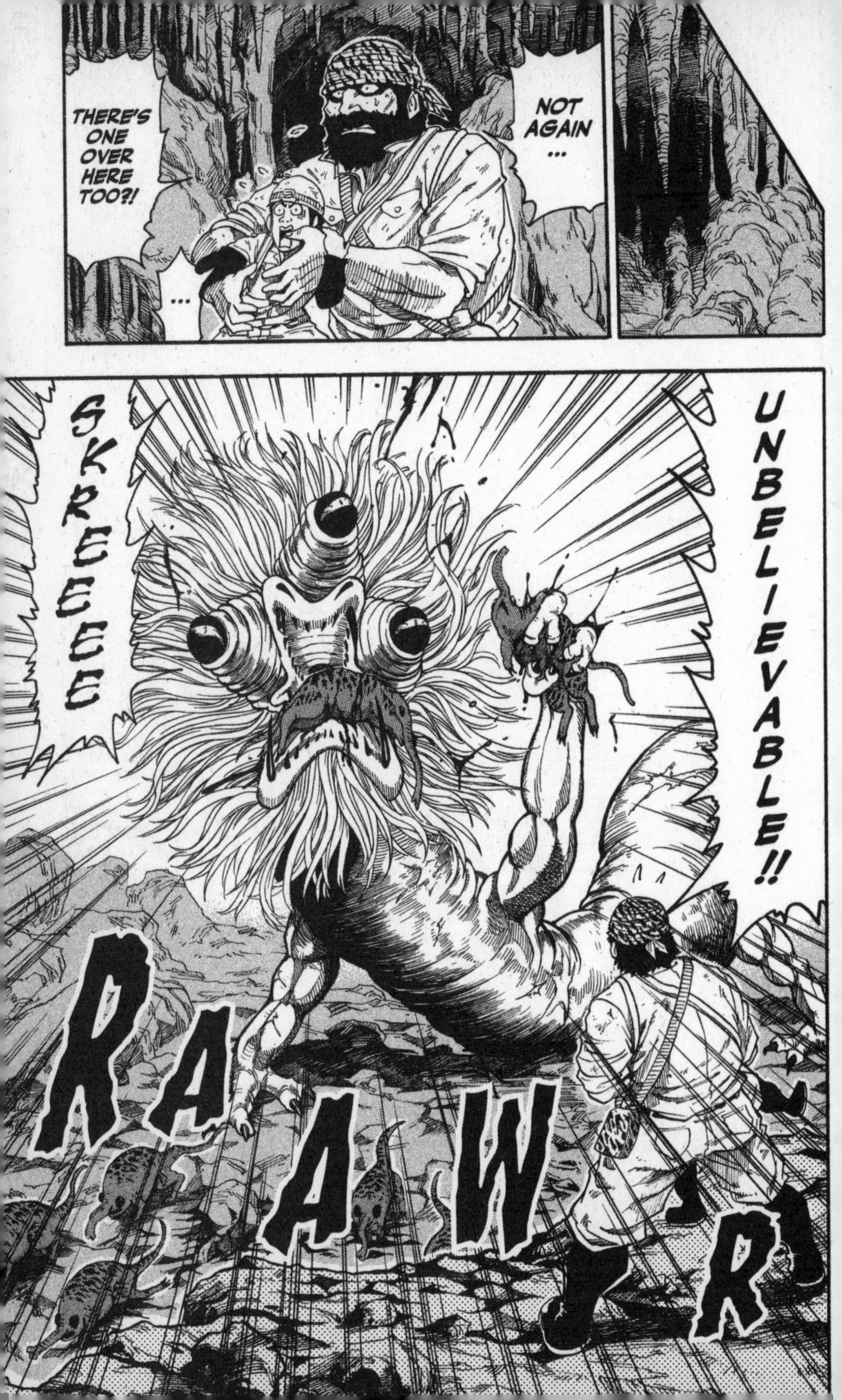

NOT AGAIN ...
THERE'S ONE OVER HERE TOO?!
...
UNBELIEVABLE!!
SKREEEEE
RAAWR

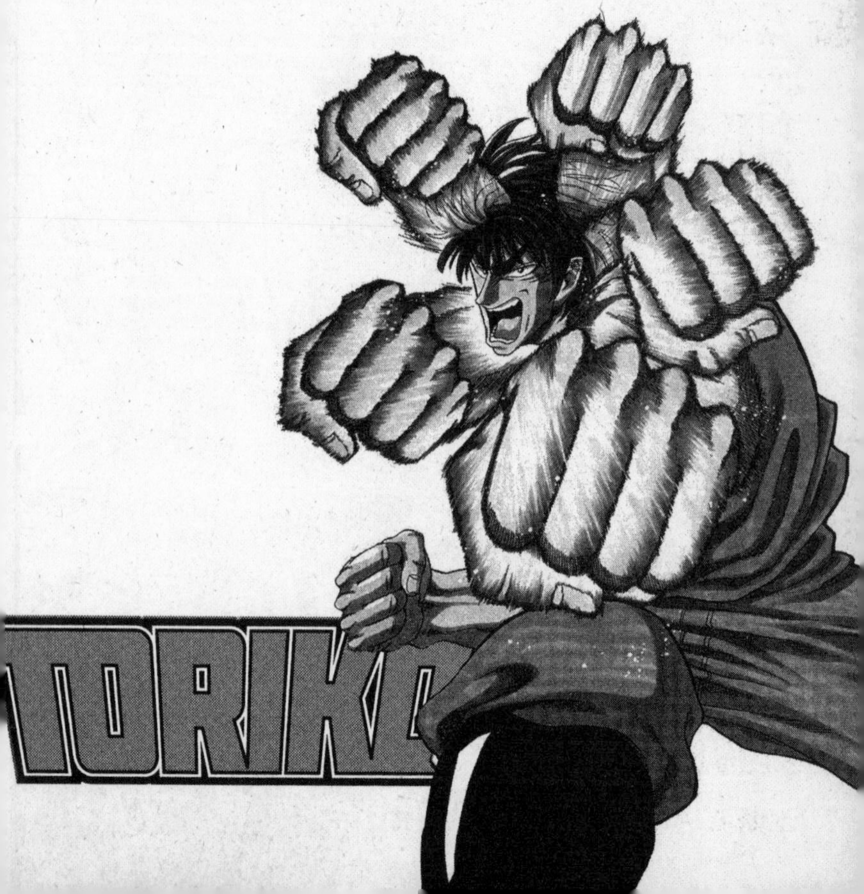
TORIKO

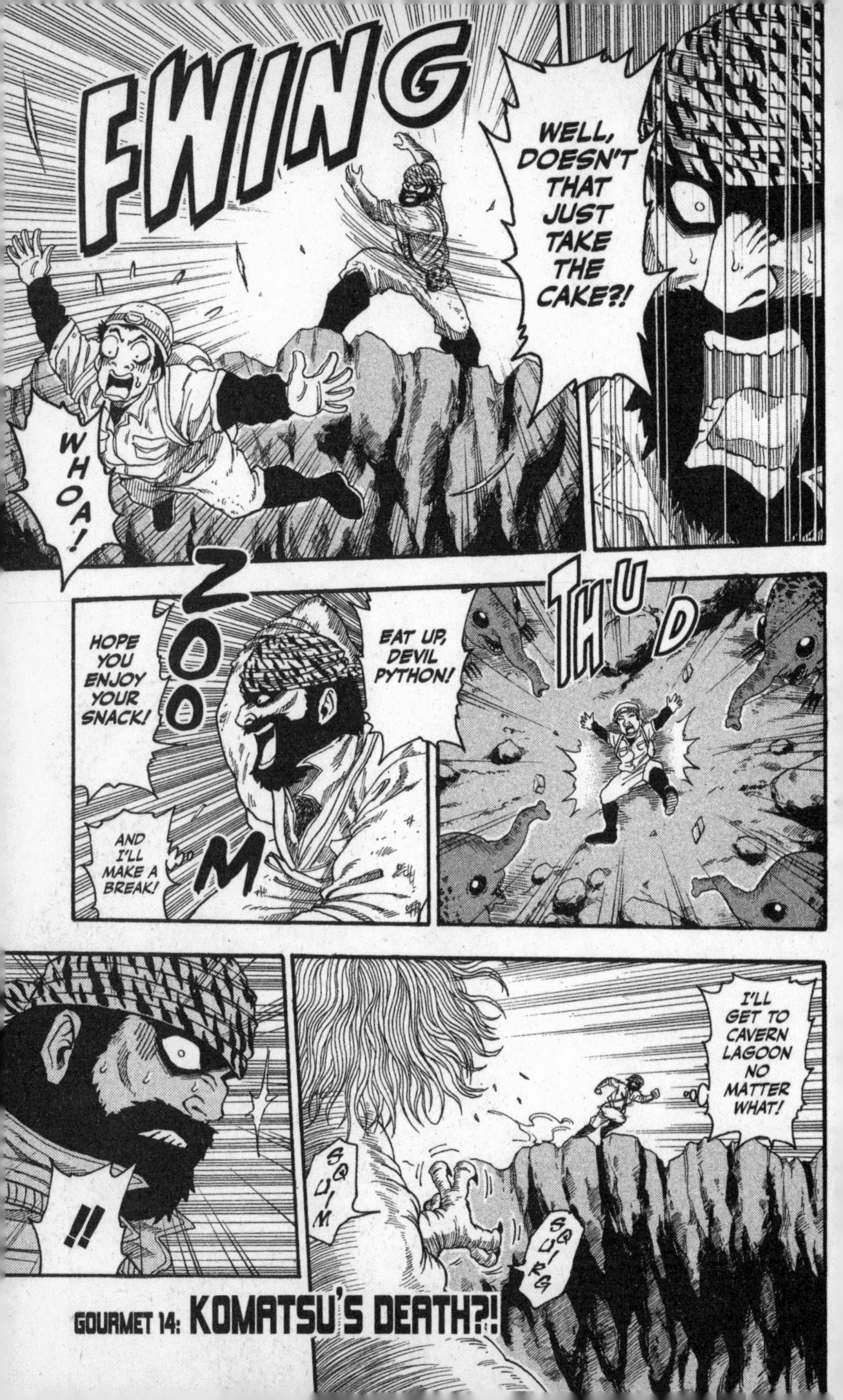
WELL, DOESN'T THAT JUST TAKE THE CAKE?!
FWING
WHOA!
THUD
EAT UP, DEVIL PYTHON!
HOPE YOU ENJOY YOUR SNACK!
ZOOOM
AND I'LL MAKE A BREAK!
I'LL GET TO CAVERN LAGOON NO MATTER WHAT!
SQUIRG
SQUIM
!!

GOURMET 14: KOMATSU'S DEATH?!

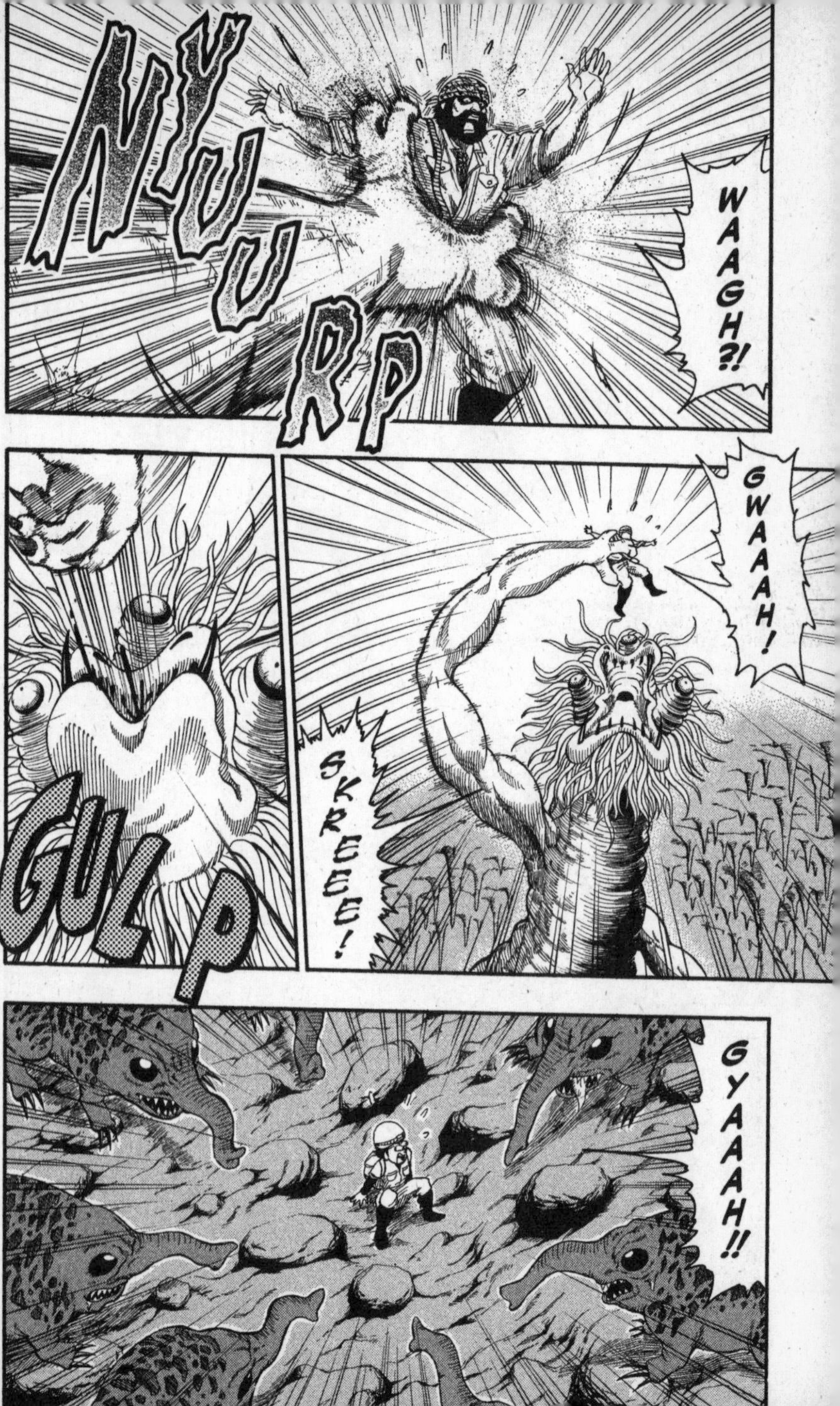
WAAAGH?!
NYUURP
GWAAAAH!
SKREEEE!
GULP
GYAAAAH!!

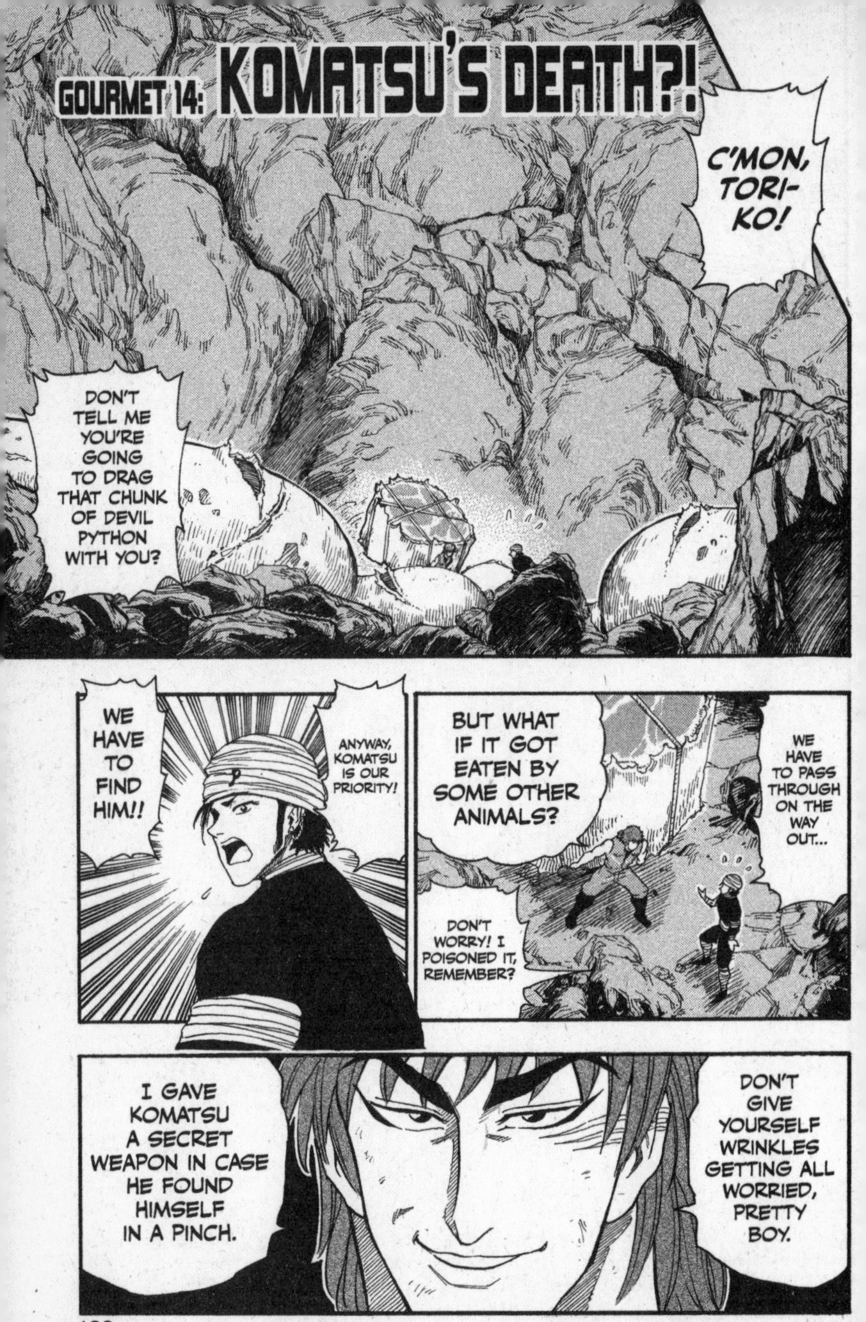
GOURMET 14: KOMATSU'S DEATH?!
C'MON, TORI-KO!
DON'T TELL ME YOU'RE GOING TO DRAG THAT CHUNK OF DEVIL PYTHON WITH YOU?
WE HAVE TO PASS THROUGH ON THE WAY OUT...
BUT WHAT IF IT GOT EATEN BY SOME OTHER ANIMALS?
DON'T WORRY! I POISONED IT, REMEMBER?
ANYWAY, KOMATSU IS OUR PRIORITY!
WE HAVE TO FIND HIM!!
DON'T GIVE YOURSELF WRINKLES GETTING ALL WORRIED, PRETTY BOY.
I GAVE KOMATSU A SECRET WEAPON IN CASE HE FOUND HIMSELF IN A PINCH.

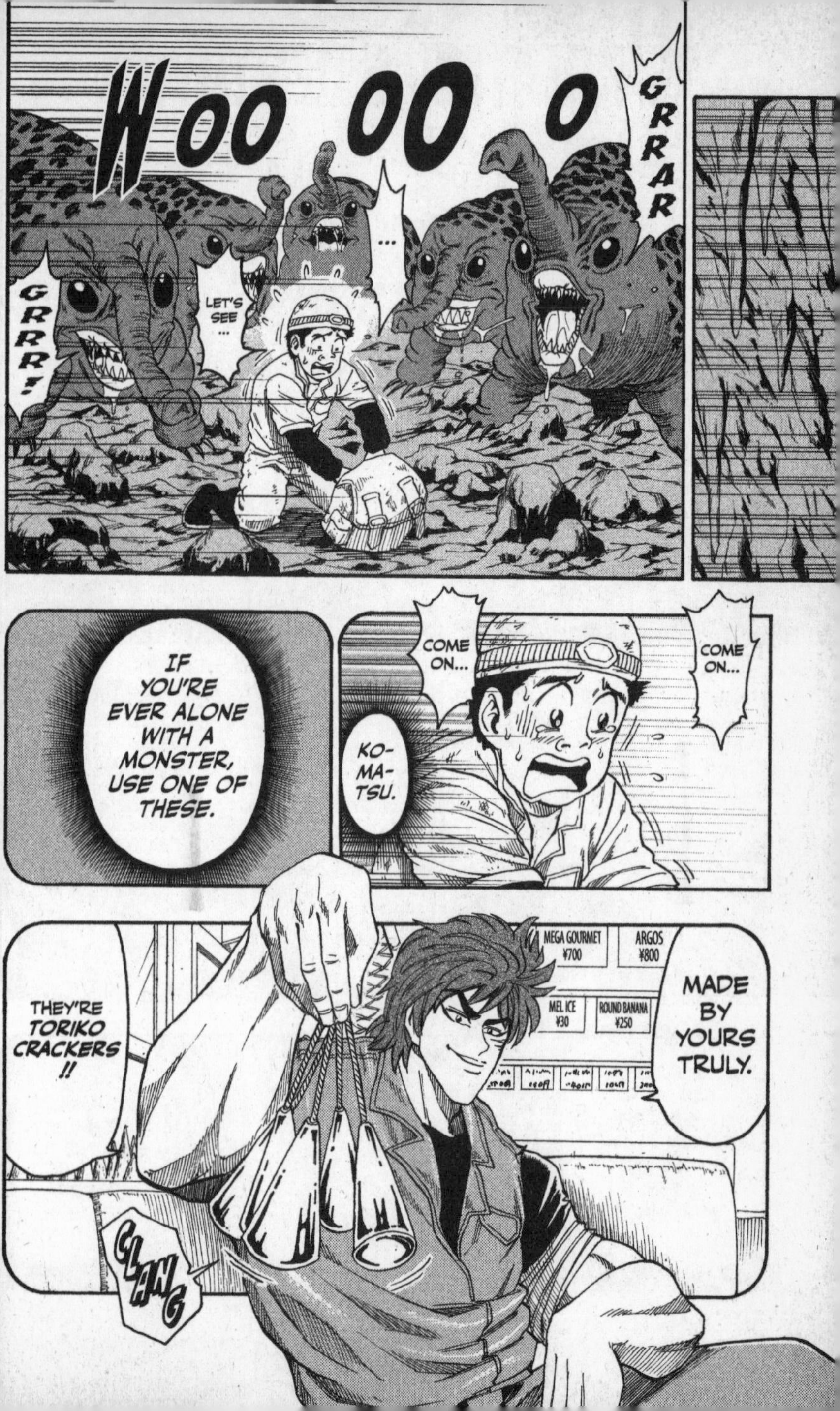
GRRAR
WOO OO O
...
LET'S SEE ...
GRRR!
COME ON...
COME ON...
KO-MA-TSU.
IF YOU'RE EVER ALONE WITH A MONSTER, USE ONE OF THESE.
MADE BY YOURS TRULY.
ARGOS ¥800
MEGA GOURMET ¥700
ROUND BANANA ¥250
MEL ICE ¥30
THEY'RE TORIKO CRACKERS !!
CLANG

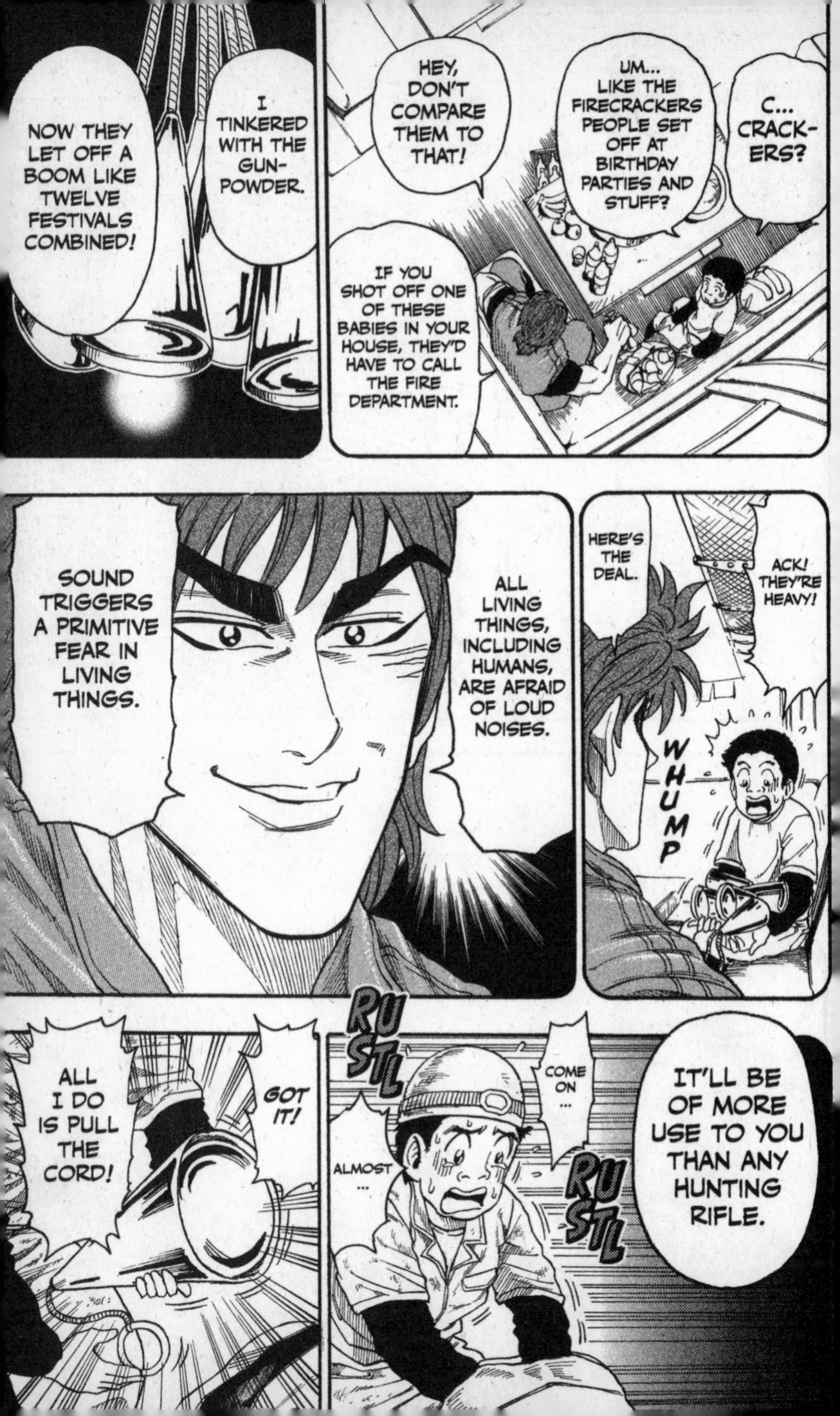
C... CRACKERS?
UM... LIKE THE FIRECRACKERS PEOPLE SET OFF AT BIRTHDAY PARTIES AND STUFF?
HEY, DON'T COMPARE THEM TO THAT!
IF YOU SHOT OFF ONE OF THESE BABIES IN YOUR HOUSE, THEY'D HAVE TO CALL THE FIRE DEPARTMENT.
I TINKERED WITH THE GUNPOWDER.
NOW THEY LET OFF A BOOM LIKE TWELVE FESTIVALS COMBINED!
ACK! THEY'RE HEAVY!
HERE'S THE DEAL.
WHUMP
ALL LIVING THINGS, INCLUDING HUMANS, ARE AFRAID OF LOUD NOISES.
SOUND TRIGGERS A PRIMITIVE FEAR IN LIVING THINGS.
IT'LL BE OF MORE USE TO YOU THAN ANY HUNTING RIFLE.
RUSTL
COME ON ...
RUSTL
ALMOST ...
GOT IT!
ALL I DO IS PULL THE CORD!

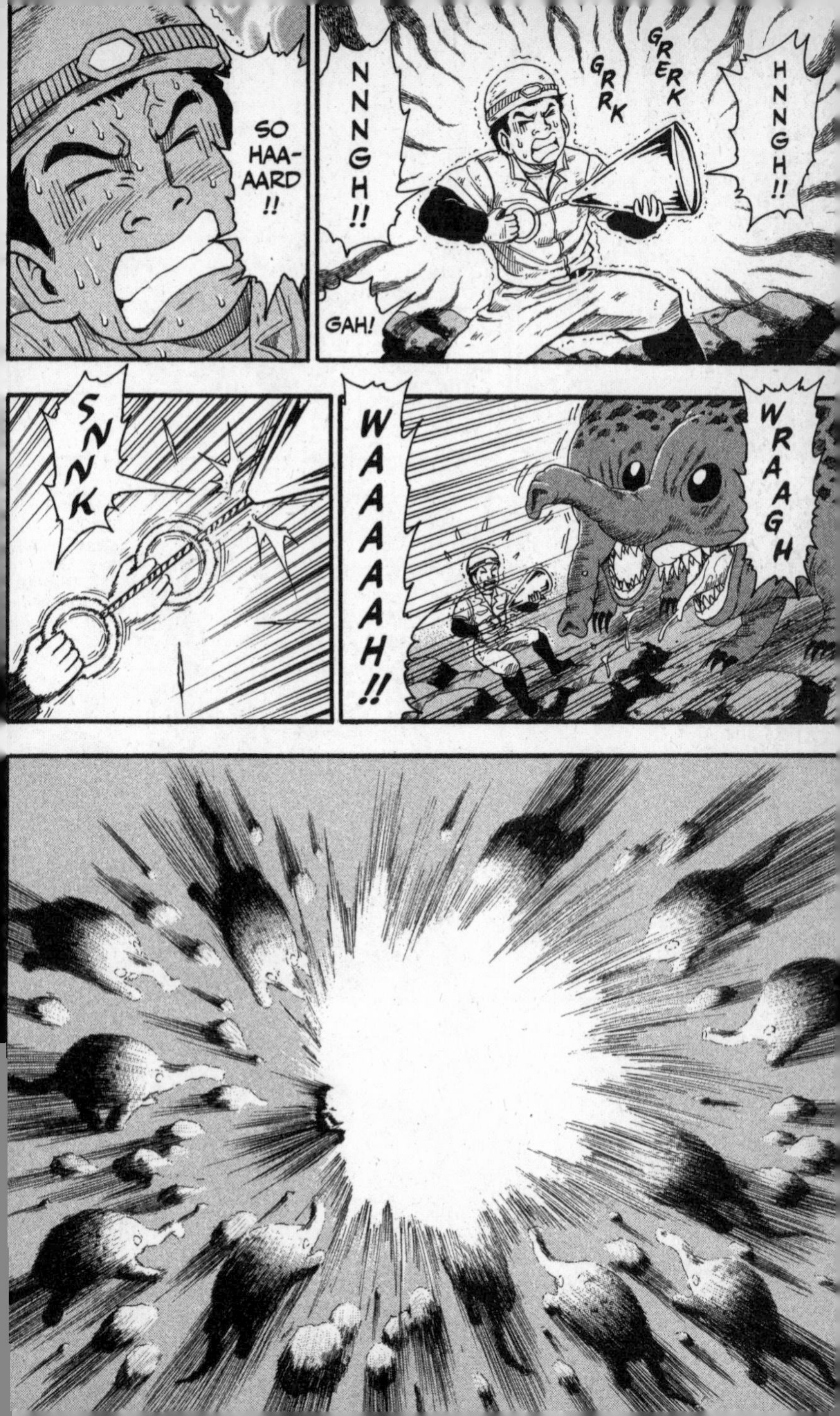
HNNGH!!
GRERK
GRRK
NNNGH!!
GAH!
SO HAA-AARD!!
WRAAGH
WAAAAAAH!!
SNNK

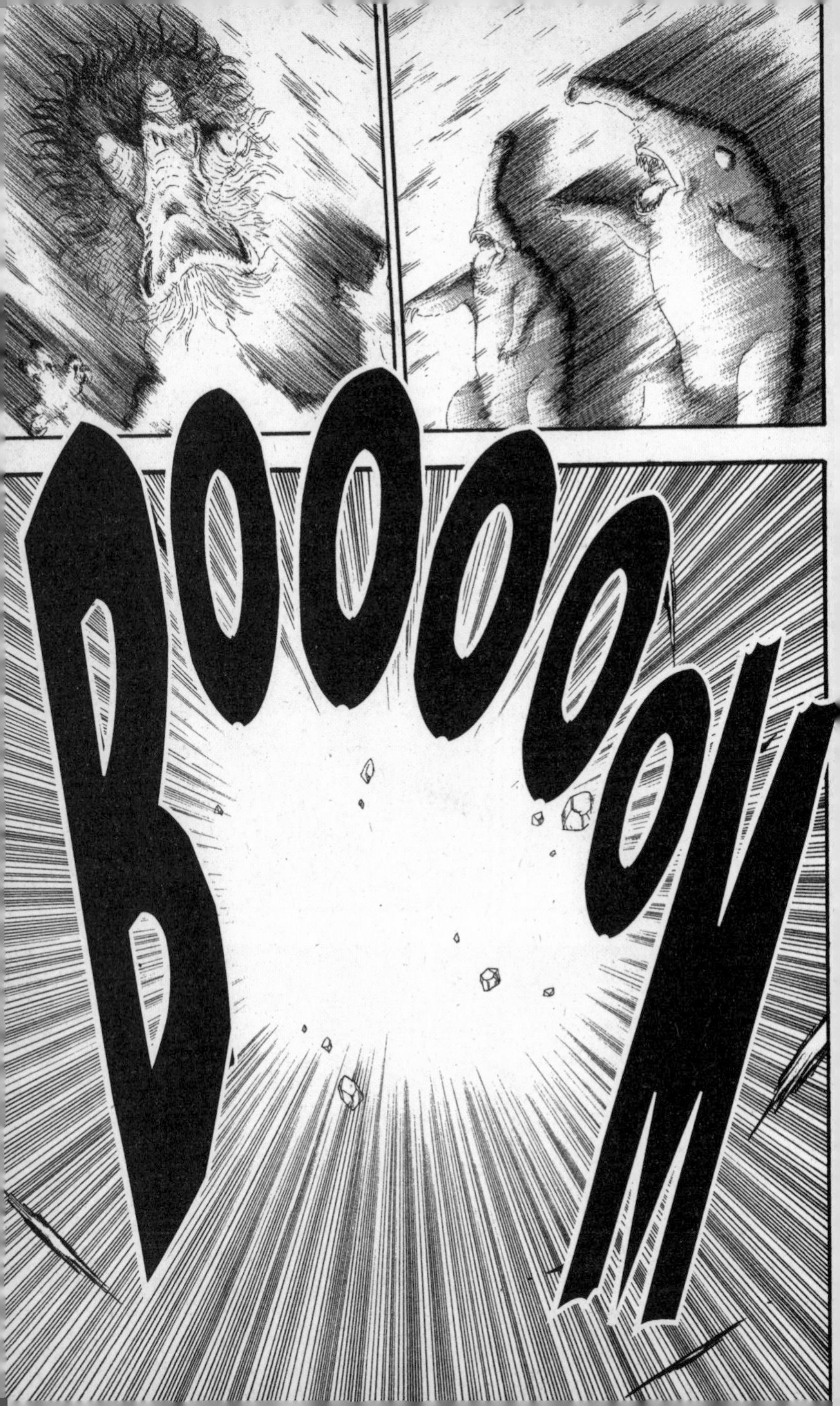
BOOOOOM

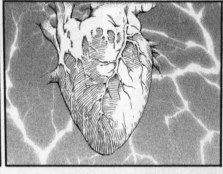

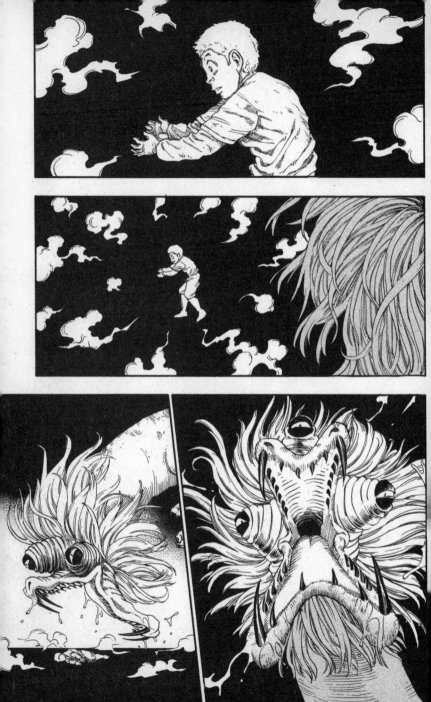

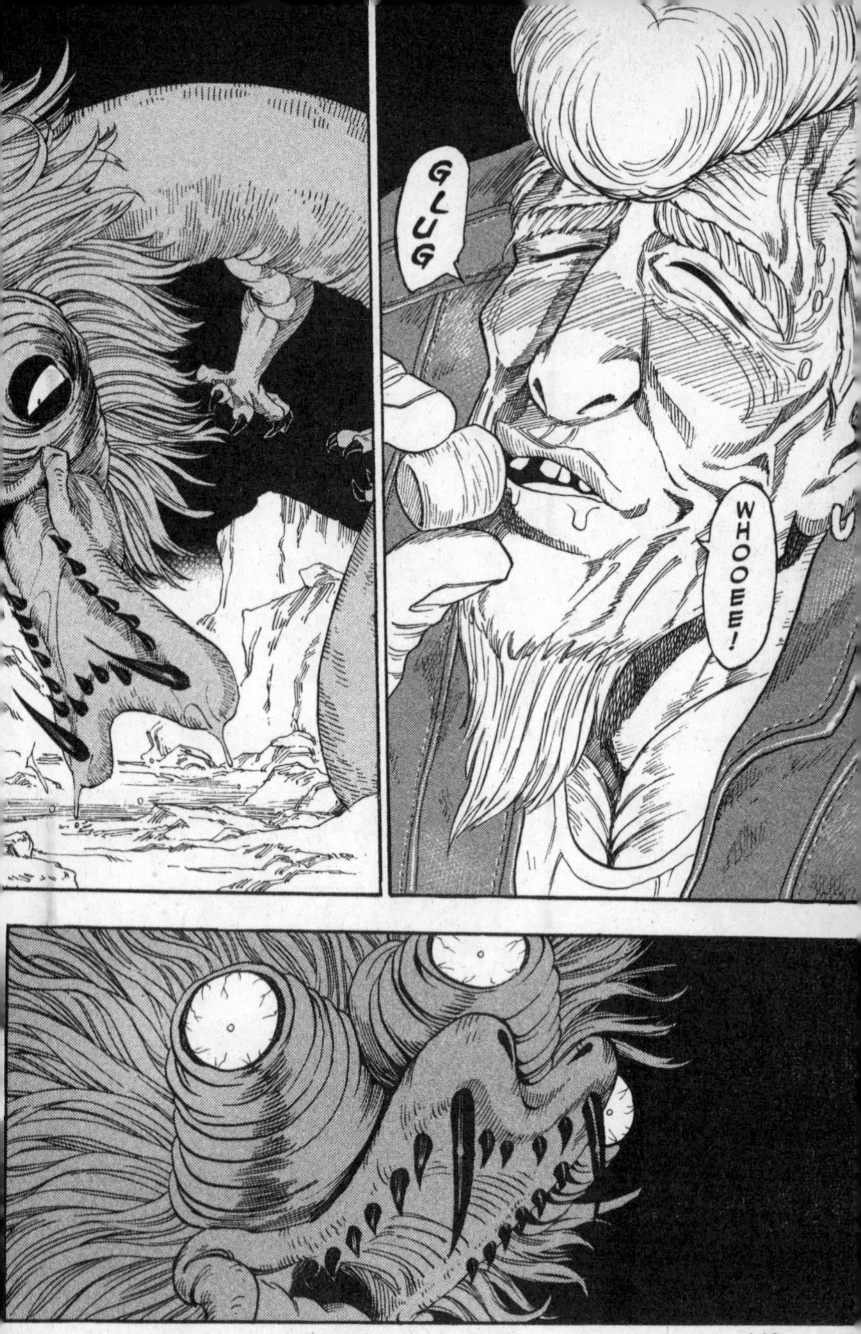
GLUG
WHOOEE!

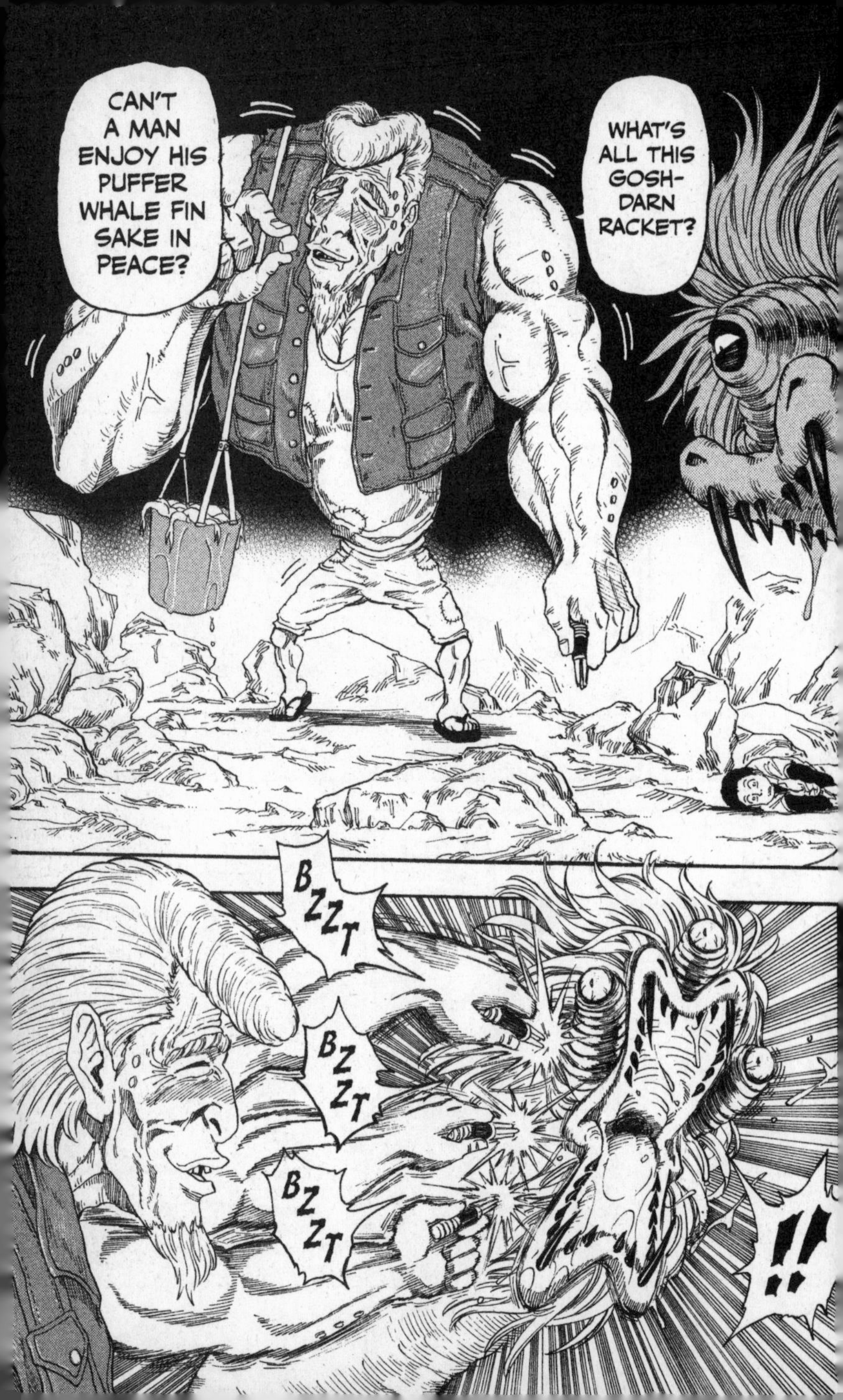
WHAT'S ALL THIS GOSH-DARN RACKET?
CAN'T A MAN ENJOY HIS PUFFER WHALE FIN SAKE IN PEACE?
BZZT
BZZT
BZZT
!!

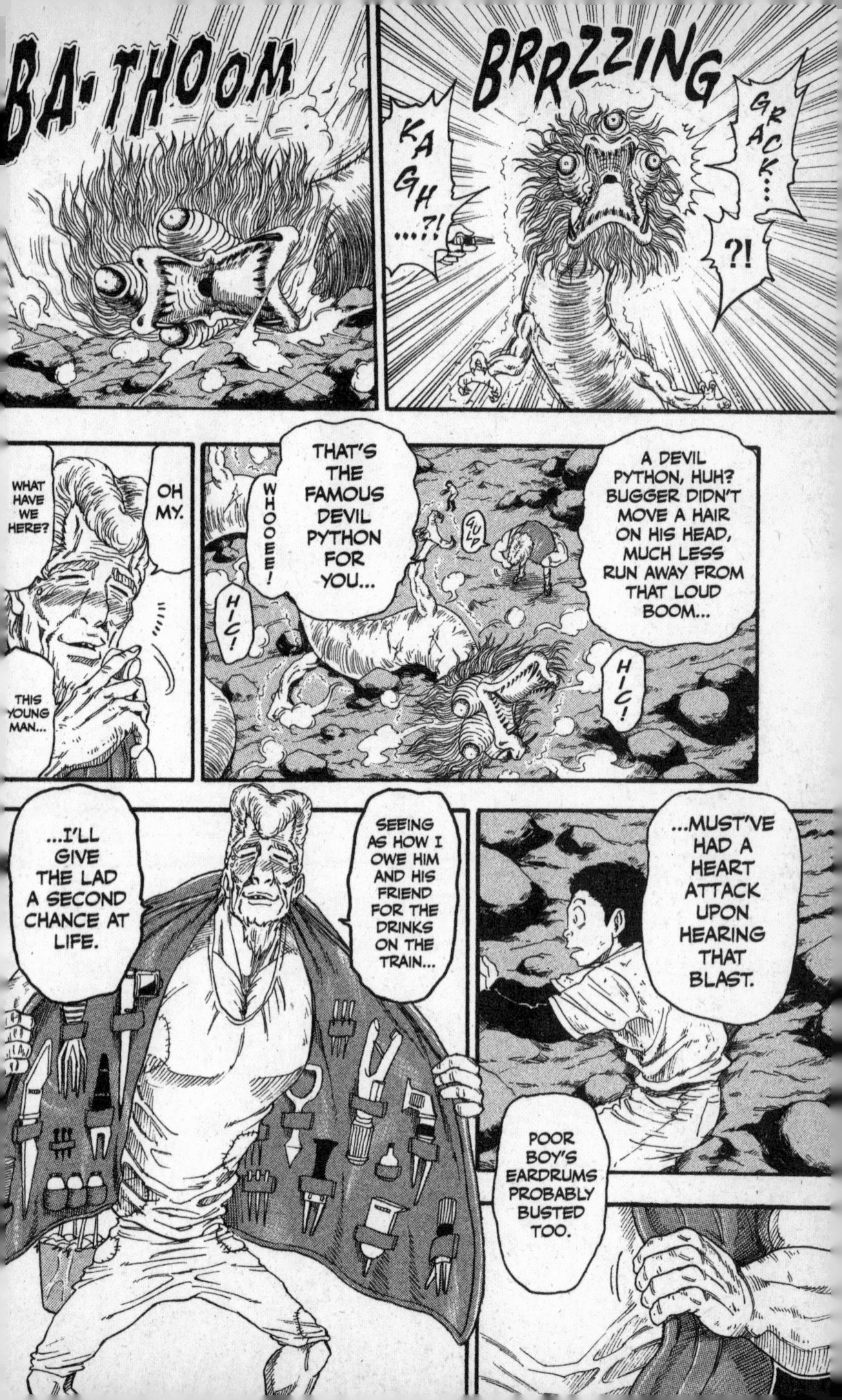
BRRZZING
GRACK...
?!
KAGH ...?!
BA-THOOM
A DEVIL PYTHON, HUH? BUGGER DIDN'T MOVE A HAIR ON HIS HEAD, MUCH LESS RUN AWAY FROM THAT LOUD BOOM...
HIC!
GULP
THAT'S THE FAMOUS DEVIL PYTHON FOR YOU...
WHOOEEE!
HIC!
OH MY.
WHAT HAVE WE HERE?
THIS YOUNG MAN...
...MUST'VE HAD A HEART ATTACK UPON HEARING THAT BLAST.
POOR BOY'S EARDRUMS PROBABLY BUSTED TOO.
SEEING AS HOW I OWE HIM AND HIS FRIEND FOR THE DRINKS ON THE TRAIN...
...I'LL GIVE THE LAD A SECOND CHANCE AT LIFE.

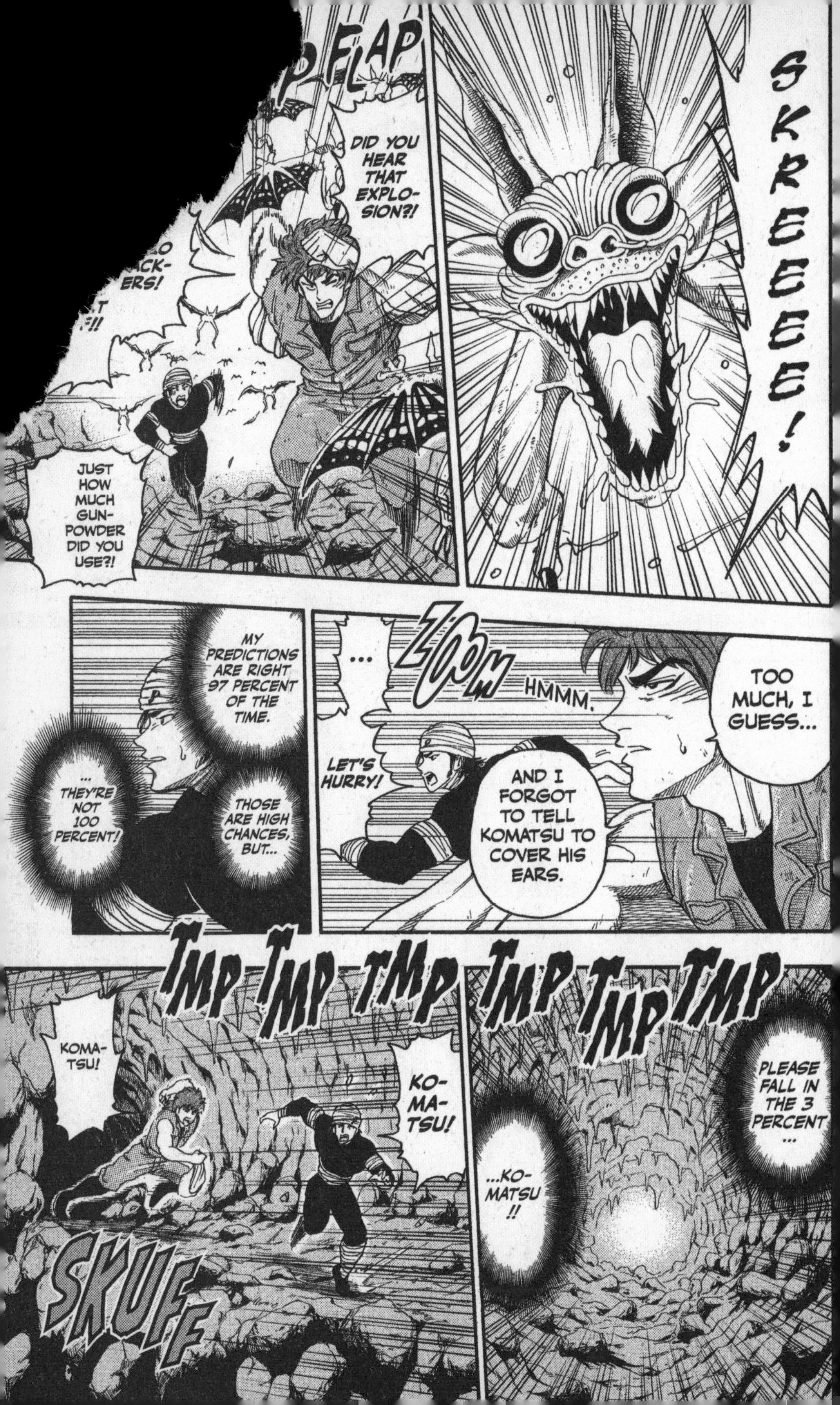
SKREEEE!
FLAP
DID YOU HEAR THAT EXPLOSION?!
JUST HOW MUCH GUNPOWDER DID YOU USE?!
TOO MUCH, I GUESS...
ZOOM
HMMM.
AND I FORGOT TO TELL KOMATSU TO COVER HIS EARS.
...
LET'S HURRY!
MY PREDICTIONS ARE RIGHT 97 PERCENT OF THE TIME.
THOSE ARE HIGH CHANCES, BUT...
...THEY'RE NOT 100 PERCENT!
TMP TMP TMP TMP TMP TMP
PLEASE FALL IN THE 3 PERCENT...
...KOMATSU!!
KOMATSU!
KOMATSU!
SKUFF

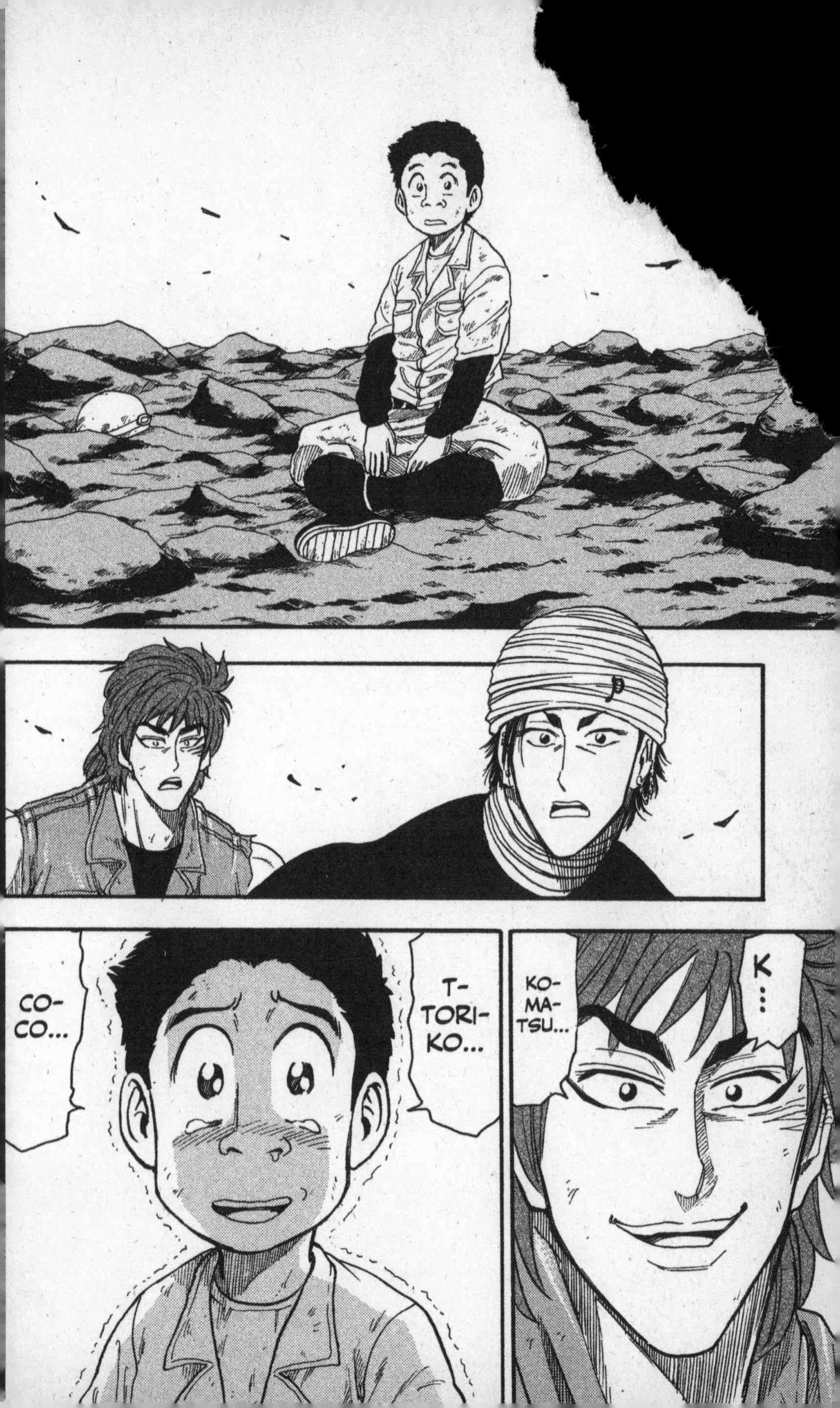
K...
KO-MA-TSU...
T-TORI-KO...
CO-CO...

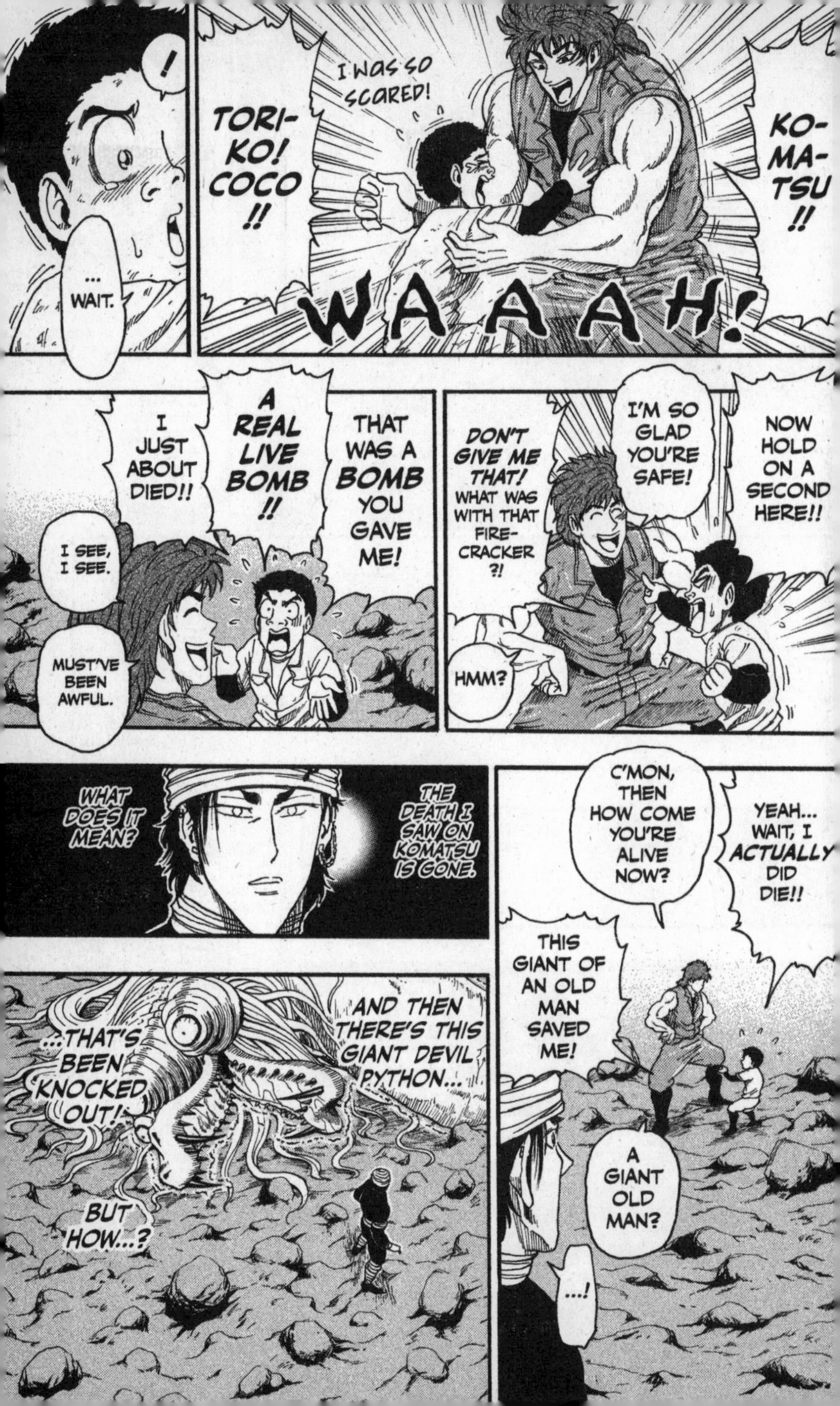
KO-MA-TSU!!
I WAS SO SCARED!
TORI-KO! COCO!!
WAAAH!
!
... WAIT.
NOW HOLD ON A SECOND HERE!!
I'M SO GLAD YOU'RE SAFE!
DON'T GIVE ME THAT! WHAT WAS WITH THAT FIRE-CRACKER?!
HMM?
THAT WAS A BOMB YOU GAVE ME!
A REAL LIVE BOMB!!
I JUST ABOUT DIED!!
I SEE, I SEE.
MUST'VE BEEN AWFUL.
YEAH... WAIT, I ACTUALLY DID DIE!!
C'MON, THEN HOW COME YOU'RE ALIVE NOW?
THIS GIANT OF AN OLD MAN SAVED ME!
A GIANT OLD MAN?
...!
THE DEATH I SAW ON KOMATSU IS GONE.
WHAT DOES IT MEAN?
AND THEN THERE'S THIS GIANT DEVIL PYTHON...
...THAT'S BEEN KNOCKED OUT!
BUT HOW...?

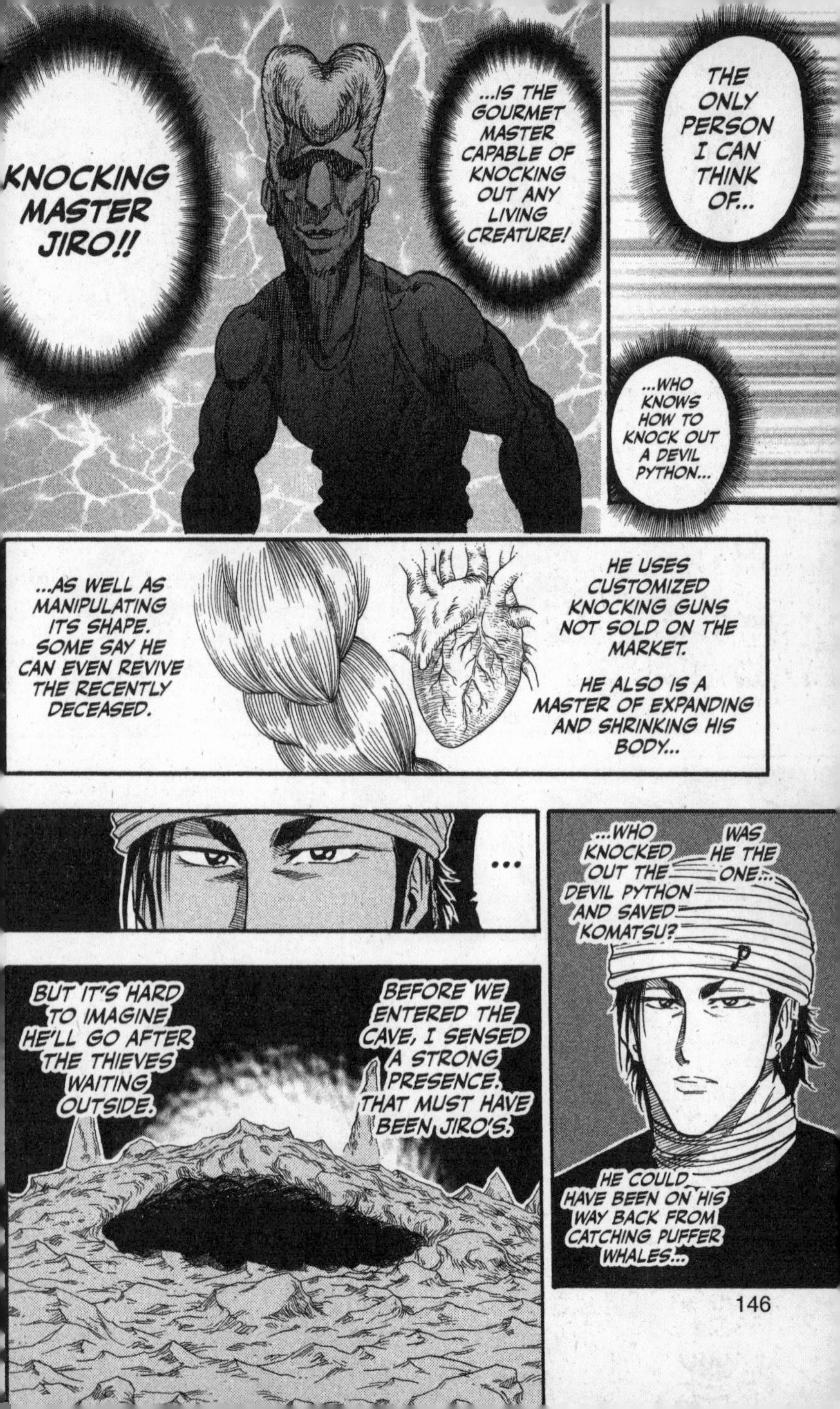
THE ONLY PERSON I CAN THINK OF...
...WHO KNOWS HOW TO KNOCK OUT A DEVIL PYTHON...
...IS THE GOURMET MASTER CAPABLE OF KNOCKING OUT ANY LIVING CREATURE!
KNOCKING MASTER JIRO!!
HE USES CUSTOMIZED KNOCKING GUNS NOT SOLD ON THE MARKET.
HE ALSO IS A MASTER OF EXPANDING AND SHRINKING HIS BODY...
...AS WELL AS MANIPULATING ITS SHAPE. SOME SAY HE CAN EVEN REVIVE THE RECENTLY DECEASED.
WAS HE THE ONE...
...WHO KNOCKED OUT THE DEVIL PYTHON AND SAVED KOMATSU?
HE COULD HAVE BEEN ON HIS WAY BACK FROM CATCHING PUFFER WHALES...
...
BEFORE WE ENTERED THE CAVE, I SENSED A STRONG PRESENCE. THAT MUST HAVE BEEN JIRO'S.
BUT IT'S HARD TO IMAGINE HE'LL GO AFTER THE THIEVES WAITING OUTSIDE.

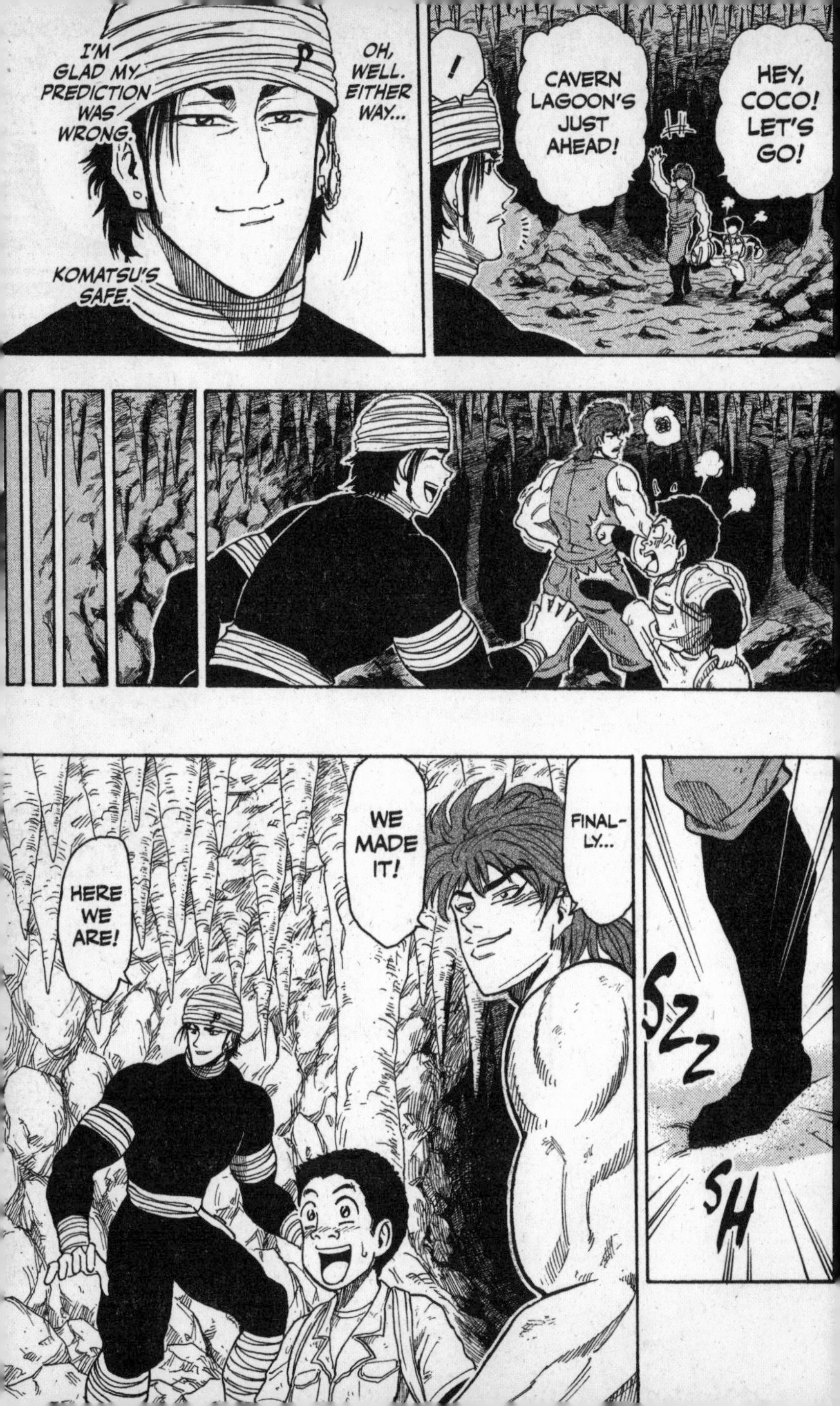
HEY, COCO! LET'S GO!
CAVERN LAGOON'S JUST AHEAD!
!
OH, WELL. EITHER WAY...
I'M GLAD MY PREDICTION WAS WRONG.
KOMATSU'S SAFE.
SZZ
SH
FINAL-LY...
WE MADE IT!
HERE WE ARE!

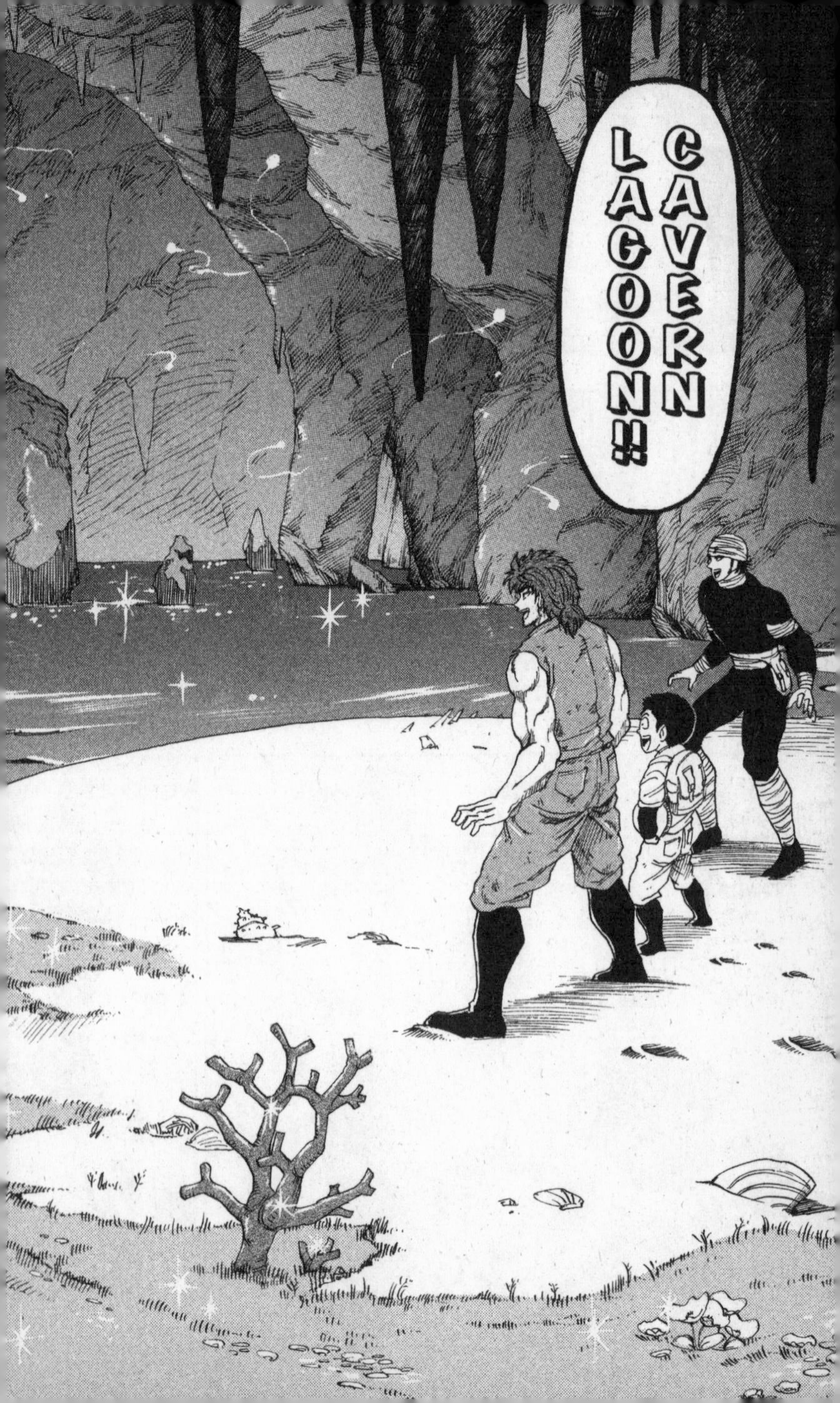
CAVERN LAGOON!!

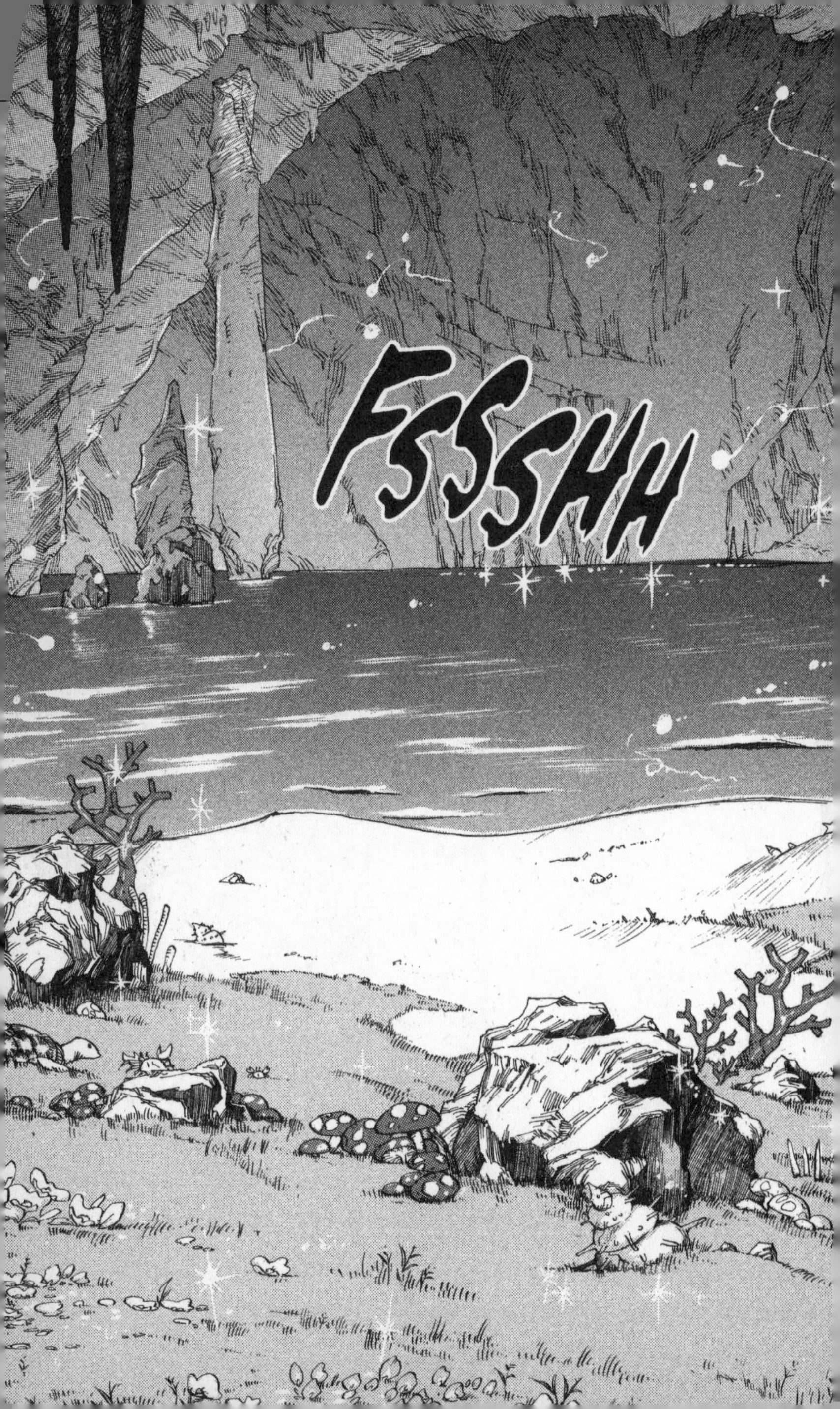
FSSSHH

JIRO

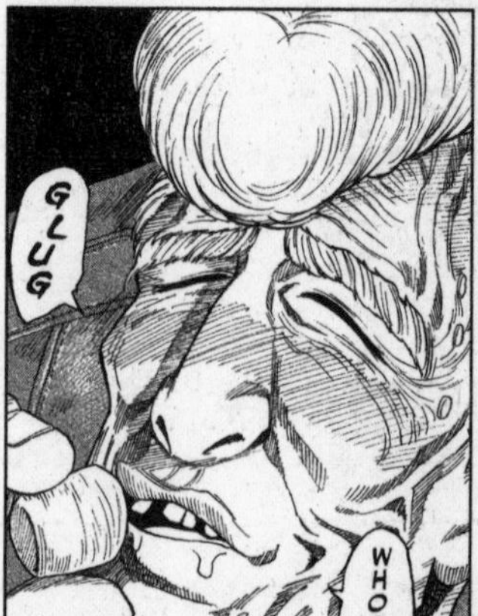

HERE WE ARE!

CAVERN LAGOON!

NOW THAT'S WHAT I CALL A SIGHT FOR SORE EYES.

FSSHH

GOURMET 15: PUFFER WHALE!!

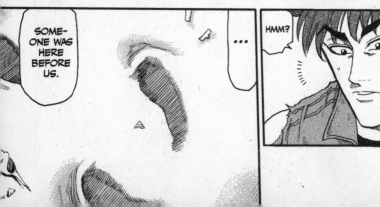

SOMEONE WAS HERE BEFORE US.

...

HMM?

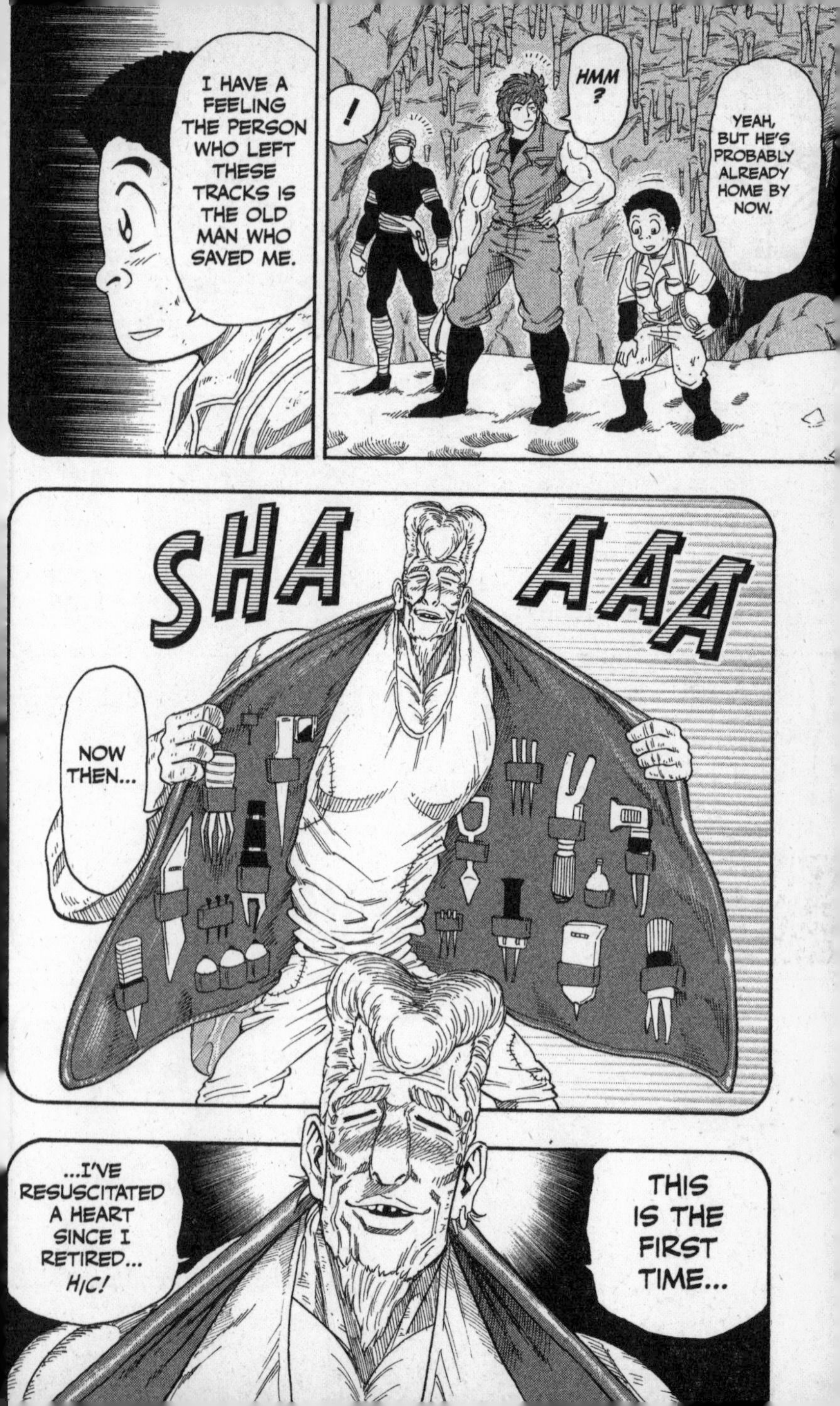

I HAVE A FEELING THE PERSON WHO LEFT THESE TRACKS IS THE OLD MAN WHO SAVED ME.
!
HMM?
YEAH, BUT HE'S PROBABLY ALREADY HOME BY NOW.
SHA AAA
NOW THEN...
THIS IS THE FIRST TIME...
...I'VE RESUSCITATED A HEART SINCE I RETIRED... HIC!

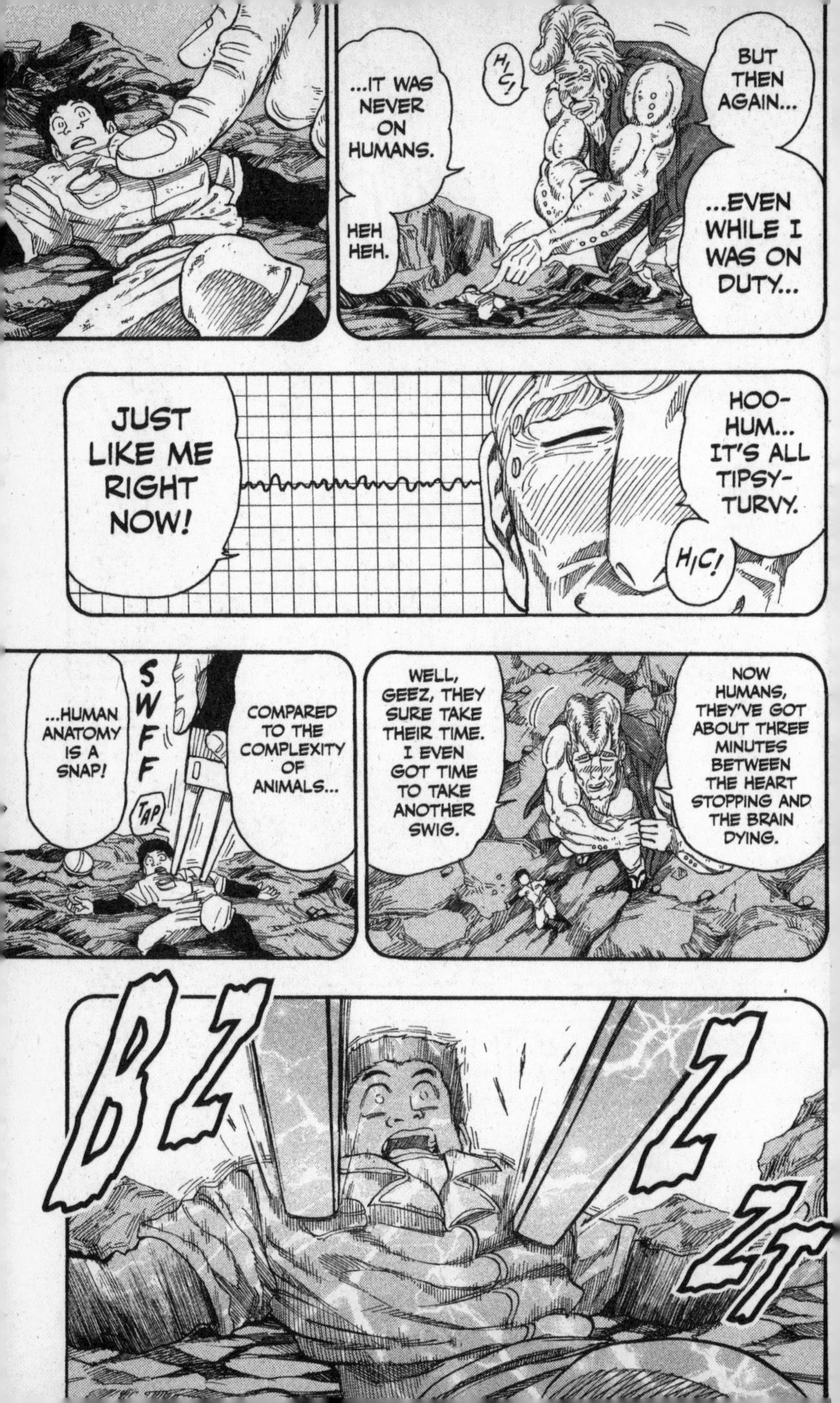
BUT THEN AGAIN...
...EVEN WHILE I WAS ON DUTY...
HIC!
...IT WAS NEVER ON HUMANS.
HEH HEH.
HOO-HUM... IT'S ALL TIPSY-TURVY.
HIC!
JUST LIKE ME RIGHT NOW!
NOW HUMANS, THEY'VE GOT ABOUT THREE MINUTES BETWEEN THE HEART STOPPING AND THE BRAIN DYING.
WELL, GEEZ, THEY SURE TAKE THEIR TIME. I EVEN GOT TIME TO TAKE ANOTHER SWIG.
COMPARED TO THE COMPLEXITY OF ANIMALS...
SWFF
TAP
...HUMAN ANATOMY IS A SNAP!
BZZZT

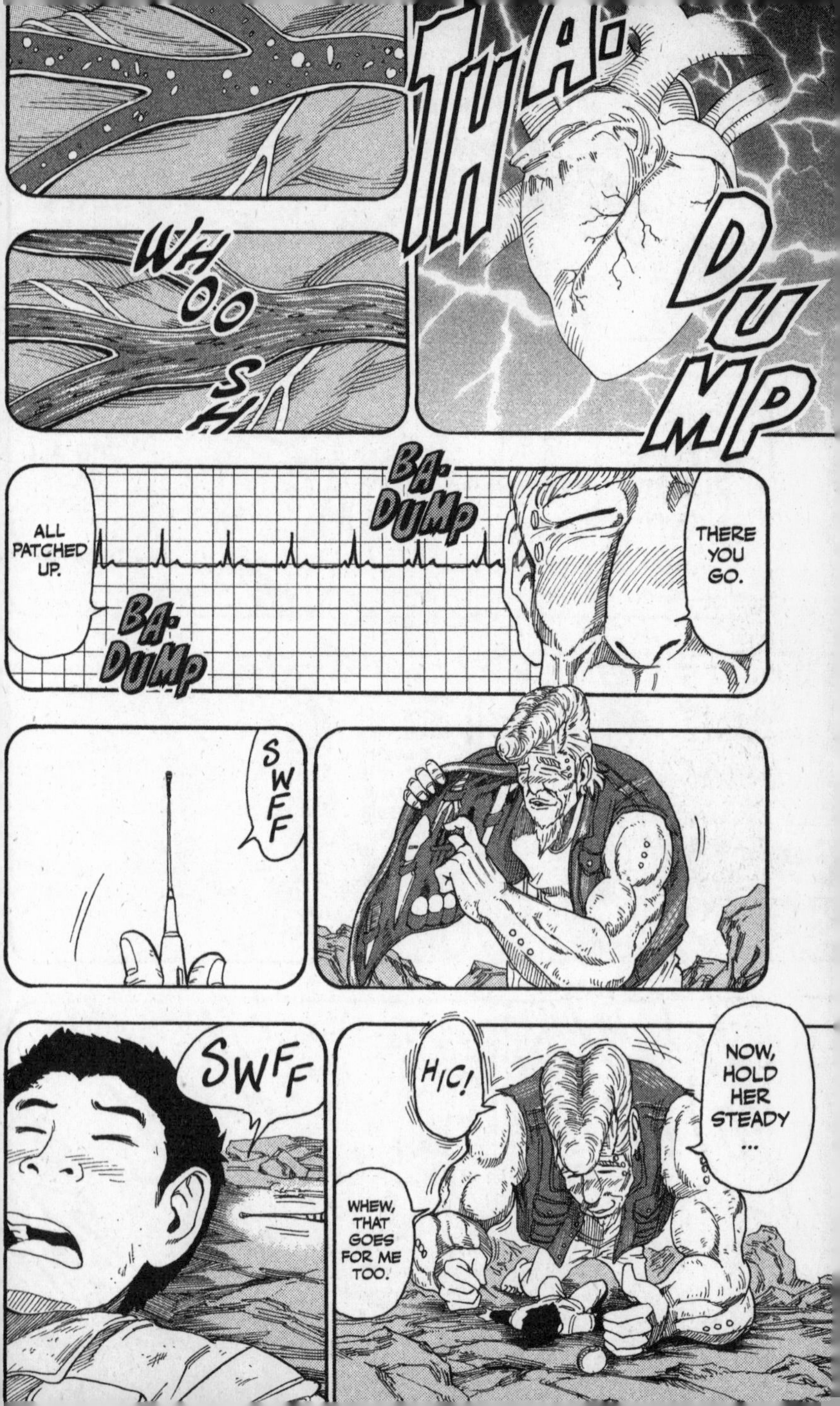
THA-DUMP
WHOOSH
THERE YOU GO.
BA-DUMP
ALL PATCHED UP.
BA-DUMP
SWFF
NOW, HOLD HER STEADY ...
HIC!
WHEW, THAT GOES FOR ME TOO.
SWFF

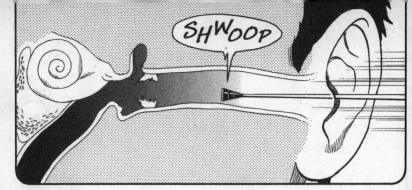

SHWOOP
SNNK
CLICK
BLOOP
PWOK
YOU HAVE THE DEEP SEA DOCTOR LOBSTER TO THANK FOR YOUR NEW EARDRUM, SONNY. I CREATED THAT FILM I INJECTED FROM THE SPECIAL POLYSACCHARIDES FOUND IN ITS HUSK.
AND THIS CREATURE'S TISSUES ADAPT BETTER TO OTHER LIVING THINGS THAN ANYTHING ELSE. YOU'LL BE ABLE TO HEAR, OR EVEN SWIM, RIGHT AWAY! HEH HEH.

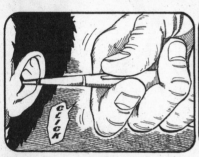

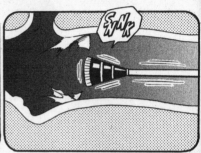

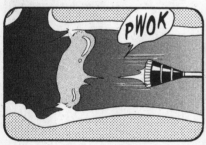

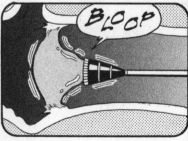

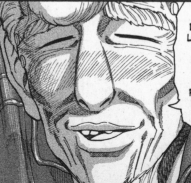

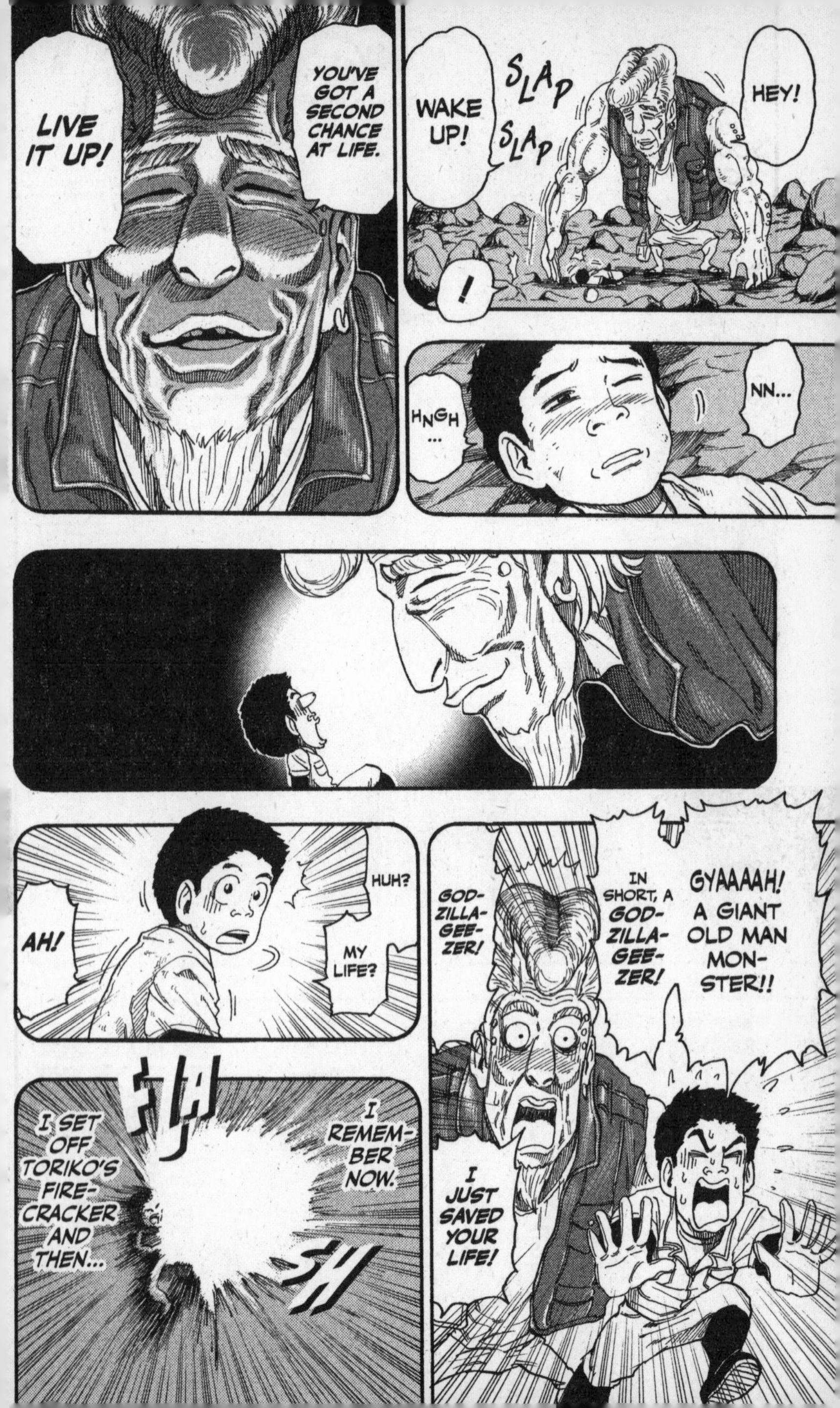
HEY!
SLAP
SLAP
WAKE UP!
!
NN...
HNGH...
YOU'VE GOT A SECOND CHANCE AT LIFE.
LIVE IT UP!
GYAAAAH! A GIANT OLD MAN MONSTER!!
IN SHORT, A GODZILLA-GEEZER!
GODZILLA-GEEZER!
I JUST SAVED YOUR LIFE!
HUH?
MY LIFE?
AH!
I REMEMBER NOW.
I SET OFF TORIKO'S FIRECRACKER AND THEN...
SH

CLUNK
GULP
WELL, TAKE CARE.
AND SAY "HI" TO YOUR PAL FOR ME TOO.
HIC!
AH ...
UM ...
--!!
OH, ONE MORE THING.
I SENSE SOME-THING BAD HEADED TOWARD CAVERN LAGOON.
AFTER YOU GET YOUR PUFFER WHALES, YOU'D BEST SKE-DADDLE ON HOME.
SEE YA!
HIC!
PUFFER...
...WHALES...

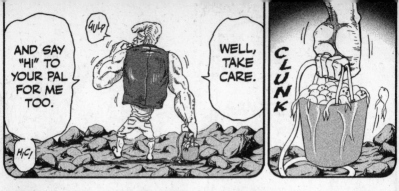

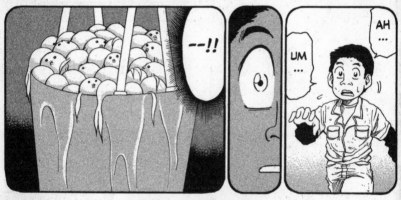

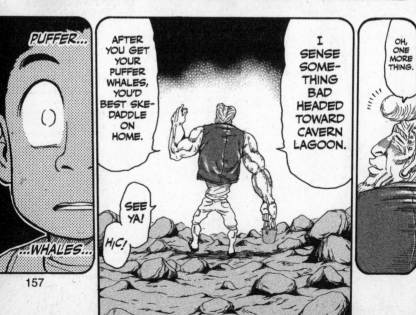

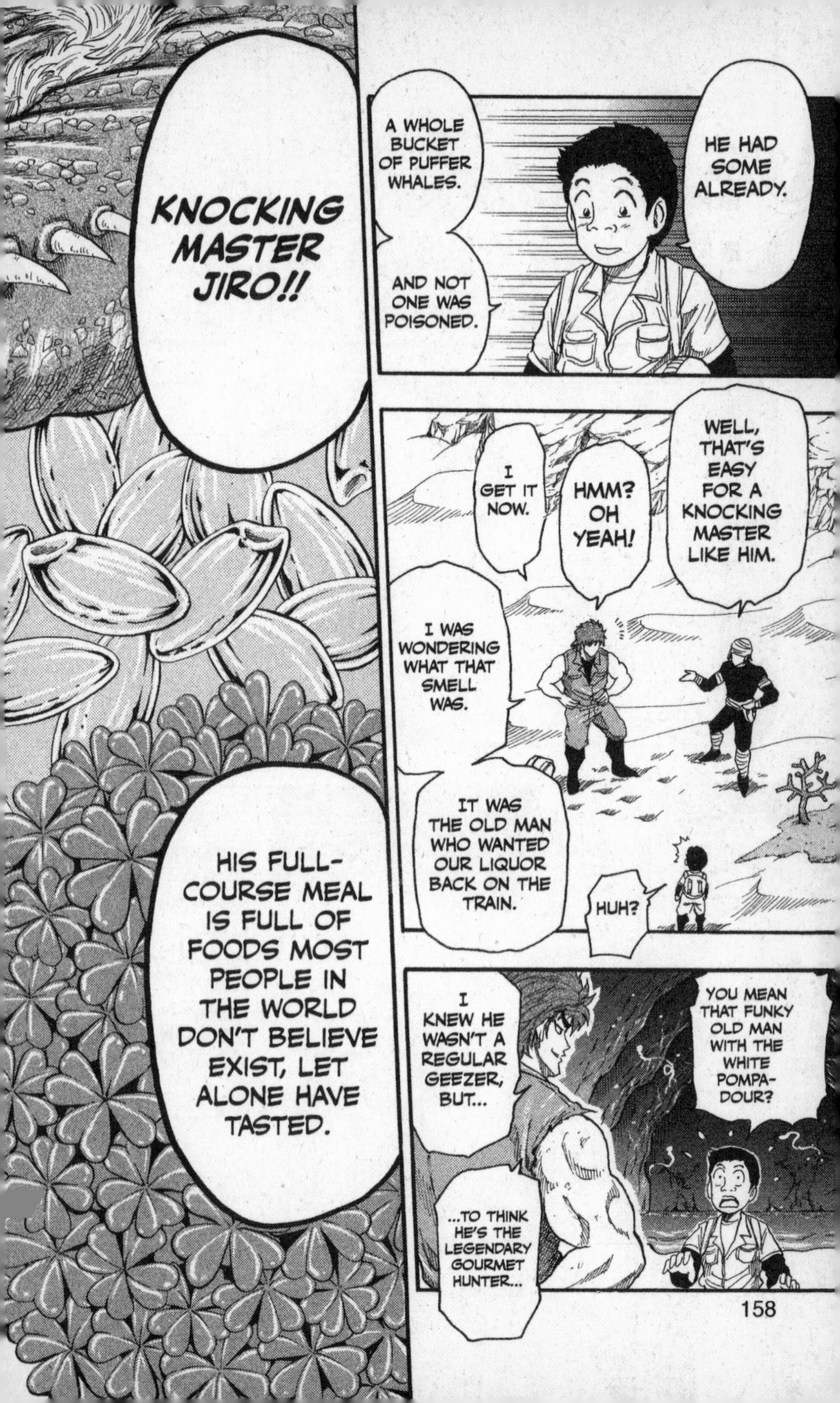
HE HAD SOME ALREADY.
A WHOLE BUCKET OF PUFFER WHALES.
AND NOT ONE WAS POISONED.
WELL, THAT'S EASY FOR A KNOCKING MASTER LIKE HIM.
HMM? OH YEAH!
I GET IT NOW.
I WAS WONDERING WHAT THAT SMELL WAS.
IT WAS THE OLD MAN WHO WANTED OUR LIQUOR BACK ON THE TRAIN.
HUH?
YOU MEAN THAT FUNKY OLD MAN WITH THE WHITE POMPADOUR?
I KNEW HE WASN'T A REGULAR GEEZER, BUT...
...TO THINK HE'S THE LEGENDARY GOURMET HUNTER...
KNOCKING MASTER JIRO!!
HIS FULL-COURSE MEAL IS FULL OF FOODS MOST PEOPLE IN THE WORLD DON'T BELIEVE EXIST, LET ALONE HAVE TASTED.

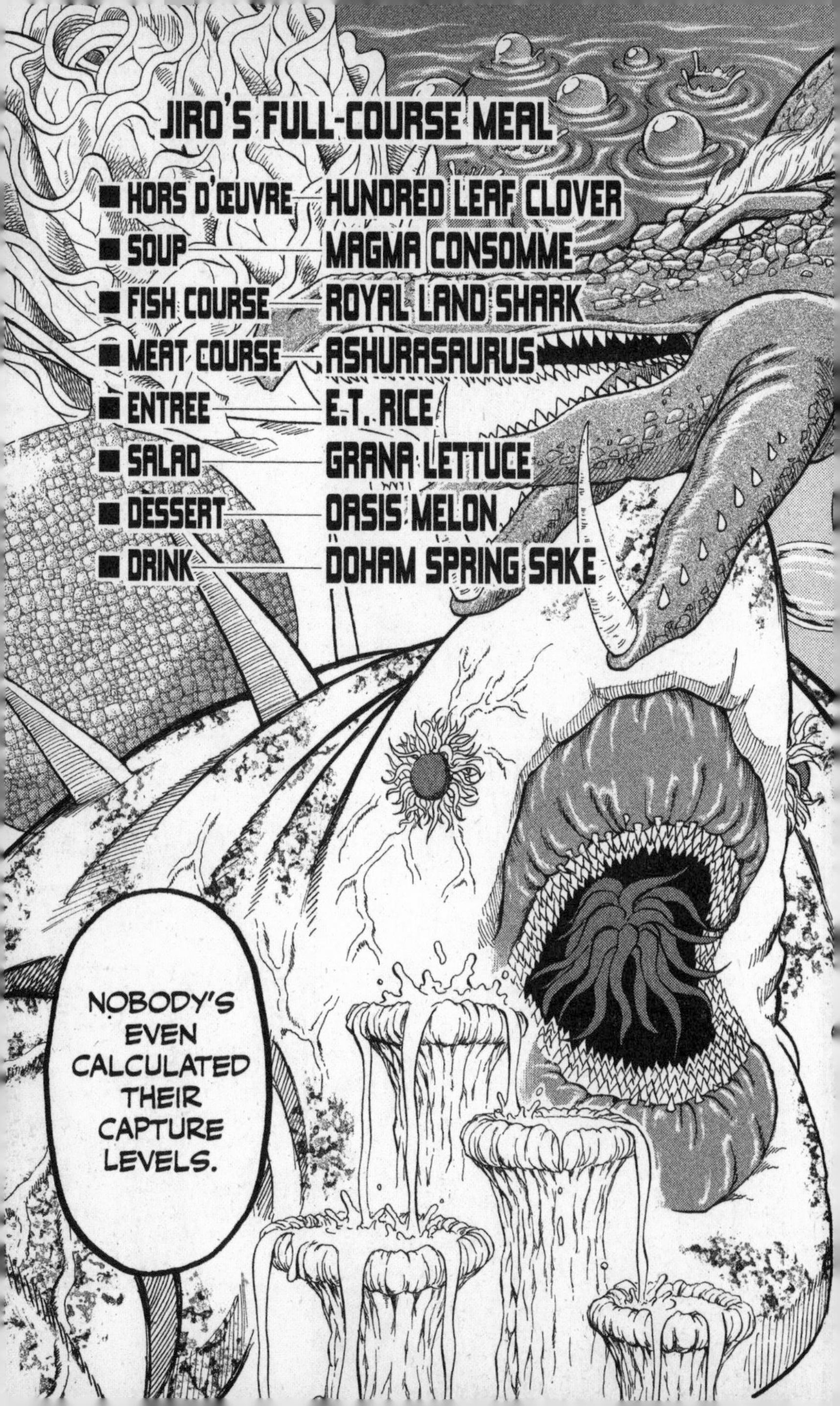
JIRO'S FULL-COURSE MEAL
■ HORS D'ŒUVRE — HUNDRED LEAF CLOVER
■ SOUP — MAGMA CONSOMME
■ FISH COURSE — ROYAL LAND SHARK
■ MEAT COURSE — ASHURASAURUS
■ ENTREE — E.T. RICE
■ SALAD — GRANA LETTUCE
■ DESSERT — OASIS MELON
■ DRINK — DOHAM SPRING SAKE
NOBODY'S EVEN CALCULATED THEIR CAPTURE LEVELS.

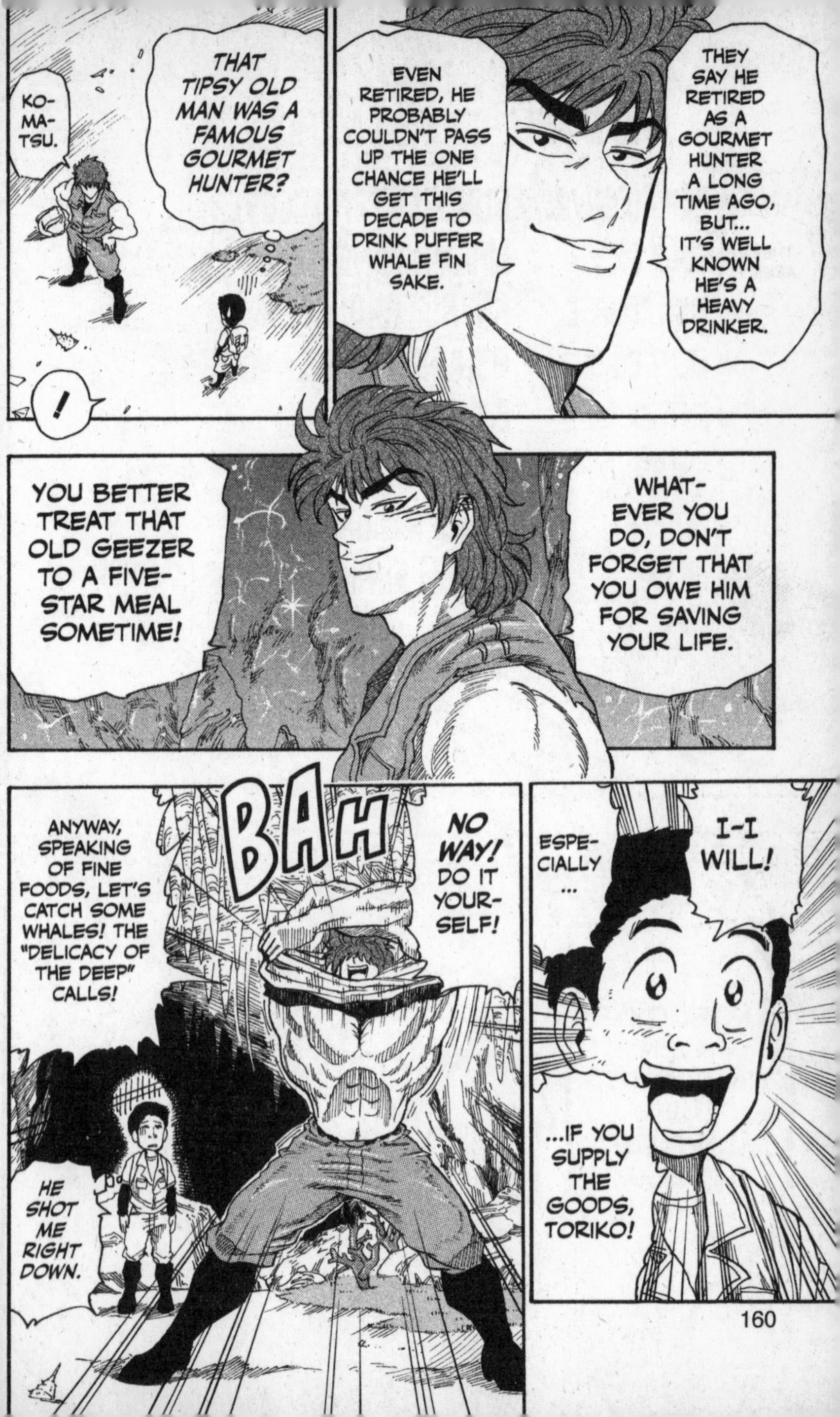
THEY SAY HE RETIRED AS A GOURMET HUNTER A LONG TIME AGO, BUT... IT'S WELL KNOWN HE'S A HEAVY DRINKER.
EVEN RETIRED, HE PROBABLY COULDN'T PASS UP THE ONE CHANCE HE'LL GET THIS DECADE TO DRINK PUFFER WHALE FIN SAKE.
THAT TIPSY OLD MAN WAS A FAMOUS GOURMET HUNTER?
KO-MA-TSU.
!
WHAT-EVER YOU DO, DON'T FORGET THAT YOU OWE HIM FOR SAVING YOUR LIFE.
YOU BETTER TREAT THAT OLD GEEZER TO A FIVE-STAR MEAL SOMETIME!
I-I WILL!
ESPE-CIALLY ...
...IF YOU SUPPLY THE GOODS, TORIKO!
NO WAY! DO IT YOUR-SELF!
BAH
ANYWAY, SPEAKING OF FINE FOODS, LET'S CATCH SOME WHALES! THE "DELICACY OF THE DEEP" CALLS!
HE SHOT ME RIGHT DOWN.

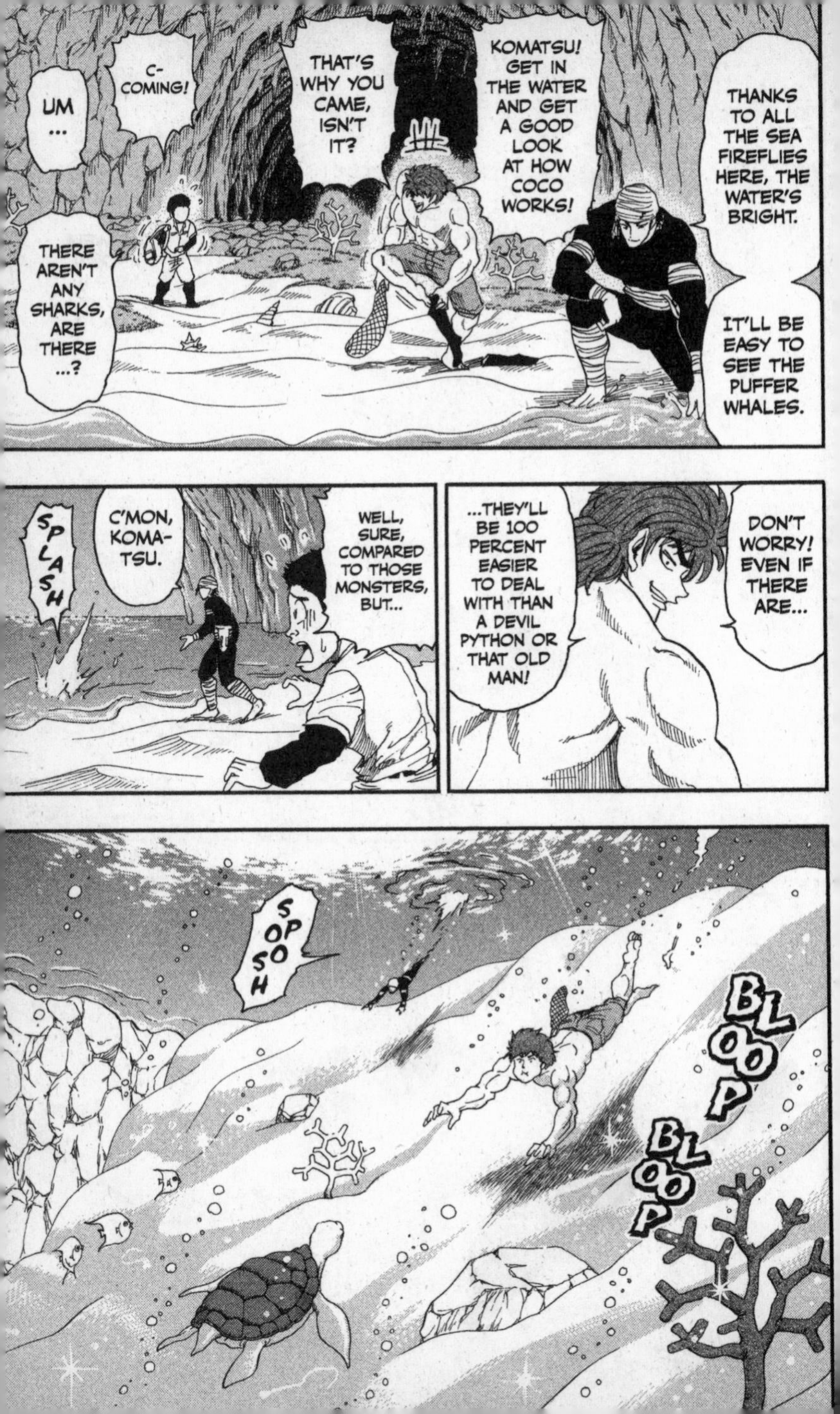
THANKS TO ALL THE SEA FIREFLIES HERE, THE WATER'S BRIGHT.
IT'LL BE EASY TO SEE THE PUFFER WHALES.
KOMATSU! GET IN THE WATER AND GET A GOOD LOOK AT HOW COCO WORKS!
THAT'S WHY YOU CAME, ISN'T IT?
C-COMING!
UM ...
THERE AREN'T ANY SHARKS, ARE THERE ...?
DON'T WORRY! EVEN IF THERE ARE...
...THEY'LL BE 100 PERCENT EASIER TO DEAL WITH THAN A DEVIL PYTHON OR THAT OLD MAN!
WELL, SURE, COMPARED TO THOSE MONSTERS, BUT...
C'MON, KOMA-TSU.
SPLASH
BLOOP
BLOOP
SPOOSH

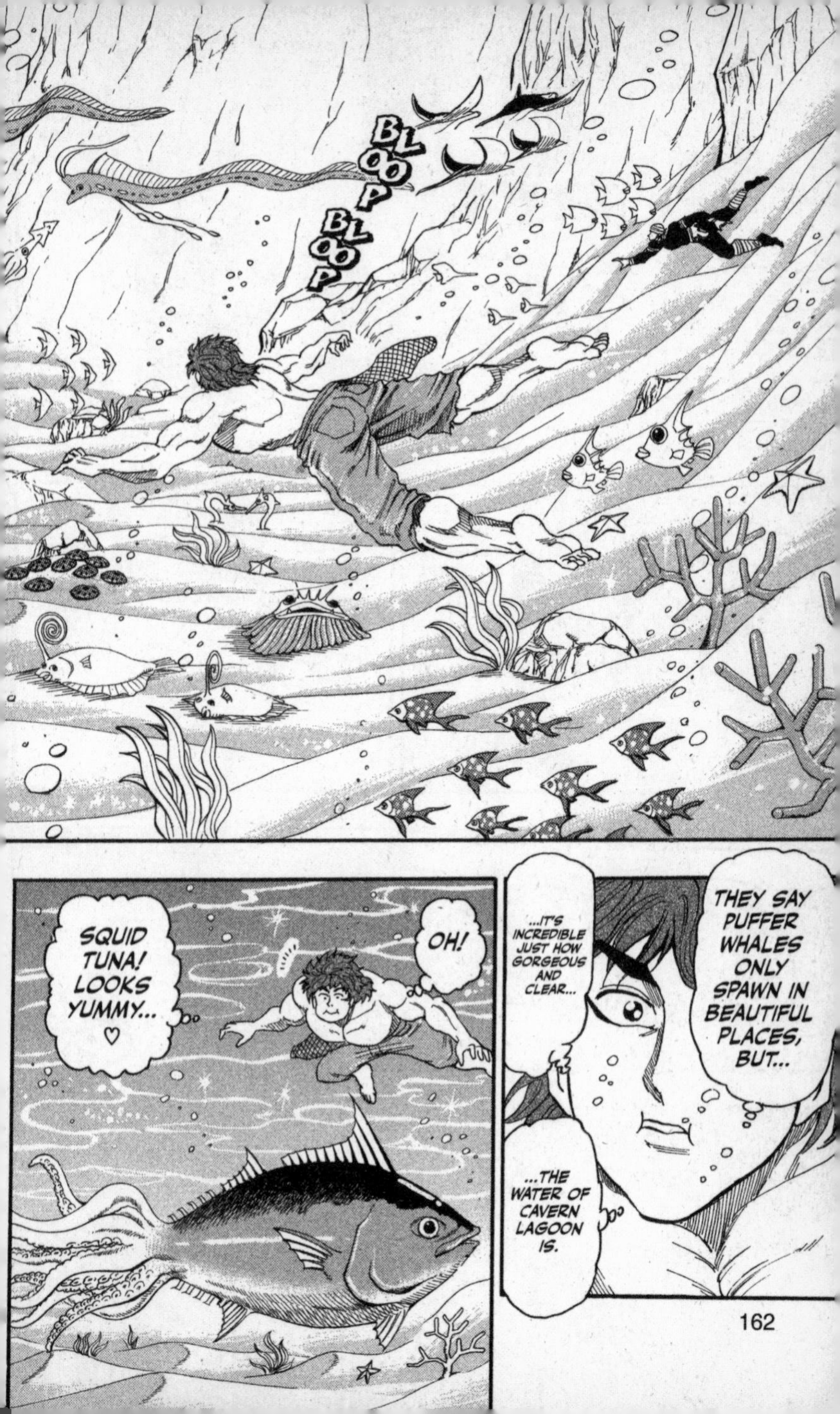
BLOOP BLOOP
THEY SAY PUFFER WHALES ONLY SPAWN IN BEAUTIFUL PLACES, BUT...
...IT'S INCREDIBLE JUST HOW GORGEOUS AND CLEAR...
...THE WATER OF CAVERN LAGOON IS.
OH!
SQUID TUNA! LOOKS YUMMY... ♡

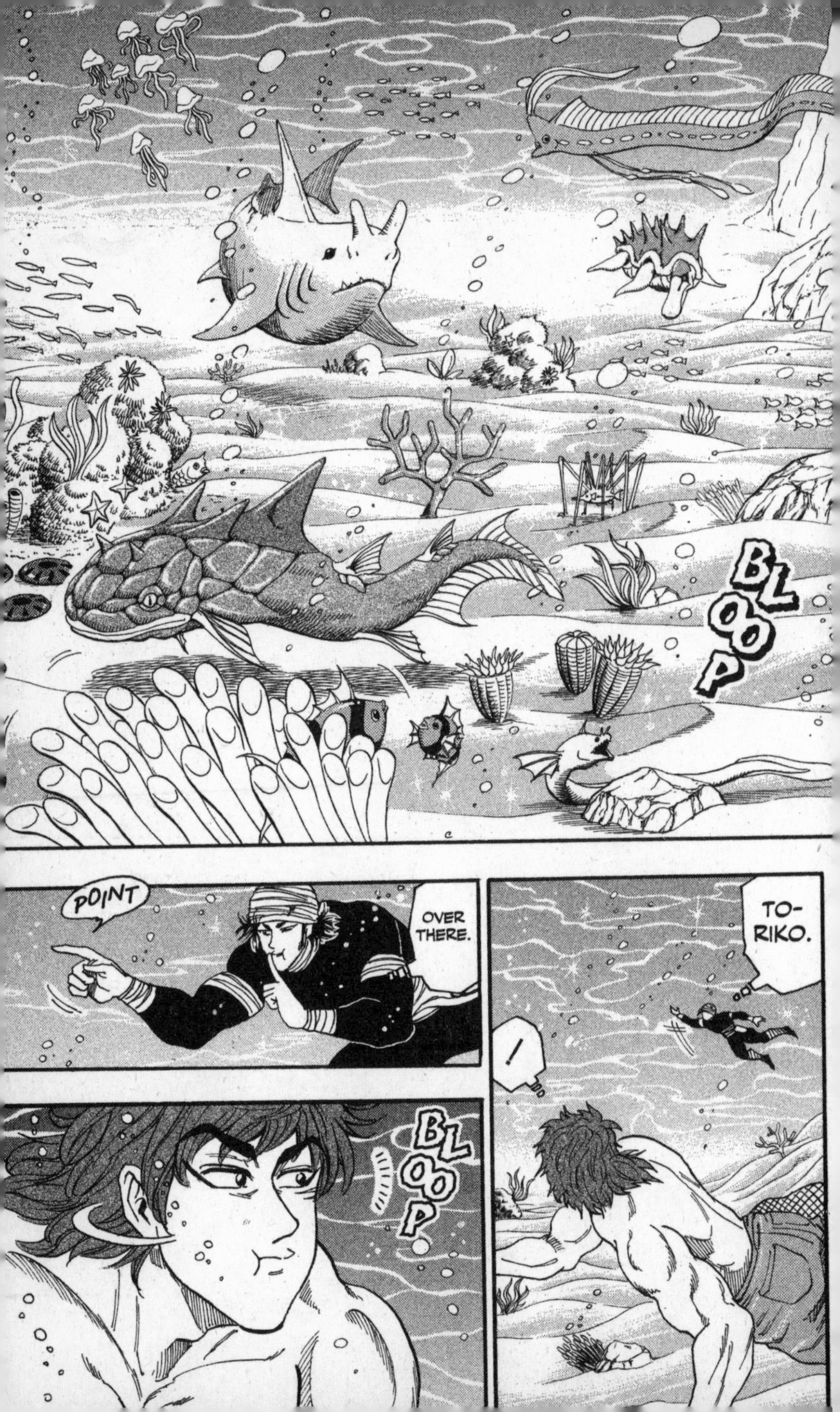
BLOOP
TO-RIKO.
!
POINT
OVER THERE.
BLOOP

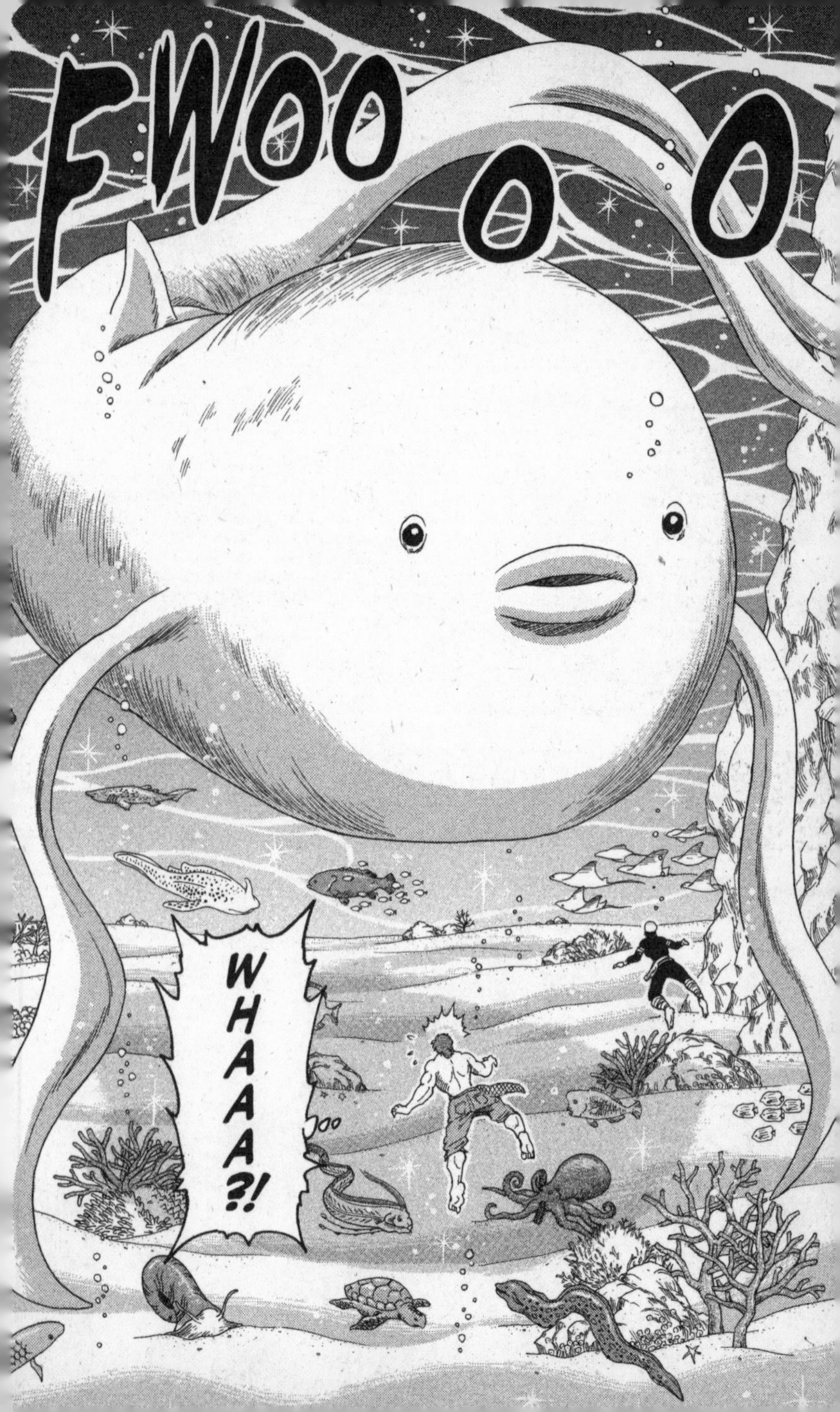
FWOO O O
WHAAAA?!

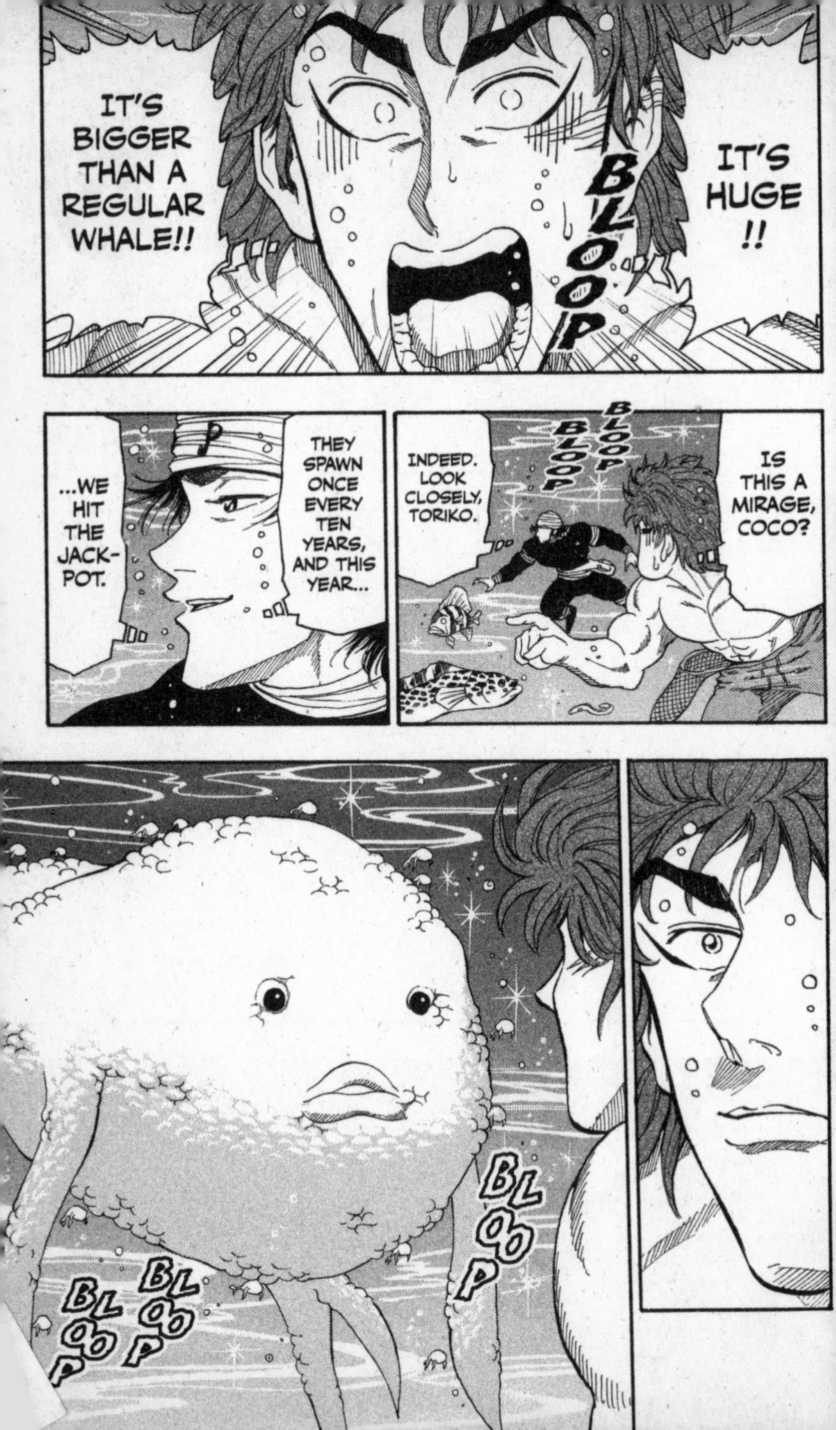
IT'S HUGE!!
BLOOP
IT'S BIGGER THAN A REGULAR WHALE!!
IS THIS A MIRAGE, COCO?
BLOOP
BLOOP
INDEED. LOOK CLOSELY, TORIKO.
THEY SPAWN ONCE EVERY TEN YEARS, AND THIS YEAR...
...WE HIT THE JACKPOT.
BLOOP
BLOOP
BLOOP

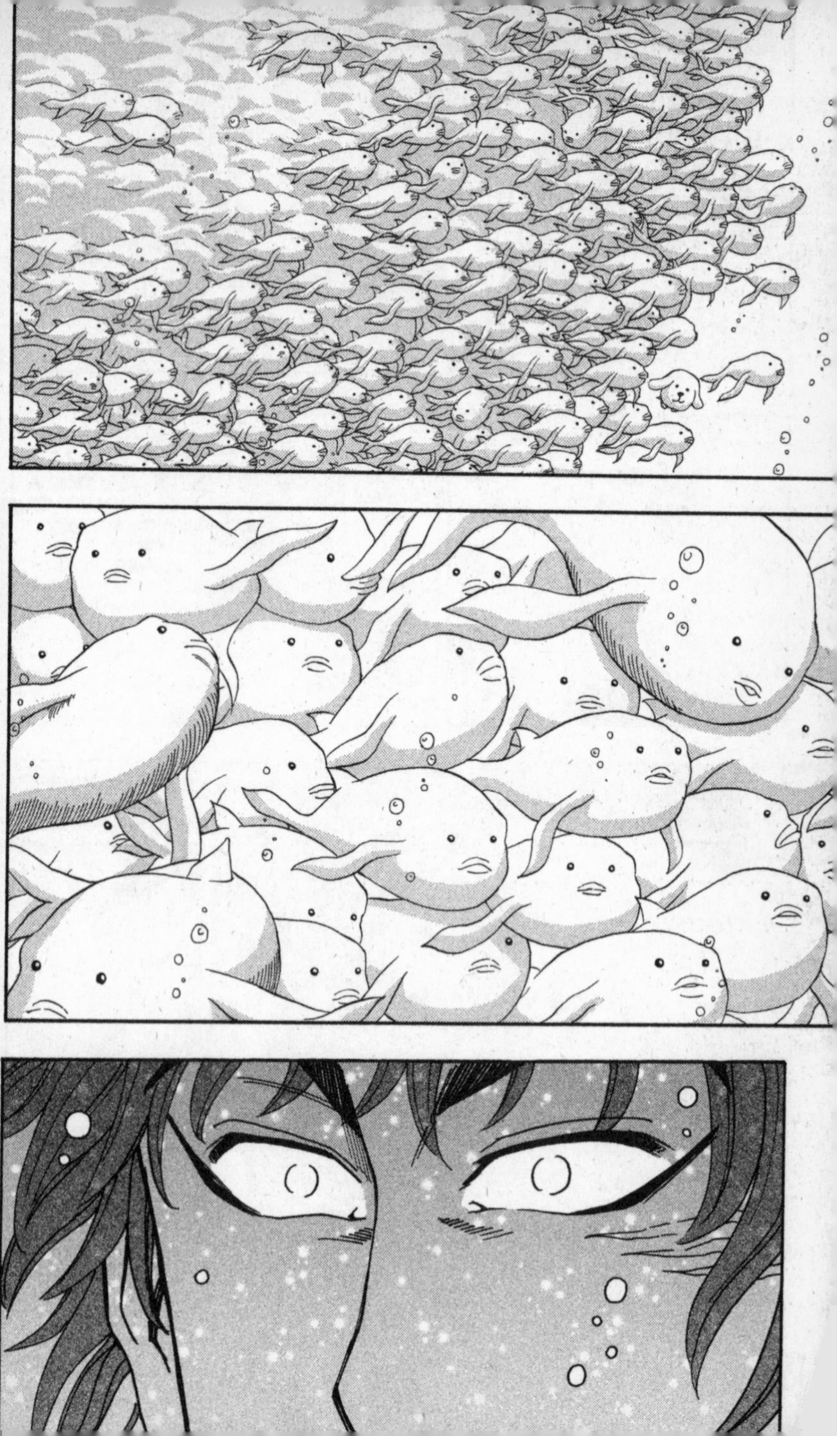

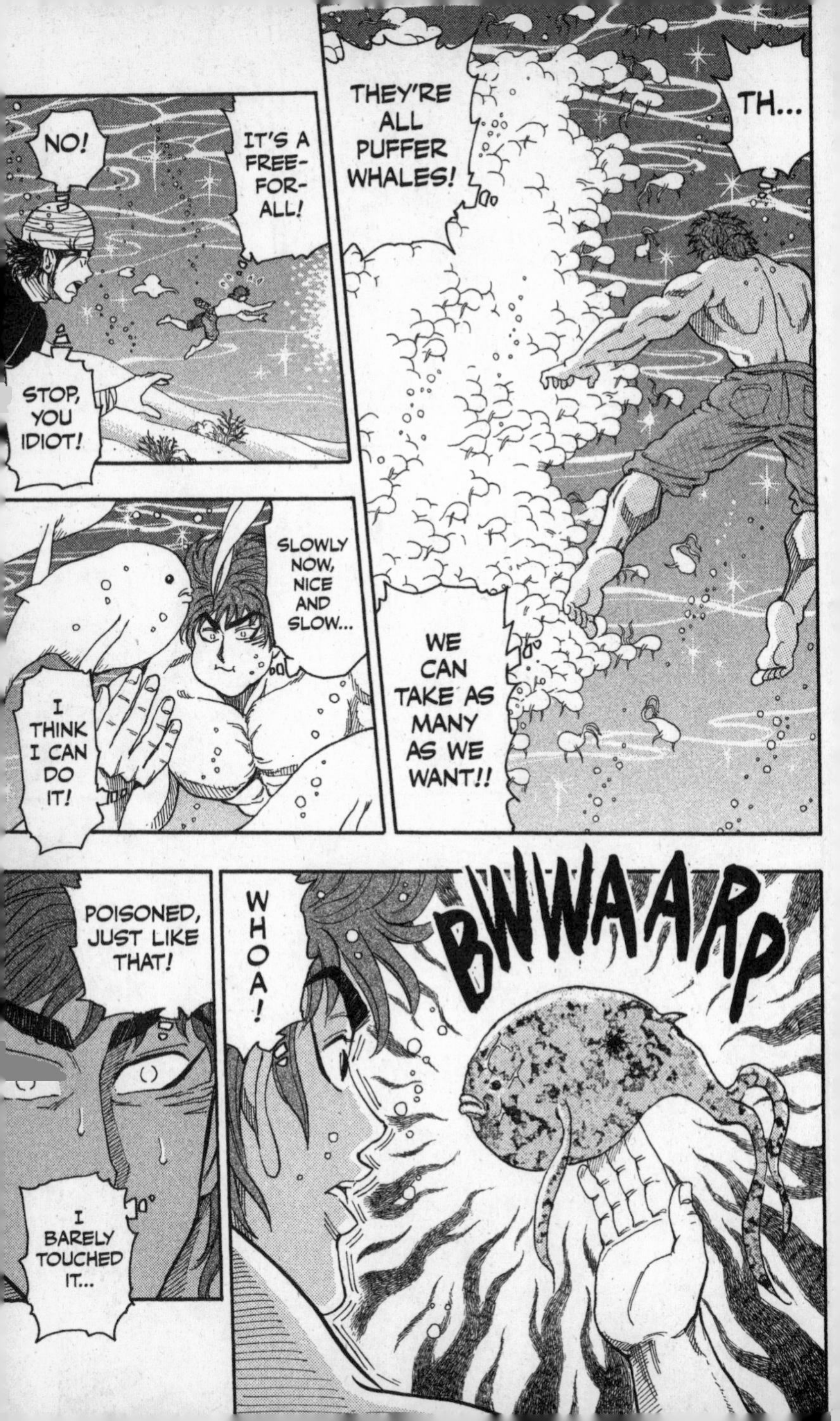
TH...
THEY'RE ALL PUFFER WHALES!
WE CAN TAKE AS MANY AS WE WANT!!
IT'S A FREE-FOR-ALL!
NO!
STOP, YOU IDIOT!
SLOWLY NOW, NICE AND SLOW...
I THINK I CAN DO IT!
BWWAARP
WHOA!
POISONED, JUST LIKE THAT!
I BARELY TOUCHED IT...

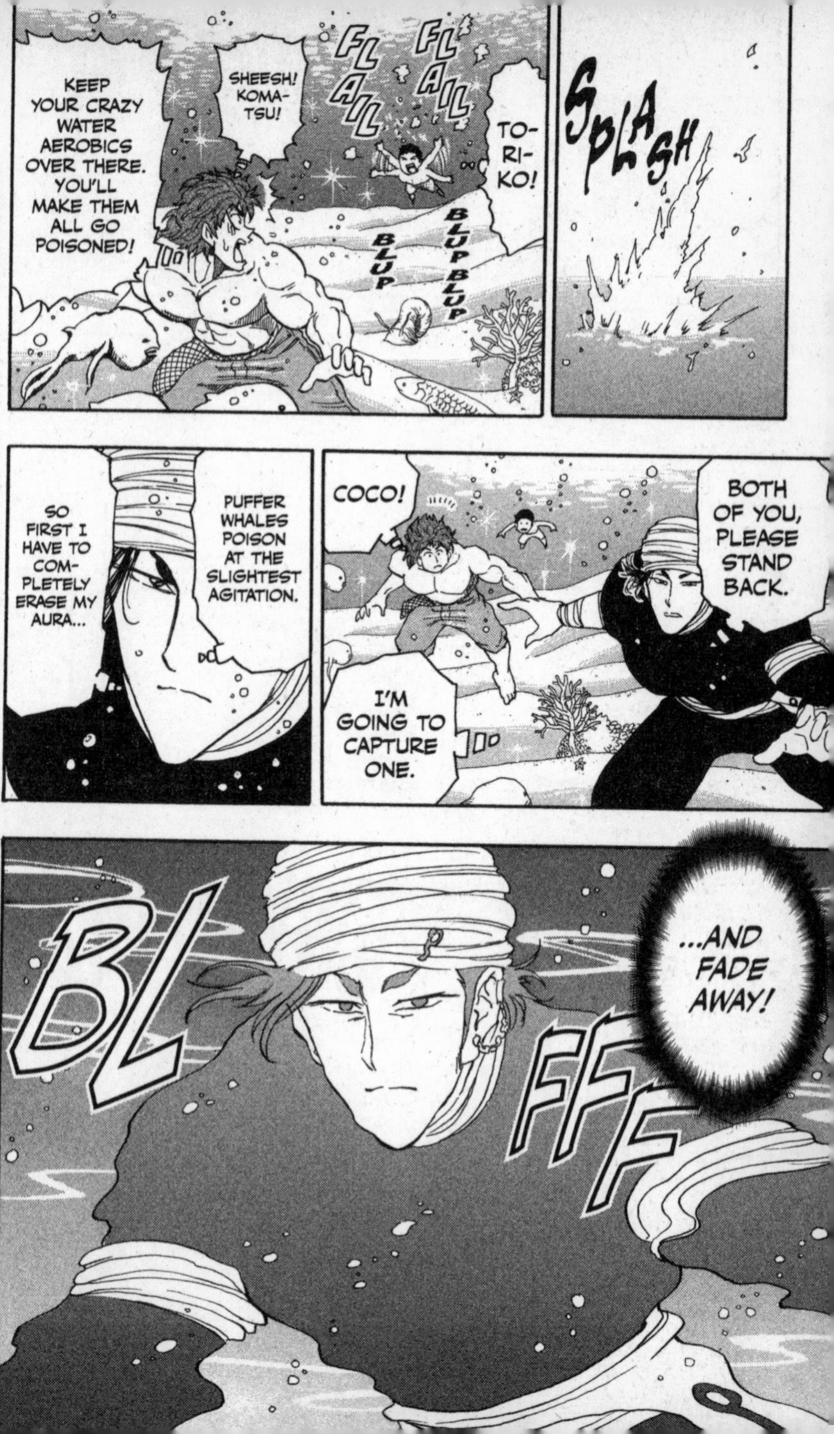
SPLASH
TO-RI-KO!
FLAIL FLAIL
SHEESH! KOMA-TSU!
KEEP YOUR CRAZY WATER AEROBICS OVER THERE. YOU'LL MAKE THEM ALL GO POISONED!
BLUP BLUP BLUP
BOTH OF YOU, PLEASE STAND BACK.
COCO!
I'M GOING TO CAPTURE ONE.
PUFFER WHALES POISON AT THE SLIGHTEST AGITATION.
SO FIRST I HAVE TO COM-PLETELY ERASE MY AURA...
...AND FADE AWAY!
BLFFF

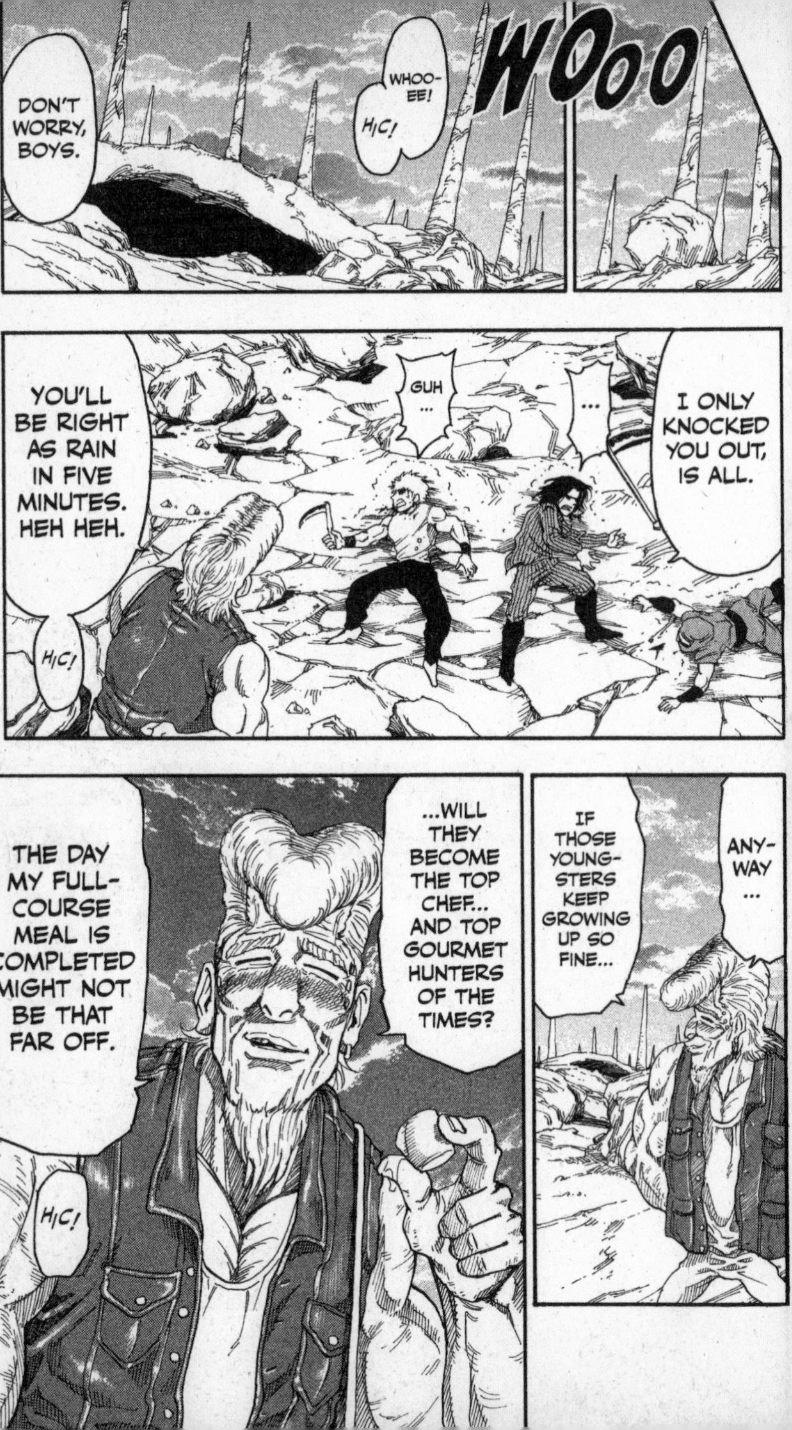
WOOO
WHOO-EE!
HIC!
DON'T WORRY, BOYS.
I ONLY KNOCKED YOU OUT, IS ALL.
...
GUH...
YOU'LL BE RIGHT AS RAIN IN FIVE MINUTES. HEH HEH.
HIC!
ANY-WAY...
IF THOSE YOUNG-STERS KEEP GROWING UP SO FINE...
...WILL THEY BECOME THE TOP CHEF... AND TOP GOURMET HUNTERS OF THE TIMES?
THE DAY MY FULL-COURSE MEAL IS COMPLETED MIGHT NOT BE THAT FAR OFF.
HIC!

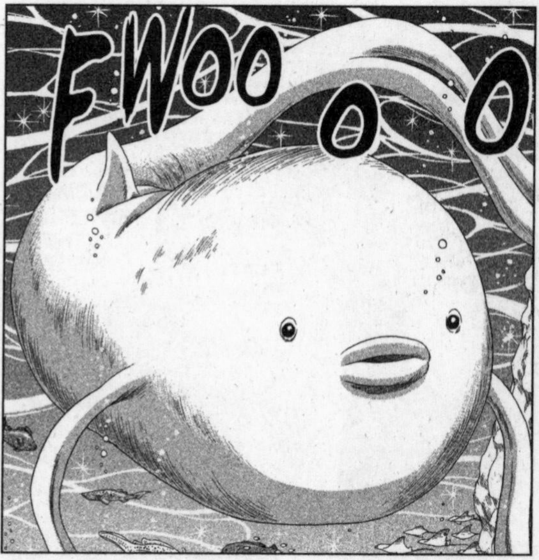
FWOO O O

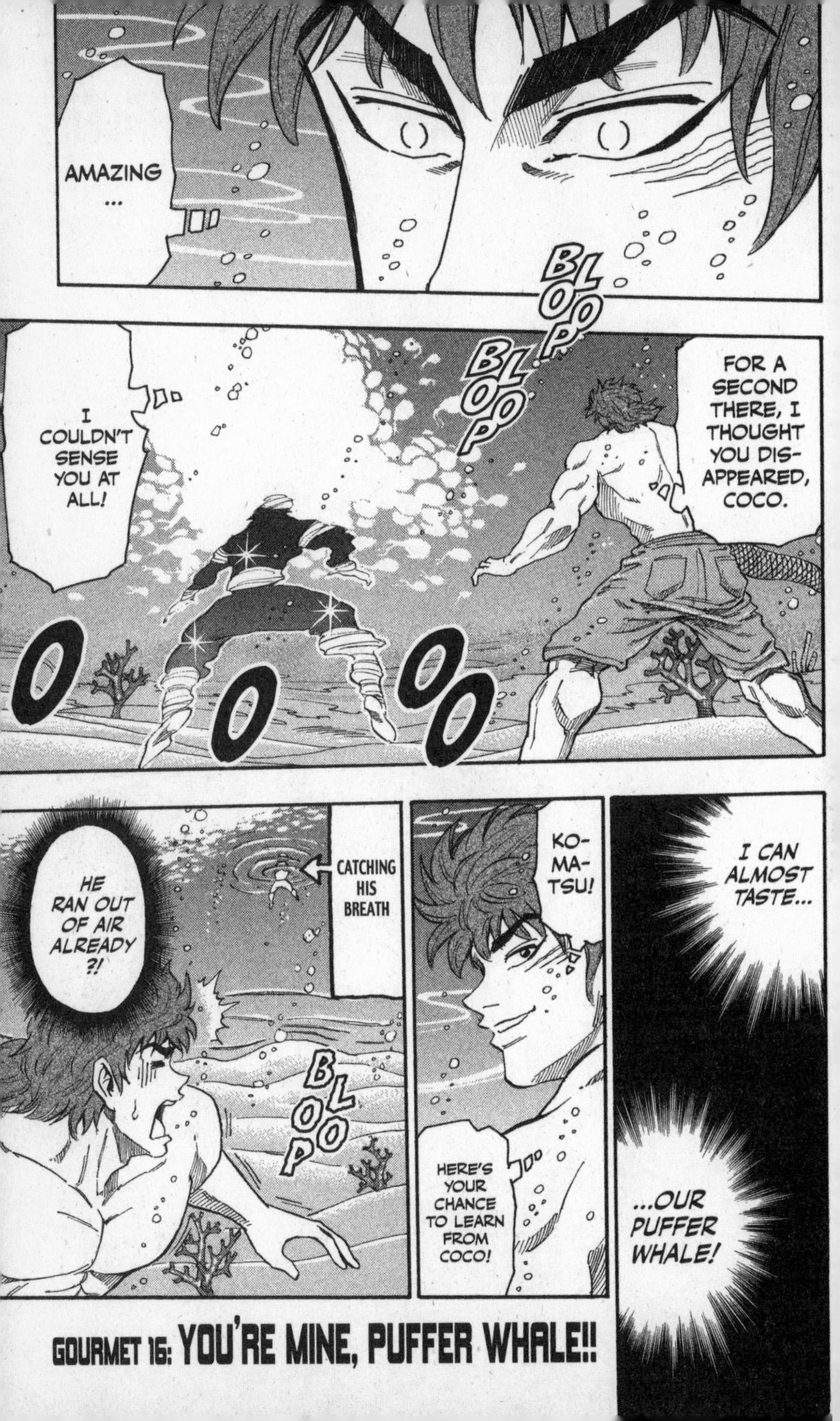
AMAZING ...
BLOOP
FOR A SECOND THERE, I THOUGHT YOU DIS-APPEARED, COCO.
BLOOP
I COULDN'T SENSE YOU AT ALL!
OOOO
I CAN ALMOST TASTE...
...OUR PUFFER WHALE!
KO-MA-TSU!
HERE'S YOUR CHANCE TO LEARN FROM COCO!
CATCHING HIS BREATH
HE RAN OUT OF AIR ALREADY ?!
BLOOP

GOURMET 16: YOU'RE MINE, PUFFER WHALE!!

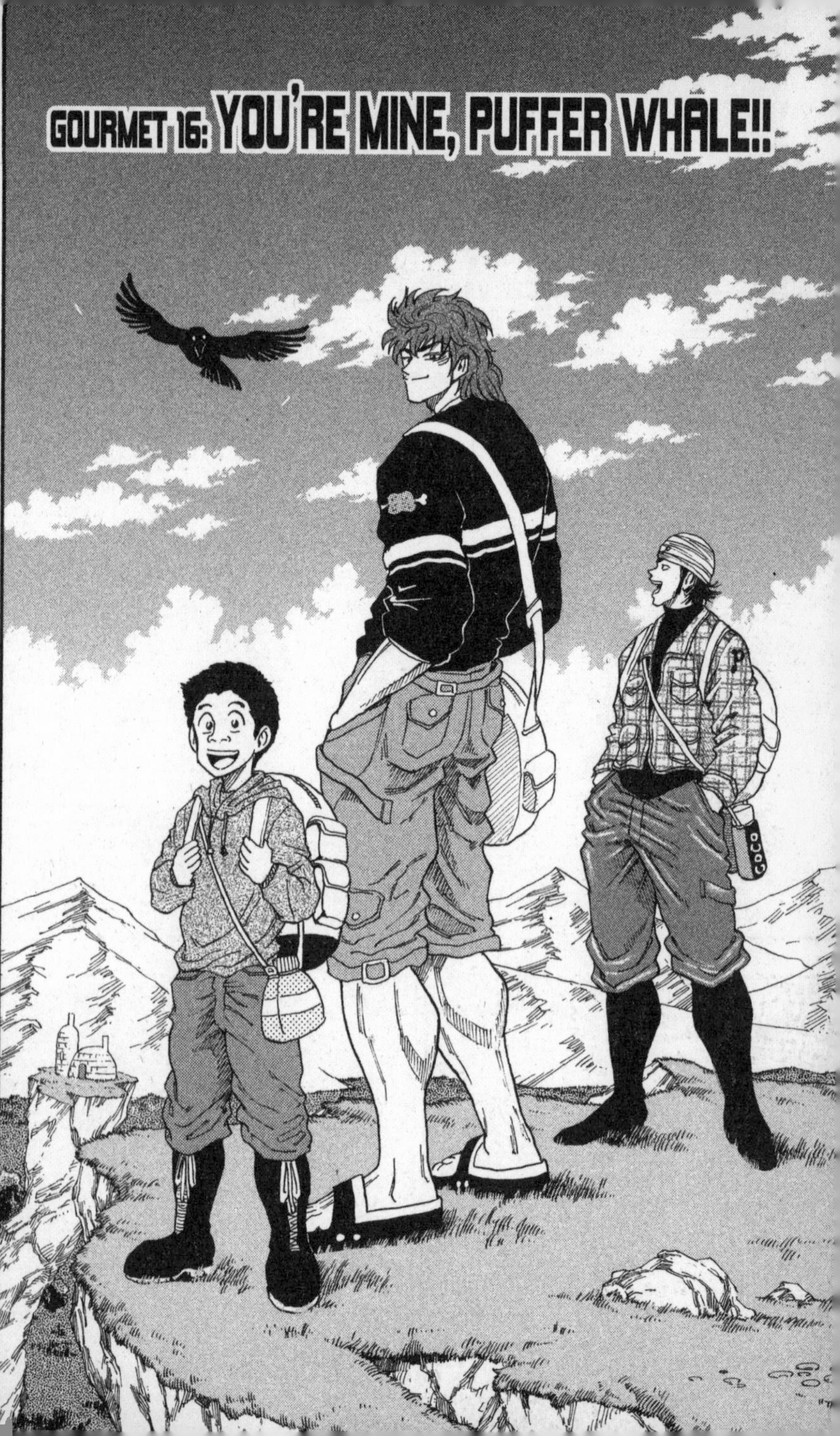
GOURMET 16: YOU'RE MINE, PUFFER WHALE!!

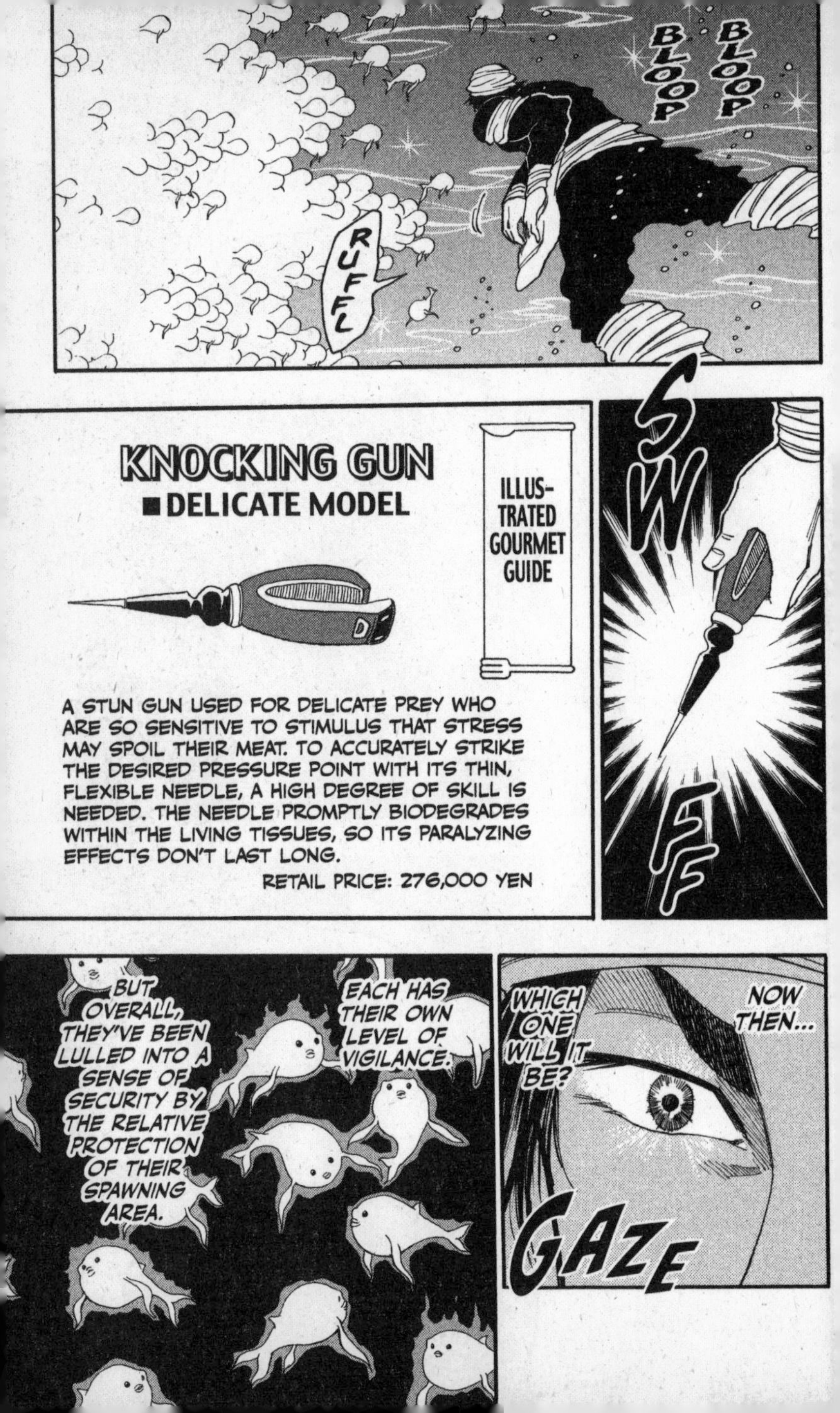
BLOOP
BLOOP
RUFFL
SWFF
KNOCKING GUN
■ DELICATE MODEL
ILLUS-TRATED GOURMET GUIDE
A STUN GUN USED FOR DELICATE PREY WHO ARE SO SENSITIVE TO STIMULUS THAT STRESS MAY SPOIL THEIR MEAT. TO ACCURATELY STRIKE THE DESIRED PRESSURE POINT WITH ITS THIN, FLEXIBLE NEEDLE, A HIGH DEGREE OF SKILL IS NEEDED. THE NEEDLE PROMPTLY BIODEGRADES WITHIN THE LIVING TISSUES, SO ITS PARALYZING EFFECTS DON'T LAST LONG.
RETAIL PRICE: 276,000 YEN
NOW THEN...
WHICH ONE WILL IT BE?
GAZE
EACH HAS THEIR OWN LEVEL OF VIGILANCE.
BUT OVERALL, THEY'VE BEEN LULLED INTO A SENSE OF SECURITY BY THE RELATIVE PROTECTION OF THEIR SPAWNING AREA.

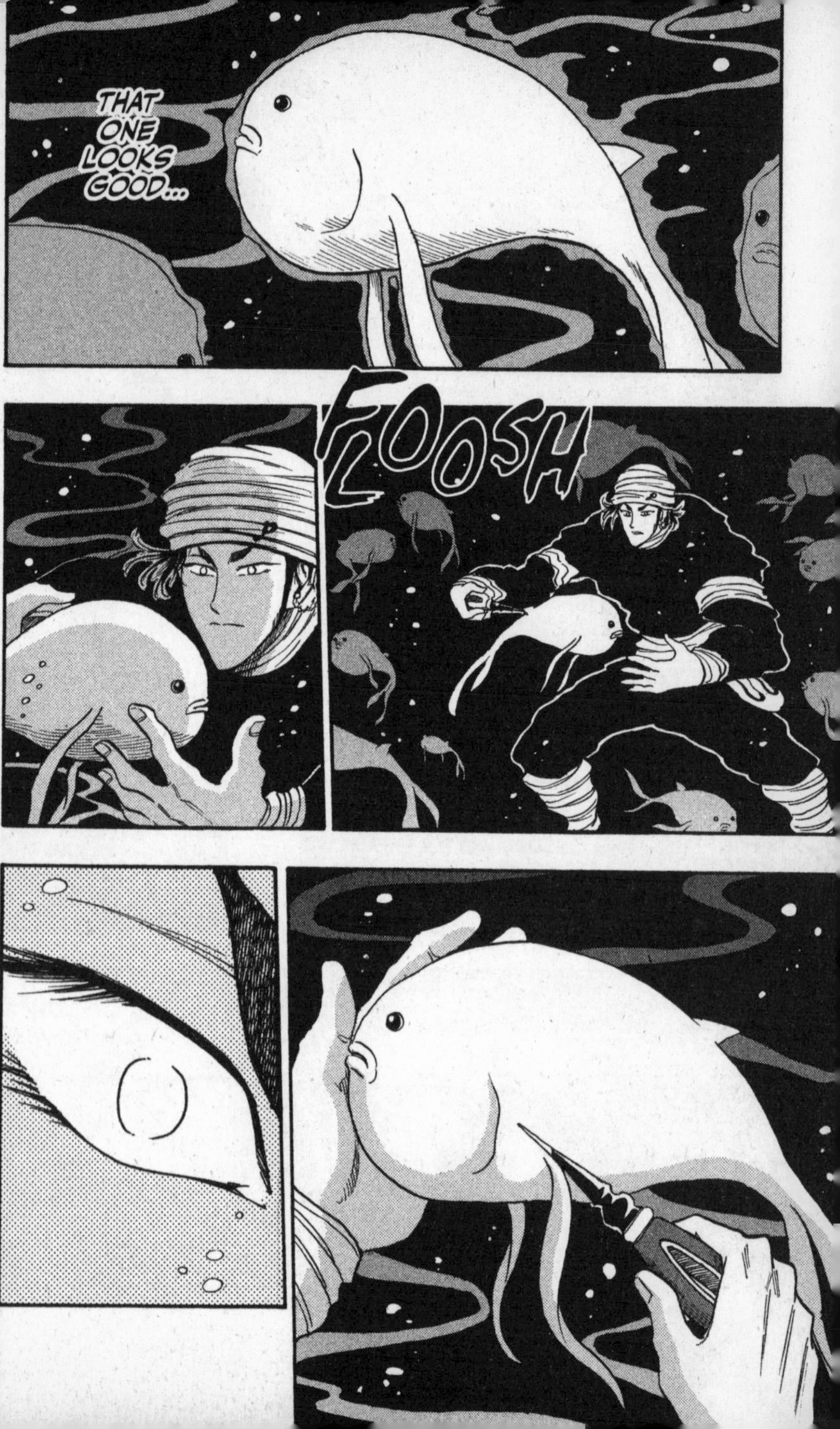
THAT ONE LOOKS GOOD...
FLOOSH

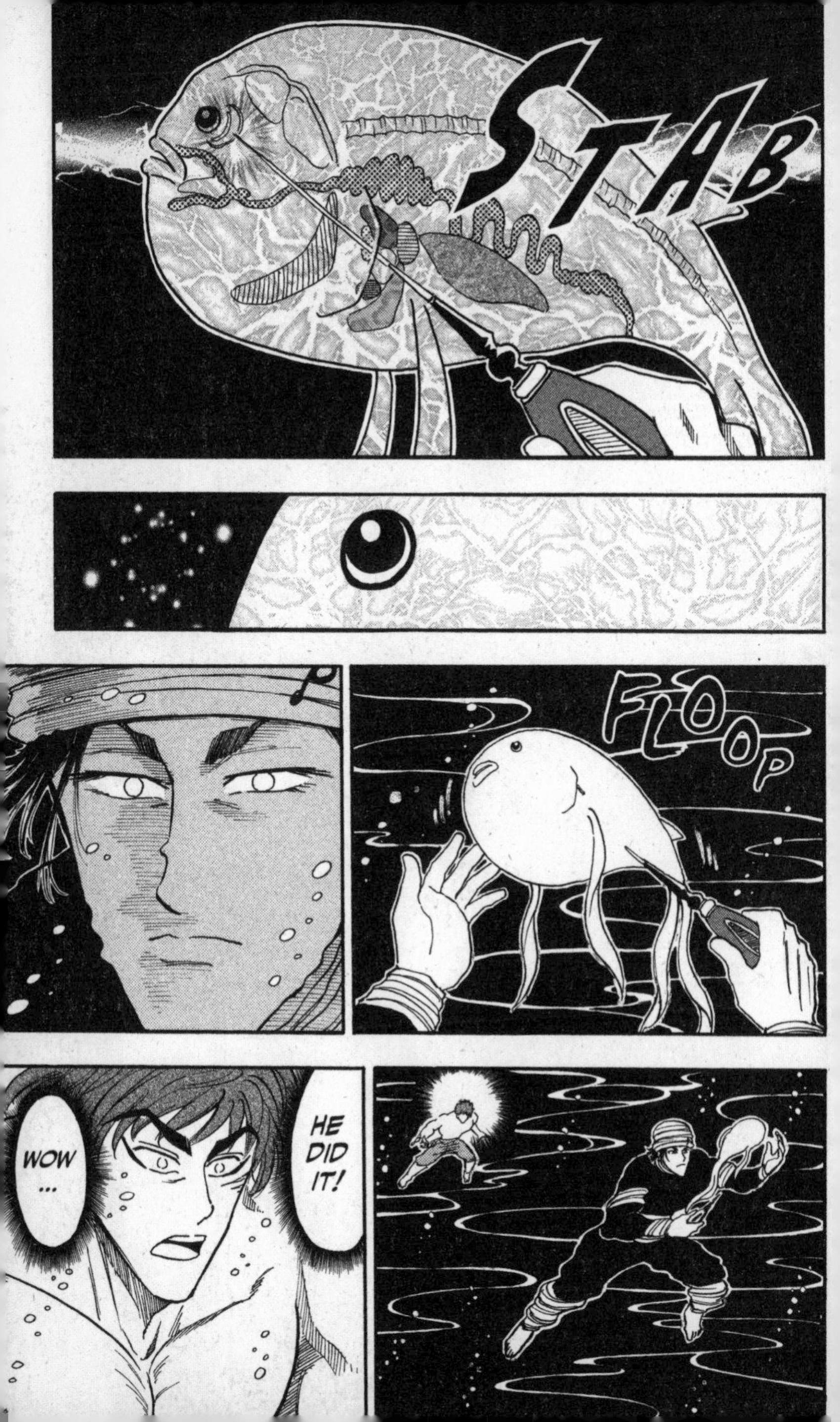
STAB
FLOOP
HE DID IT!
WOW ...

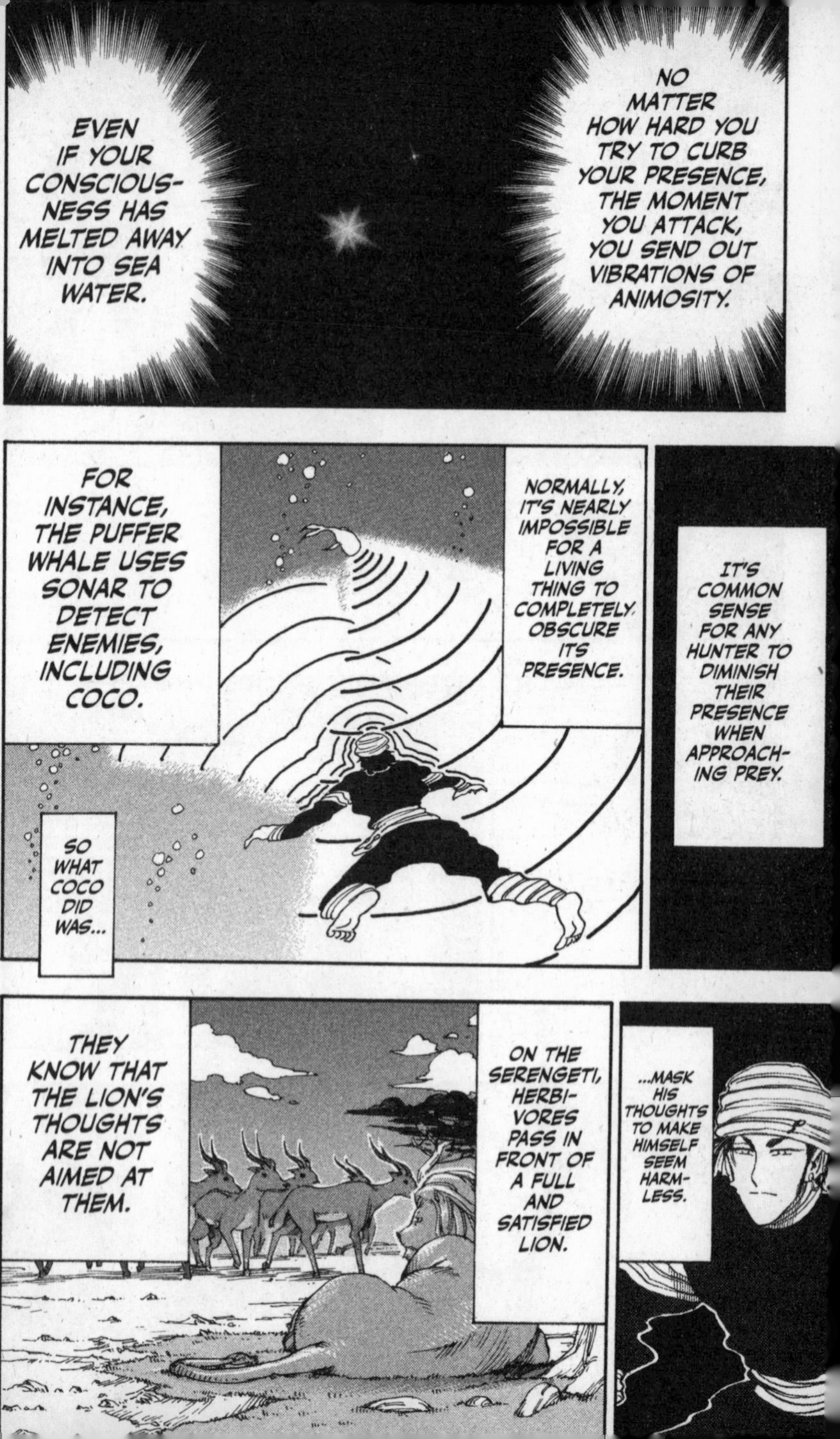
NO MATTER HOW HARD YOU TRY TO CURB YOUR PRESENCE, THE MOMENT YOU ATTACK, YOU SEND OUT VIBRATIONS OF ANIMOSITY.
EVEN IF YOUR CONSCIOUS-NESS HAS MELTED AWAY INTO SEA WATER.
IT'S COMMON SENSE FOR ANY HUNTER TO DIMINISH THEIR PRESENCE WHEN APPROACH-ING PREY.
NORMALLY, IT'S NEARLY IMPOSSIBLE FOR A LIVING THING TO COMPLETELY OBSCURE ITS PRESENCE.
FOR INSTANCE, THE PUFFER WHALE USES SONAR TO DETECT ENEMIES, INCLUDING COCO.
SO WHAT COCO DID WAS...
...MASK HIS THOUGHTS TO MAKE HIMSELF SEEM HARM-LESS.
ON THE SERENGETI, HERBI-VORES PASS IN FRONT OF A FULL AND SATISFIED LION.
THEY KNOW THAT THE LION'S THOUGHTS ARE NOT AIMED AT THEM.

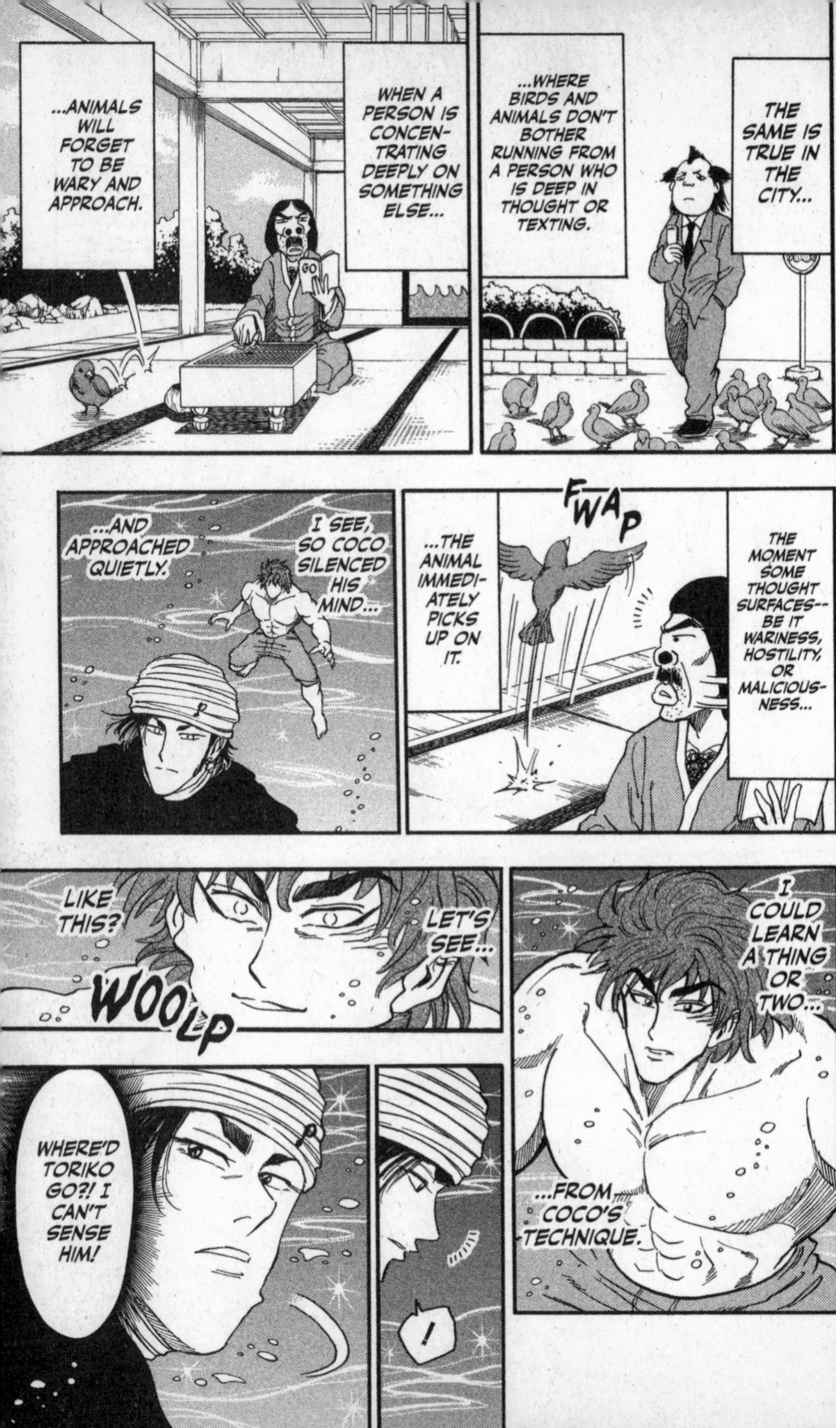
THE SAME IS TRUE IN THE CITY...
...WHERE BIRDS AND ANIMALS DON'T BOTHER RUNNING FROM A PERSON WHO IS DEEP IN THOUGHT OR TEXTING.
WHEN A PERSON IS CONCENTRATING DEEPLY ON SOMETHING ELSE...
...ANIMALS WILL FORGET TO BE WARY AND APPROACH.
GO
THE MOMENT SOME THOUGHT SURFACES-- BE IT WARINESS, HOSTILITY, OR MALICIOUSNESS...
FWAP
...THE ANIMAL IMMEDIATELY PICKS UP ON IT.
I SEE, SO COCO SILENCED HIS MIND...
...AND APPROACHED QUIETLY.
I COULD LEARN A THING OR TWO...
...FROM COCO'S TECHNIQUE.
LET'S SEE...
LIKE THIS?
WOOLP
!
WHERE'D TORIKO GO?! I CAN'T SENSE HIM!

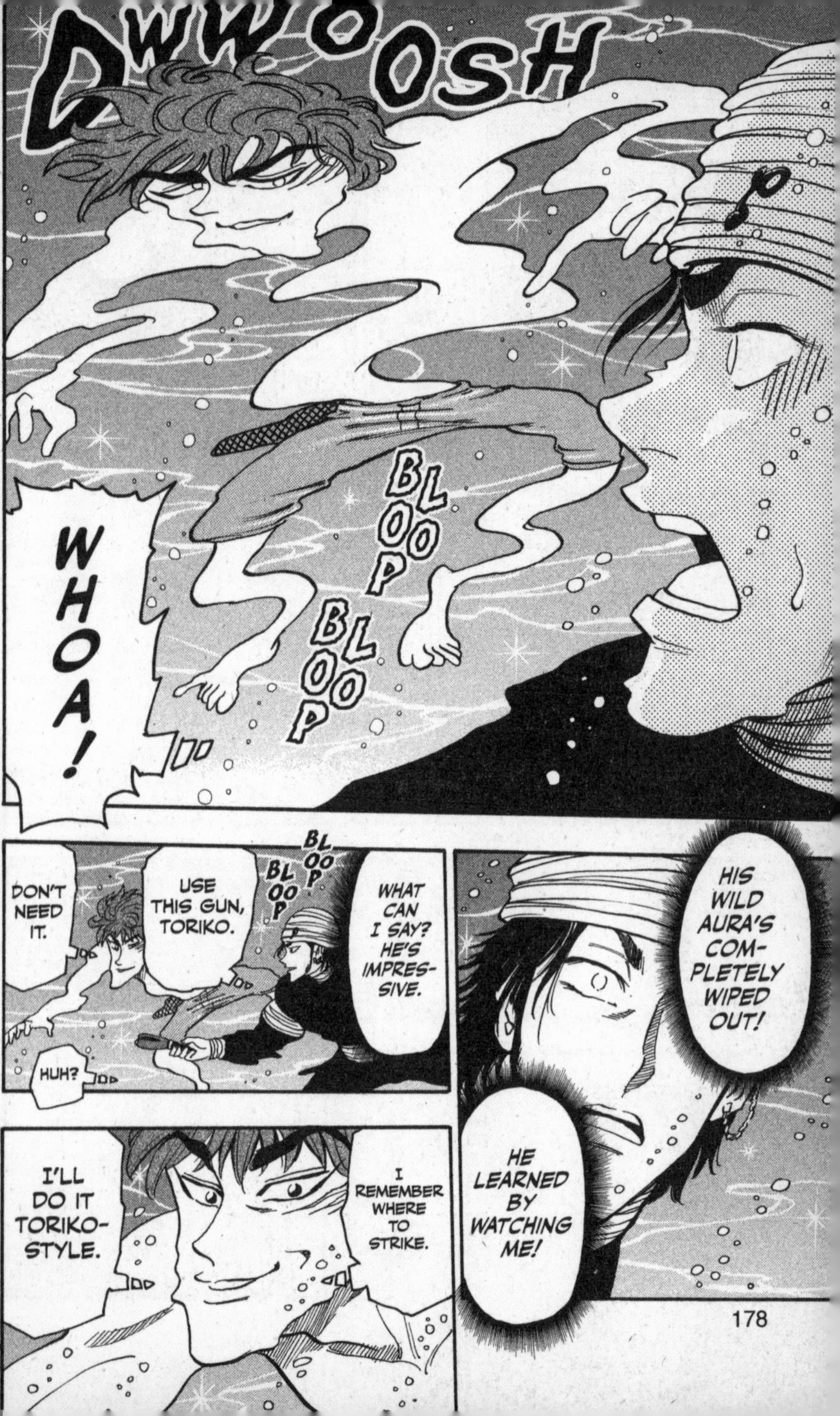
DWWOOSH
BLOOP BLOOP
BLOOP BLOOP
WHOA!
HIS WILD AURA'S COMPLETELY WIPED OUT!
HE LEARNED BY WATCHING ME!
WHAT CAN I SAY? HE'S IMPRESSIVE.
BLOOP BLOOP
USE THIS GUN, TORIKO.
DON'T NEED IT.
HUH?
I REMEMBER WHERE TO STRIKE.
I'LL DO IT TORIKO-STYLE.

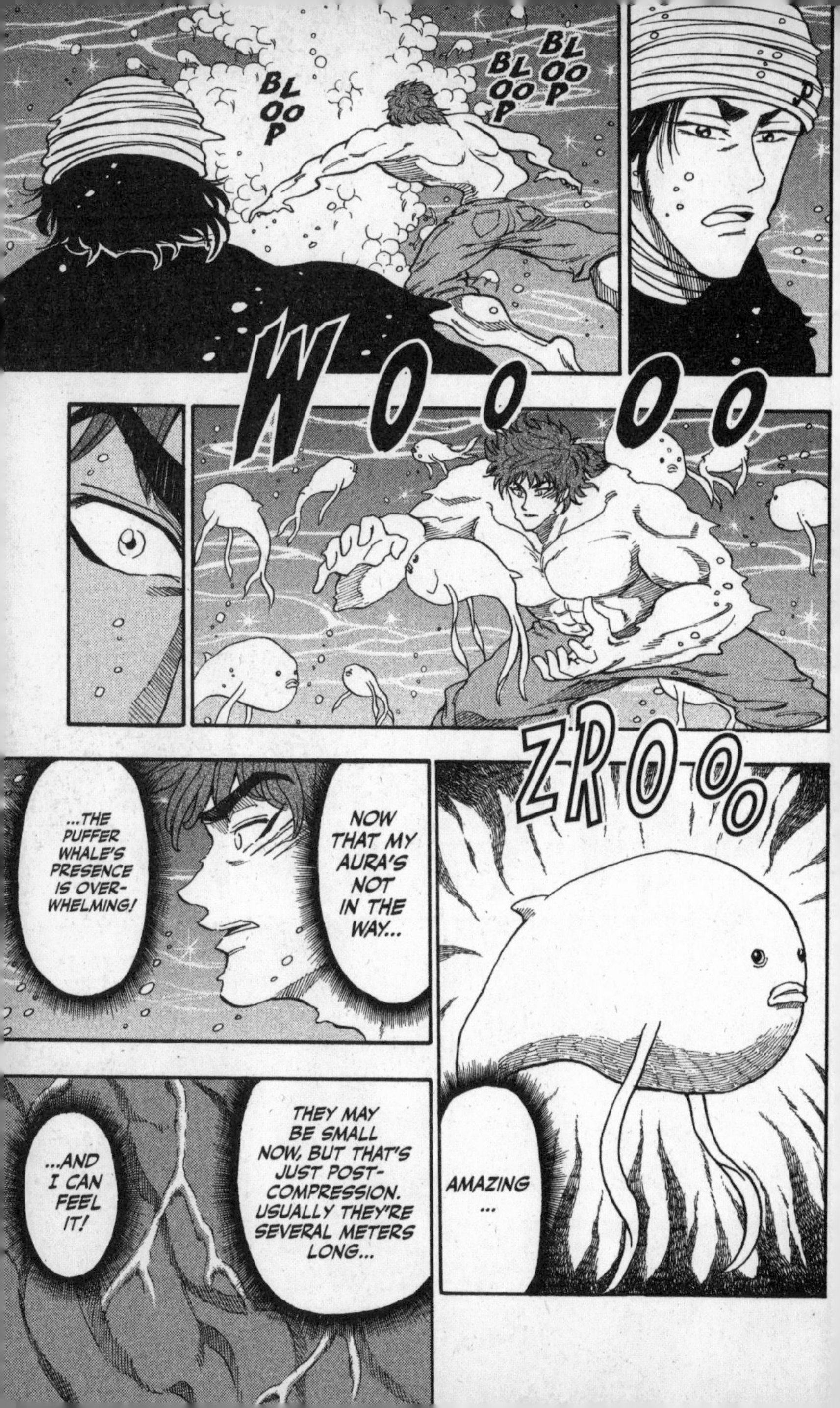
BLOOP BLOOP
BLOOP
WOOOO
ZROOOO
AMAZING ...
NOW THAT MY AURA'S NOT IN THE WAY...
...THE PUFFER WHALE'S PRESENCE IS OVER-WHELMING!
THEY MAY BE SMALL NOW, BUT THAT'S JUST POST-COMPRESSION. USUALLY THEY'RE SEVERAL METERS LONG...
...AND I CAN FEEL IT!

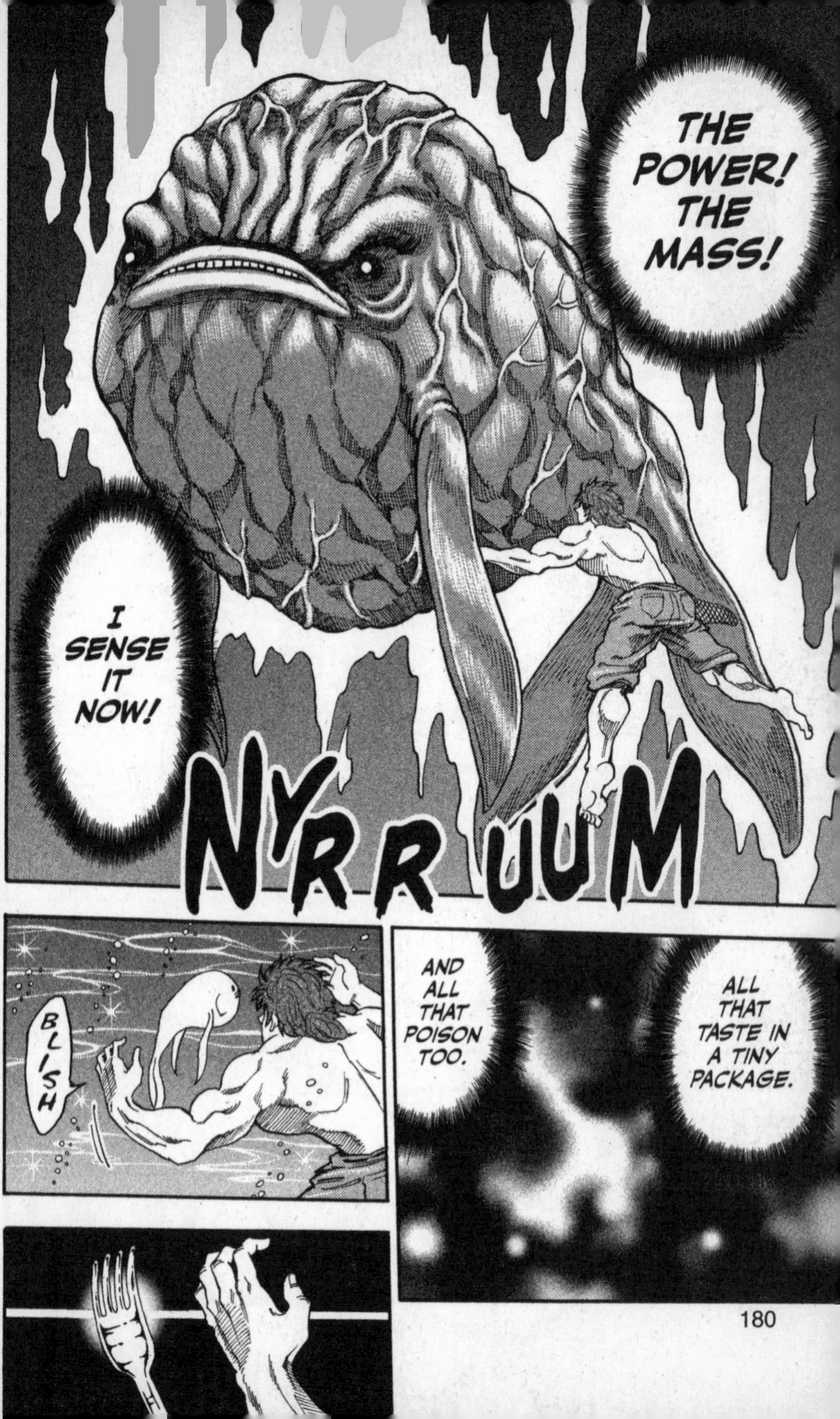
THE POWER! THE MASS!
I SENSE IT NOW!
NYRRUUM
ALL THAT TASTE IN A TINY PACKAGE.
AND ALL THAT POISON TOO.
BLISH

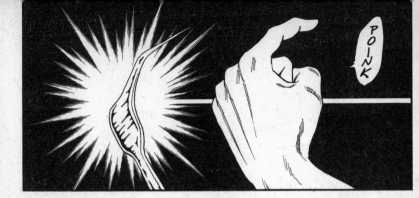

POINK
!
YOU'RE GONNA TRY IT BARE-HANDED?
YOU'LL POISON IT!
ALL I NEED TO DO...
...IS A TINY AND QUICK POKE!
FROM THE GILL TO THE INNER BRAIN...
...IS A 45 DEGREE DIAGONAL ANGLE.

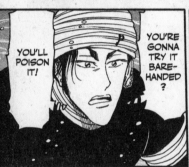

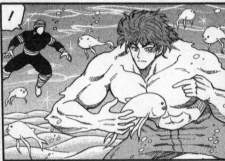

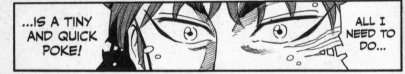

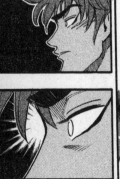

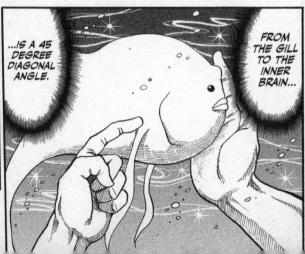

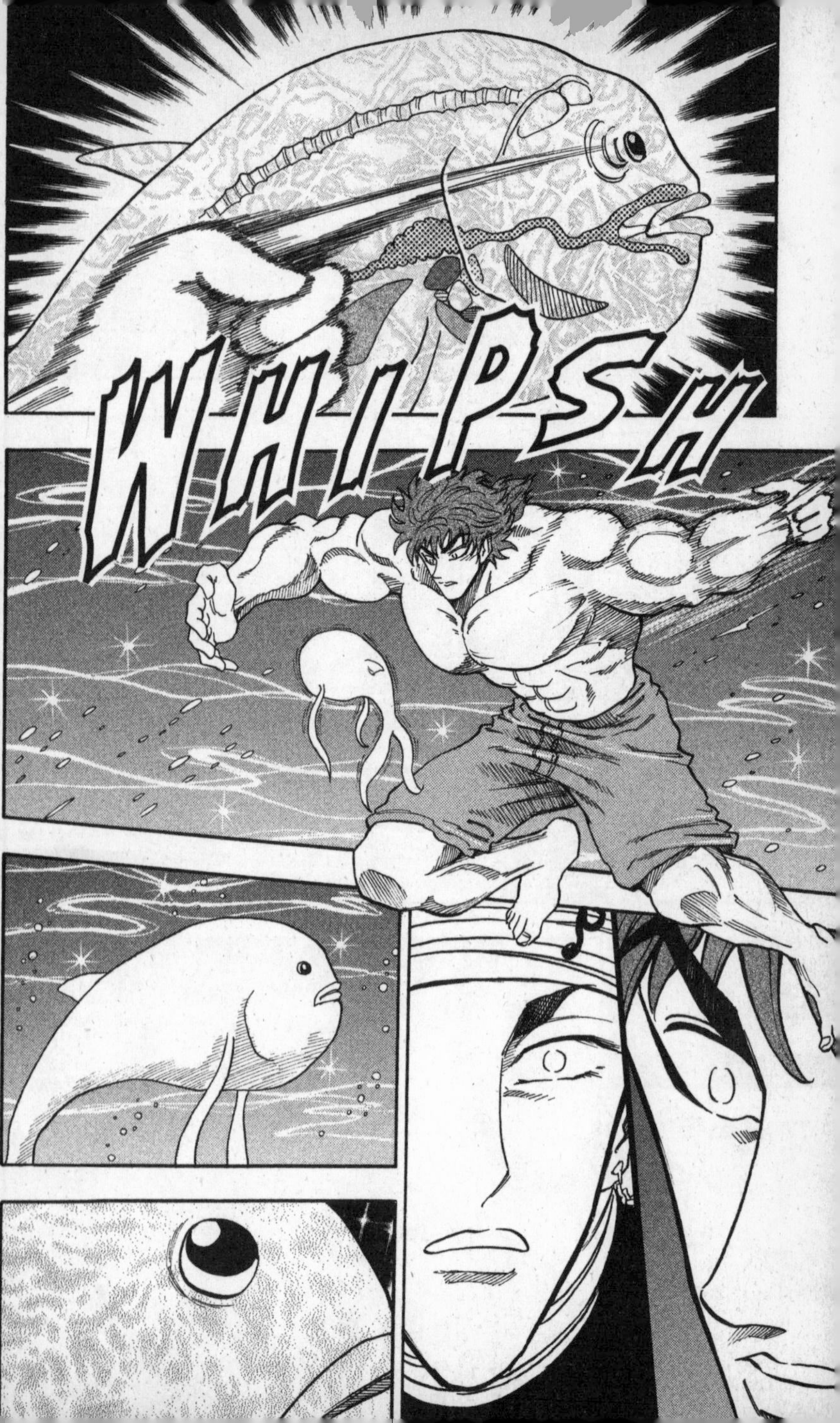
WHIPSH

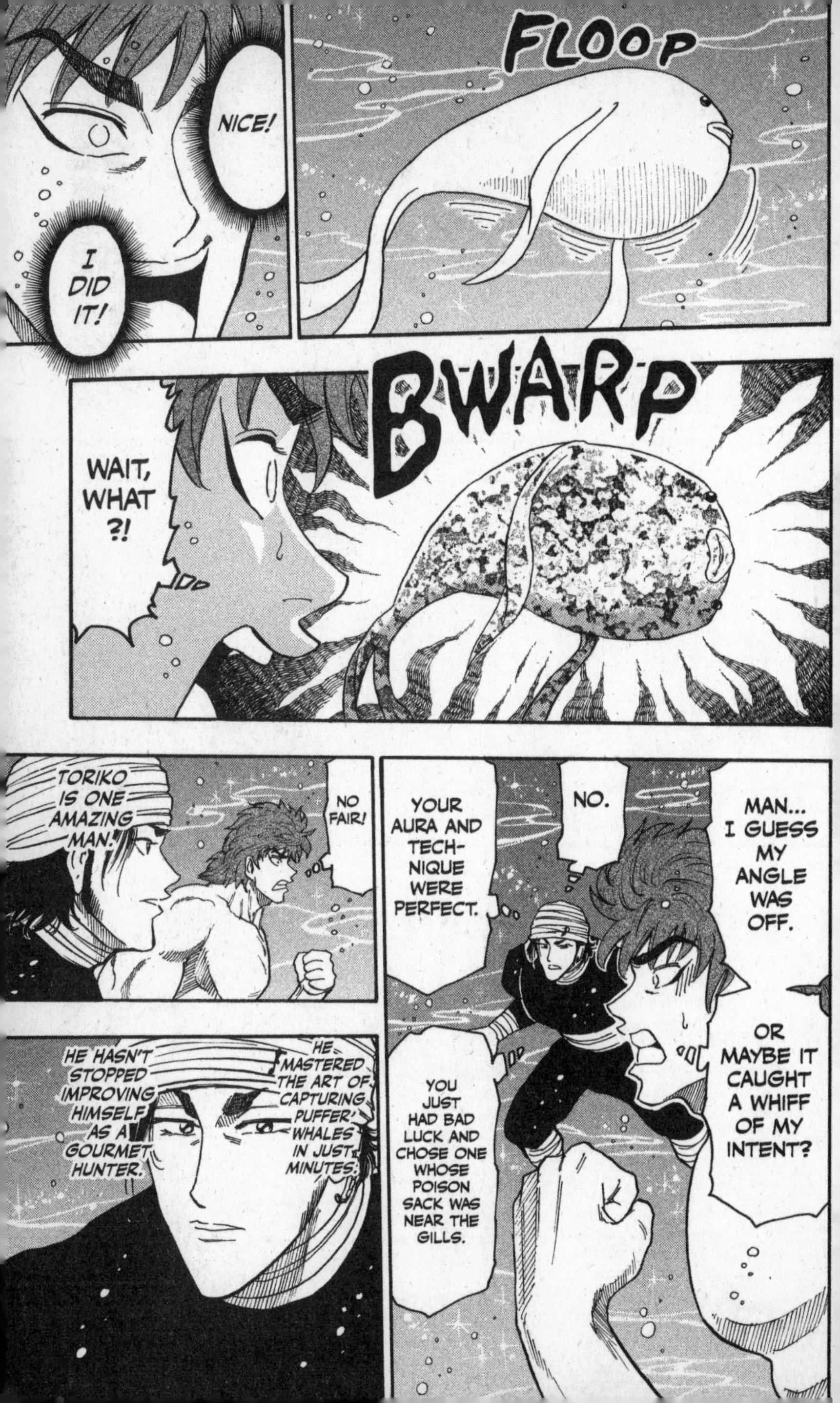
FLOOP
NICE!
I DID IT!
BWARP
WAIT, WHAT?!
MAN... I GUESS MY ANGLE WAS OFF.
NO.
YOUR AURA AND TECH-NIQUE WERE PERFECT.
OR MAYBE IT CAUGHT A WHIFF OF MY INTENT?
YOU JUST HAD BAD LUCK AND CHOSE ONE WHOSE POISON SACK WAS NEAR THE GILLS.
NO FAIR!
TORIKO IS ONE AMAZING MAN.
HE MASTERED THE ART OF CAPTURING PUFFER WHALES IN JUST MINUTES.
HE HASN'T STOPPED IMPROVING HIMSELF AS A GOURMET HUNTER.

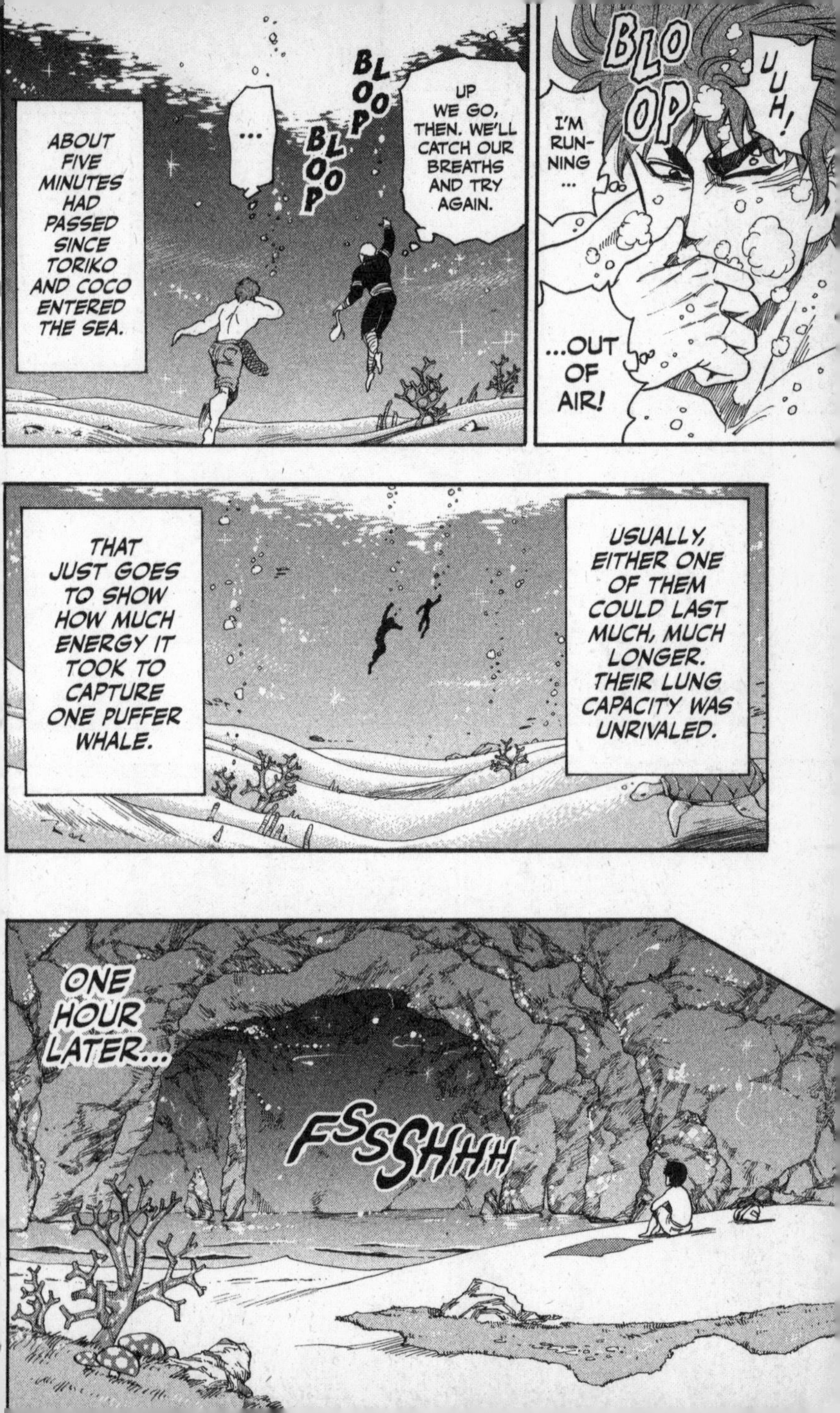
BLOOP
UUH!
I'M RUNNING...
...OUT OF AIR!
UP WE GO, THEN. WE'LL CATCH OUR BREATHS AND TRY AGAIN.
BLOOP BLOOP
...
ABOUT FIVE MINUTES HAD PASSED SINCE TORIKO AND COCO ENTERED THE SEA.
USUALLY, EITHER ONE OF THEM COULD LAST MUCH, MUCH LONGER. THEIR LUNG CAPACITY WAS UNRIVALED.
THAT JUST GOES TO SHOW HOW MUCH ENERGY IT TOOK TO CAPTURE ONE PUFFER WHALE.
ONE HOUR LATER...
FSSSHHH

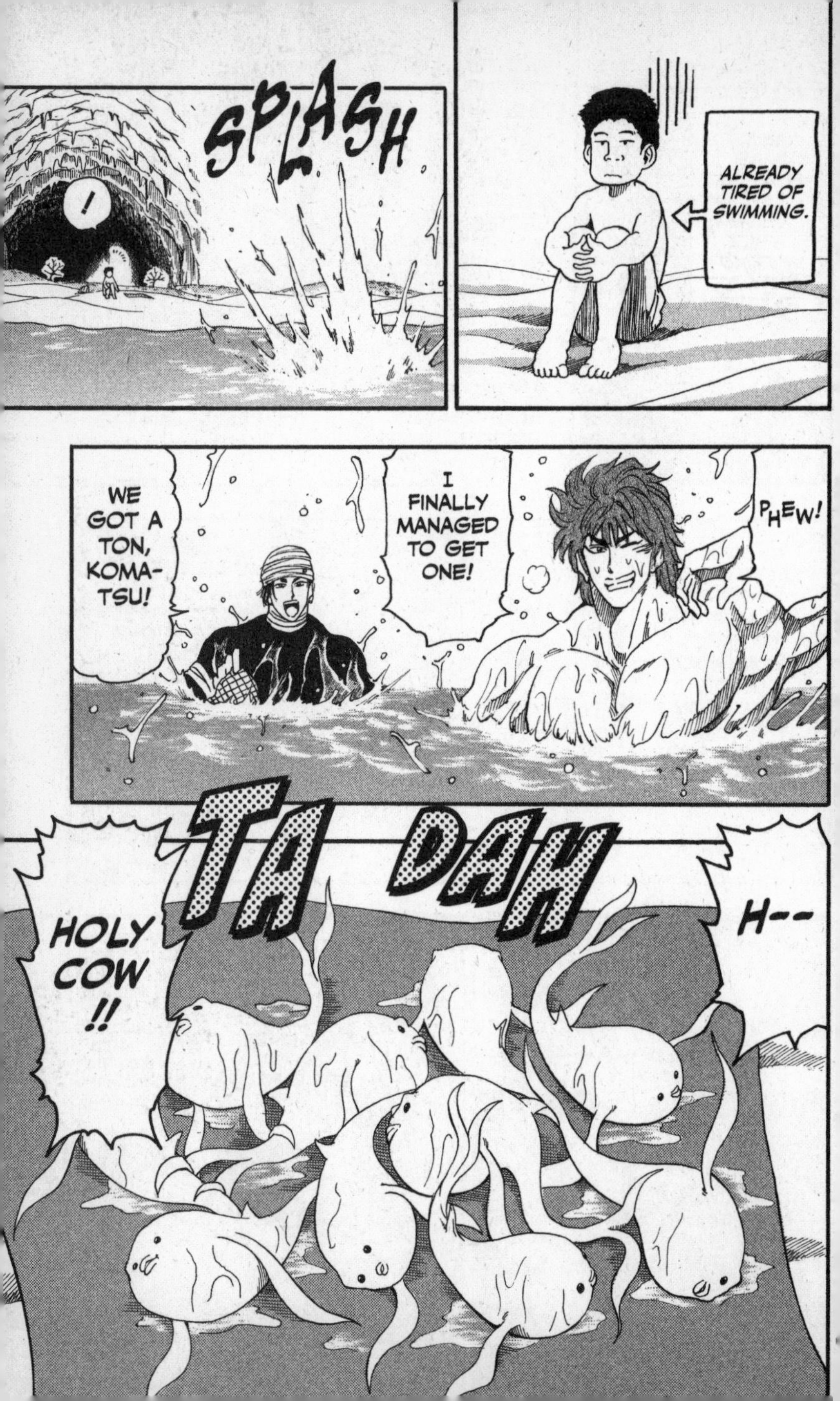
ALREADY TIRED OF SWIMMING.
SPLASH
!
PHEW!
I FINALLY MANAGED TO GET ONE!
WE GOT A TON, KOMATSU!
H--
TA DAH
HOLY COW !!

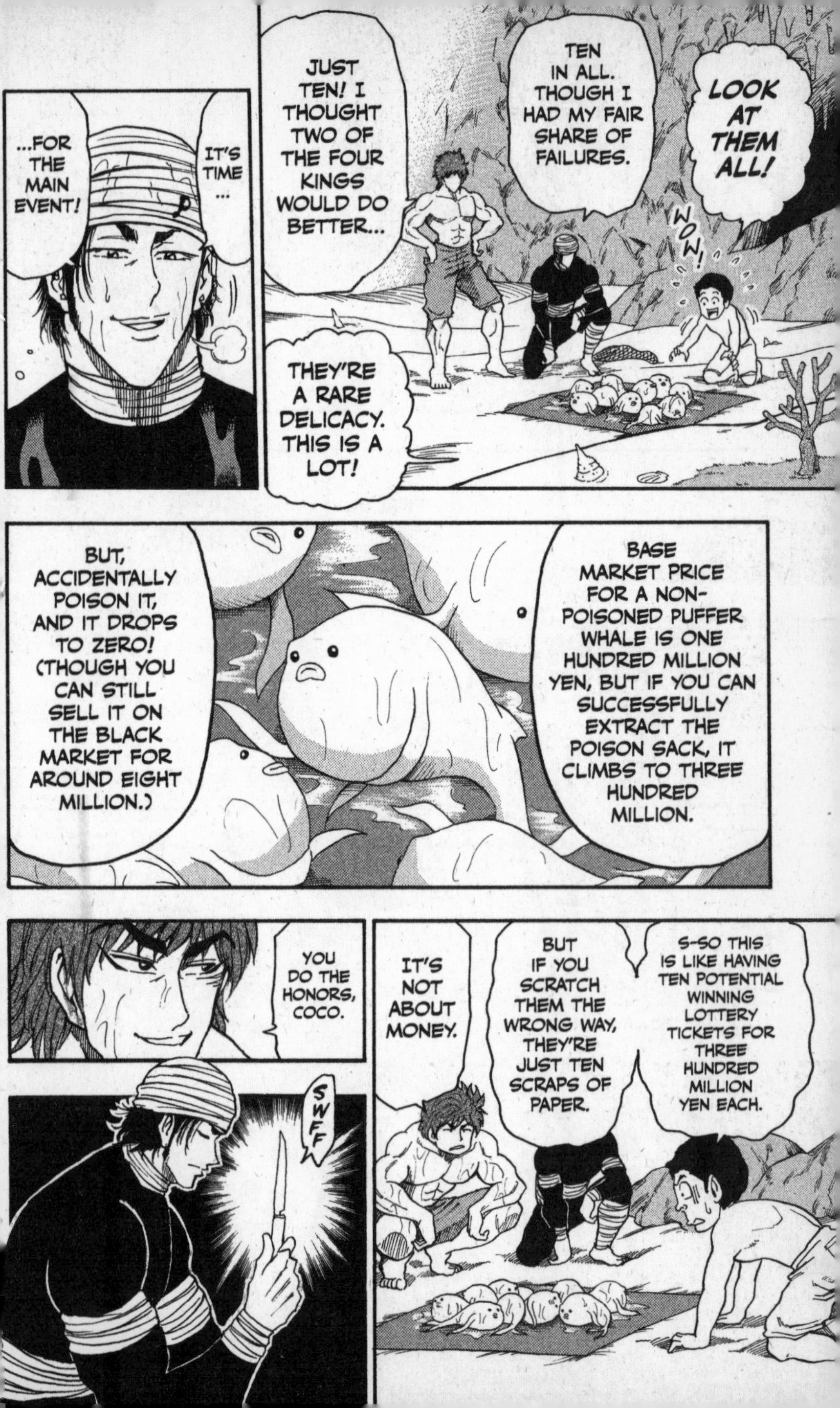
LOOK AT THEM ALL!
WOW!
TEN IN ALL. THOUGH I HAD MY FAIR SHARE OF FAILURES.
JUST TEN! I THOUGHT TWO OF THE FOUR KINGS WOULD DO BETTER...
THEY'RE A RARE DELICACY. THIS IS A LOT!
IT'S TIME ...
...FOR THE MAIN EVENT!
BASE MARKET PRICE FOR A NON-POISONED PUFFER WHALE IS ONE HUNDRED MILLION YEN, BUT IF YOU CAN SUCCESSFULLY EXTRACT THE POISON SACK, IT CLIMBS TO THREE HUNDRED MILLION.
BUT, ACCIDENTALLY POISON IT, AND IT DROPS TO ZERO! (THOUGH YOU CAN STILL SELL IT ON THE BLACK MARKET FOR AROUND EIGHT MILLION.)
S-SO THIS IS LIKE HAVING TEN POTENTIAL WINNING LOTTERY TICKETS FOR THREE HUNDRED MILLION YEN EACH.
BUT IF YOU SCRATCH THEM THE WRONG WAY, THEY'RE JUST TEN SCRAPS OF PAPER.
IT'S NOT ABOUT MONEY.
YOU DO THE HONORS, COCO.
SWFF

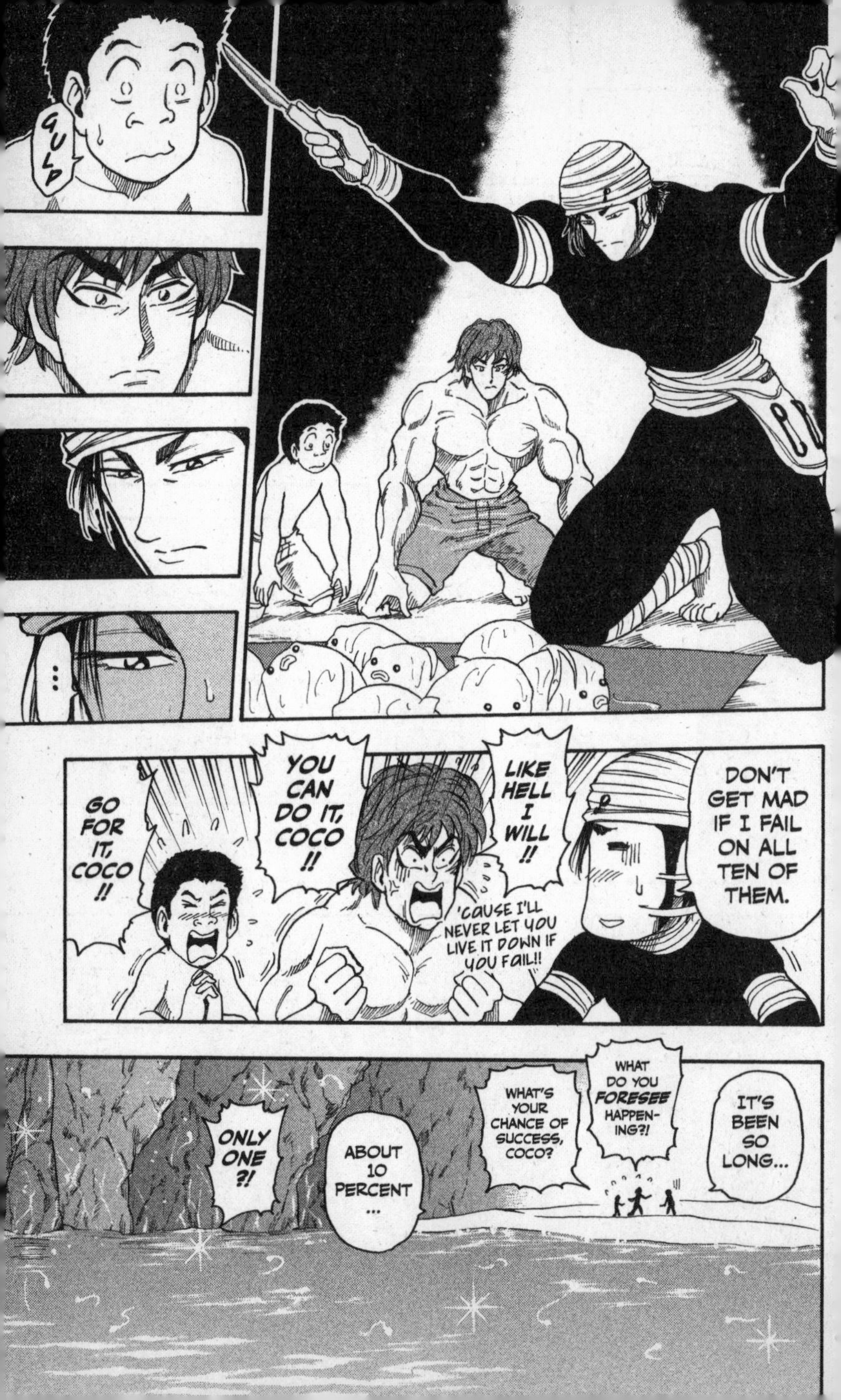
GULP
...
DON'T GET MAD IF I FAIL ON ALL TEN OF THEM.
LIKE HELL I WILL!!
'CAUSE I'LL NEVER LET YOU LIVE IT DOWN IF YOU FAIL!!
YOU CAN DO IT, COCO!!
GO FOR IT, COCO!!
IT'S BEEN SO LONG...
WHAT DO YOU FORESEE HAPPENING?!
WHAT'S YOUR CHANCE OF SUCCESS, COCO?
ABOUT 10 PERCENT...
ONLY ONE?!

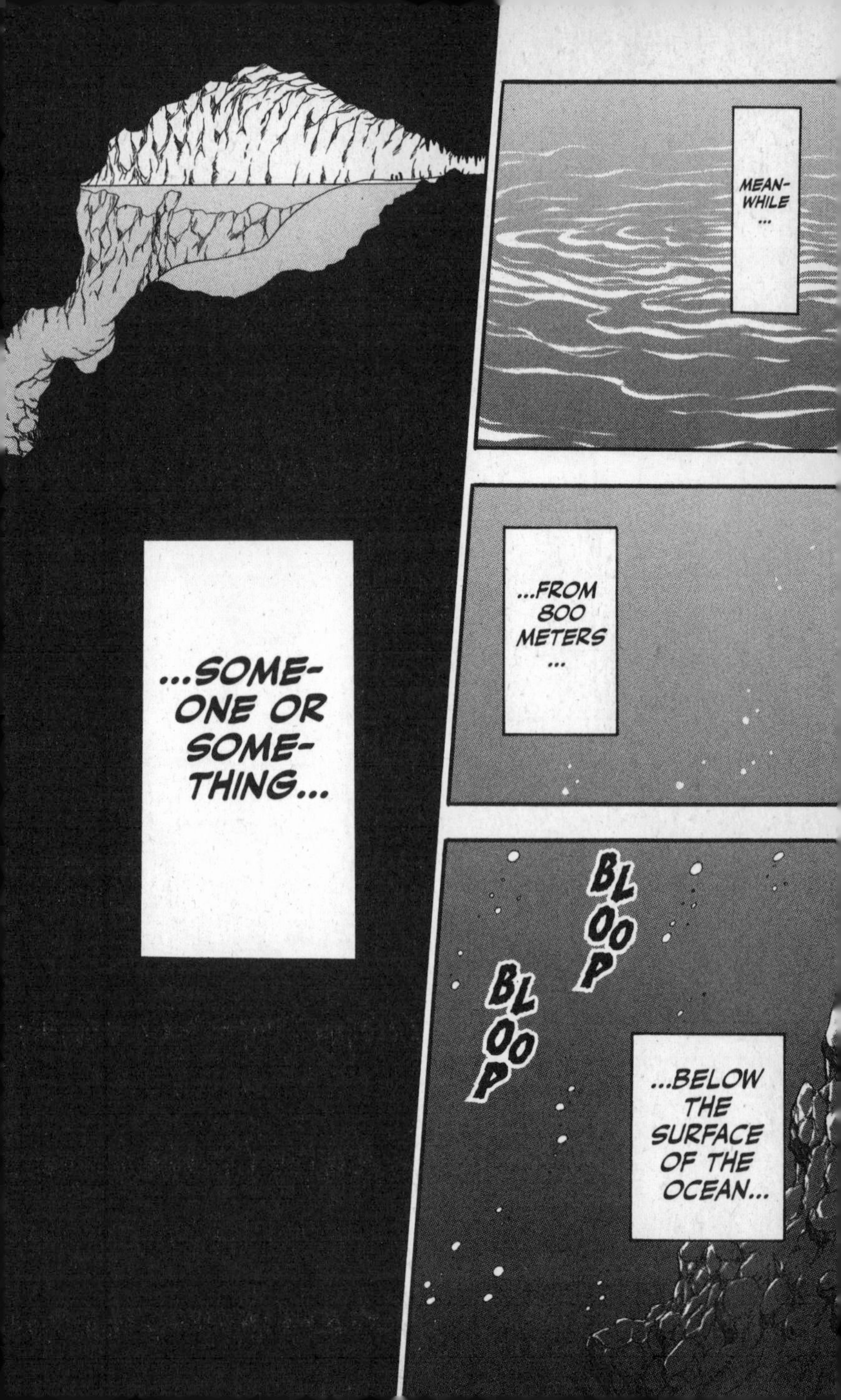
MEAN-WHILE ...
...FROM 800 METERS ...
BLOOP
BLOOP
...BELOW THE SURFACE OF THE OCEAN...
...SOME-ONE OR SOME-THING...

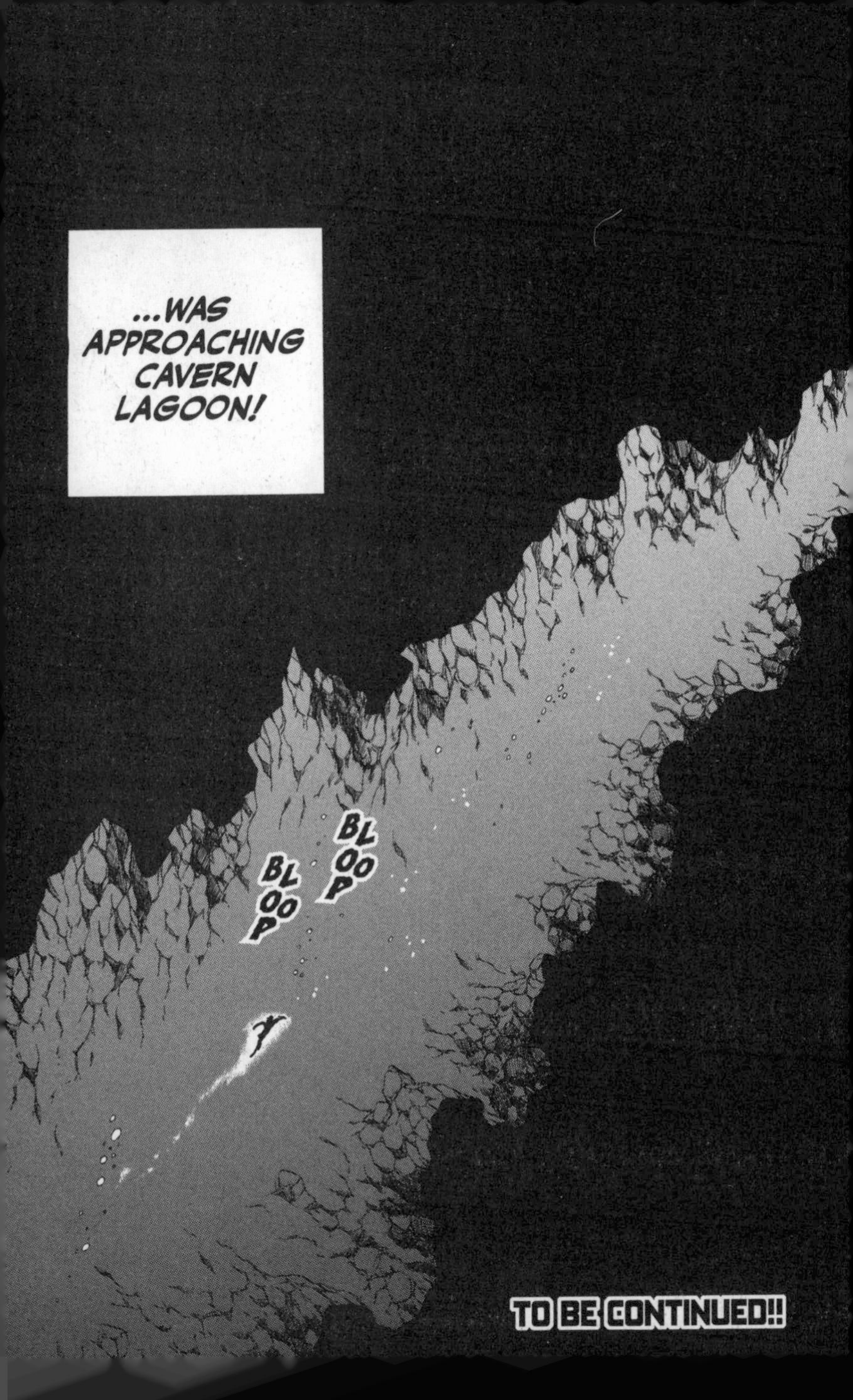
...WAS APPROACHING CAVERN LAGOON!
BLOOP
BLOOP
TO BE CONTINUED!!

COMING NEXT VOLUME

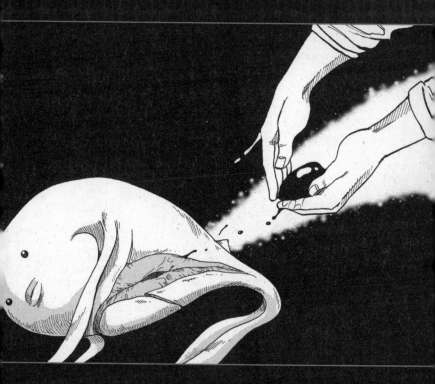

NEW CHALLENGES

Catching the Puffer Whale was easy compared to removing the poison and eating it. Komatsu's skills with a knife may come in handy, but will the combined efforts of the team lead to an awesome meal? And will Toriko finally meet an animal that's too powerful for even him to handle?

AVAILABLE DECEMBER 2010!